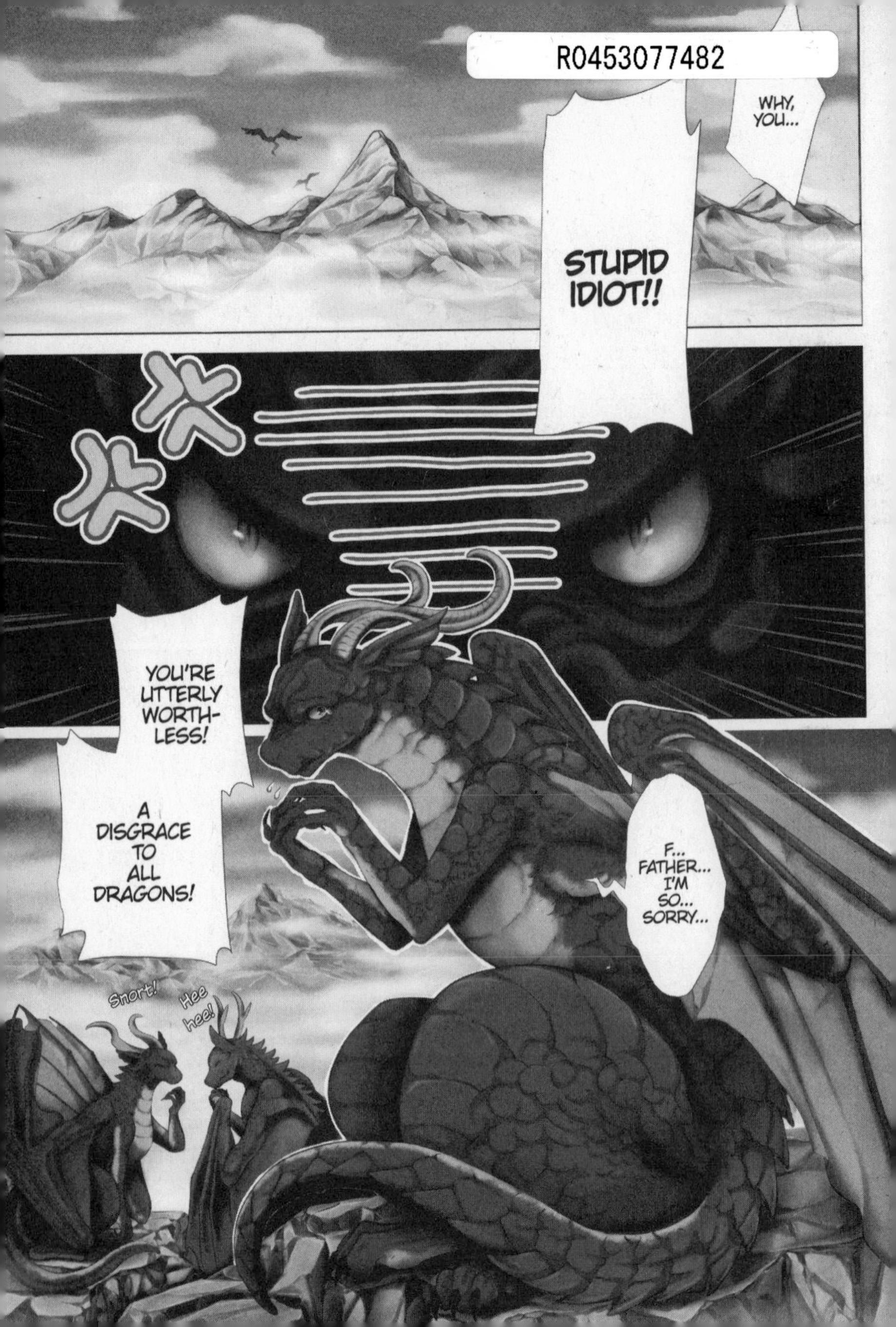
WHY, YOU...
STUPID IDIOT!!
YOU'RE UTTERLY WORTH-LESS!
A DISGRACE TO ALL DRAGONS!
F... FATHER... I'M SO... SORRY...
Hee hee!
Snort!

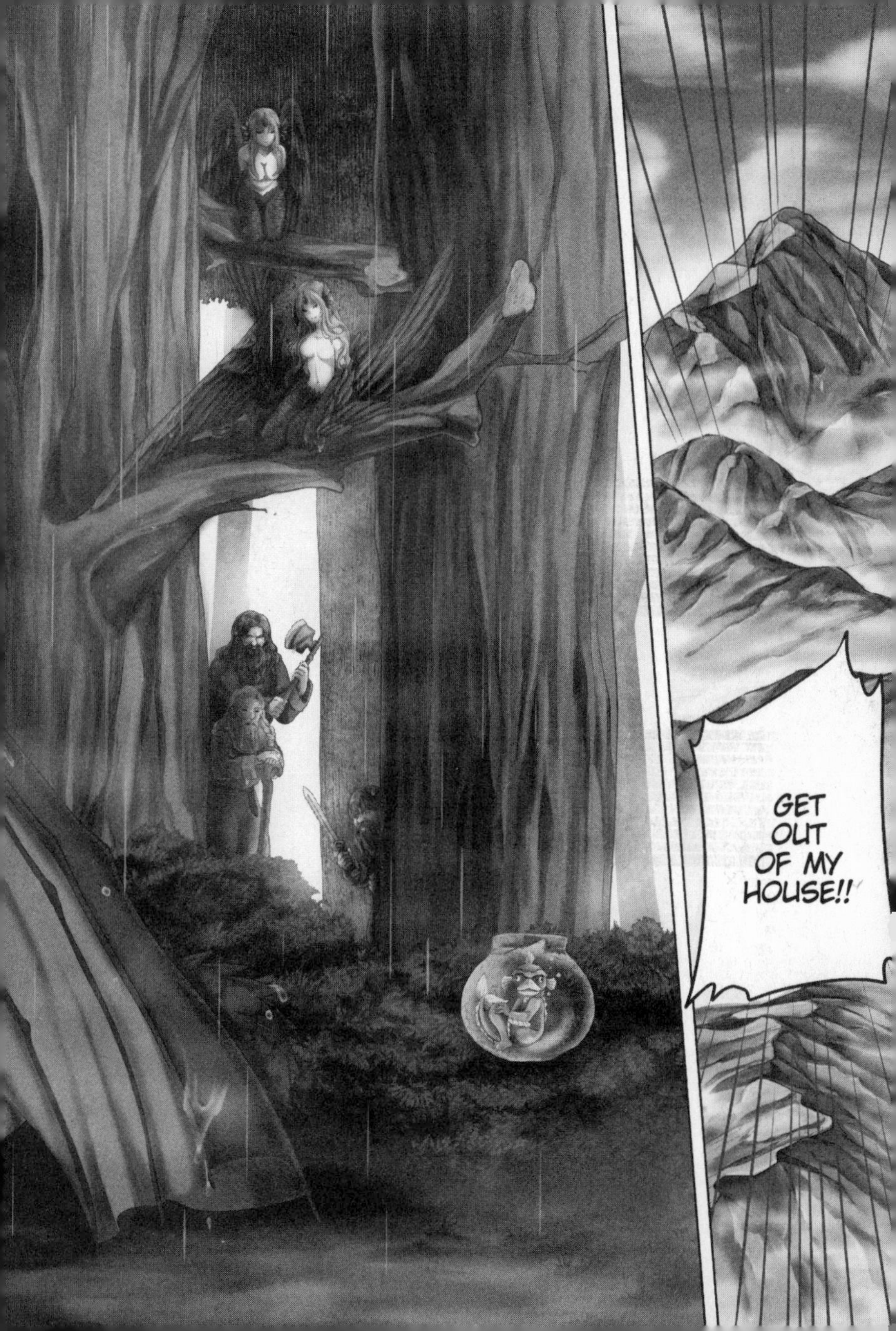
GET OUT OF MY HOUSE!!

House 1: Many Different Homes

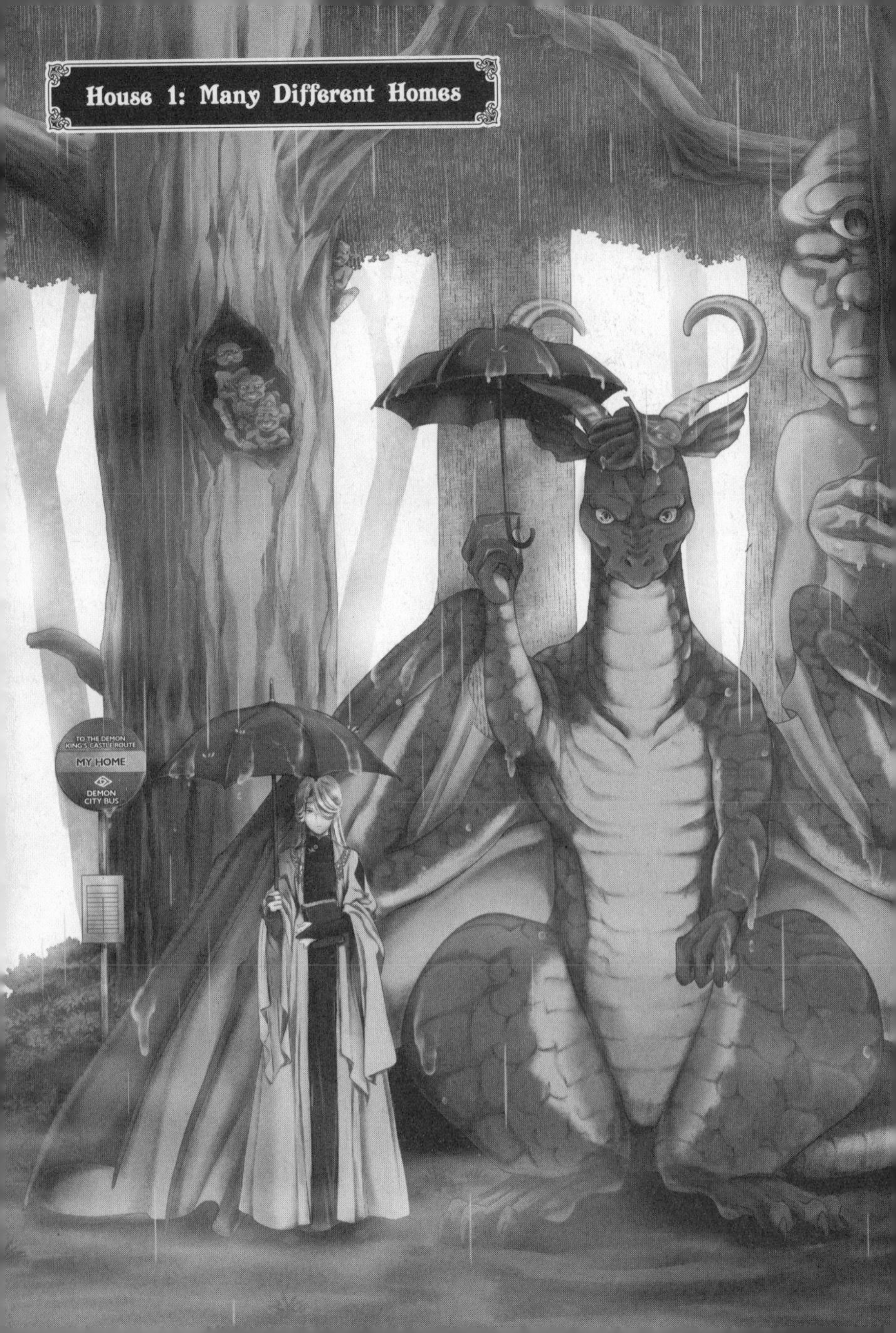
TO THE DEMON KING'S CASTLE ROUTE
MY HOME
DEMON CITY BUS

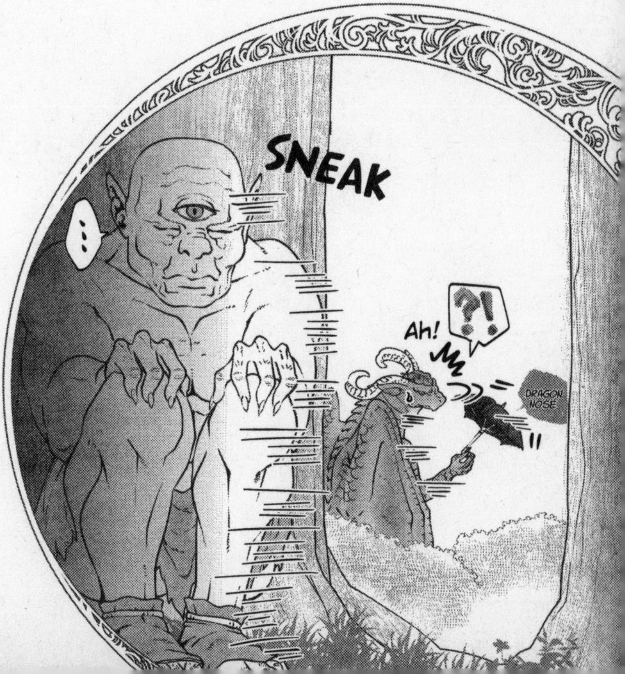
SNEAK
...
Ah!
?!
DRAGON NOSE

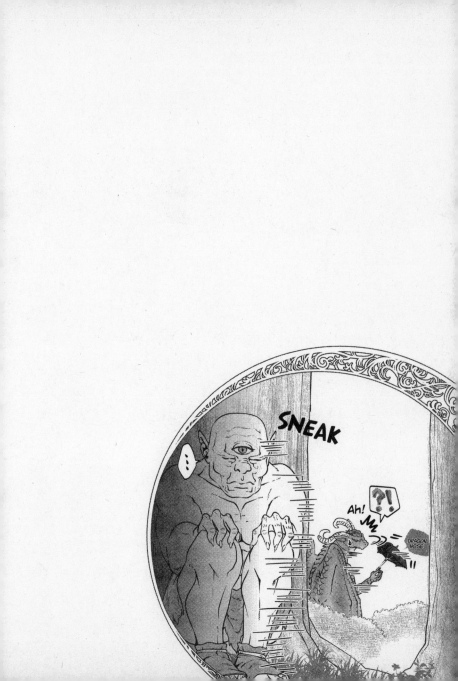

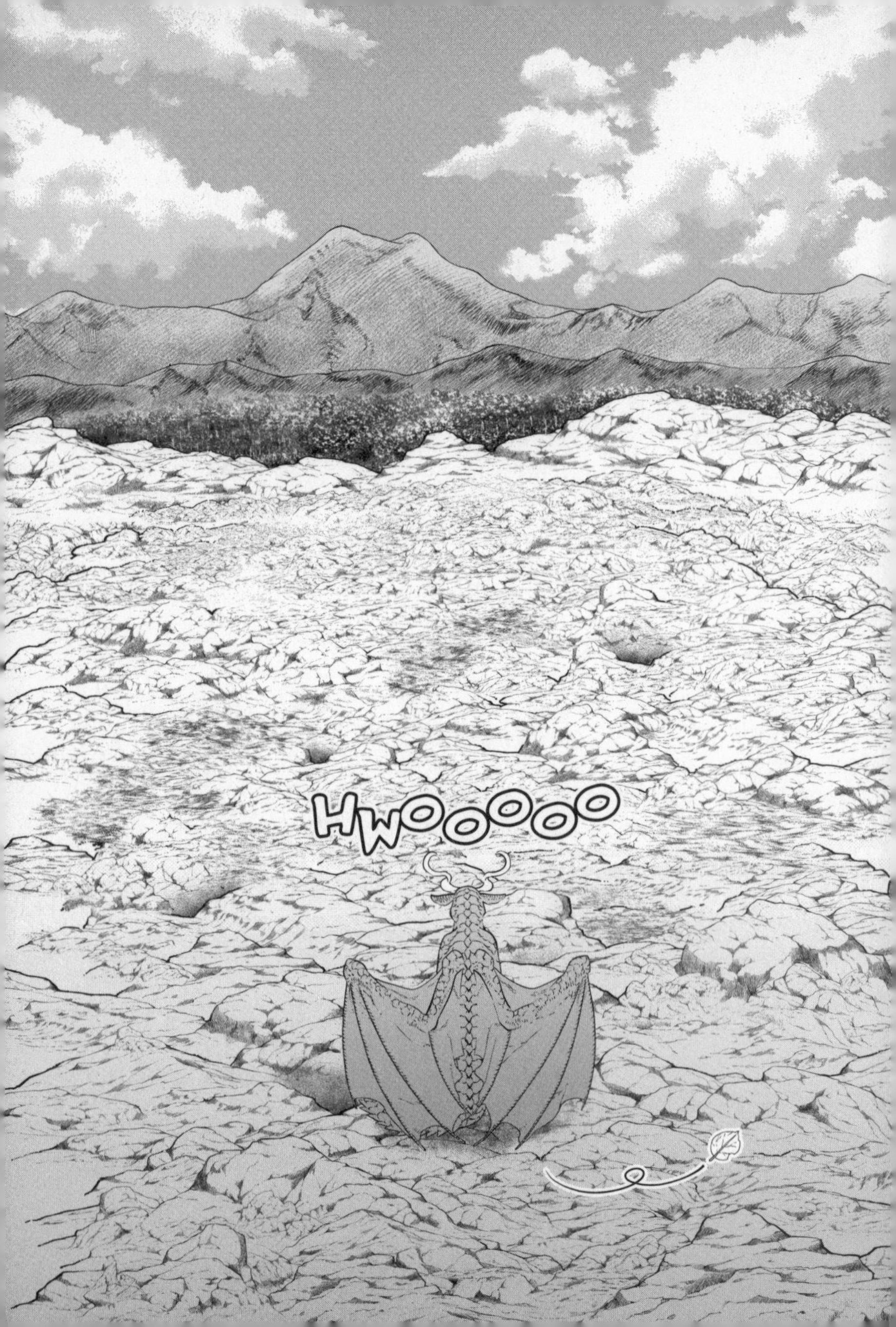
HWOOOOOO

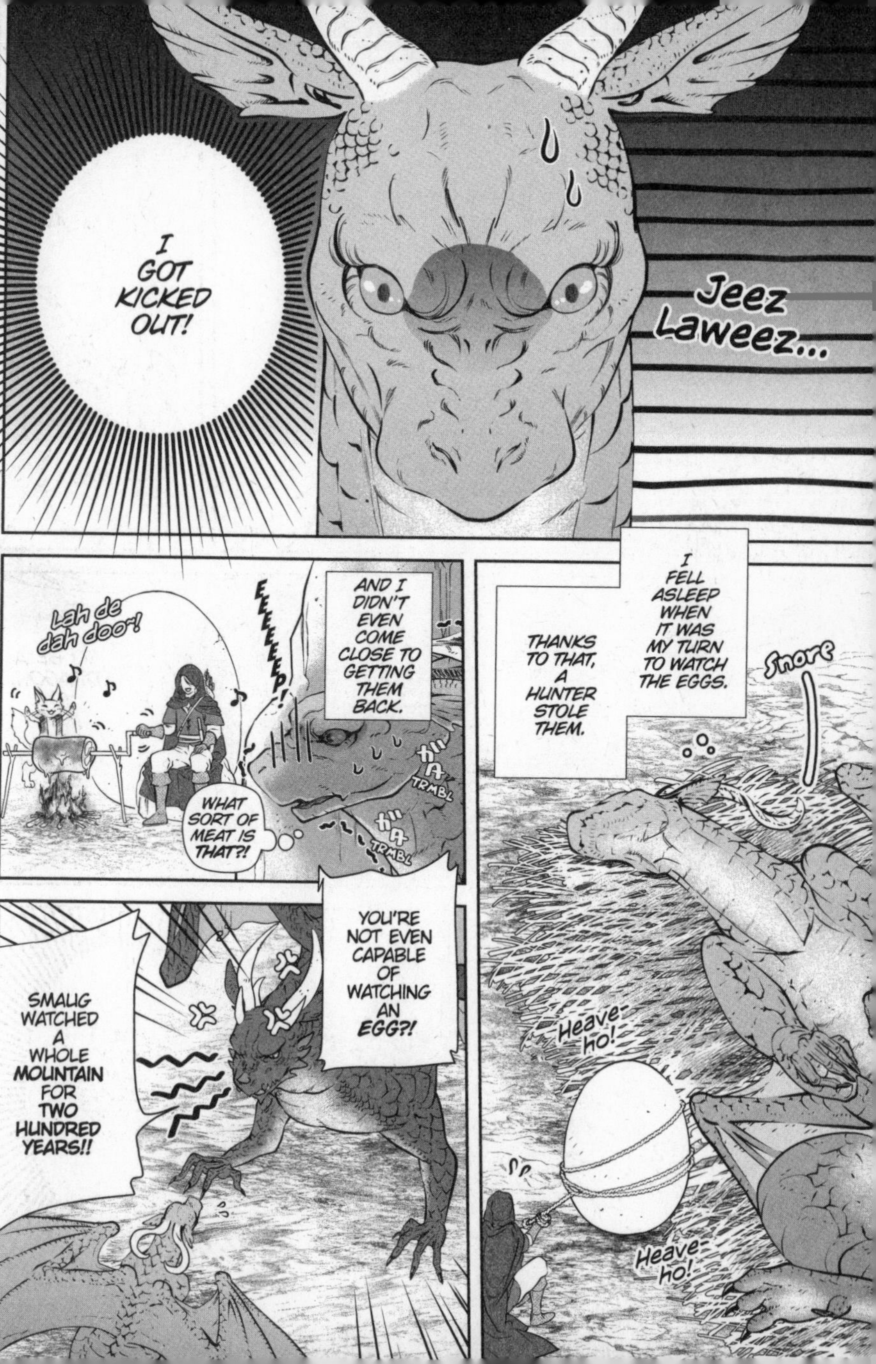
Jeez Laweez...
I GOT KICKED OUT!
I FELL ASLEEP WHEN IT WAS MY TURN TO WATCH THE EGGS.
THANKS TO THAT, A HUNTER STOLE THEM.
Snore
Heave-ho!
Heave-ho!
AND I DIDN'T EVEN COME CLOSE TO GETTING THEM BACK.
EEEEEEEP!
Lah de dah doo~!
TRMBL
WHAT SORT OF MEAT IS THAT?!
TRMBL
YOU'RE NOT EVEN CAPABLE OF WATCHING AN EGG?!
SMAUG WATCHED A WHOLE MOUNTAIN FOR TWO HUNDRED YEARS!!

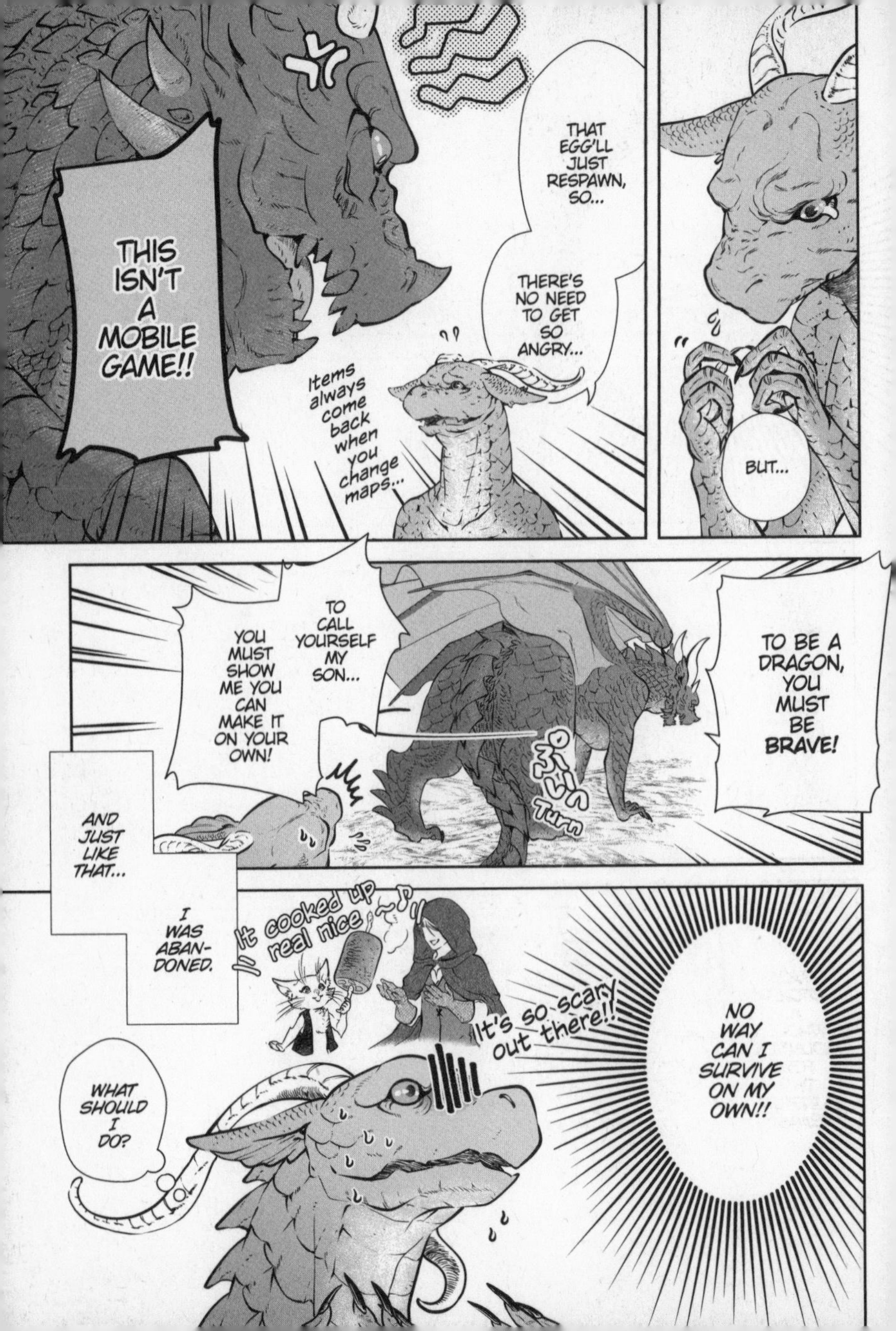
BUT...
THAT EGG'LL JUST RESPAWN, SO...
THERE'S NO NEED TO GET SO ANGRY...
Items always come back when you change maps...
THIS ISN'T A MOBILE GAME!!
TO BE A DRAGON, YOU MUST BE BRAVE!
TO CALL YOURSELF MY SON...
YOU MUST SHOW ME YOU CAN MAKE IT ON YOUR OWN!
Turn
AND JUST LIKE THAT...
I WAS ABAN-DONED.
NO WAY CAN I SURVIVE ON MY OWN!!
It's so scary out there!!
It cooked up real nice~♪
WHAT SHOULD I DO?

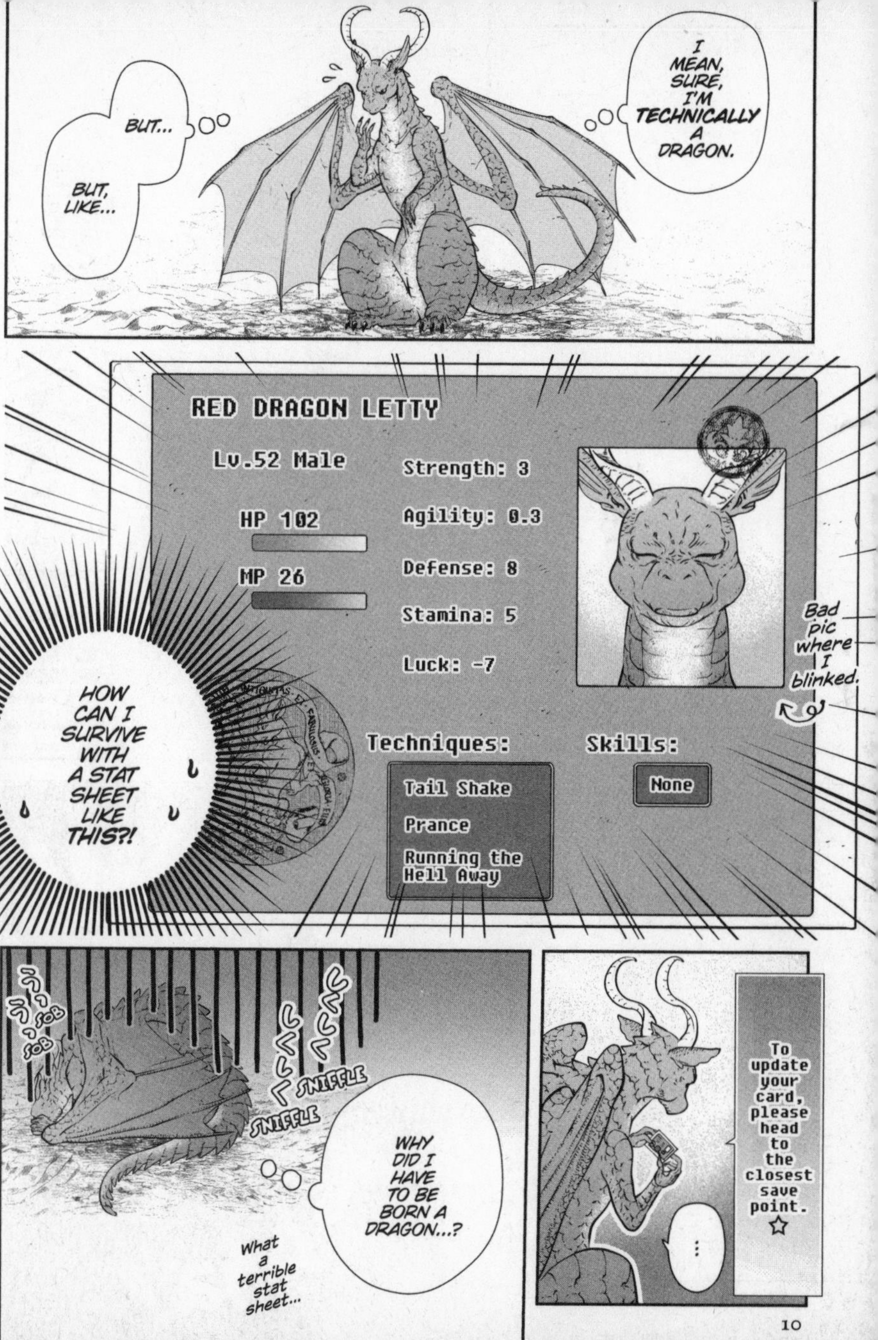

I MEAN, SURE, I'M TECHNICALLY A DRAGON.
BUT...
BUT, LIKE...
RED DRAGON LETTY
Lv.52 Male
HP 102
MP 26
Strength: 3
Agility: 0.3
Defense: 8
Stamina: 5
Luck: -7
Techniques:
Tail Shake
Prance
Running the Hell Away
Skills:
None
Bad pic where I blinked.
HOW CAN I SURVIVE WITH A STAT SHEET LIKE THIS?!
To update your card, please head to the closest save point. ☆
...
SOB SOB
SNIFFLE SNIFFLE
WHY DID I HAVE TO BE BORN A DRAGON...?
What a terrible stat sheet...

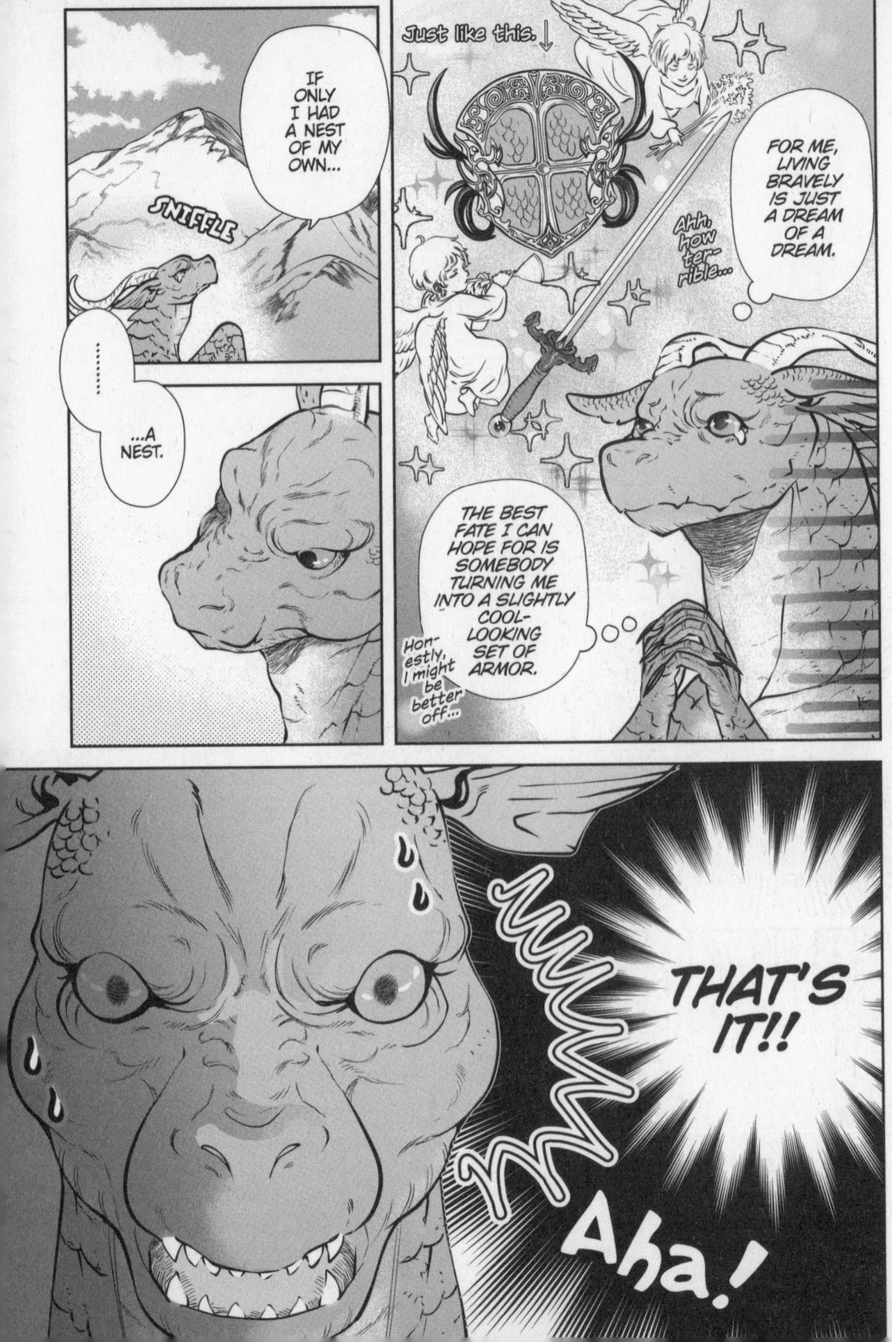
Just like this. ↓
FOR ME, LIVING BRAVELY IS JUST A DREAM OF A DREAM.
Ahh, how terrible...
THE BEST FATE I CAN HOPE FOR IS SOMEBODY TURNING ME INTO A SLIGHTLY COOL-LOOKING SET OF ARMOR.
Honestly, I might be better off...
IF ONLY I HAD A NEST OF MY OWN...
SNIFFLE
......
...A NEST.
THAT'S IT!!
Aha!

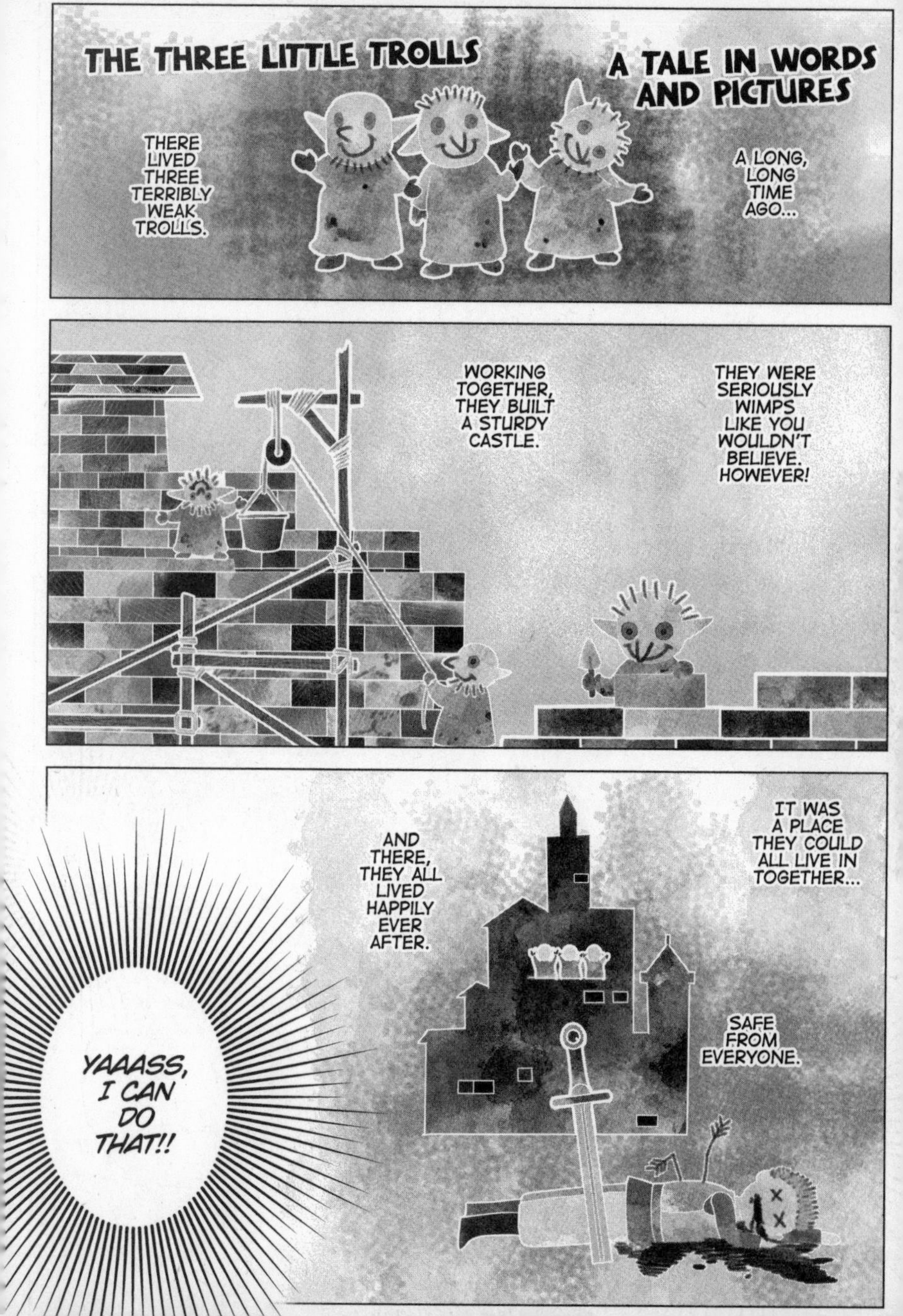
THE THREE LITTLE TROLLS
A TALE IN WORDS AND PICTURES
A LONG, LONG TIME AGO...
THERE LIVED THREE TERRIBLY WEAK TROLLS.
THEY WERE SERIOUSLY WIMPS LIKE YOU WOULDN'T BELIEVE. HOWEVER!
WORKING TOGETHER, THEY BUILT A STURDY CASTLE.
IT WAS A PLACE THEY COULD ALL LIVE IN TOGETHER...
SAFE FROM EVERYONE.
AND THERE, THEY ALL LIVED HAPPILY EVER AFTER.
YAAASS, I CAN DO THAT!!

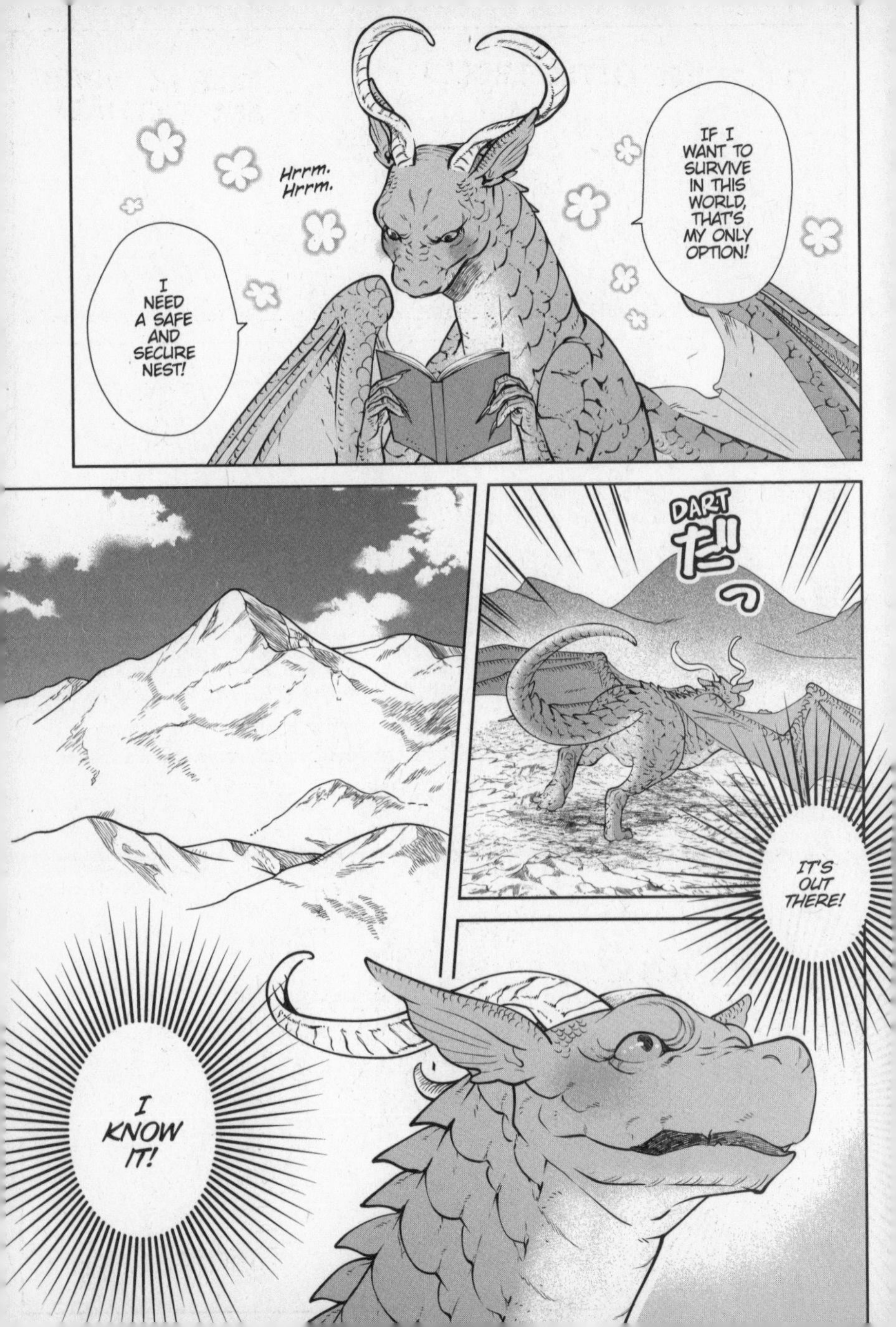
IF I WANT TO SURVIVE IN THIS WORLD, THAT'S MY ONLY OPTION!
Hrrm. Hrrm.
I NEED A SAFE AND SECURE NEST!
DART
だっ
IT'S OUT THERE!
I KNOW IT!

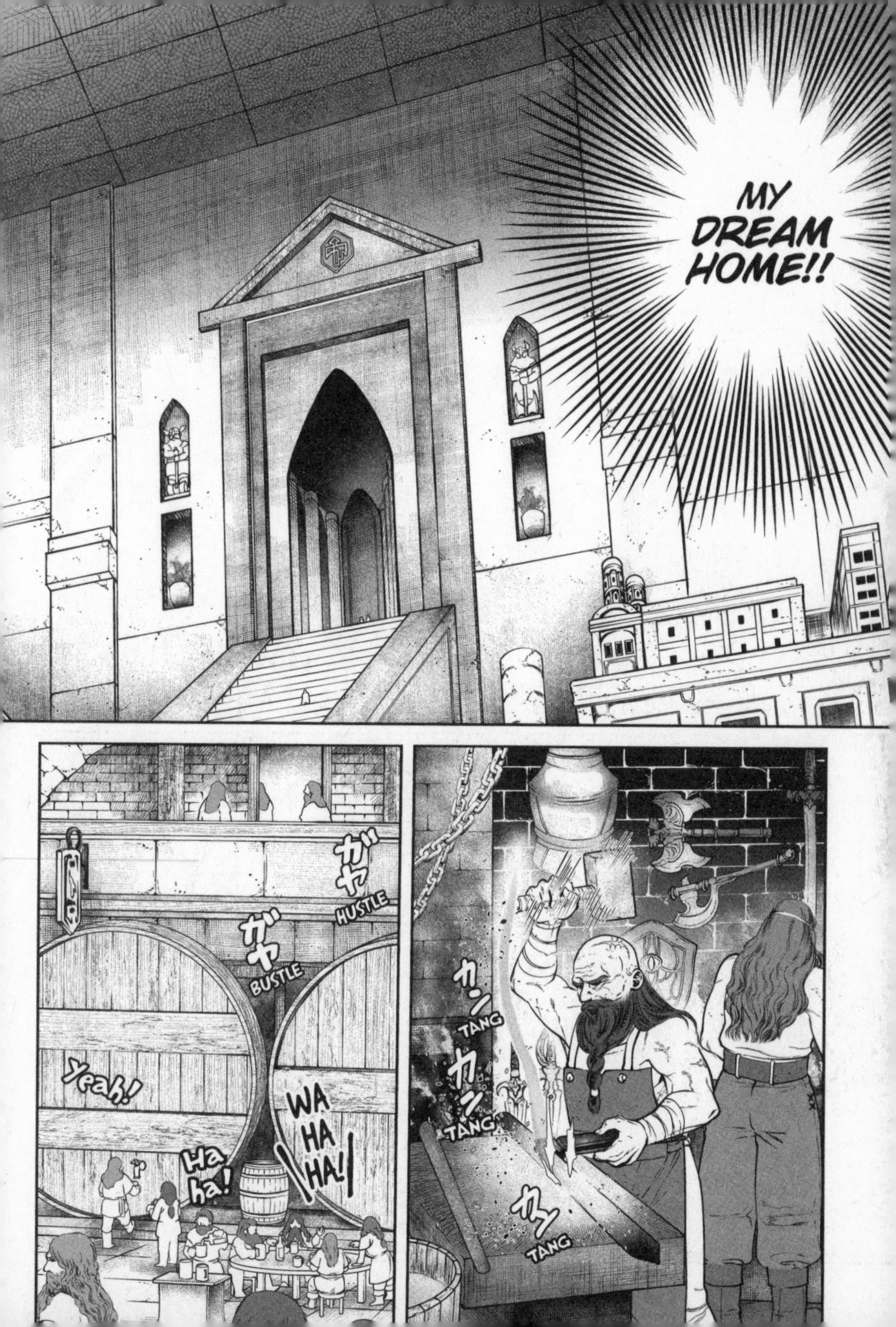
MY DREAM HOME!!
カン
TANG
カン
TANG
カン
TANG
ガヤ
HUSTLE
ガヤ
BUSTLE
Yeah!
WA HA HA!
Ha ha!

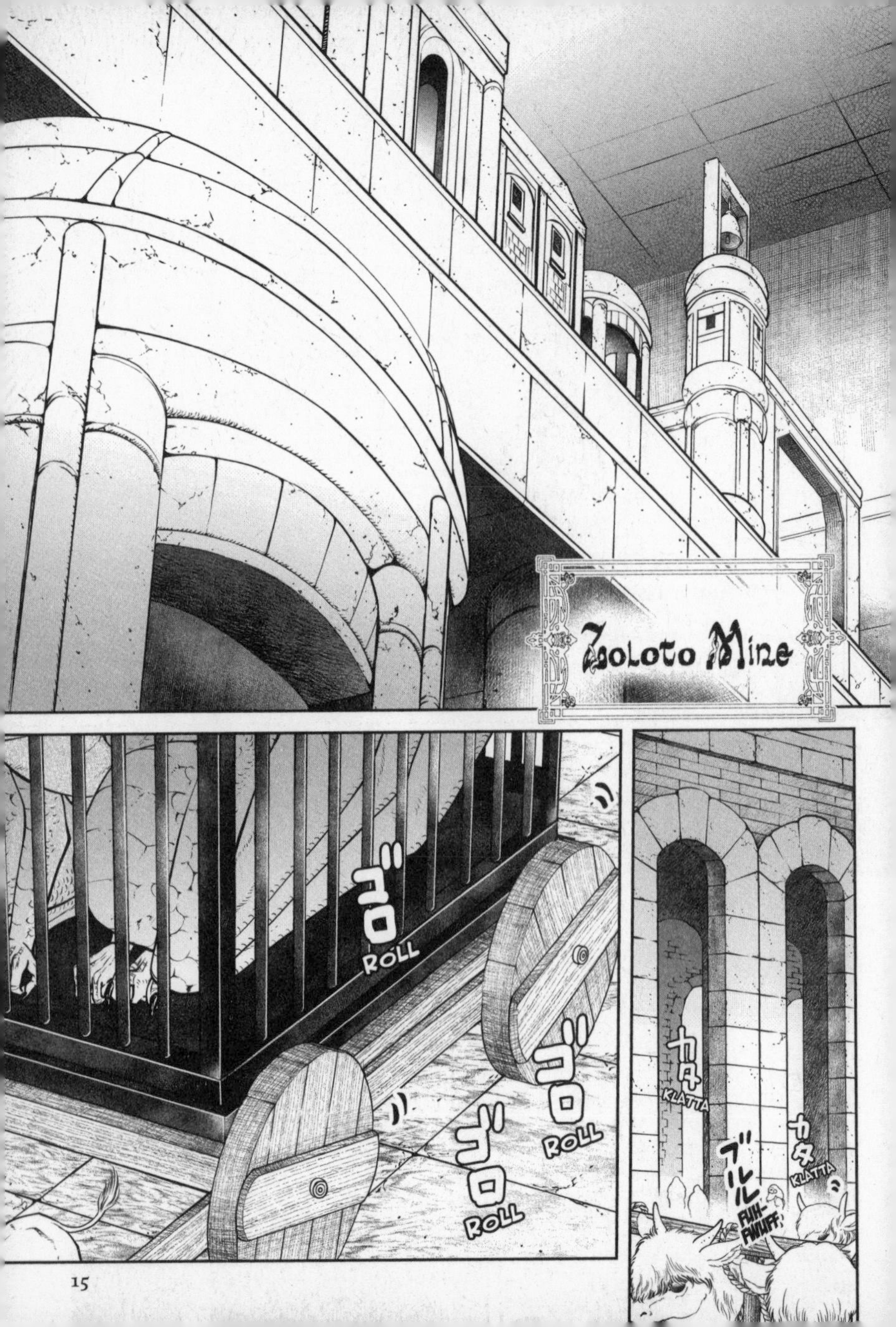
Zoloto Mine
カタ
KLATTA
カタ
KLATTA
ブルル
FUH-FWUFF
ゴロ
ROLL
ゴロ
ROLL
ゴロ
ROLL

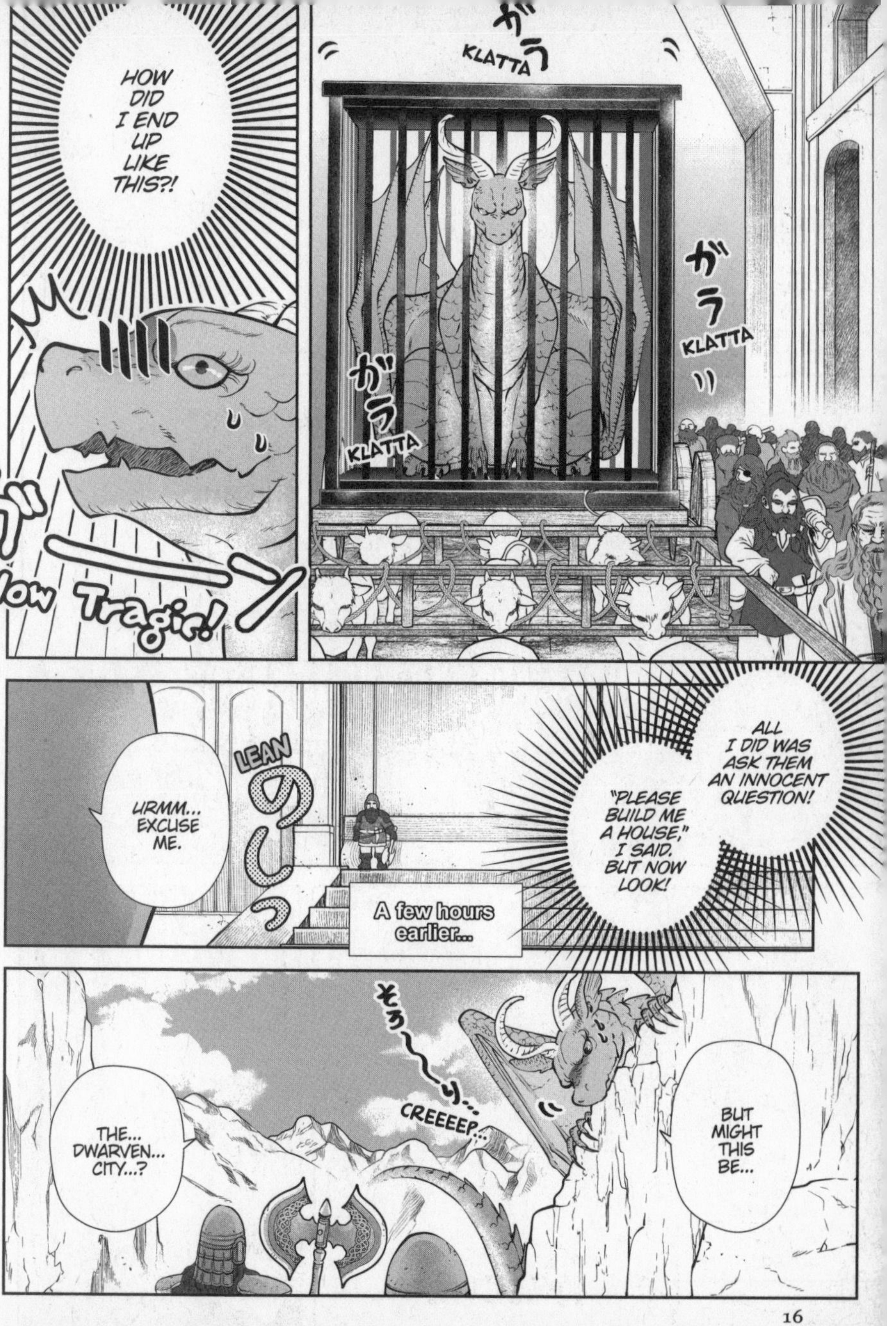
ガラ
KLATTA
ガラ
KLATTA
ガラ
KLATTA
HOW DID I END UP LIKE THIS?!
ガーン
How Tragic!
ALL I DID WAS ASK THEM AN INNOCENT QUESTION!
"PLEASE BUILD ME A HOUSE," I SAID. BUT NOW LOOK!
のしっ
LEAN
URMM... EXCUSE ME.
A few hours earlier...
BUT MIGHT THIS BE...
そろ～～り...
CREEEEP...
THE... DWARVEN... CITY...?

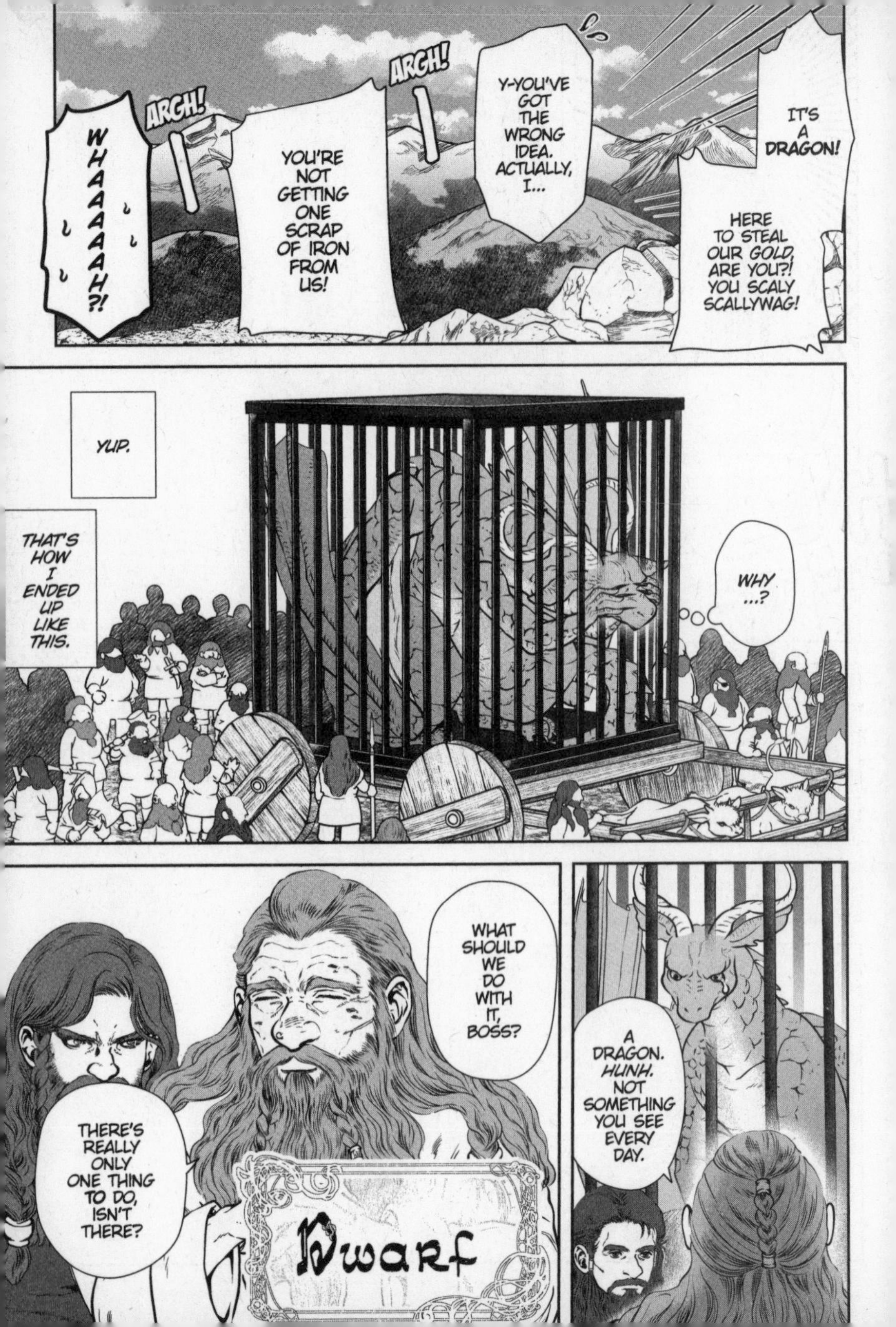
IT'S A DRAGON!
HERE TO STEAL OUR GOLD, ARE YOU?! YOU SCALY SCALLYWAG!
Y-YOU'VE GOT THE WRONG IDEA. ACTUALLY, I...
ARGH!
YOU'RE NOT GETTING ONE SCRAP OF IRON FROM US!
ARGH!
WHAAAAAAH?!
WHY ...?
YUP.
THAT'S HOW I ENDED UP LIKE THIS.
A DRAGON. HUNH. NOT SOMETHING YOU SEE EVERY DAY.
WHAT SHOULD WE DO WITH IT, BOSS?
THERE'S REALLY ONLY ONE THING TO DO, ISN'T THERE?
Dwarf

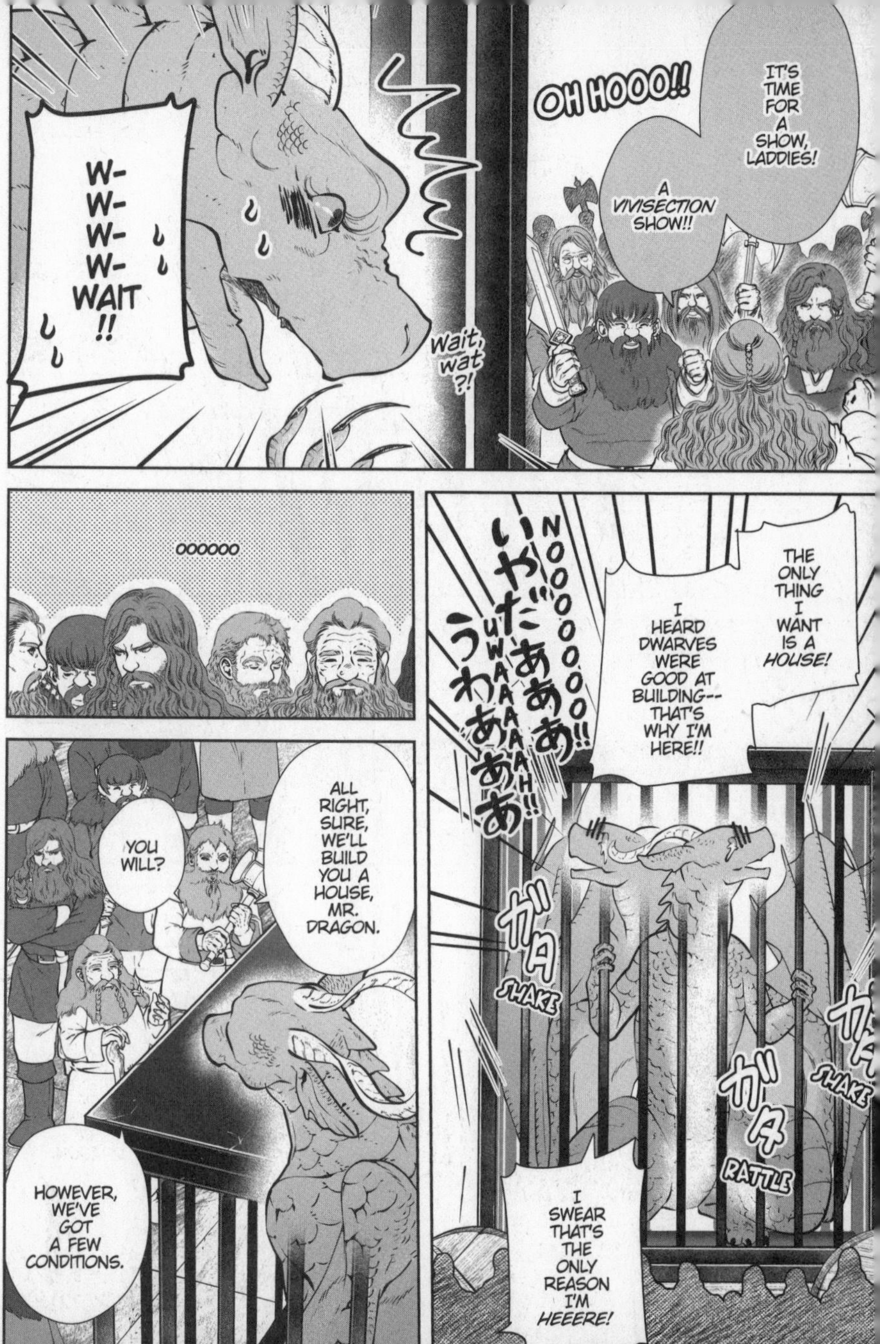
OH HOOO!!
IT'S TIME FOR A SHOW, LADDIES!
A VIVISECTION SHOW!!
W-W-W-W-WAIT!!
Wait, wat?!
THE ONLY THING I WANT IS A HOUSE!
I HEARD DWARVES WERE GOOD AT BUILDING-- THAT'S WHY I'M HERE!!
NOOOOOOOOO!!
いやだあああ
UWAAAAAH!!
うわあああ
ガタ
SHAKE
ガタ
SHAKE
ガタ
RATTLE
I SWEAR THAT'S THE ONLY REASON I'M HEEERE!
oooooo
ALL RIGHT, SURE, WE'LL BUILD YOU A HOUSE, MR. DRAGON.
YOU WILL?
HOWEVER, WE'VE GOT A FEW CONDITIONS.

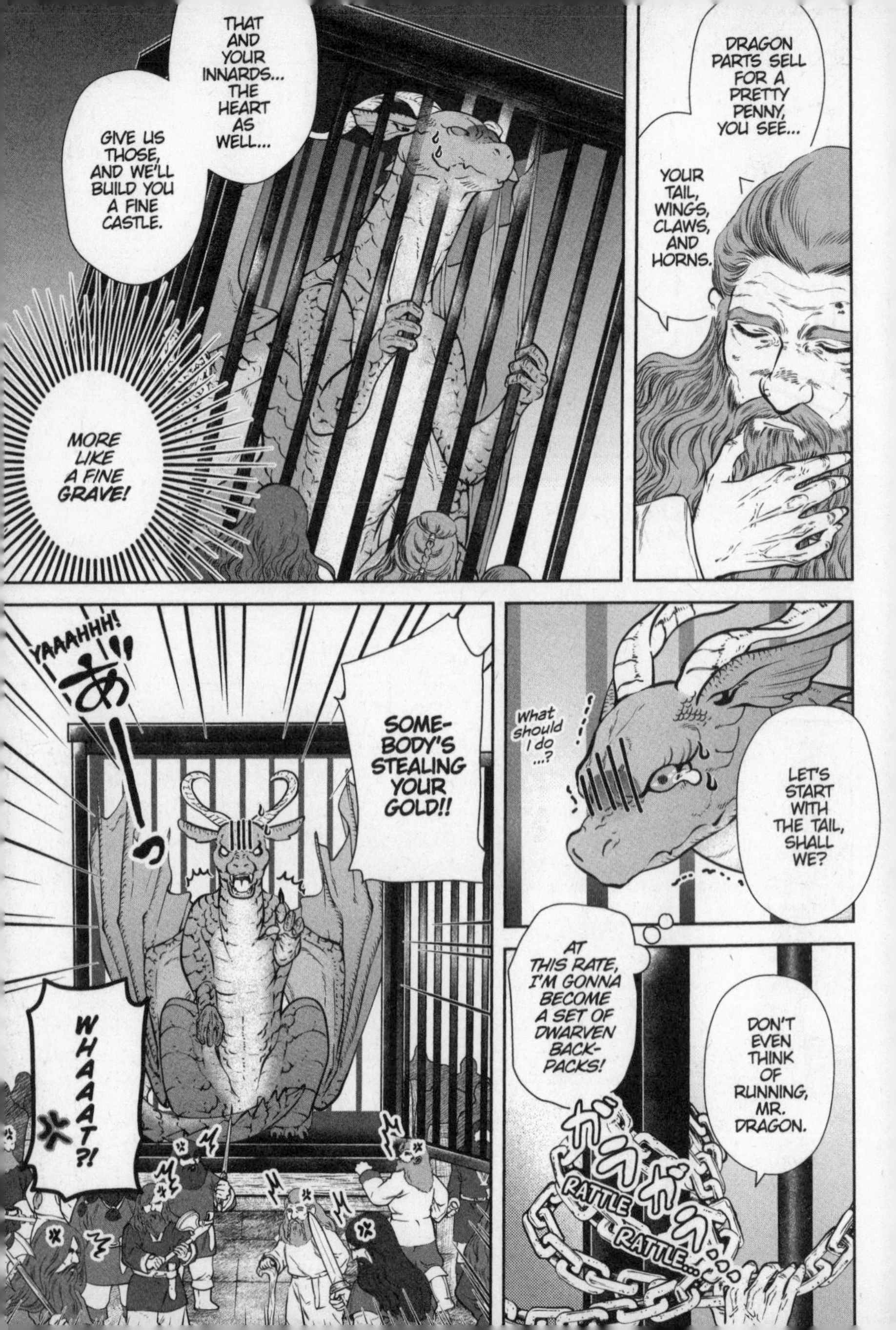
DRAGON PARTS SELL FOR A PRETTY PENNY, YOU SEE...
YOUR TAIL, WINGS, CLAWS, AND HORNS.
THAT AND YOUR INNARDS... THE HEART AS WELL...
GIVE US THOSE, AND WE'LL BUILD YOU A FINE CASTLE.
MORE LIKE A FINE GRAVE!
LET'S START WITH THE TAIL, SHALL WE?
What should I do ...?
DON'T EVEN THINK OF RUNNING, MR. DRAGON.
AT THIS RATE, I'M GONNA BECOME A SET OF DWARVEN BACK-PACKS!
RATTLE RATTLE...
SOME-BODY'S STEALING YOUR GOLD!!
YAAAHHH!
あ!!
WHAAAAT?!

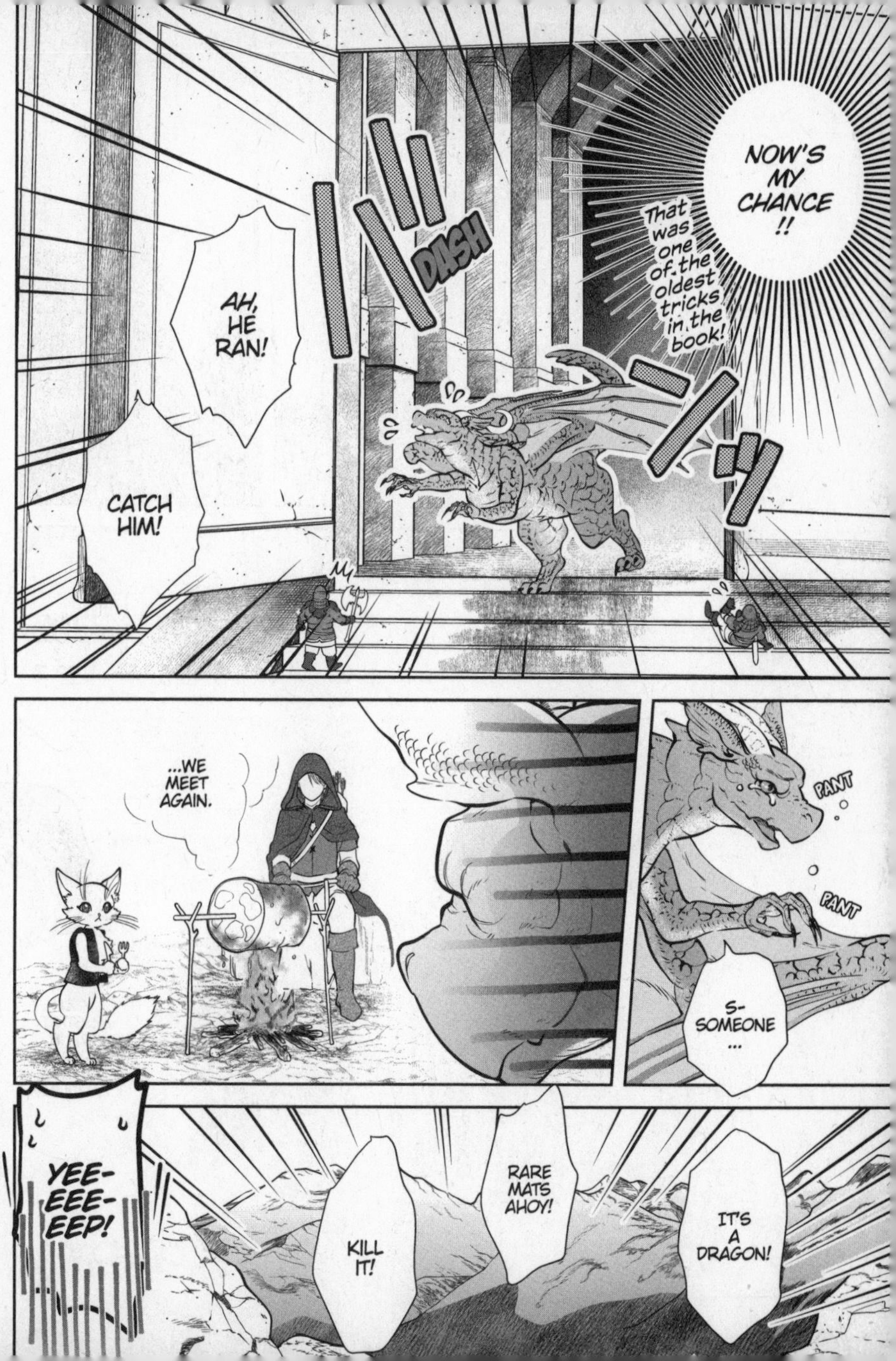
NOW'S MY CHANCE!!
That was one of the oldest tricks in the book!
DASH
AH, HE RAN!
CATCH HIM!
PANT
PANT
S-SOMEONE...
...WE MEET AGAIN.
IT'S A DRAGON!
RARE MATS AHOY!
KILL IT!
YEE-EEE-EEP!

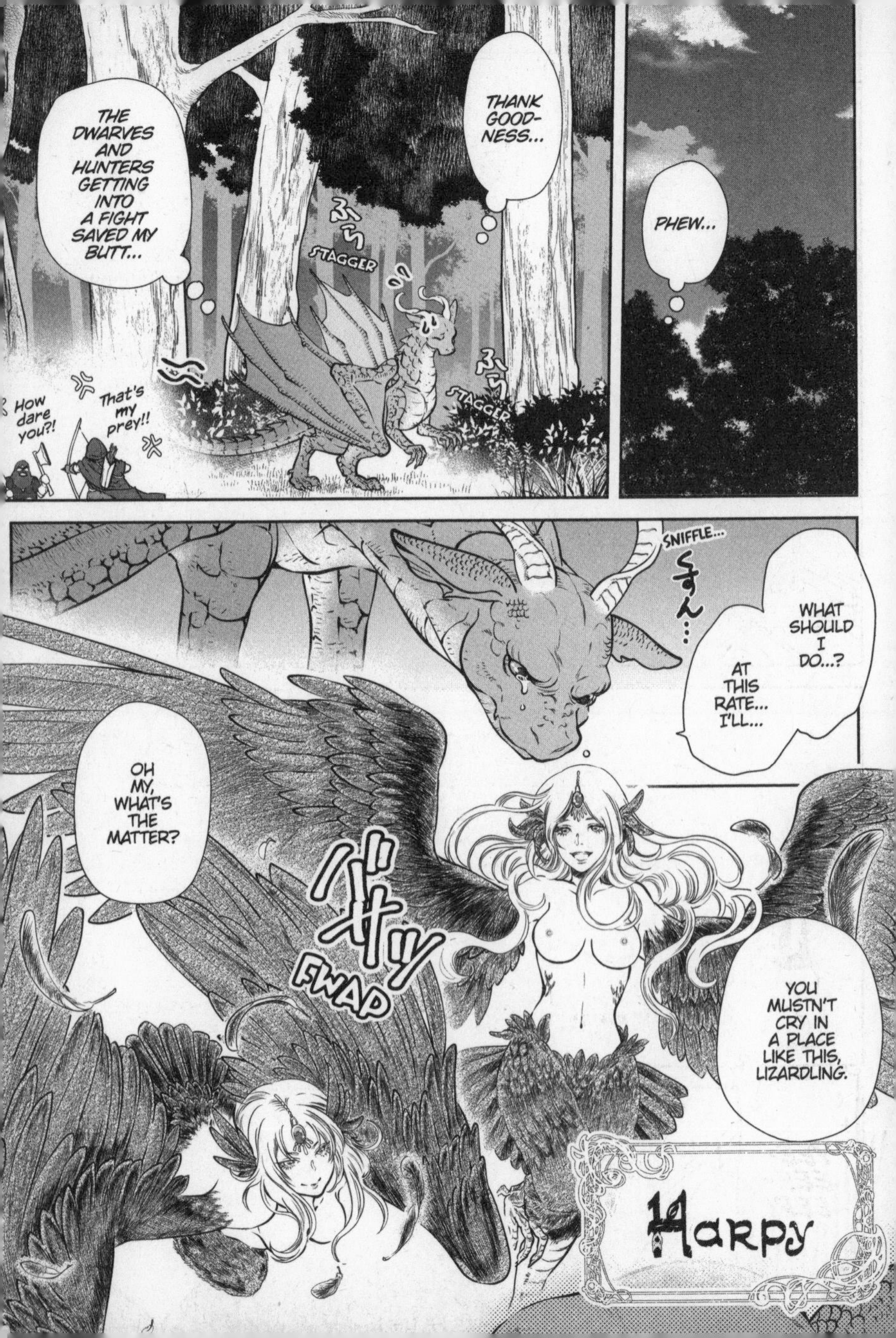
PHEW...
THANK GOODNESS...
THE DWARVES AND HUNTERS GETTING INTO A FIGHT SAVED MY BUTT...
ふら
STAGGER
ふら
STAGGER
That's my prey!!
How dare you?!
SNIFFLE...
くすん…
WHAT SHOULD I DO...?
AT THIS RATE... I'LL...
OH MY, WHAT'S THE MATTER?
バサッ
FWAP
YOU MUSTN'T CRY IN A PLACE LIKE THIS, LIZARDLING.
Harpy

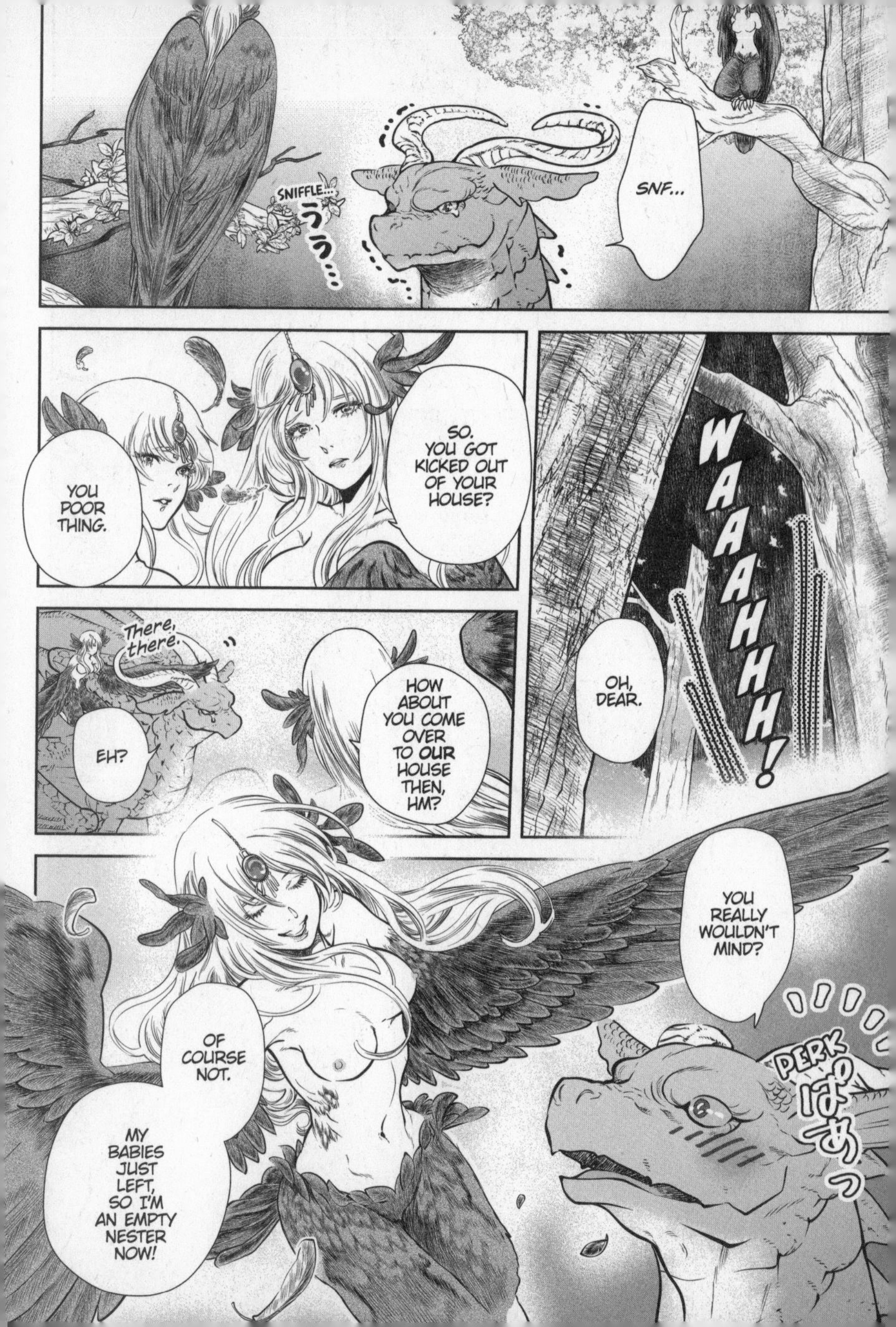
SNF...
SNIFFLE... うう...
WAAAHHH!
OH, DEAR.
SO. YOU GOT KICKED OUT OF YOUR HOUSE?
YOU POOR THING.
HOW ABOUT YOU COME OVER TO **OUR** HOUSE THEN, HM?
There, there.
EH?
YOU REALLY WOULDN'T MIND?
PERK ぱあっ
OF COURSE NOT.
MY BABIES JUST LEFT, SO I'M AN EMPTY NESTER NOW!

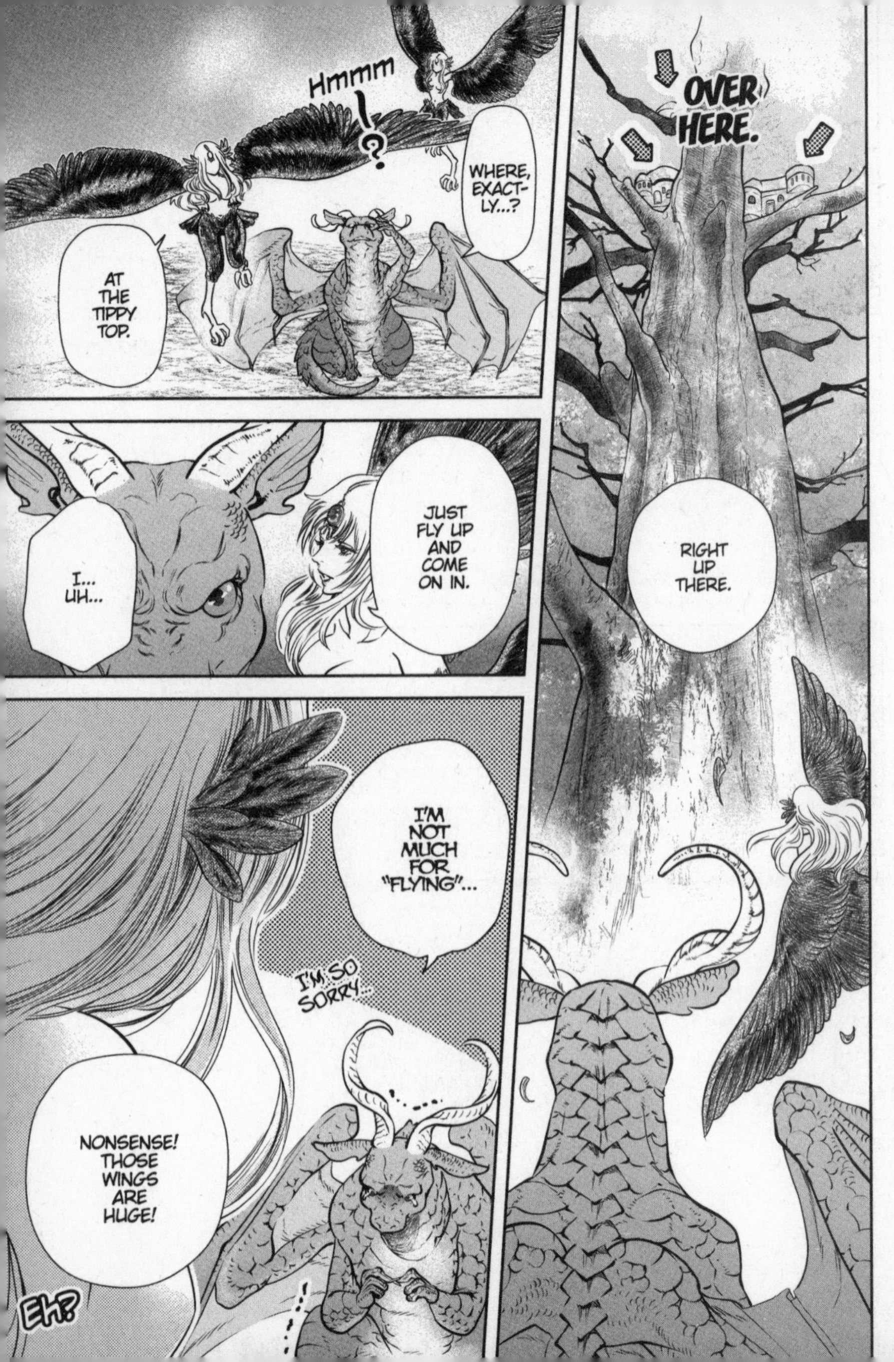
OVER HERE.
RIGHT UP THERE.
Hmmm?
WHERE, EXACTLY...?
AT THE TIPPY TOP.
JUST FLY UP AND COME ON IN.
I... UH...
I'M NOT MUCH FOR "FLYING"...
I'M SO SORRY...
NONSENSE! THOSE WINGS ARE HUGE!
Eh?

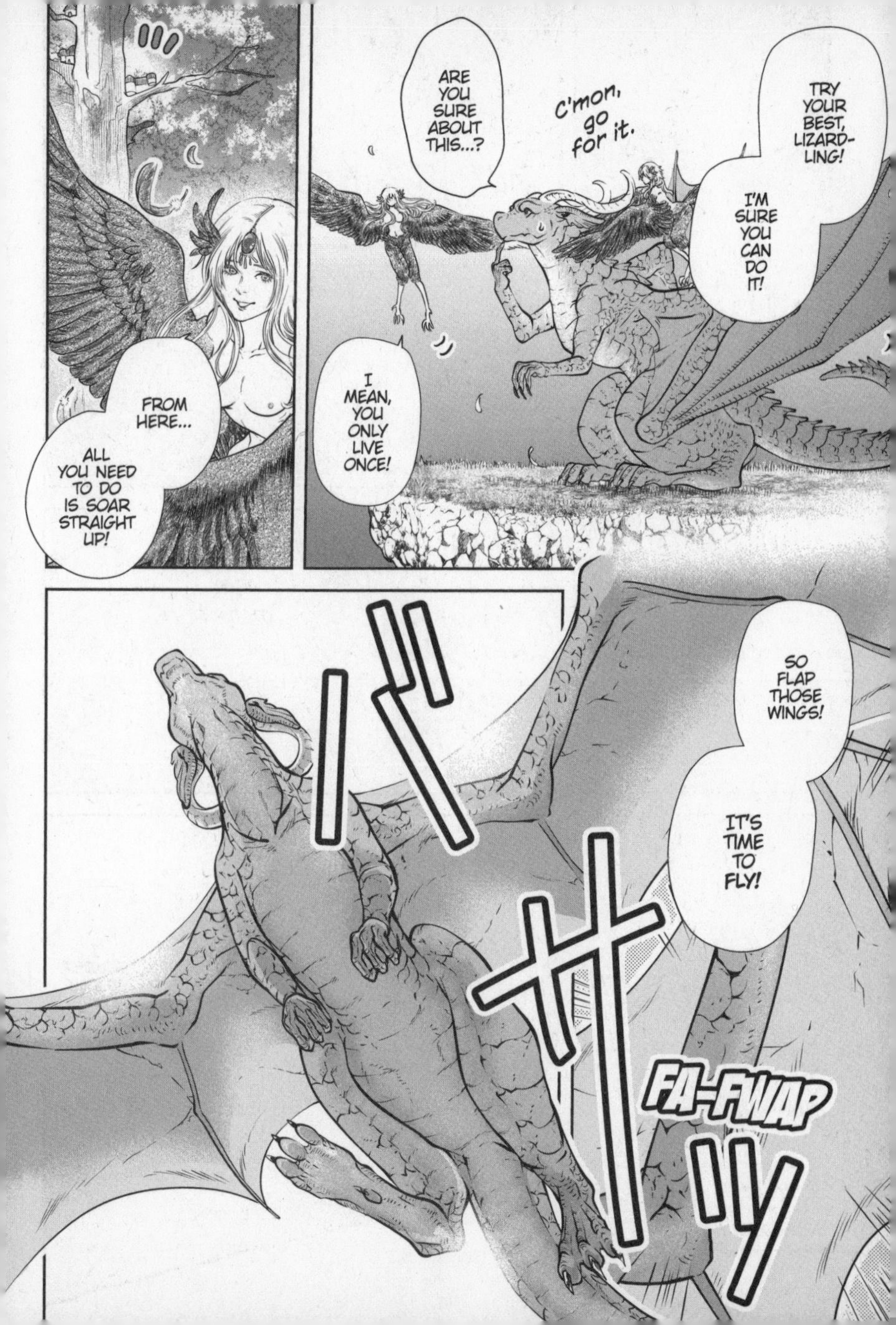
TRY YOUR BEST, LIZARD-LING!
I'M SURE YOU CAN DO IT!
C'mon, go for it.
ARE YOU SURE ABOUT THIS...?
I MEAN, YOU ONLY LIVE ONCE!
FROM HERE...
ALL YOU NEED TO DO IS SOAR STRAIGHT UP!
SO FLAP THOSE WINGS!
IT'S TIME TO FLY!
FA-FWAP

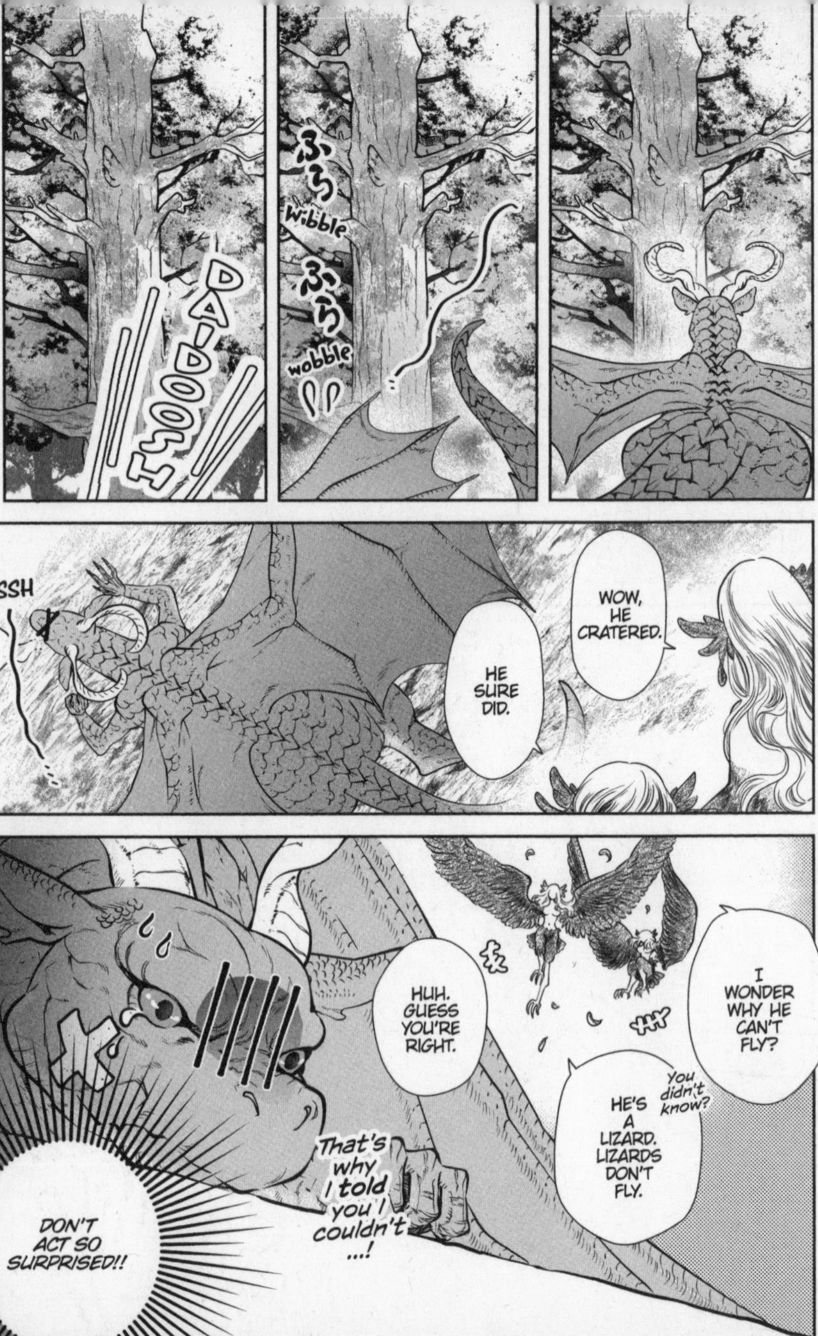
ふら
wibble
ふら
wobble
DAIDOOSH
WOW, HE CRATERED.
HE SURE DID.
FSSH
I WONDER WHY HE CAN'T FLY?
You didn't know?
HE'S A LIZARD. LIZARDS DON'T FLY.
HUH. GUESS YOU'RE RIGHT.
That's why I told you I couldn't ...!
DON'T ACT SO SURPRISED!!

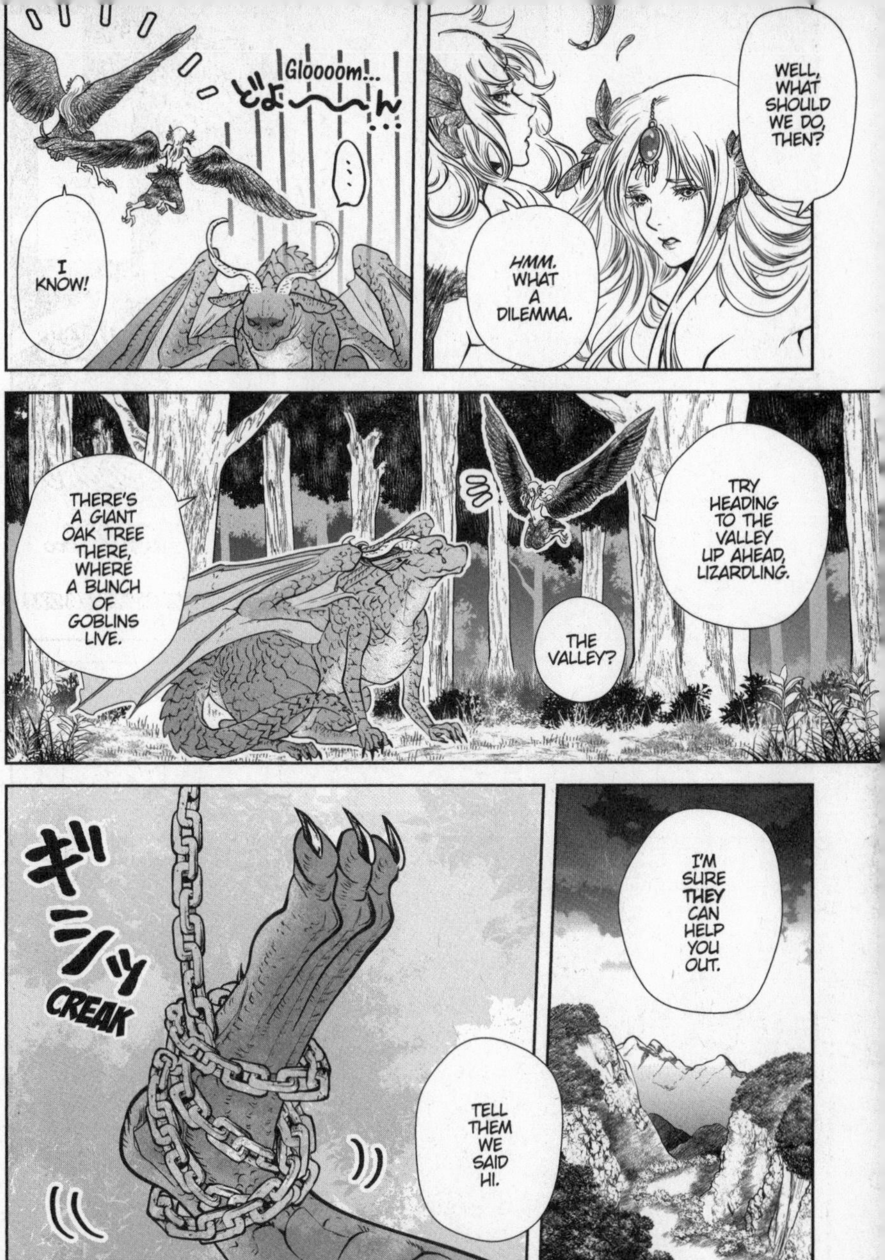
WELL, WHAT SHOULD WE DO, THEN?
HMM. WHAT A DILEMMA.
Gloooom!..
どよ〜〜ん…
…
I KNOW!
TRY HEADING TO THE VALLEY UP AHEAD, LIZARDLING.
THE VALLEY?
THERE'S A GIANT OAK TREE THERE, WHERE A BUNCH OF GOBLINS LIVE.
I'M SURE THEY CAN HELP YOU OUT.
TELL THEM WE SAID HI.
ギシッ
CREAK

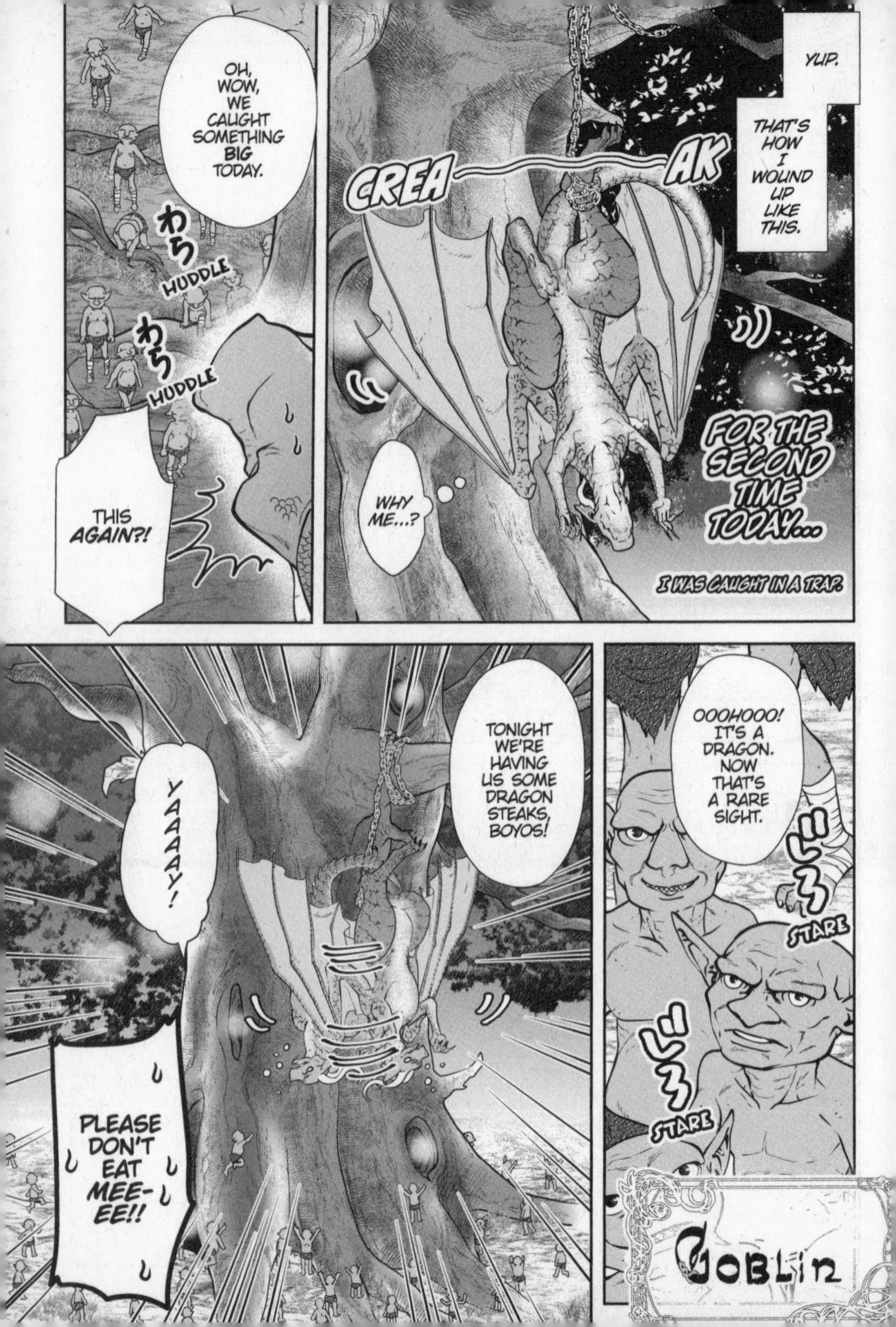
YUP.
THAT'S HOW I WOUND UP LIKE THIS.
CREA—AK
FOR THE SECOND TIME TODAY...
I WAS CAUGHT IN A TRAP.
WHY ME...?
OH, WOW, WE CAUGHT SOMETHING BIG TODAY.
わら
HUDDLE
わら
HUDDLE
THIS AGAIN?!
OOOHOOO! IT'S A DRAGON. NOW THAT'S A RARE SIGHT.
じろ
STARE
じろ
STARE
GOBLIN
TONIGHT WE'RE HAVING US SOME DRAGON STEAKS, BOYOS!
YAAAAY!
PLEASE DON'T EAT MEEE-EE!!

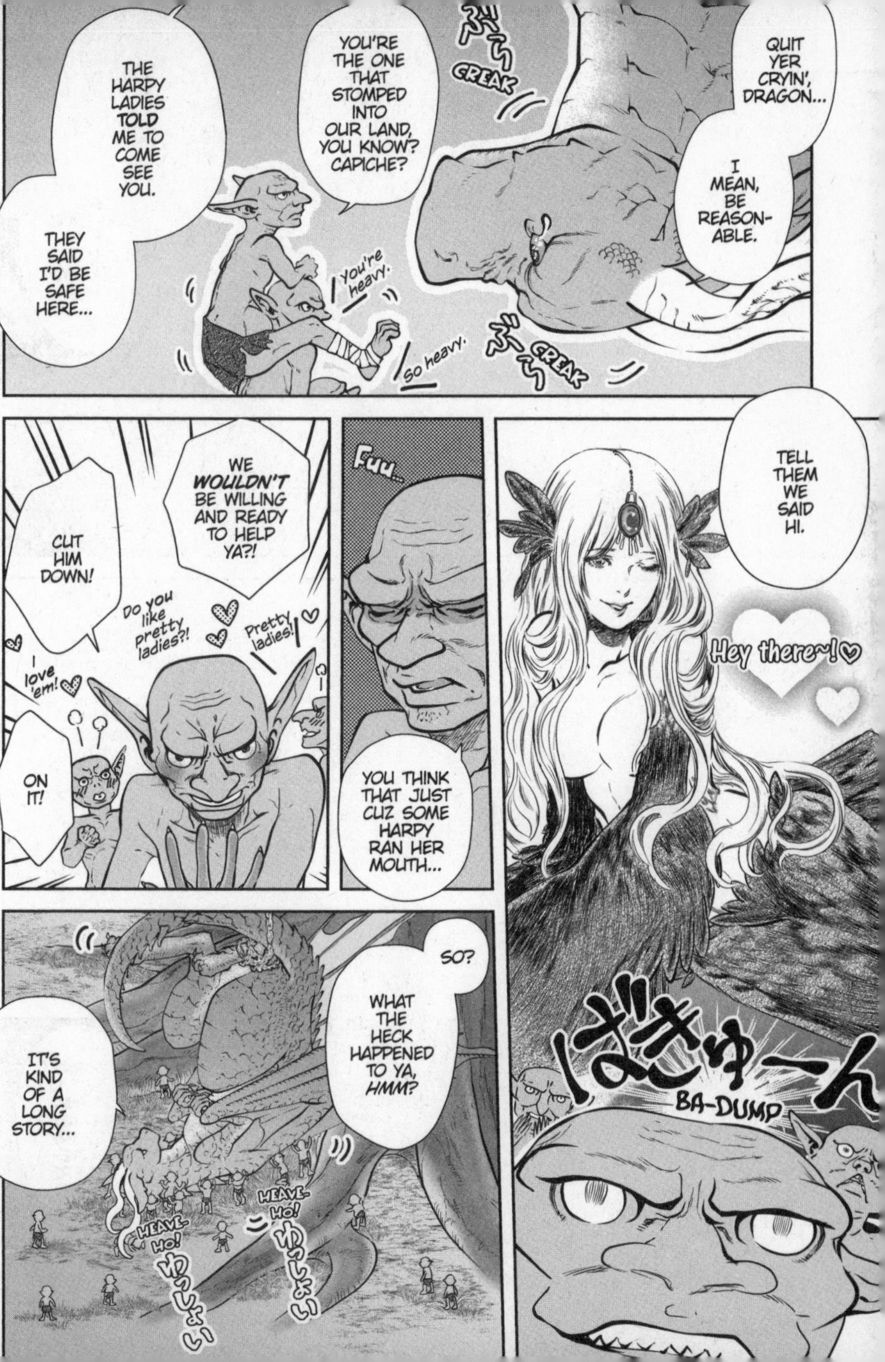
QUIT YER CRYIN', DRAGON...
I MEAN, BE REASON-ABLE.
CREAK
CREAK
YOU'RE THE ONE THAT STOMPED INTO OUR LAND, YOU KNOW? CAPICHE?
You're heavy.
So heavy.
THE HARPY LADIES TOLD ME TO COME SEE YOU.
THEY SAID I'D BE SAFE HERE...
TELL THEM WE SAID HI.
Hey there~!♡
ばきゅーん
BA-DUMP
Fuu...
YOU THINK THAT JUST CUZ SOME HARPY RAN HER MOUTH...
WE WOULDN'T BE WILLING AND READY TO HELP YA?!
CUT HIM DOWN!
Do you like pretty ladies?!
Pretty ladies!
I love 'em!
ON IT!
SO?
WHAT THE HECK HAPPENED TO YA, HMM?
IT'S KIND OF A LONG STORY...
HEAVE-HO! わっしょい
HEAVE-HO! わっしょい

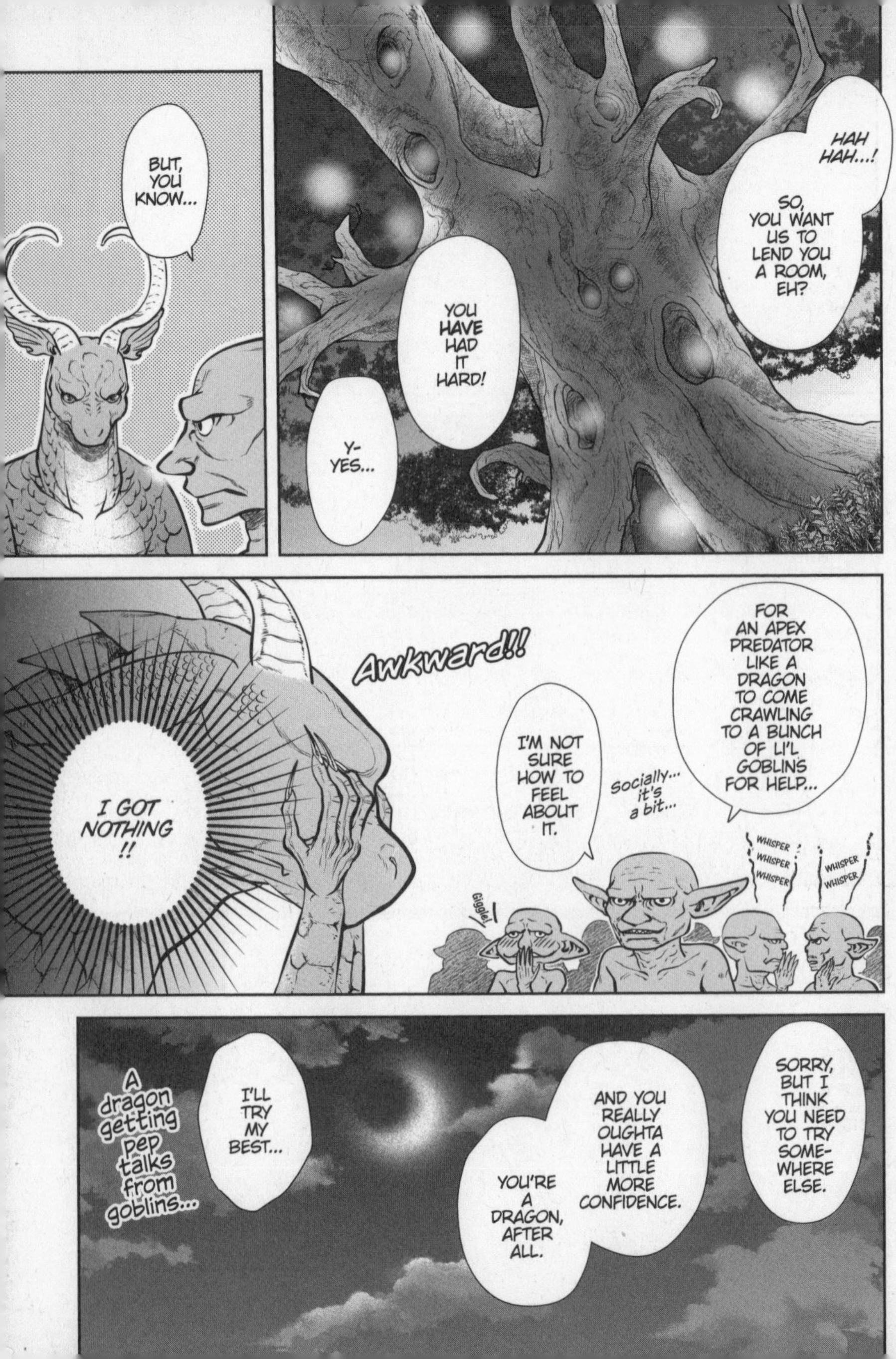
HAH HAH...!
SO, YOU WANT US TO LEND YOU A ROOM, EH?
YOU HAVE HAD IT HARD!
Y-YES...
BUT, YOU KNOW...
FOR AN APEX PREDATOR LIKE A DRAGON TO COME CRAWLING TO A BUNCH OF LI'L GOBLINS FOR HELP...
WHISPER WHISPER WHISPER
WHISPER WHISPER
Socially... it's a bit...
I'M NOT SURE HOW TO FEEL ABOUT IT.
Giggle
Awkward!!
I GOT NOTHING!!
SORRY, BUT I THINK YOU NEED TO TRY SOME-WHERE ELSE.
AND YOU REALLY OUGHTA HAVE A LITTLE MORE CONFIDENCE.
YOU'RE A DRAGON, AFTER ALL.
I'LL TRY MY BEST...
A dragon getting pep talks from goblins...

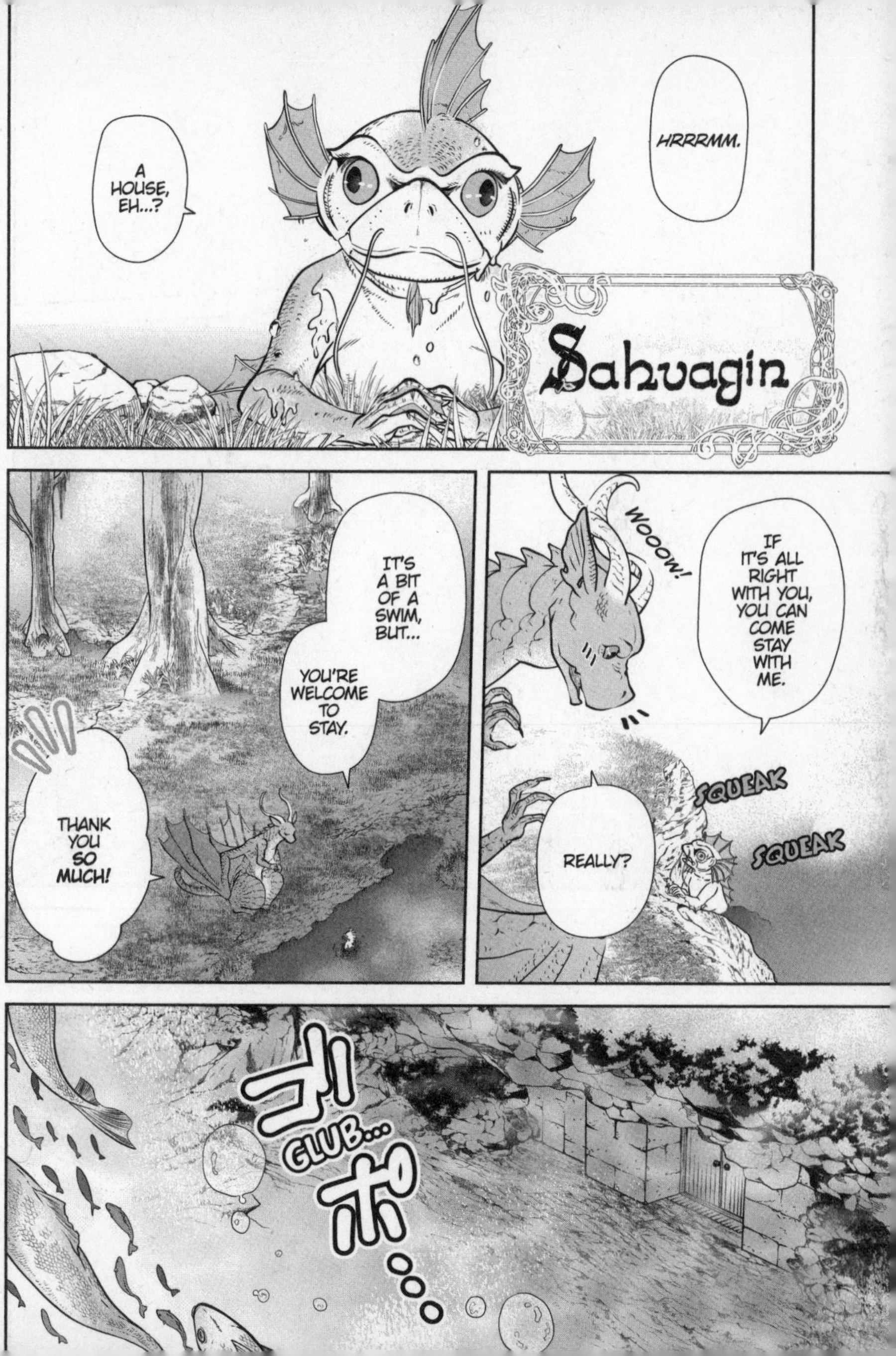
HRRRMM.
A HOUSE, EH...?
Sahuagin
WOOOW!
IF IT'S ALL RIGHT WITH YOU, YOU CAN COME STAY WITH ME.
SQUEAK
SQUEAK
REALLY?
IT'S A BIT OF A SWIM, BUT...
YOU'RE WELCOME TO STAY.
THANK YOU SO MUCH!
ゴポ…
GLUB...

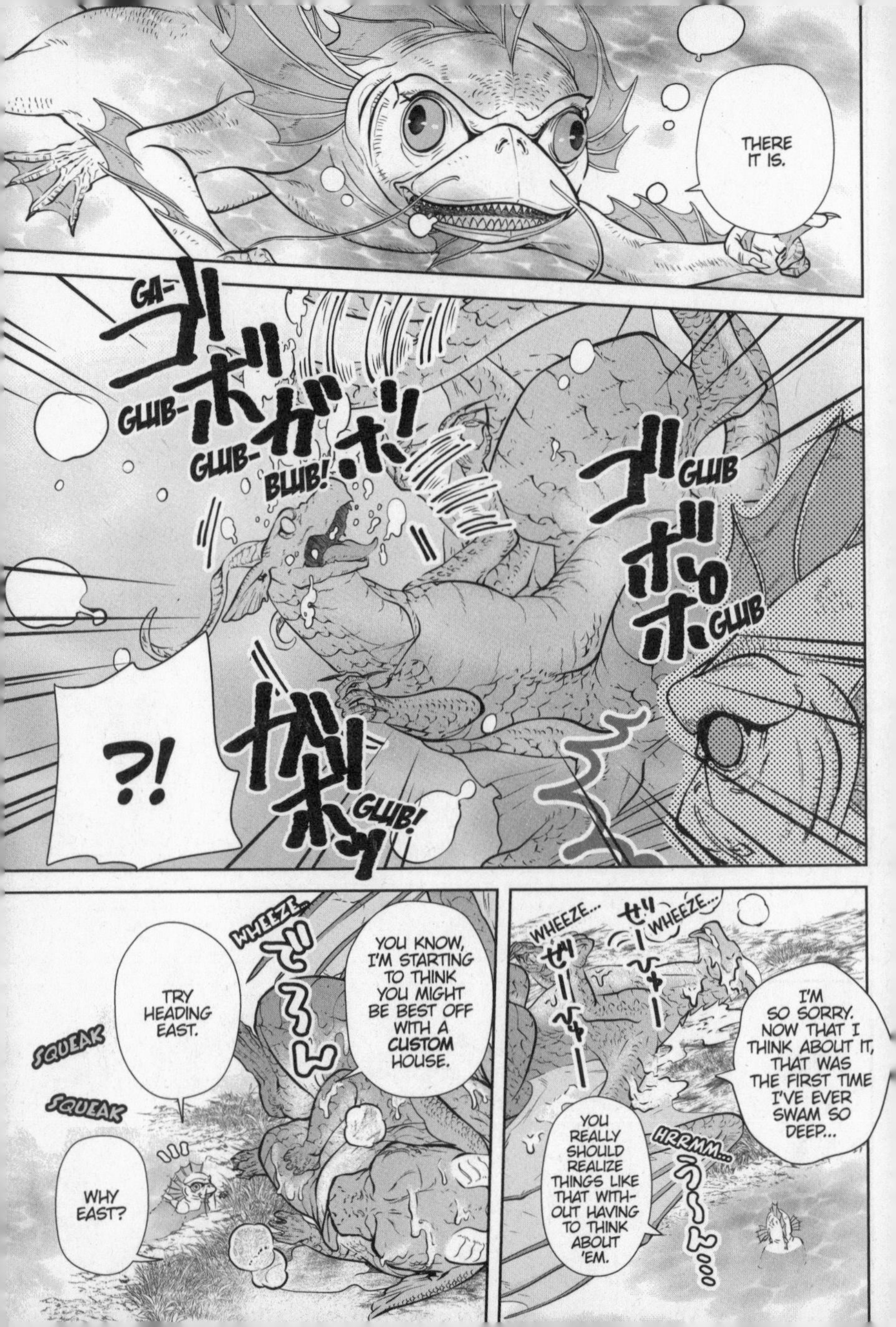
THERE IT IS.
GLUB
GLUB
GA-
GLUB-
GLUB-
BLUB!
?!
GLUB!
WHEEZE...
WHEEZE...
I'M SO SORRY. NOW THAT I THINK ABOUT IT, THAT WAS THE FIRST TIME I'VE EVER SWAM SO DEEP...
HRRMM...
YOU REALLY SHOULD REALIZE THINGS LIKE THAT WITH-OUT HAVING TO THINK ABOUT 'EM.
WHEEZE...
YOU KNOW, I'M STARTING TO THINK YOU MIGHT BE BEST OFF WITH A CUSTOM HOUSE.
TRY HEADING EAST.
SQUEAK
SQUEAK
WHY EAST?

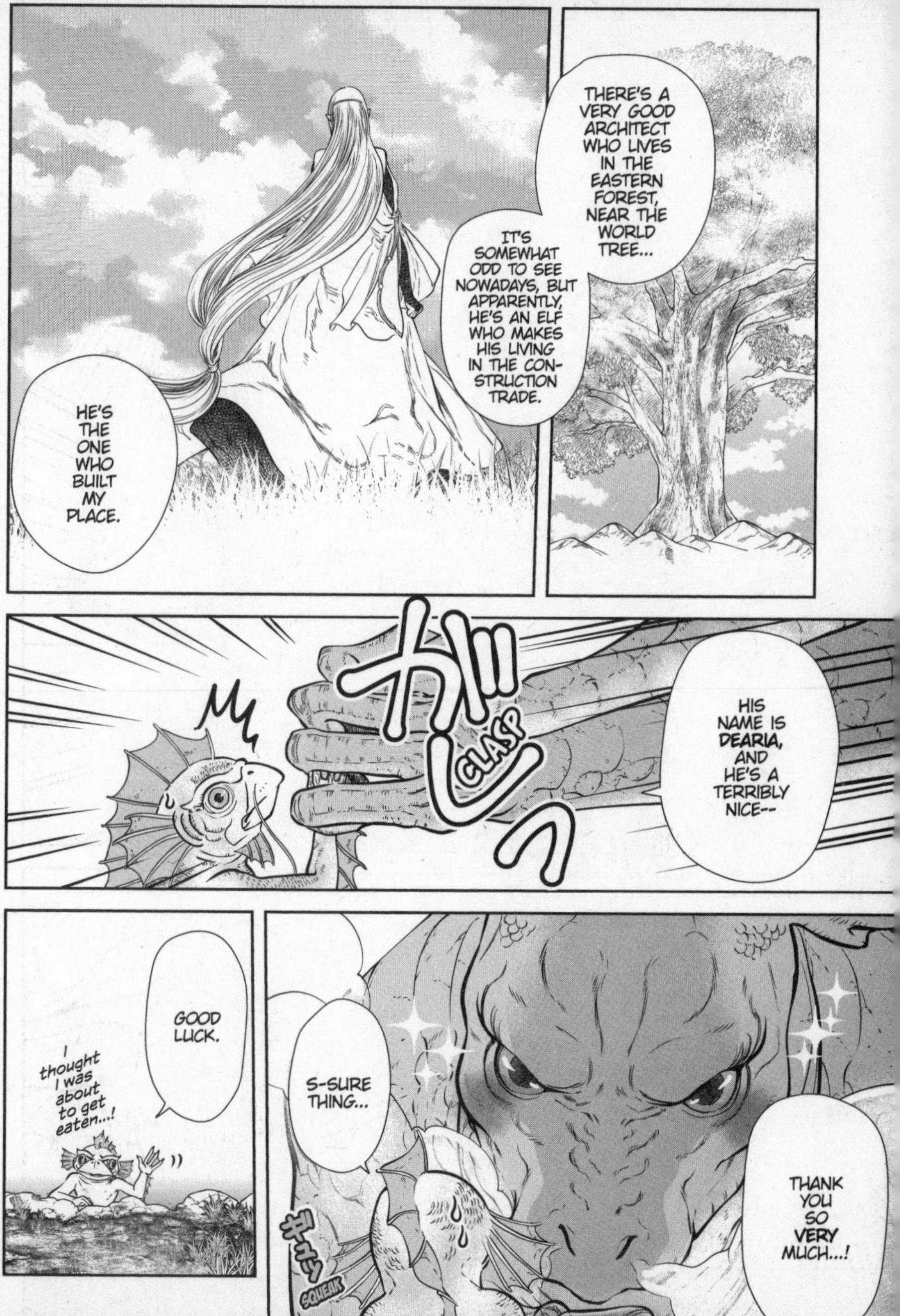
THERE'S A VERY GOOD ARCHITECT WHO LIVES IN THE EASTERN FOREST, NEAR THE WORLD TREE...
IT'S SOMEWHAT ODD TO SEE NOWADAYS, BUT APPARENTLY, HE'S AN ELF WHO MAKES HIS LIVING IN THE CONSTRUCTION TRADE.
HE'S THE ONE WHO BUILT MY PLACE.
HIS NAME IS **DEARIA,** AND HE'S A TERRIBLY NICE--
CLASP
THANK YOU SO **VERY** MUCH...!
S-SURE THING...
SQUEAK
GOOD LUCK.
I thought I was about to get eaten...!

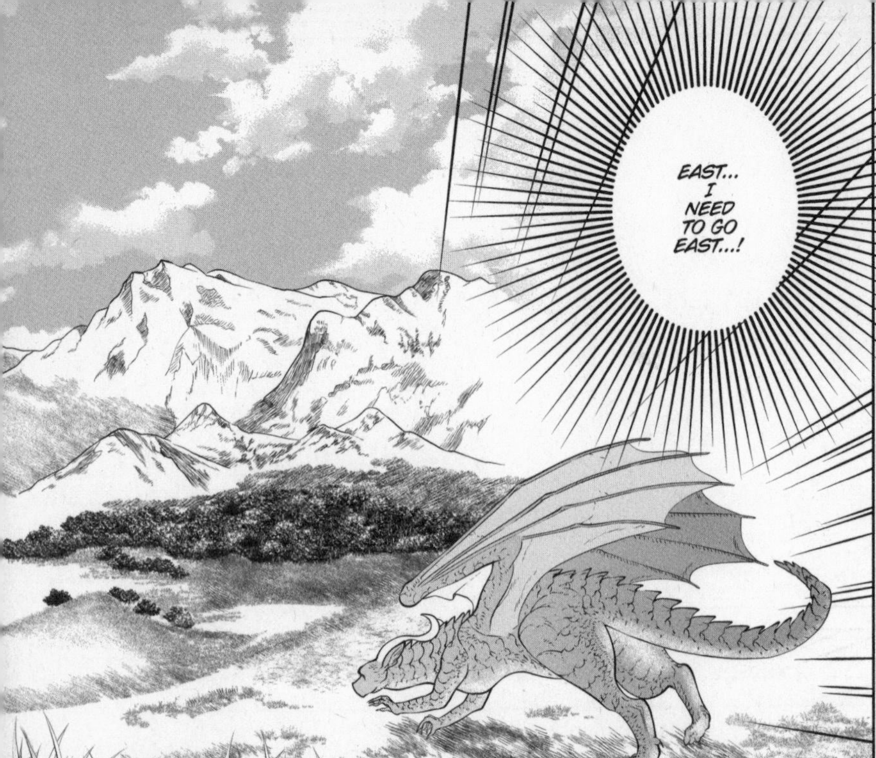
EAST... I NEED TO GO EAST...!

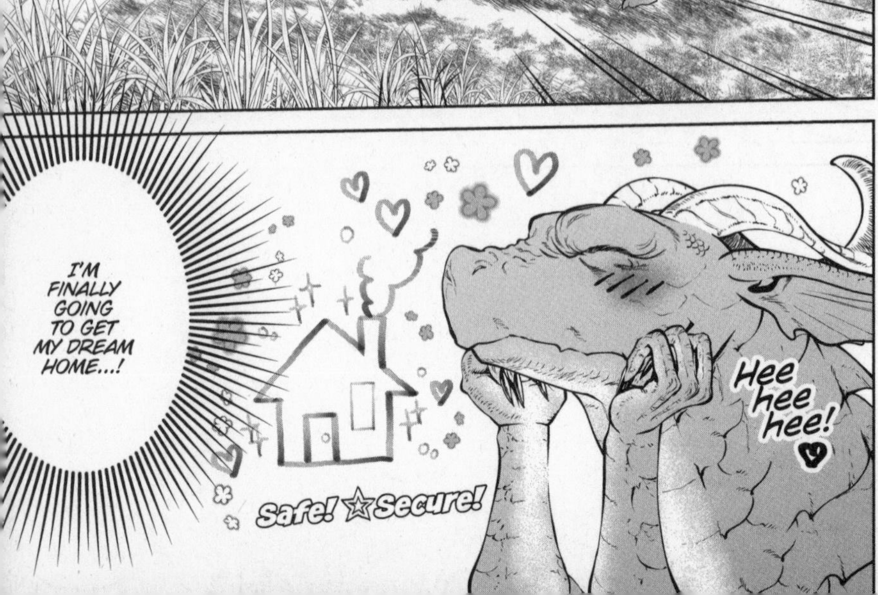
I'M FINALLY GOING TO GET MY DREAM HOME...!
Safe! ☆ Secure!
Hee hee hee!

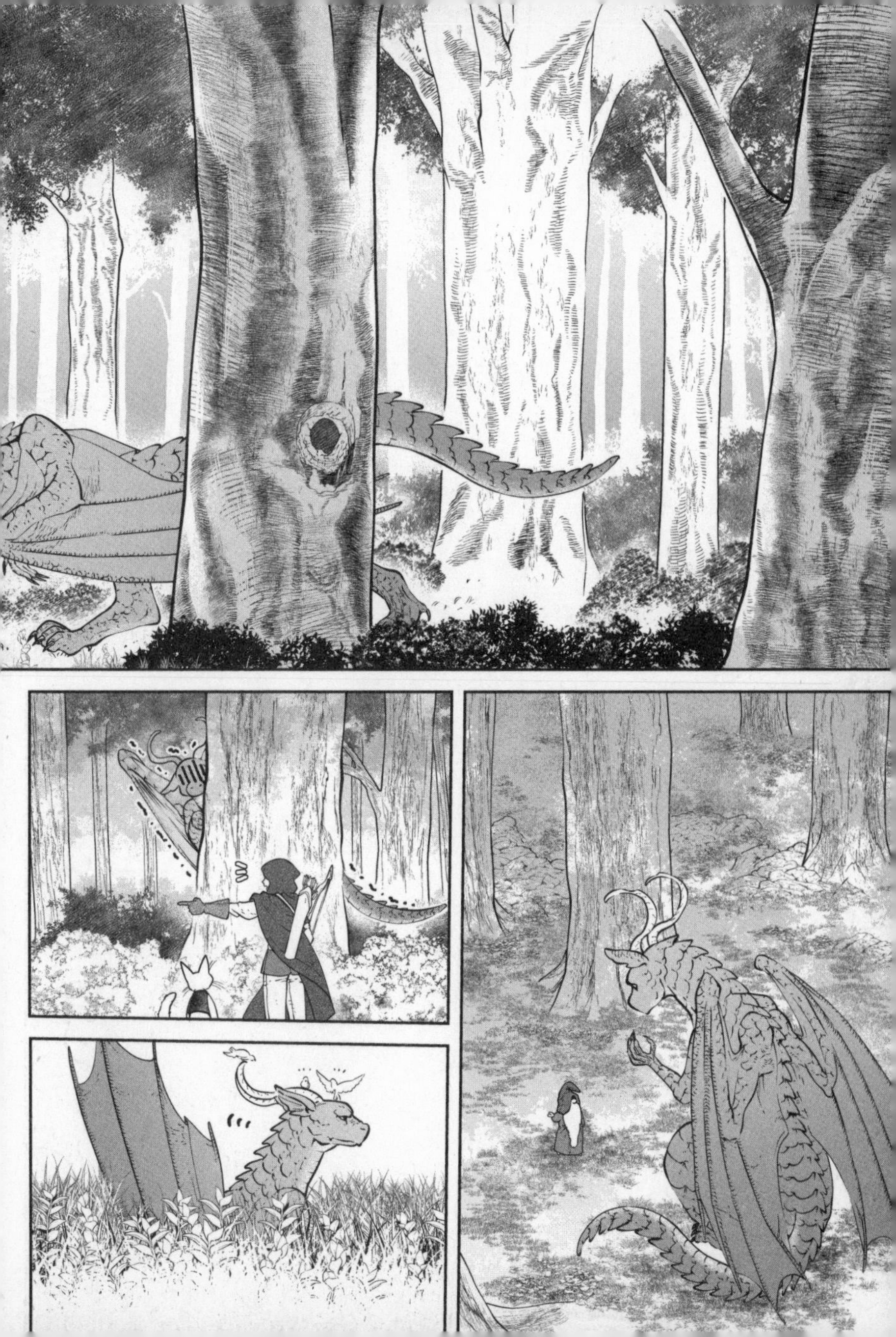

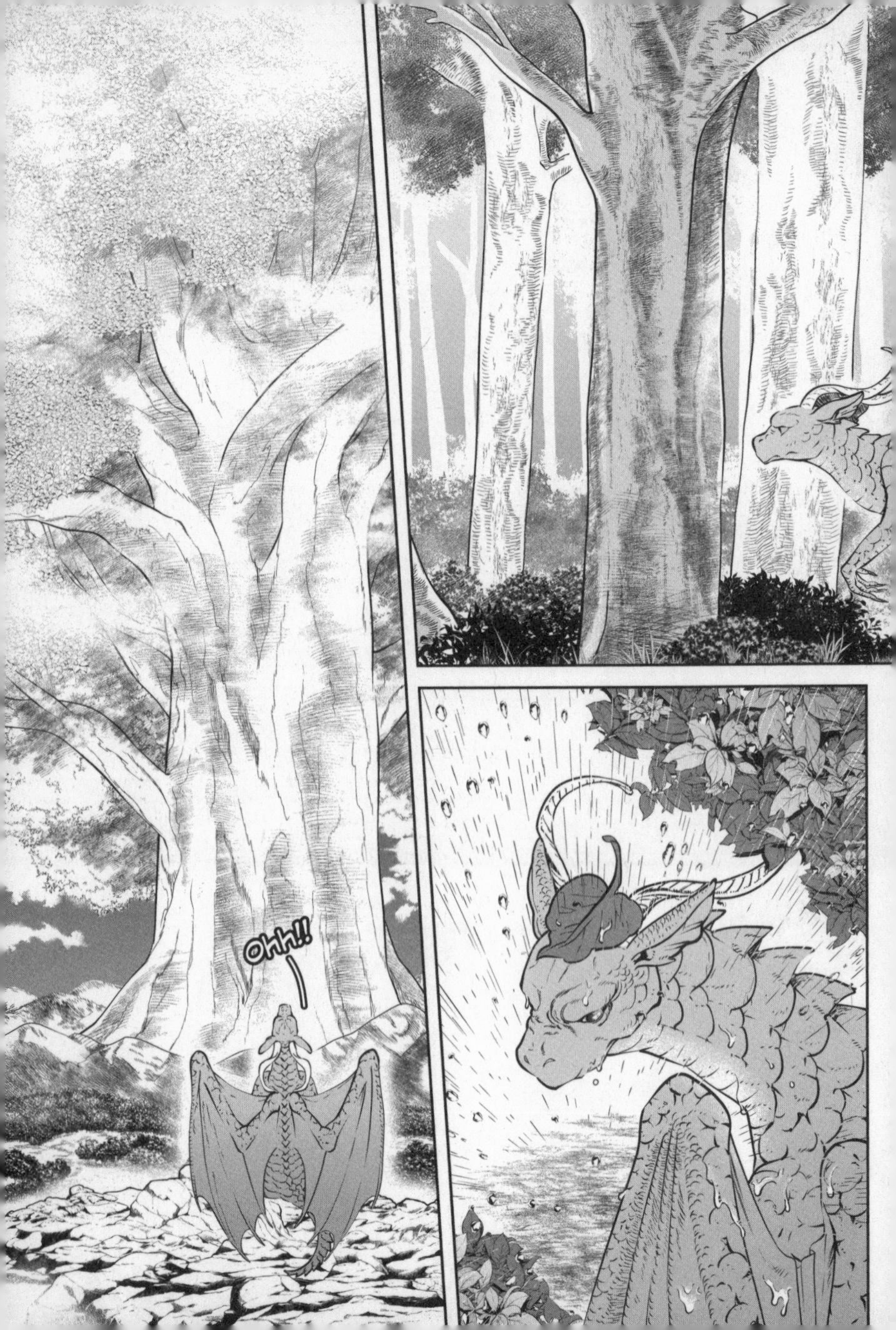
Ohh!!

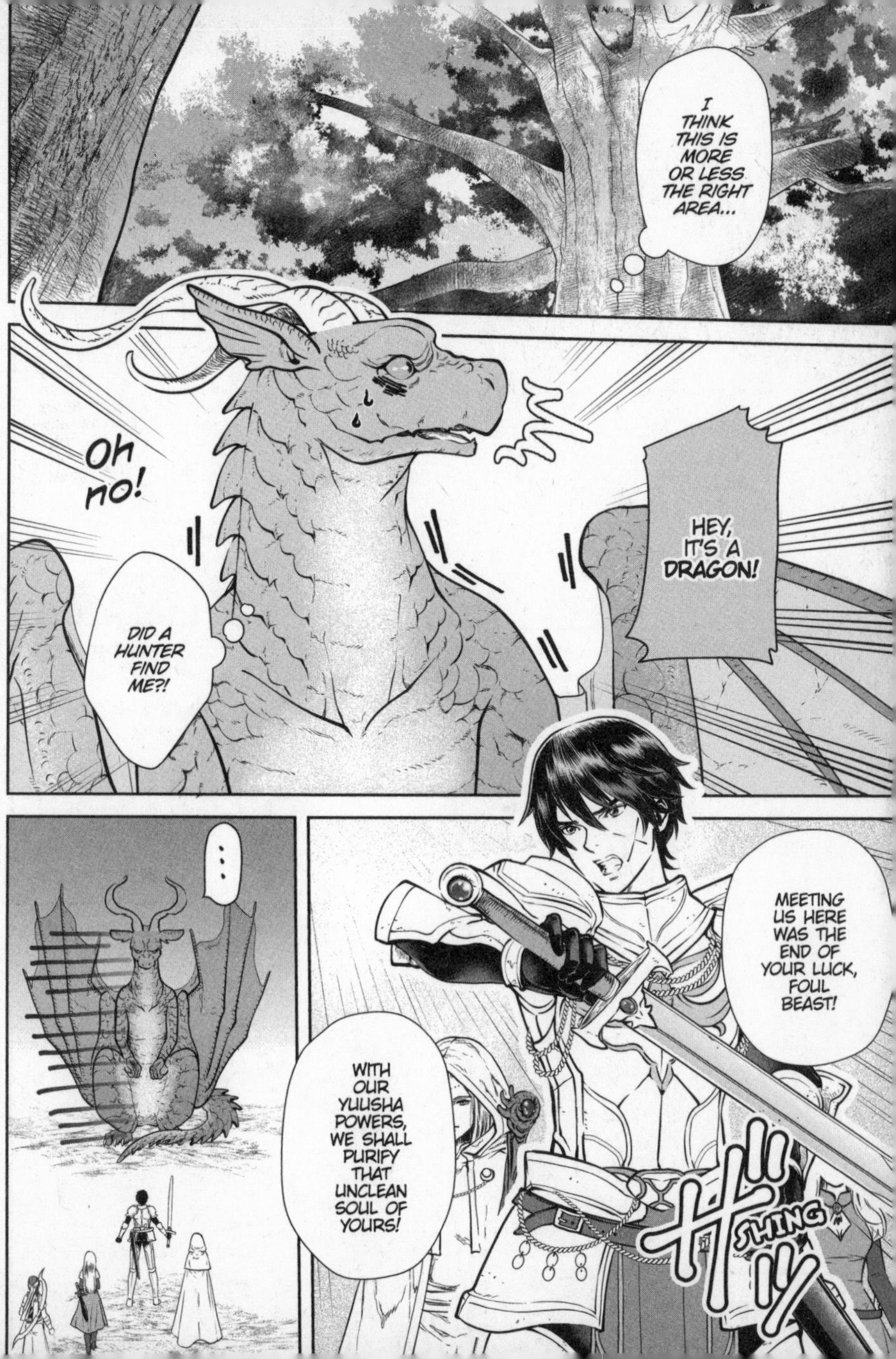
I THINK THIS IS MORE OR LESS THE RIGHT AREA...
HEY, IT'S A DRAGON!
Oh no!
DID A HUNTER FIND ME?!
MEETING US HERE WAS THE END OF YOUR LUCK, FOUL BEAST!
WITH OUR YUUSHA POWERS, WE SHALL PURIFY THAT UNCLEAN SOUL OF YOURS!
SHING
...

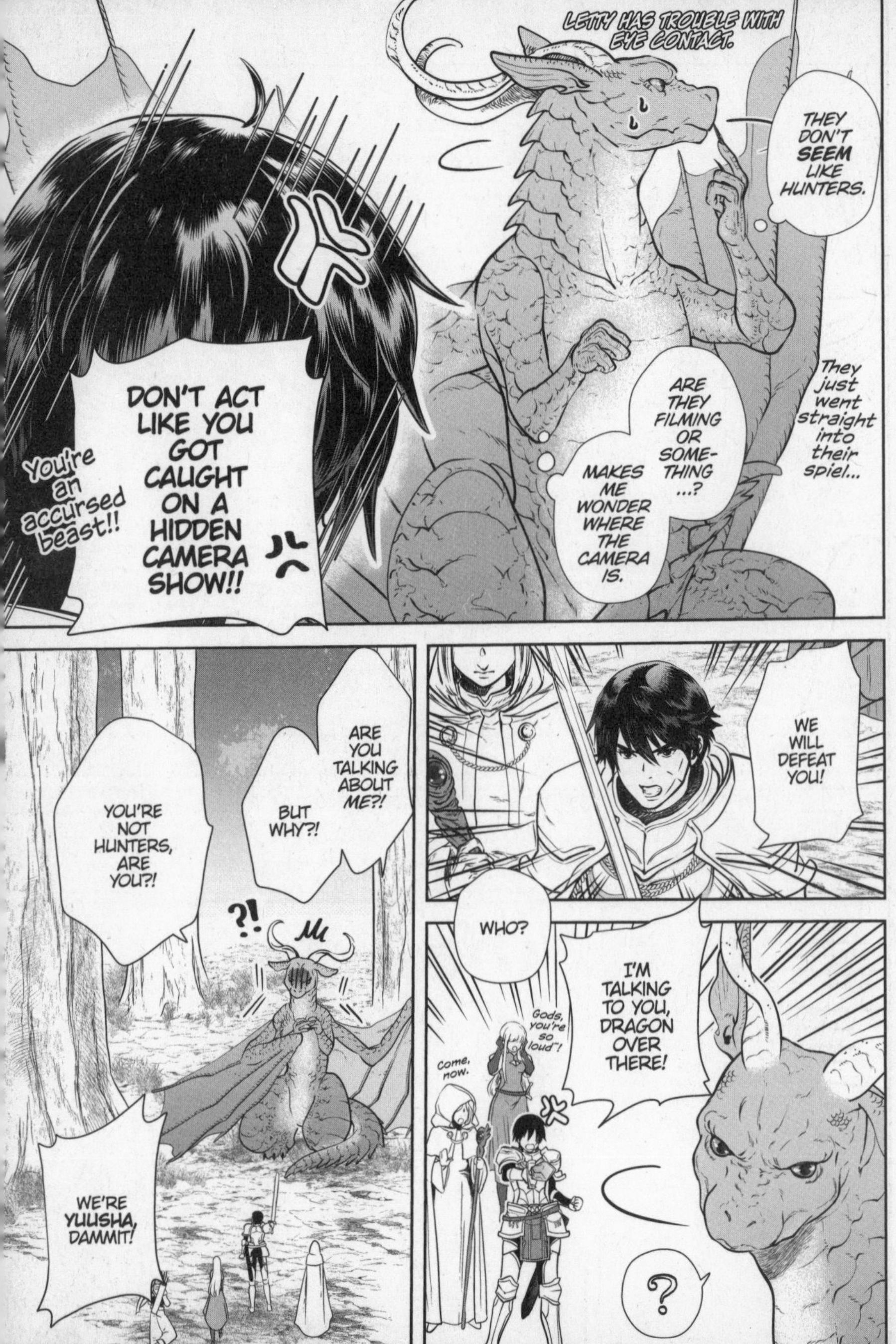
LETTY HAS TROUBLE WITH EYE CONTACT.
THEY DON'T SEEM LIKE HUNTERS.
They just went straight into their spiel...
ARE THEY FILMING OR SOME-THING...?
MAKES ME WONDER WHERE THE CAMERA IS.
DON'T ACT LIKE YOU GOT CAUGHT ON A HIDDEN CAMERA SHOW!!
You're an accursed beast!!
WE WILL DEFEAT YOU!
WHO?
I'M TALKING TO YOU, DRAGON OVER THERE!
Gods, you're so loud~!
Come, now.
?
ARE YOU TALKING ABOUT ME?!
BUT WHY?!
YOU'RE NOT HUNTERS, ARE YOU?!
?!
WE'RE YUUSHA, DAMMIT!

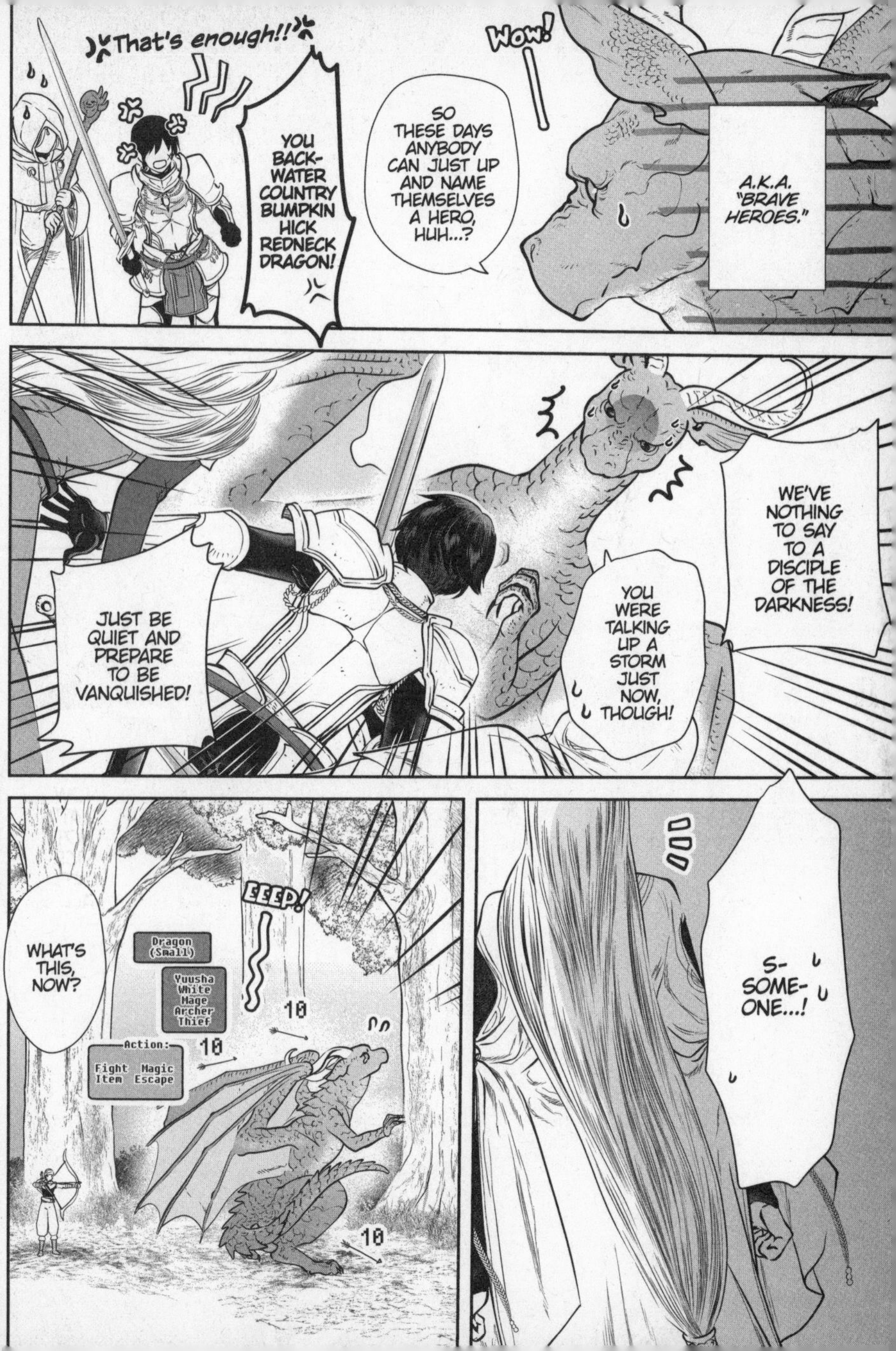
A.K.A. "BRAVE HEROES."
Wow!
SO THESE DAYS ANYBODY CAN JUST UP AND NAME THEMSELVES A HERO, HUH...?
That's enough!!
YOU BACK-WATER COUNTRY BUMPKIN HICK REDNECK DRAGON!
WE'VE NOTHING TO SAY TO A DISCIPLE OF THE DARKNESS!
YOU WERE TALKING UP A STORM JUST NOW, THOUGH!
JUST BE QUIET AND PREPARE TO BE VANQUISHED!
S-SOME-ONE...!
EEEP!
WHAT'S THIS, NOW?
Dragon (Small)
Yuusha White Mage Archer Thief
Action:
Fight Magic Item Escape
10
10
10

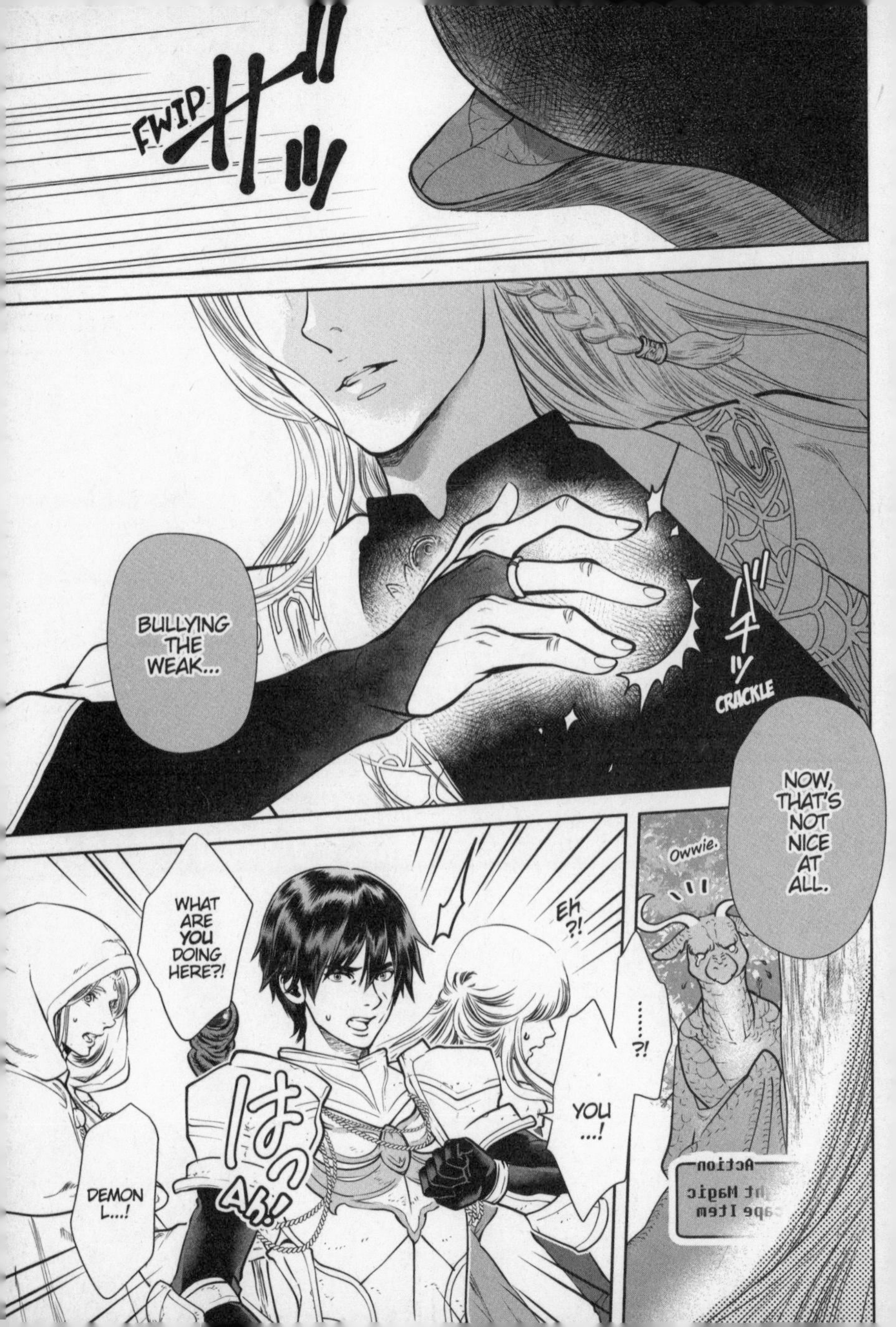
FWIP
CRACKLE
BULLYING THE WEAK...
NOW, THAT'S NOT NICE AT ALL.
Owwie.
Action
ht Magic
ape Item
Eh?!
......?!
YOU...!
WHAT ARE YOU DOING HERE?!
Ah!
DEMON L...!

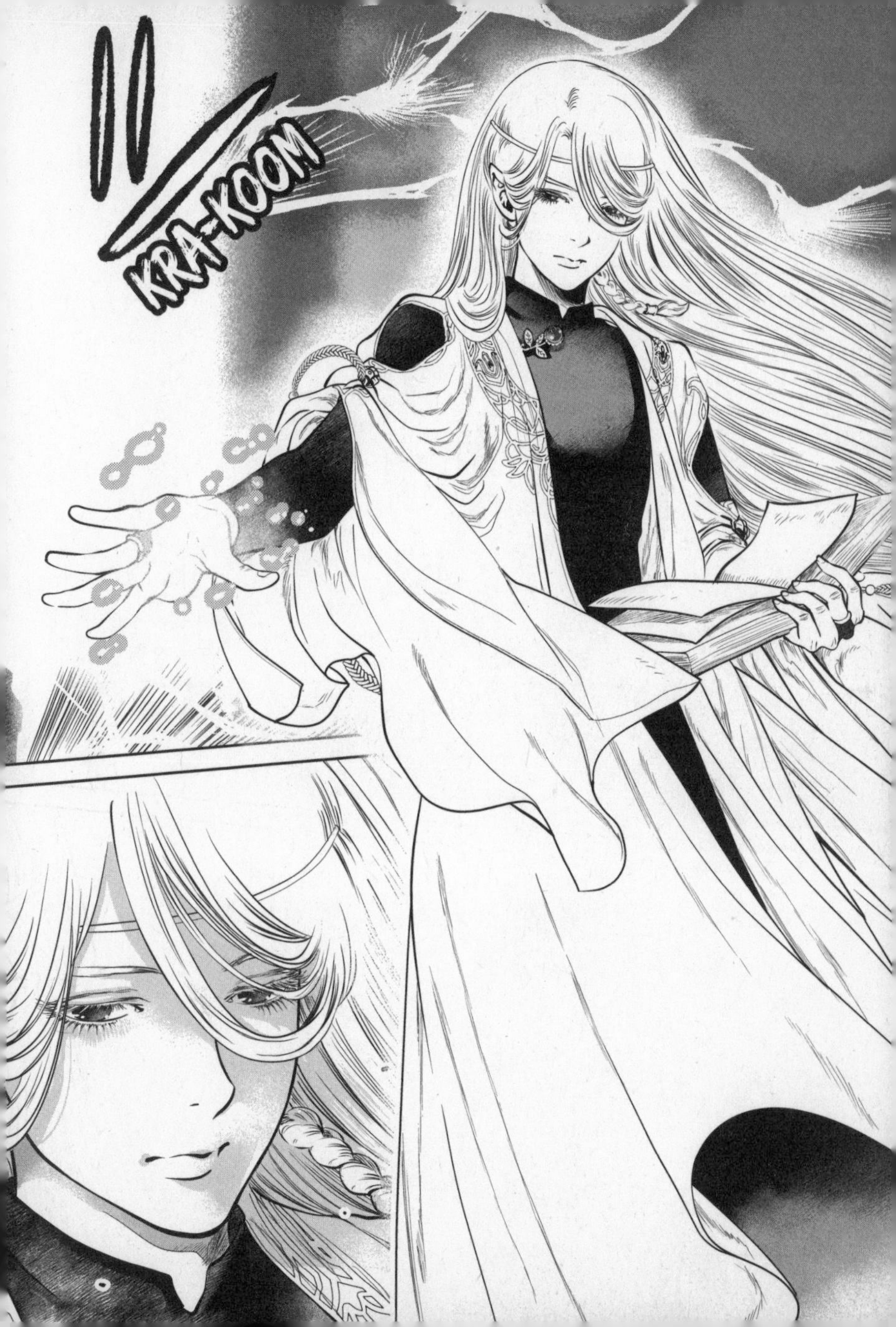
KRA-KOOM

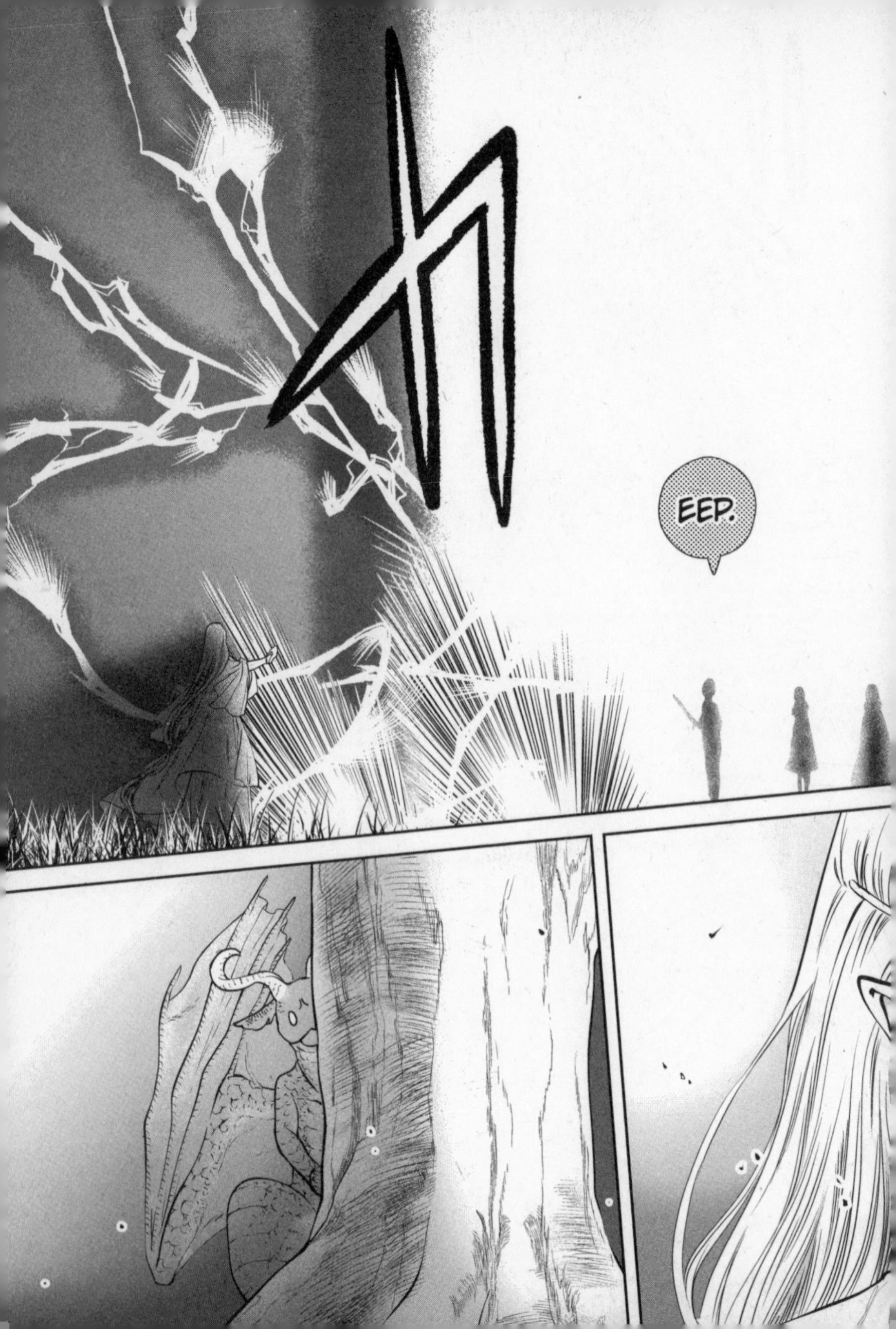
EEP.

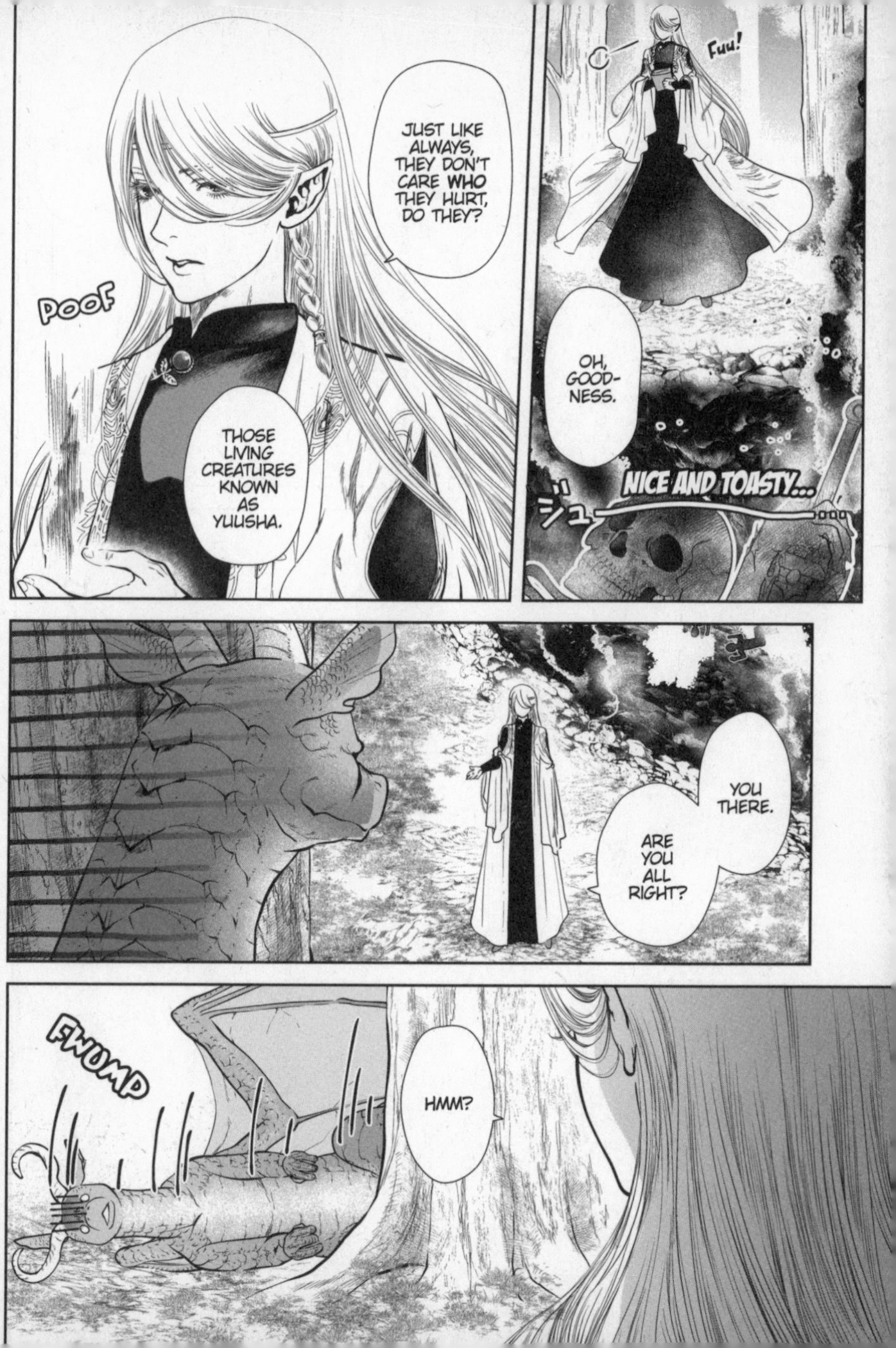
Fuu!
OH, GOODNESS.
NICE AND TOASTY...
ジュ
JUST LIKE ALWAYS, THEY DON'T CARE WHO THEY HURT, DO THEY?
THOSE LIVING CREATURES KNOWN AS YUUSHA.
POOF
YOU THERE.
ARE YOU ALL RIGHT?
HMM?
FWUMP

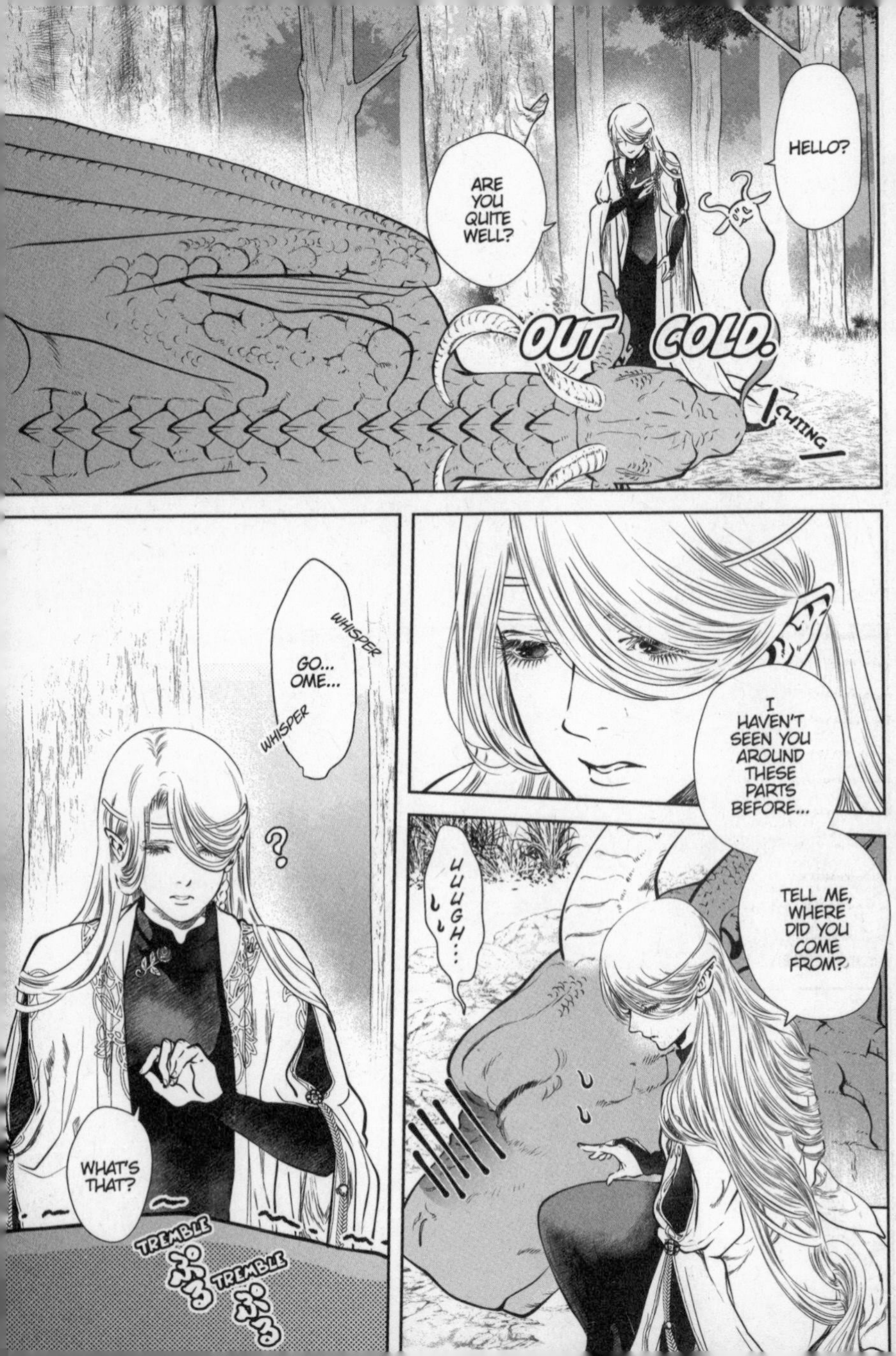
HELLO?
ARE YOU QUITE WELL?
OUT COLD.
CHIIING
I HAVEN'T SEEN YOU AROUND THESE PARTS BEFORE...
TELL ME, WHERE DID YOU COME FROM?
UUUGH...
WHISPER
GO... OME...
WHISPER
?
WHAT'S THAT?
TREMBLE
ぶる
TREMBLE
ぶる

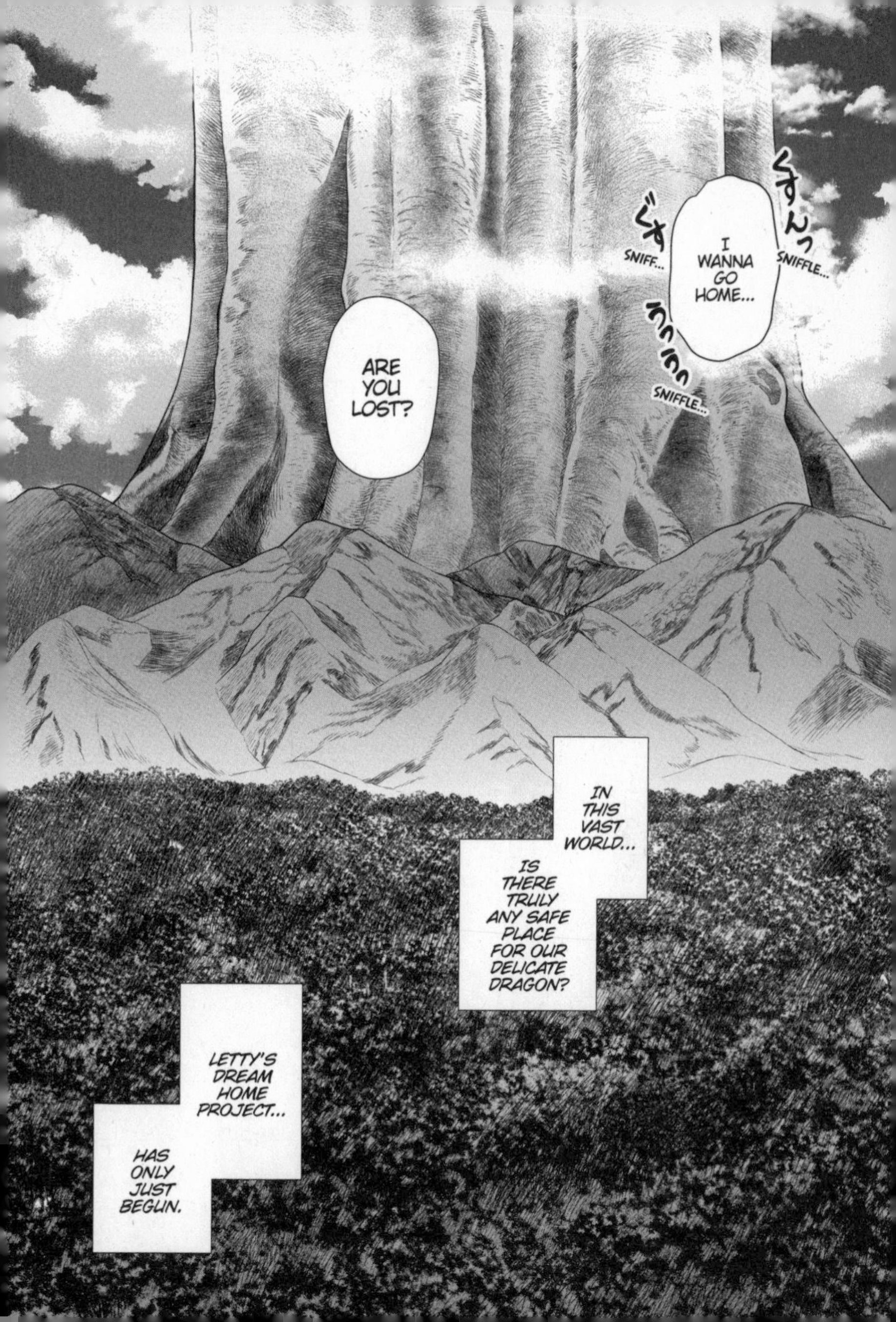
SNIFFLE...
I WANNA GO HOME...
SNIFF...
SNIFFLE...
ARE YOU LOST?
IN THIS VAST WORLD...
IS THERE TRULY ANY SAFE PLACE FOR OUR DELICATE DRAGON?
LETTY'S DREAM HOME PROJECT...
HAS ONLY JUST BEGUN.

I Picked Up a Lost Dragon

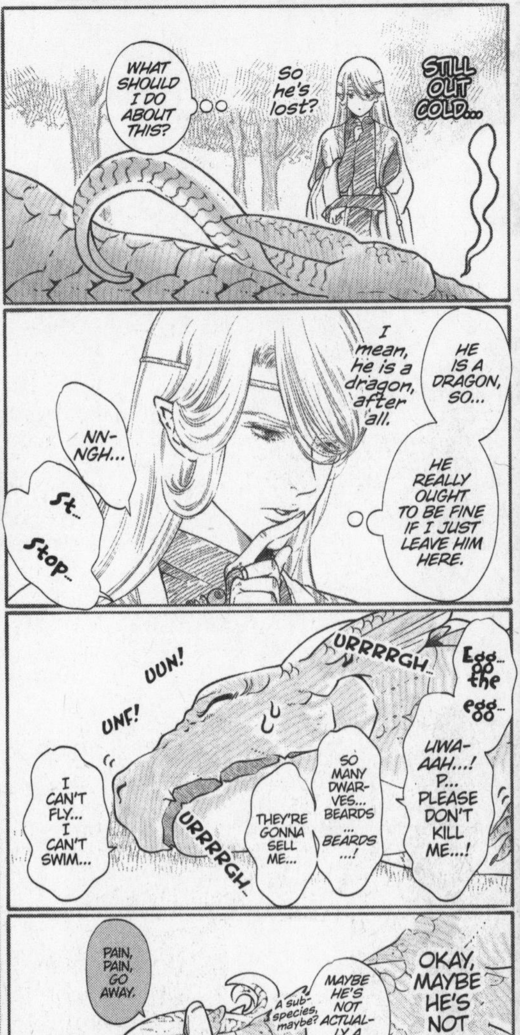

STILL OUT COLD...
So he's lost?
WHAT SHOULD I DO ABOUT THIS?
HE IS A DRAGON, SO...
I mean, he is a dragon, after all.
HE REALLY OUGHT TO BE FINE IF I JUST LEAVE HIM HERE.
NN-NGH...
St... Stop...
Egg... the egg...
URRRRGH...
UWA-AAH...! P... PLEASE DON'T KILL ME...!
UUN!
SO MANY DWAR-VES... BEARDS... BEARDS...!
THEY'RE GONNA SELL ME...
UNF!
I CAN'T FLY... I CAN'T SWIM...
URRRRGH...
OKAY, MAYBE HE'S NOT GONNA BE FINE.
MAYBE HE'S NOT ACTUAL-LY A DRAGON...?
A sub-species, maybe?
PAIN, PAIN, GO AWAY.
THERE, THERE.
SNIFFLE...

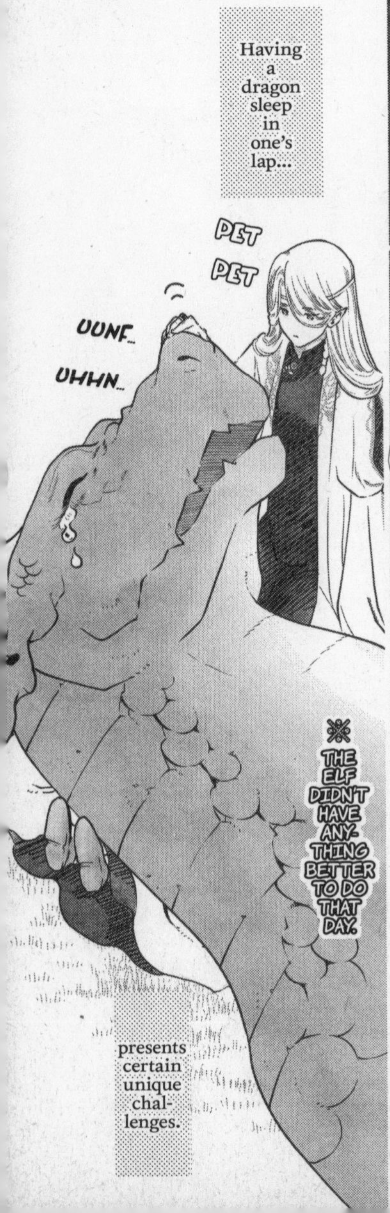

Having a dragon sleep in one's lap...
PET
PET
UUNF...
UHHN...
※ THE ELF DIDN'T HAVE ANY-THING BETTER TO DO THAT DAY.
presents certain unique chal-lenges.

Dragon Goes House-Hunting

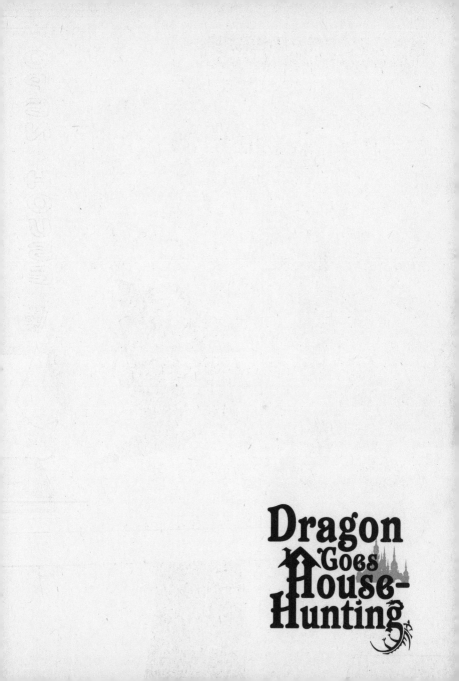

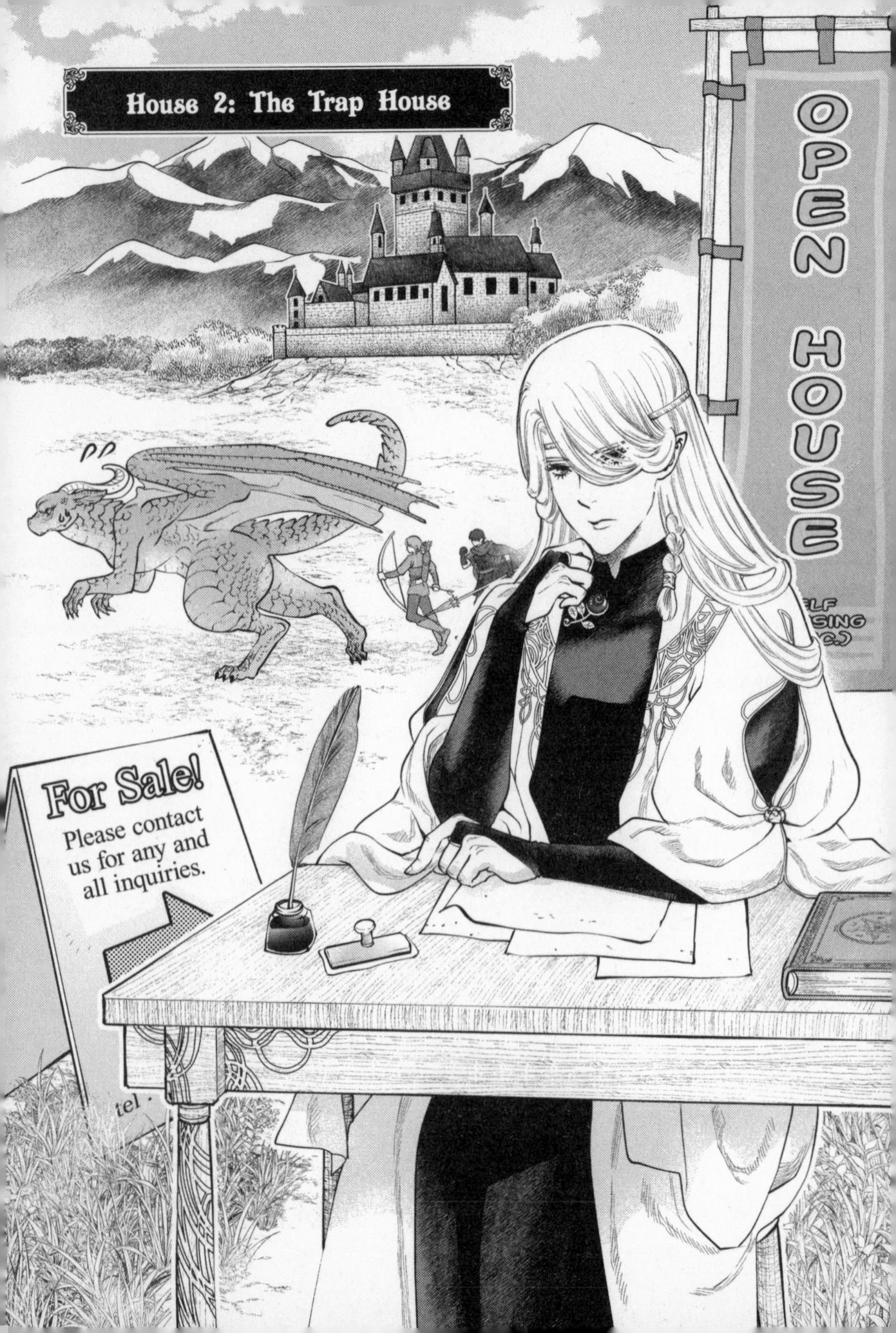
House 2: The Trap House
OPEN HOUSE
For Sale!
Please contact us for any and all inquiries.
tel .

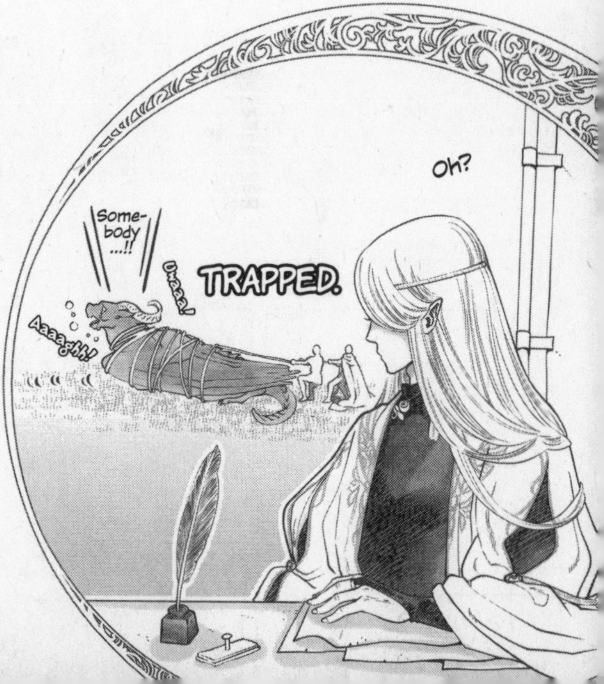
Oh?
TRAPPED.
Uwaaa!
Some-body ...!!
Aaaaghh!

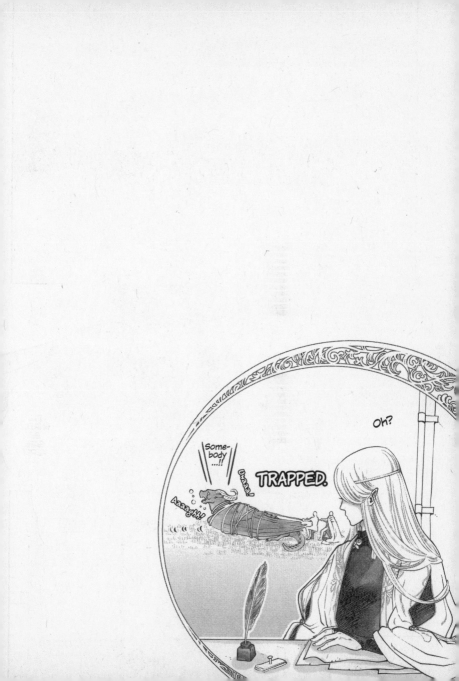

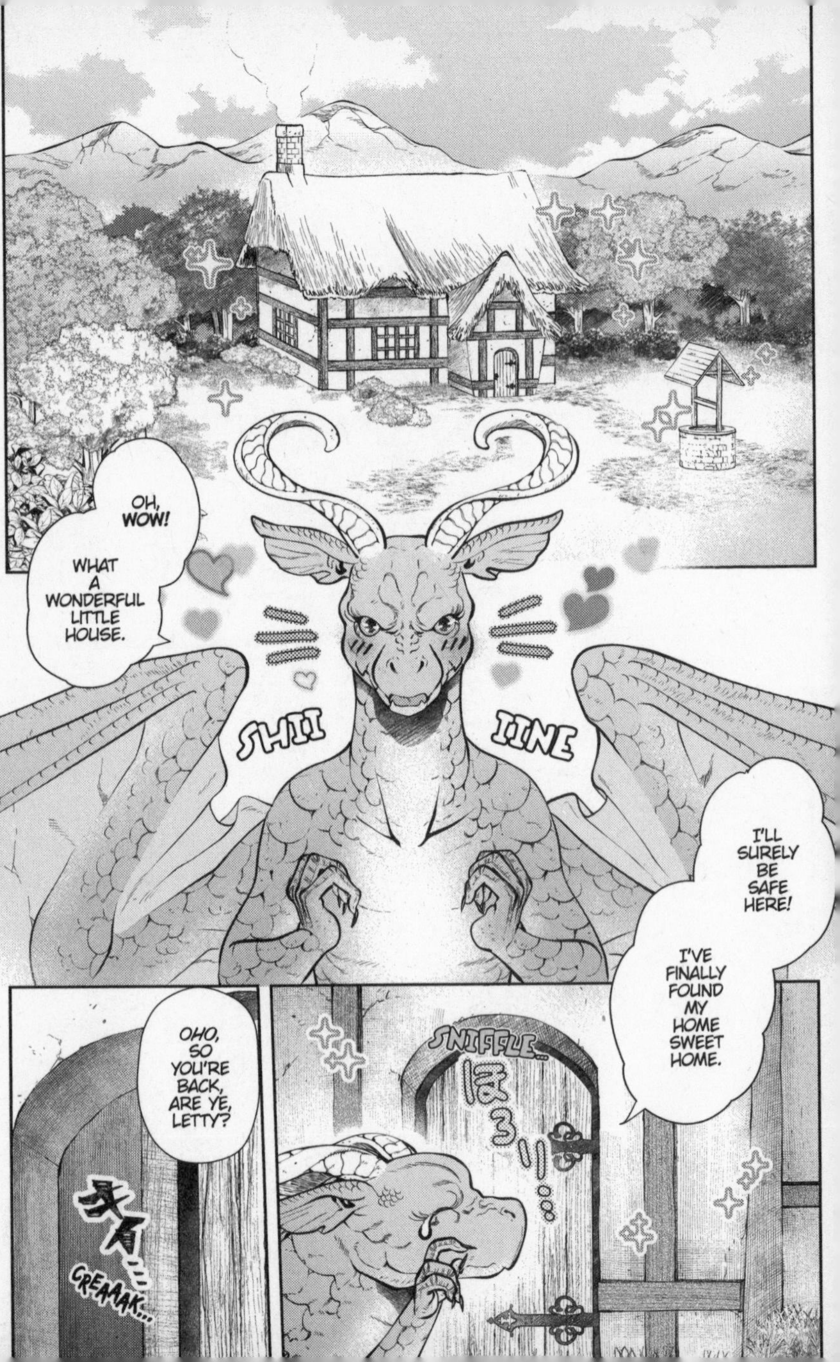
OH, WOW!
WHAT A WONDERFUL LITTLE HOUSE.
SHII IINE
I'LL SURELY BE SAFE HERE!
I'VE FINALLY FOUND MY HOME SWEET HOME.
SNIFFLE...
ほろり…
OHO, SO YOU'RE BACK, ARE YE, LETTY?
CREAAAK...

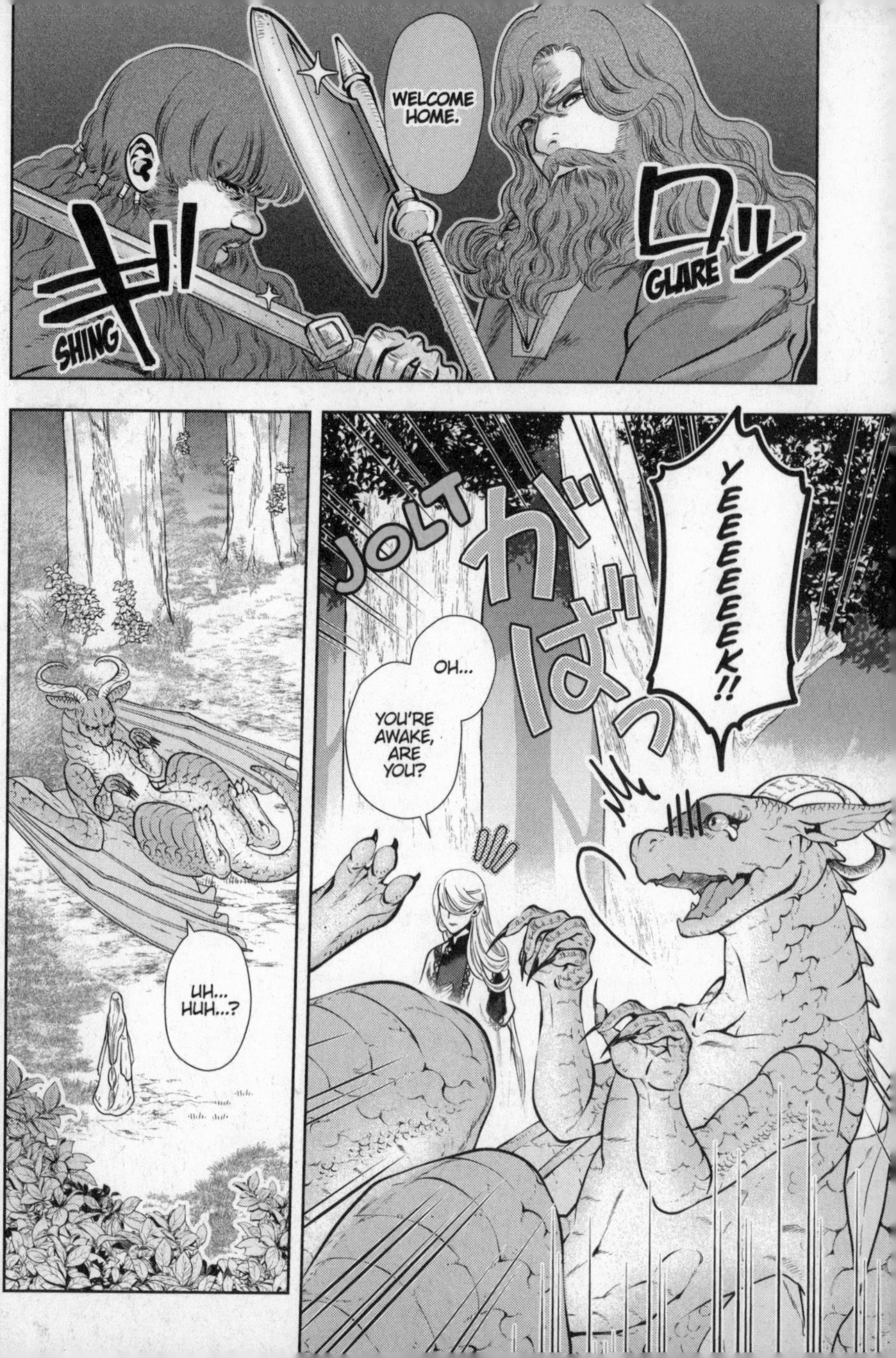
SHING
ギッ
WELCOME HOME.
GLARE
ワッ
UH... HUH...?
JOLT
がばっ
YEEEEEEEK!!
OH...
YOU'RE AWAKE, ARE YOU?

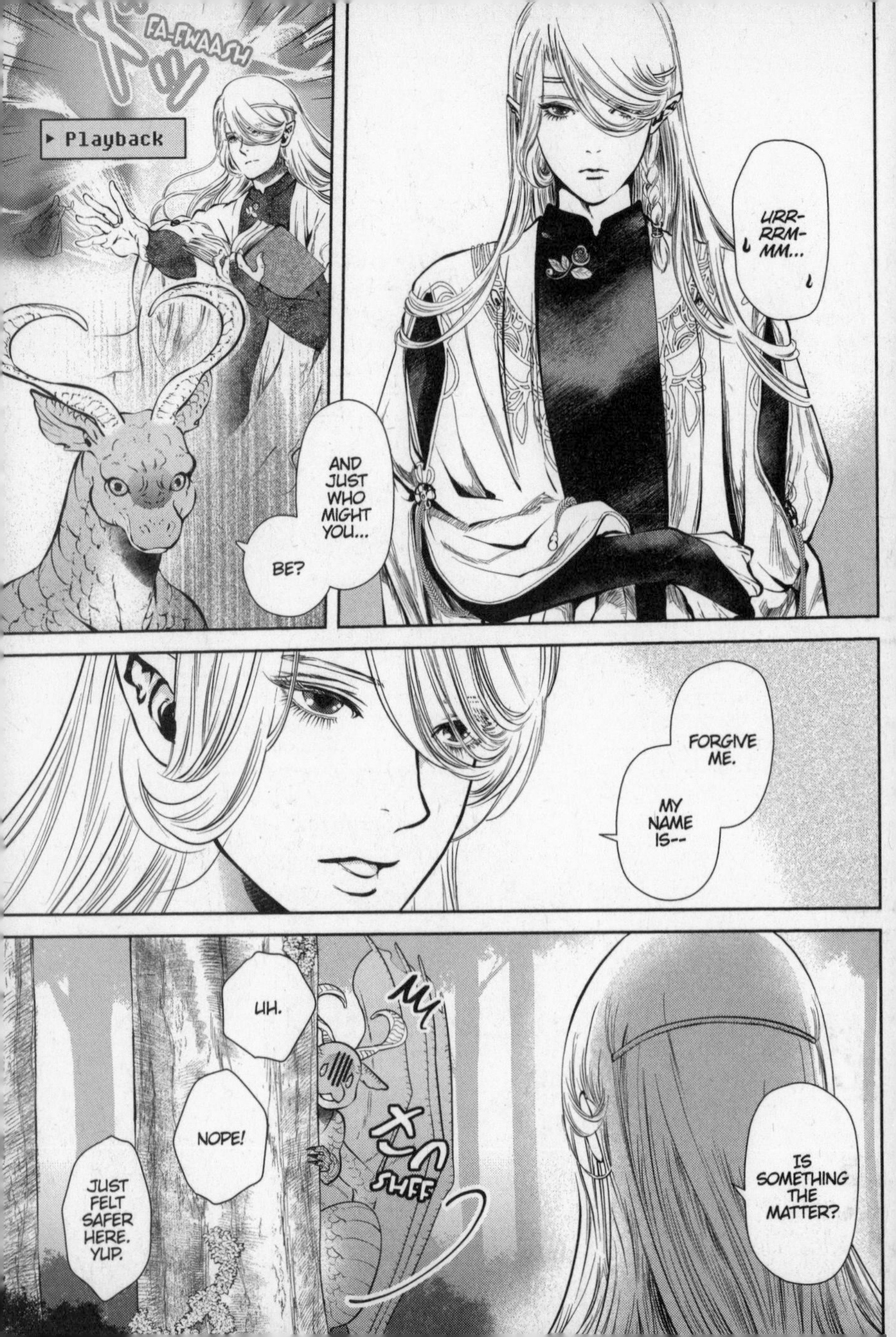

URRR-RRM-MM...
FA-FWAASH
▸ Playback
AND JUST WHO MIGHT YOU...
BE?
FORGIVE ME.
MY NAME IS--
IS SOMETHING THE MATTER?
UH.
SHFF
NOPE!
JUST FELT SAFER HERE. YUP.

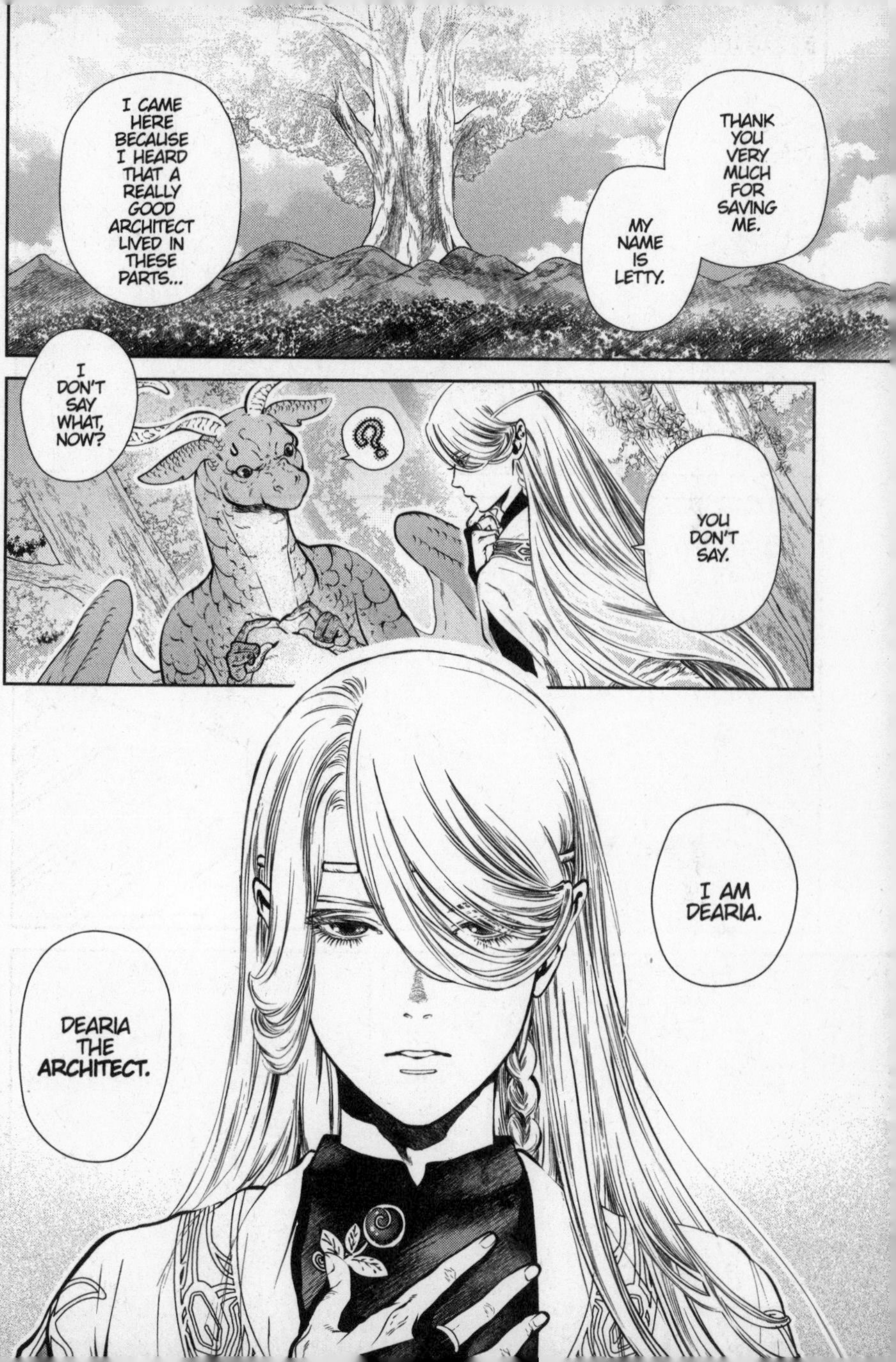
THANK YOU VERY MUCH FOR SAVING ME.
MY NAME IS LETTY.
I CAME HERE BECAUSE I HEARD THAT A REALLY GOOD ARCHITECT LIVED IN THESE PARTS...
YOU DON'T SAY.
?
I DON'T SAY WHAT, NOW?
I AM DEARIA.
DEARIA THE ARCHITECT.

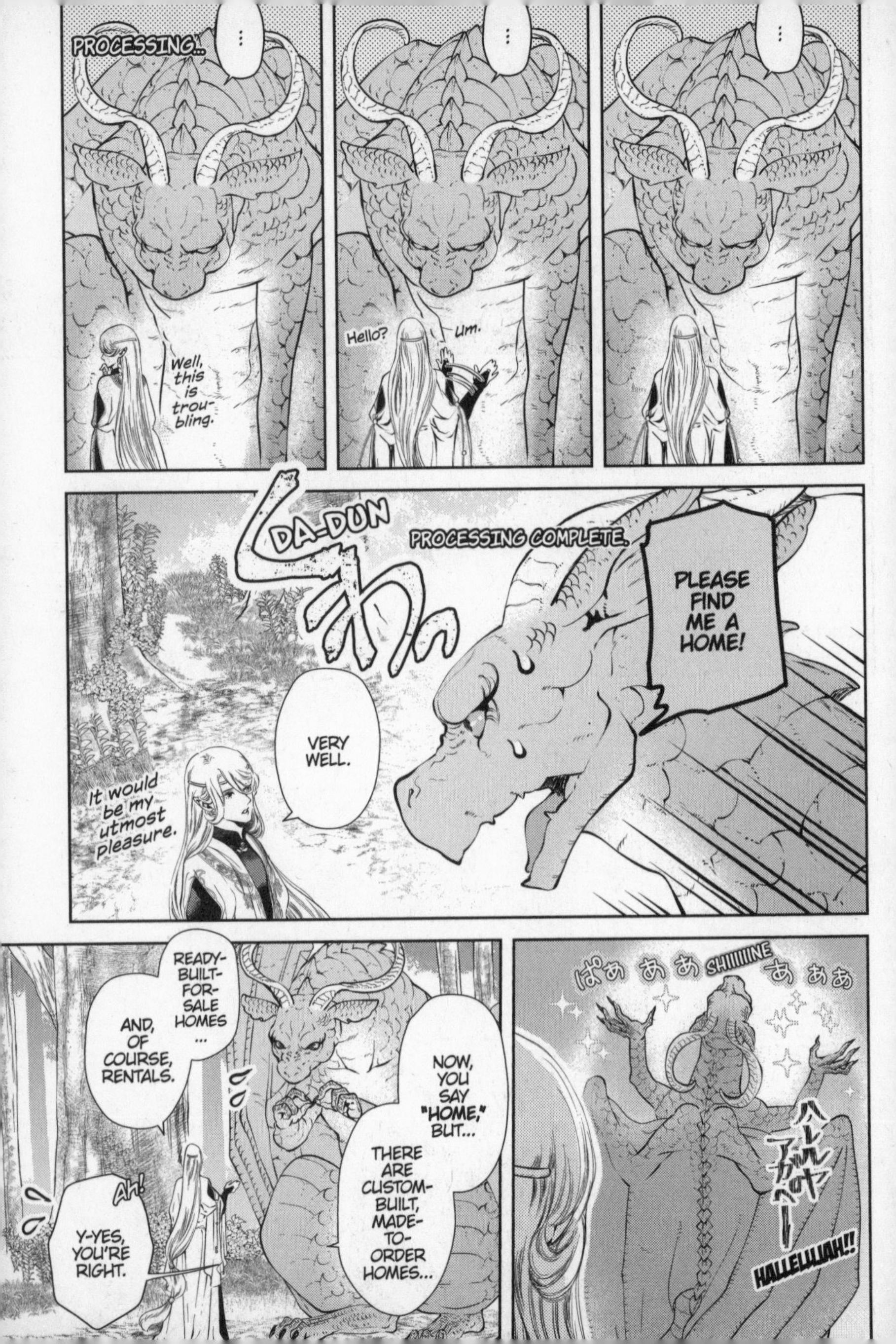
…
…
Um.
Hello?
PROCESSING…
…
Well, this is troubling.
DA-DUN
PROCESSING COMPLETE.
PLEASE FIND ME A HOME!
VERY WELL.
It would be my utmost pleasure.
SHIIIIIINE
HALLELUJAH!!
NOW, YOU SAY "HOME," BUT...
THERE ARE CUSTOM-BUILT, MADE-TO-ORDER HOMES...
READY-BUILT-FOR-SALE HOMES...
AND, OF COURSE, RENTALS.
Ah!
Y-YES, YOU'RE RIGHT.

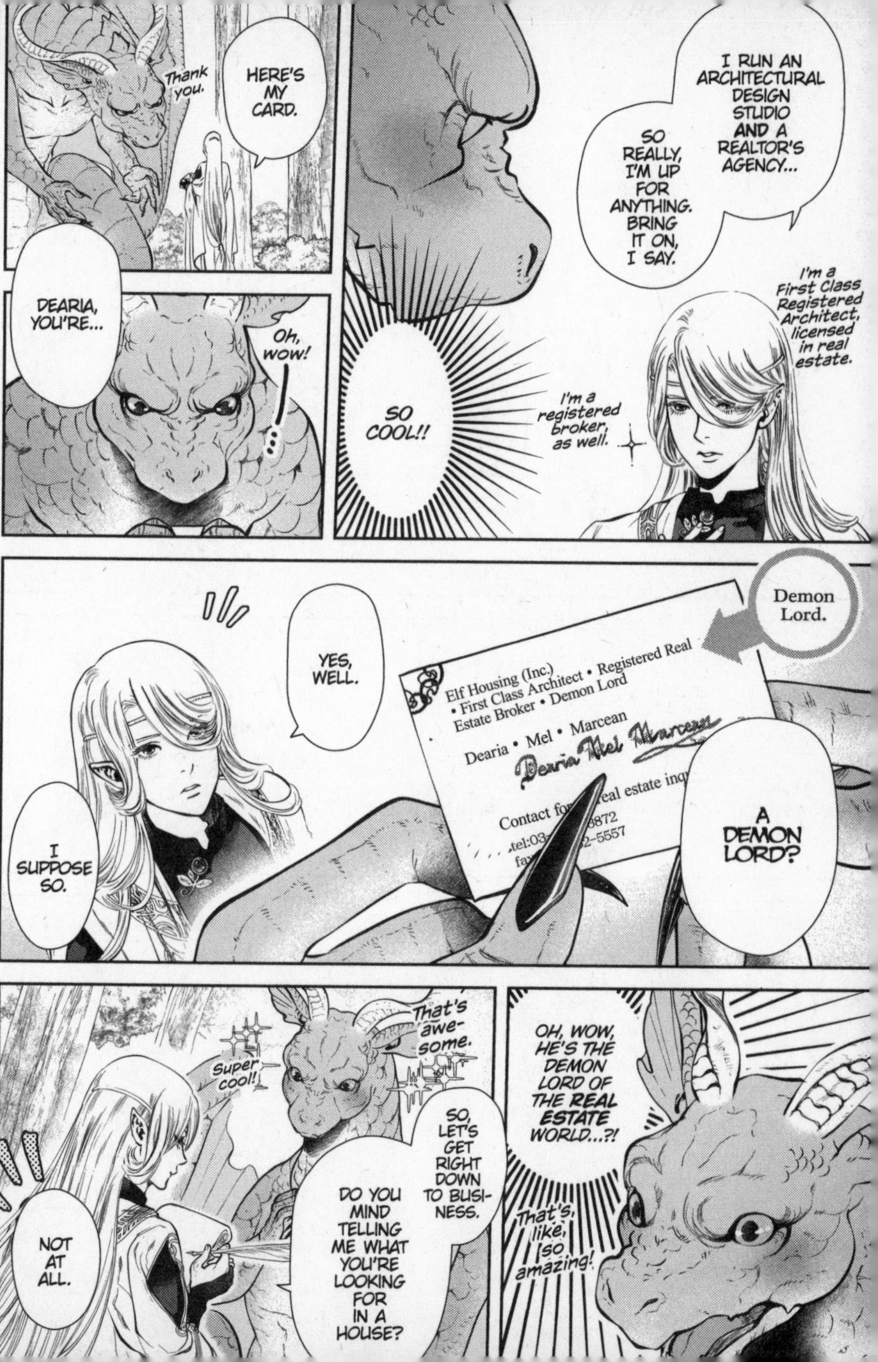
I RUN AN ARCHITECTURAL DESIGN STUDIO AND A REALTOR'S AGENCY...
SO REALLY, I'M UP FOR ANYTHING. BRING IT ON, I SAY.
I'm a First Class Registered Architect, licensed in real estate.
I'm a registered broker, as well.
SO COOL!!
HERE'S MY CARD.
Thank you.
DEARIA, YOU'RE...
Oh, wow!
...
Demon Lord.
Elf Housing (Inc.)
• First Class Architect • Registered Real Estate Broker • Demon Lord
Dearia • Mel • Marcean
A DEMON LORD?
YES, WELL.
I SUPPOSE SO.
OH, WOW, HE'S THE DEMON LORD OF THE REAL ESTATE WORLD...?!
That's, like, so amazing!
That's awe-some.
Super cool!
SO, LET'S GET RIGHT DOWN TO BUSI-NESS.
DO YOU MIND TELLING ME WHAT YOU'RE LOOKING FOR IN A HOUSE?
NOT AT ALL.

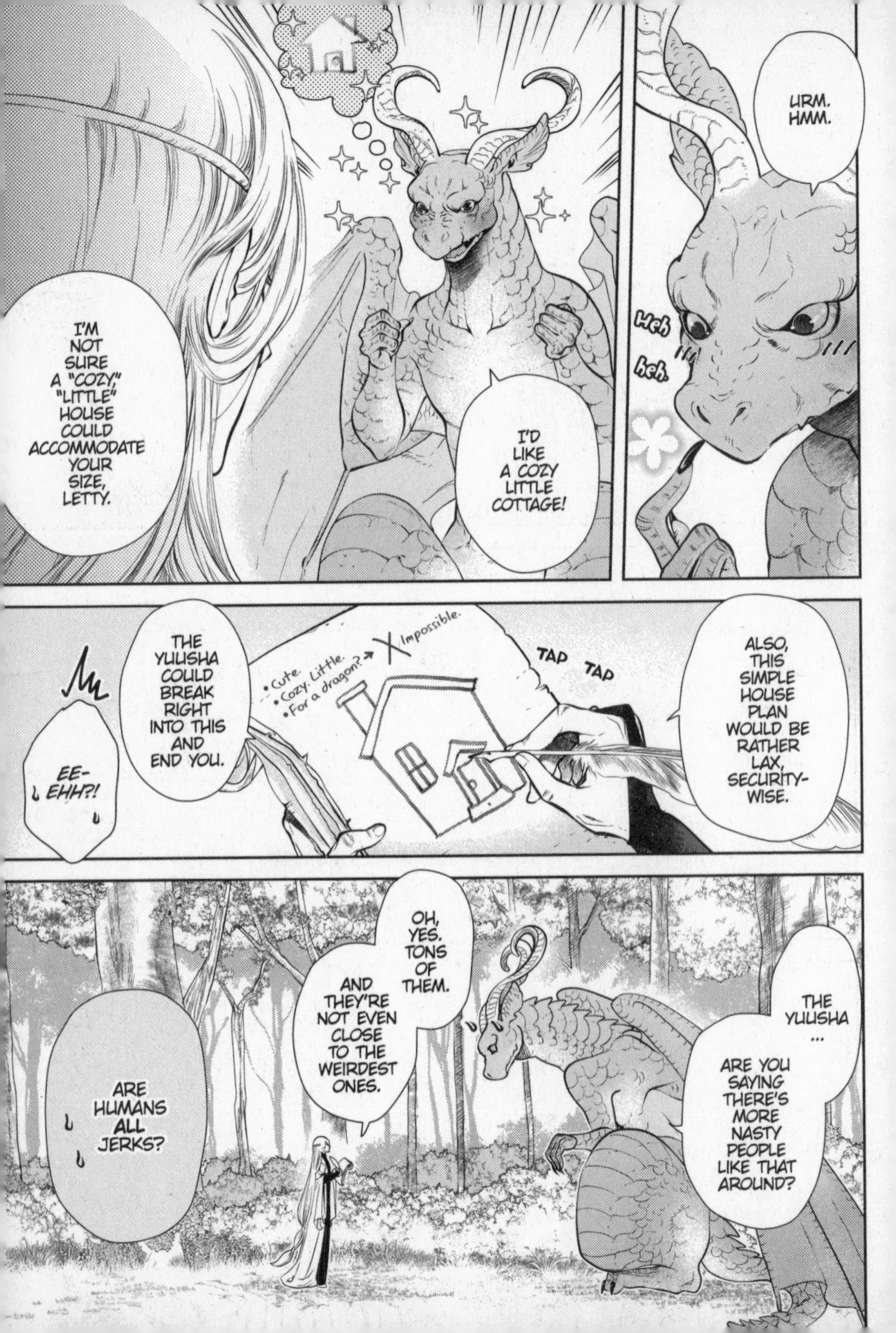
URM. HMM.
Heh heh.
I'D LIKE A COZY LITTLE COTTAGE!
I'M NOT SURE A "COZY," "LITTLE" HOUSE COULD ACCOMMODATE YOUR SIZE, LETTY.
ALSO, THIS SIMPLE HOUSE PLAN WOULD BE RATHER LAX, SECURITY-WISE.
TAP TAP
• Cute. • Cozy. Little. • For a dragon? → Impossible.
THE YUUSHA COULD BREAK RIGHT INTO THIS AND END YOU.
EE-EHH?!
THE YUUSHA ...
ARE YOU SAYING THERE'S MORE NASTY PEOPLE LIKE THAT AROUND?
OH, YES. TONS OF THEM.
AND THEY'RE NOT EVEN CLOSE TO THE WEIRDEST ONES.
ARE HUMANS ALL JERKS?

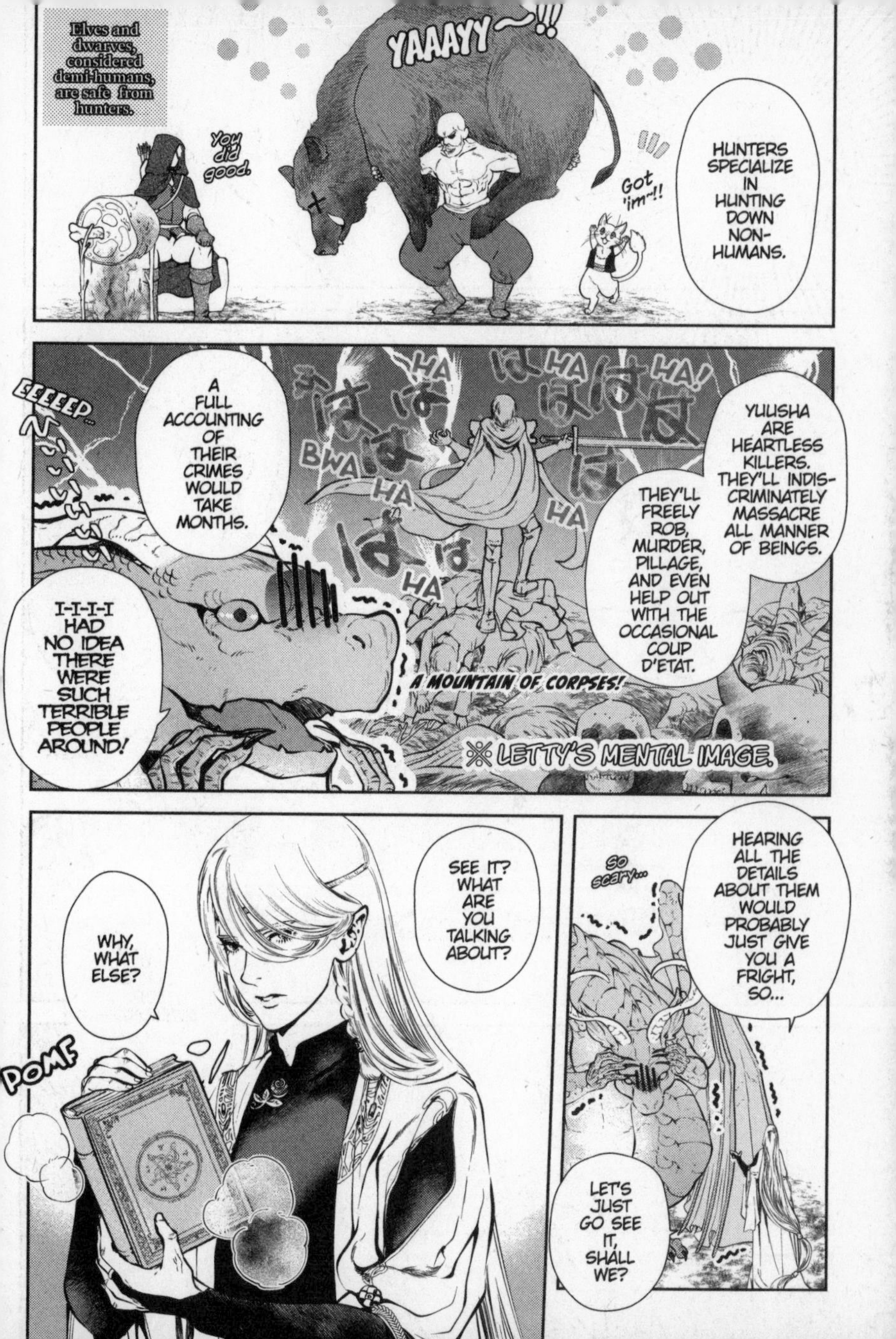
HUNTERS SPECIALIZE IN HUNTING DOWN NON-HUMANS.
YAAAYY~!!!
Got 'im~!!
You did good.
Elves and dwarves, considered demi-humans, are safe from hunters.
YUUSHA ARE HEARTLESS KILLERS. THEY'LL INDIS-CRIMINATELY MASSACRE ALL MANNER OF BEINGS.
THEY'LL FREELY ROB, MURDER, PILLAGE, AND EVEN HELP OUT WITH THE OCCASIONAL COUP D'ETAT.
HA HA HA! BWA HA HA HA HA
A FULL ACCOUNTING OF THEIR CRIMES WOULD TAKE MONTHS.
EEEEEP...
I-I-I-I HAD NO IDEA THERE WERE SUCH TERRIBLE PEOPLE AROUND!
A MOUNTAIN OF CORPSES!
※LETTY'S MENTAL IMAGE.
HEARING ALL THE DETAILS ABOUT THEM WOULD PROBABLY JUST GIVE YOU A FRIGHT, SO...
So scary...
LET'S JUST GO SEE IT, SHALL WE?
SEE IT? WHAT ARE YOU TALKING ABOUT?
WHY, WHAT ELSE?
POMF

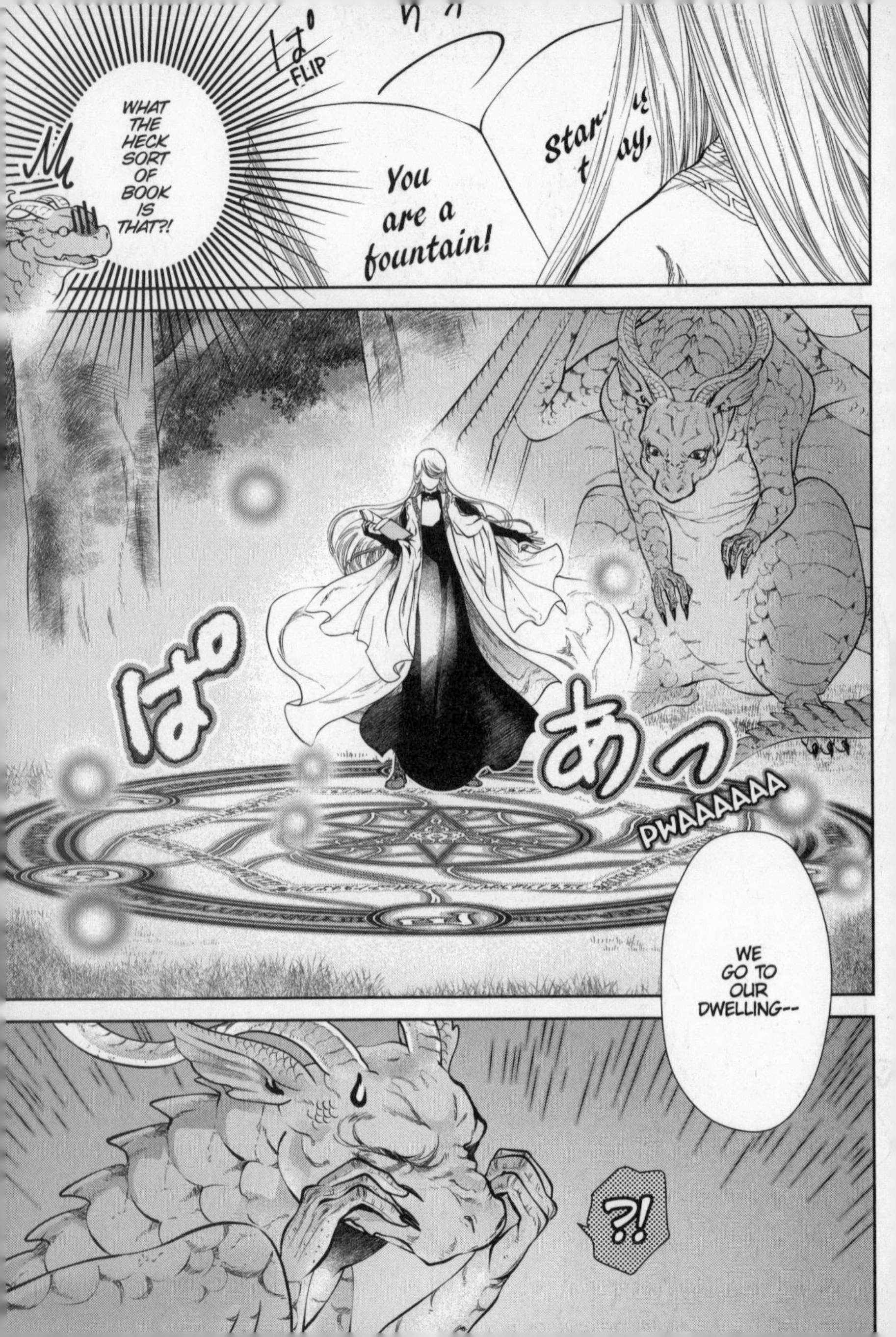
You are a fountain!
FLIP
WHAT THE HECK SORT OF BOOK IS THAT?!
ぱあっ
PWAAAAAA
WE GO TO OUR DWELLING--
?!

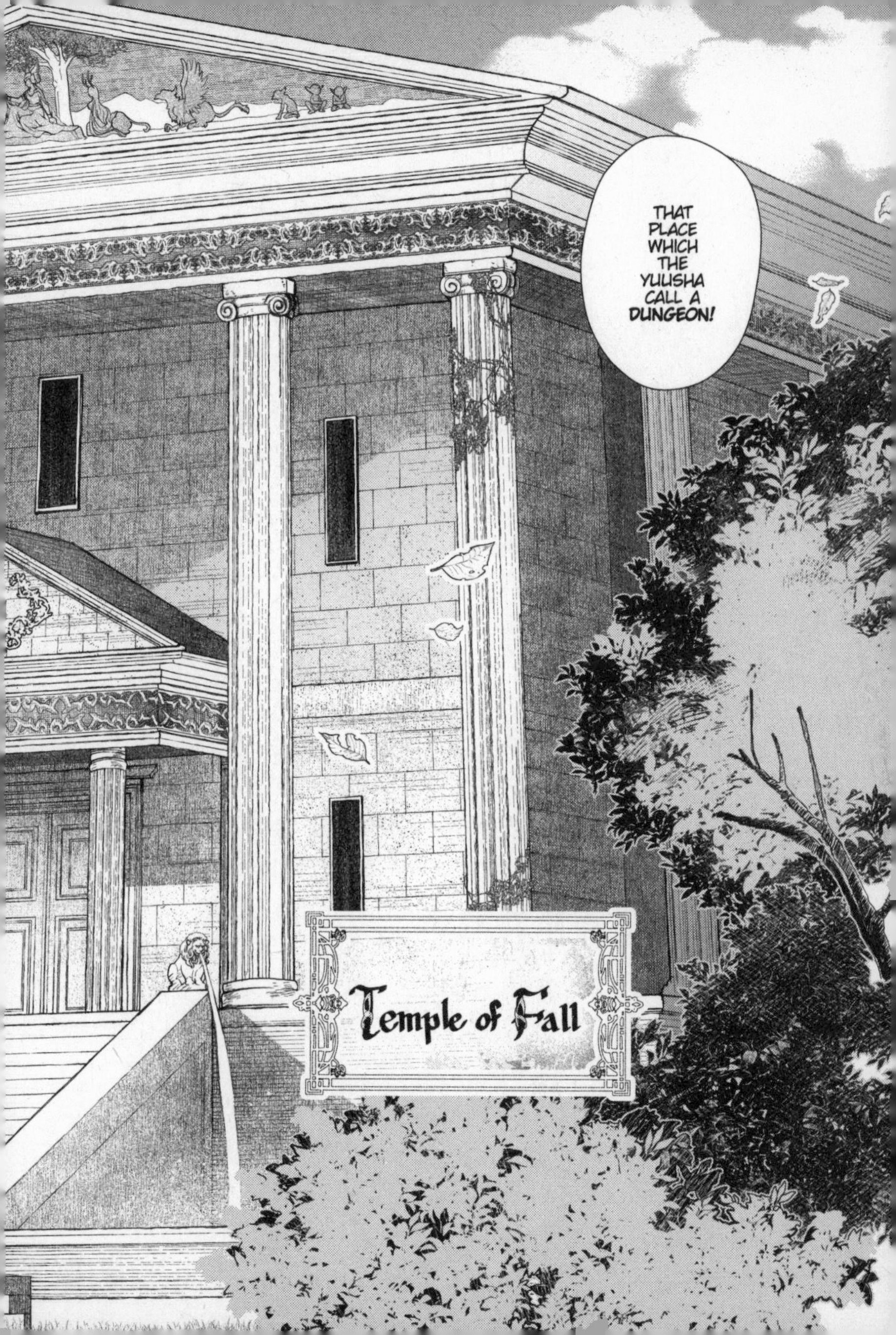
THAT PLACE WHICH THE YUUSHA CALL A DUNGEON!
Temple of Fall

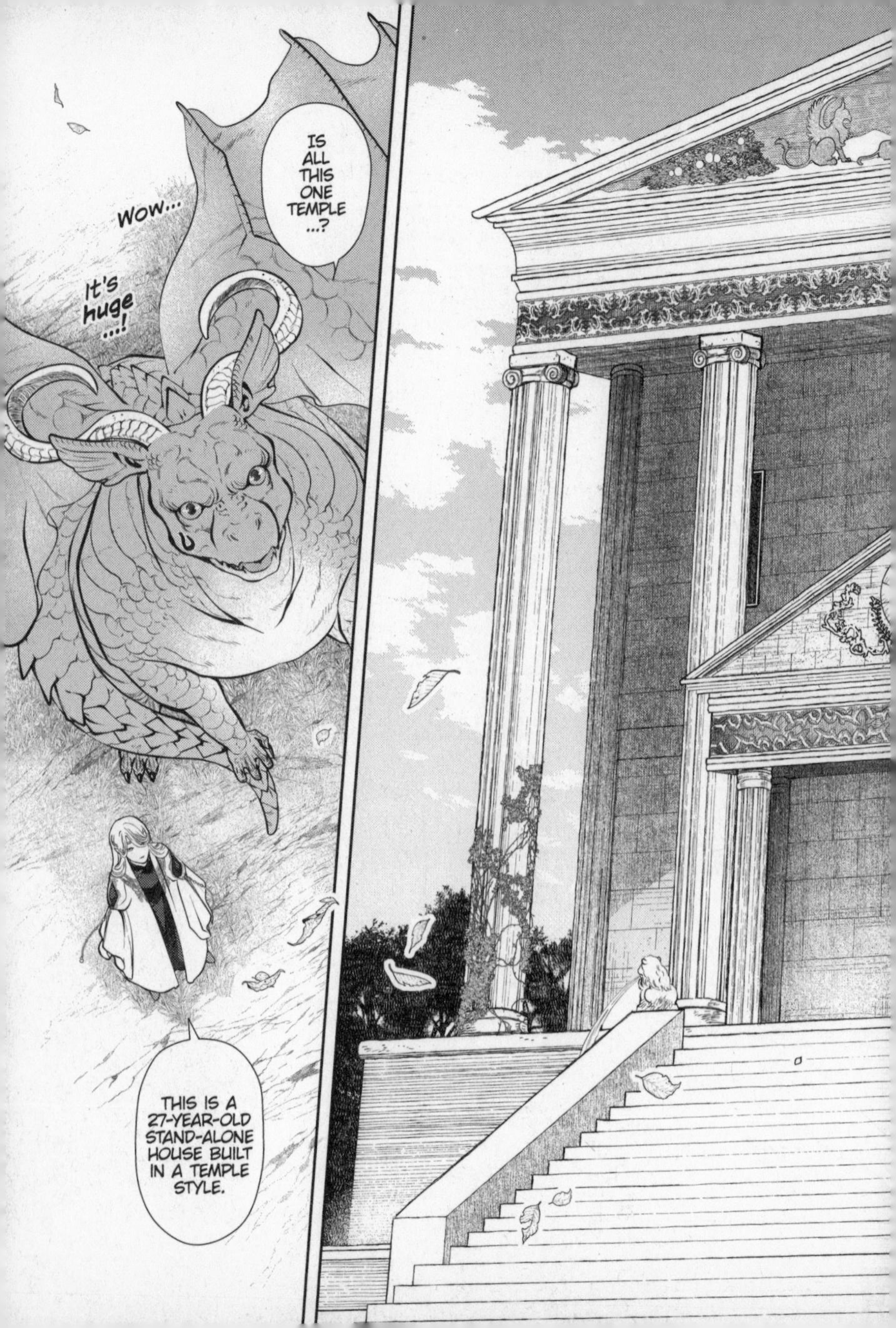
IS ALL THIS ONE TEMPLE ...?
Wow...
It's huge ...!
THIS IS A 27-YEAR-OLD STAND-ALONE HOUSE BUILT IN A TEMPLE STYLE.

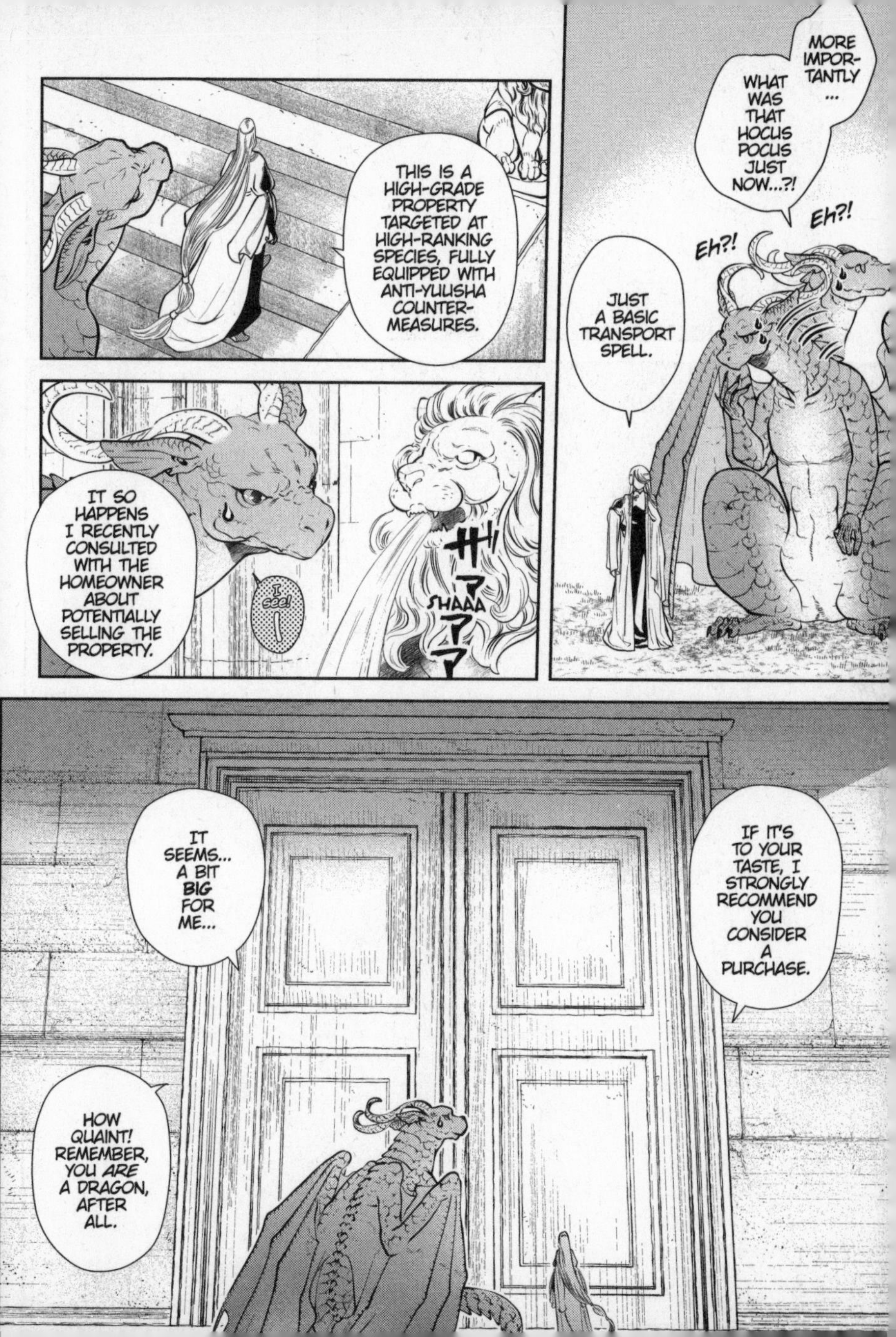
MORE IMPORTANTLY...
WHAT WAS THAT HOCUS POCUS JUST NOW...?!
Eh?!
Eh?!
JUST A BASIC TRANSPORT SPELL.
THIS IS A HIGH-GRADE PROPERTY TARGETED AT HIGH-RANKING SPECIES, FULLY EQUIPPED WITH ANTI-YUUSHA COUNTER-MEASURES.
ザァァ SHAAA
I see!
IT SO HAPPENS I RECENTLY CONSULTED WITH THE HOMEOWNER ABOUT POTENTIALLY SELLING THE PROPERTY.
IF IT'S TO YOUR TASTE, I STRONGLY RECOMMEND YOU CONSIDER A PURCHASE.
IT SEEMS... A BIT BIG FOR ME...
HOW QUAINT! REMEMBER, YOU *ARE* A DRAGON, AFTER ALL.

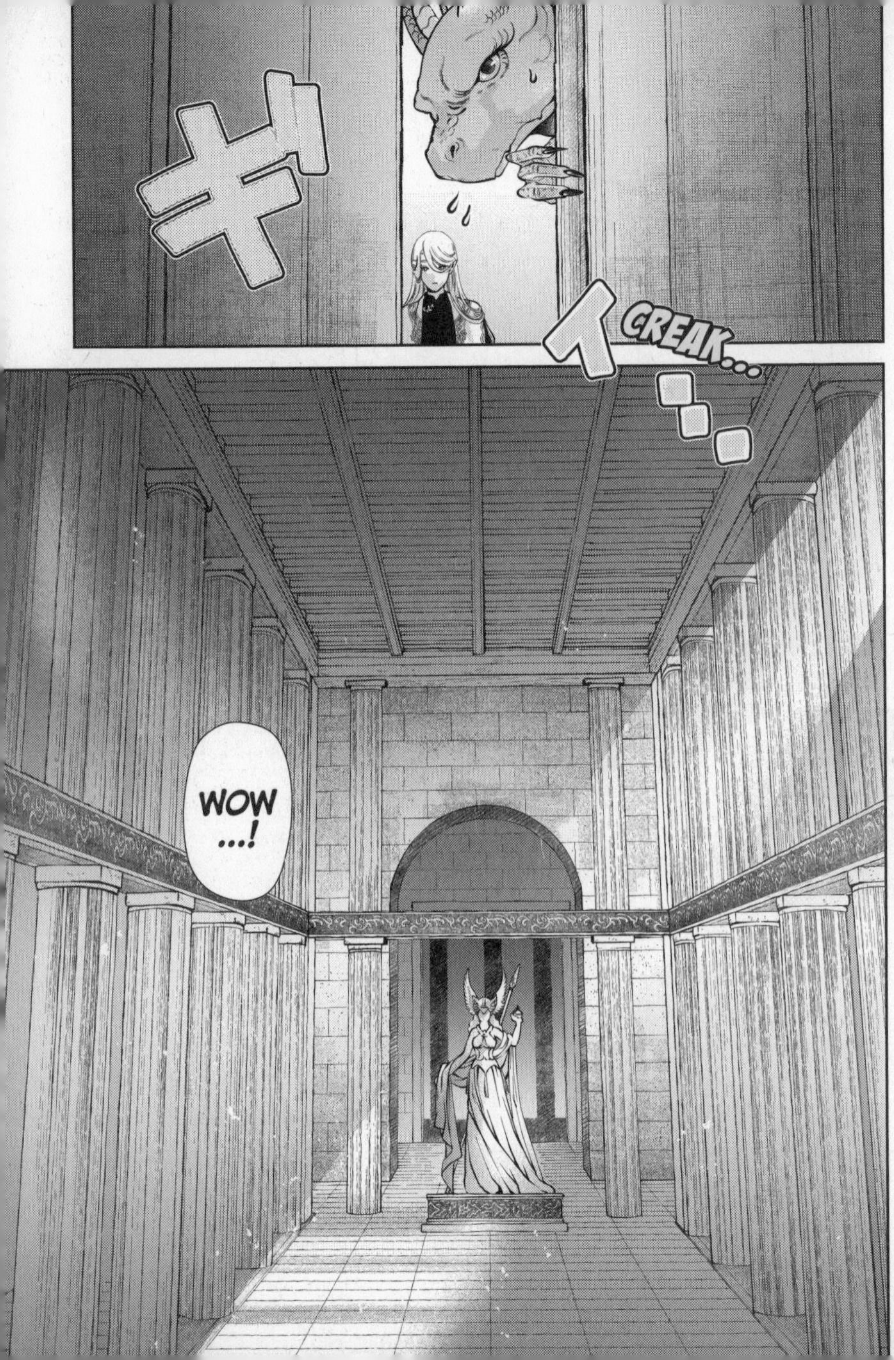
ギイ…
CREAK…
WOW ...!

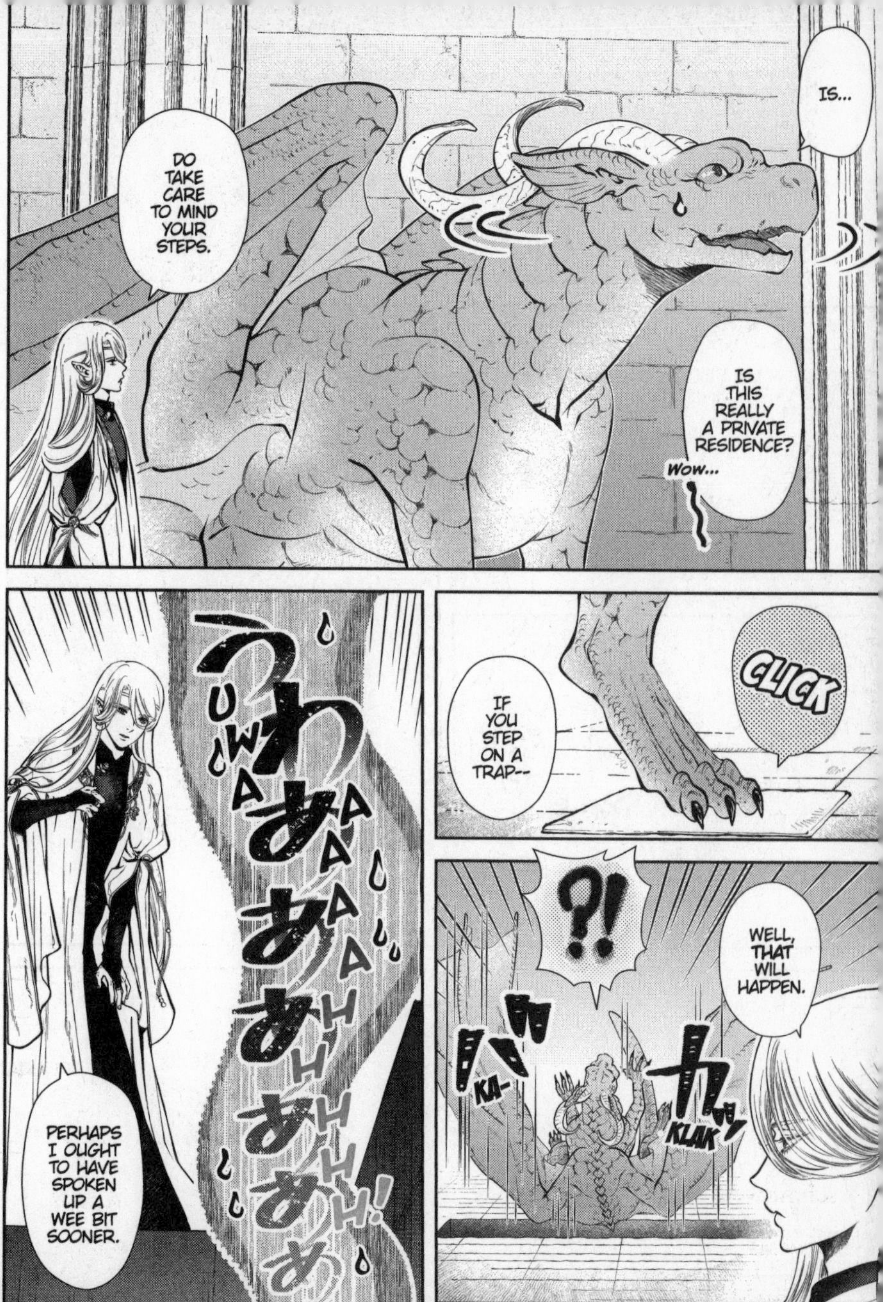
IS...
IS THIS REALLY A PRIVATE RESIDENCE?
WOW...
DO TAKE CARE TO MIND YOUR STEPS.
CLICK
IF YOU STEP ON A TRAP--
?!
WELL, THAT WILL HAPPEN.
KA-
KLAK
UWAAAAAHHHHHH!
PERHAPS I OUGHT TO HAVE SPOKEN UP A WEE BIT SOONER.

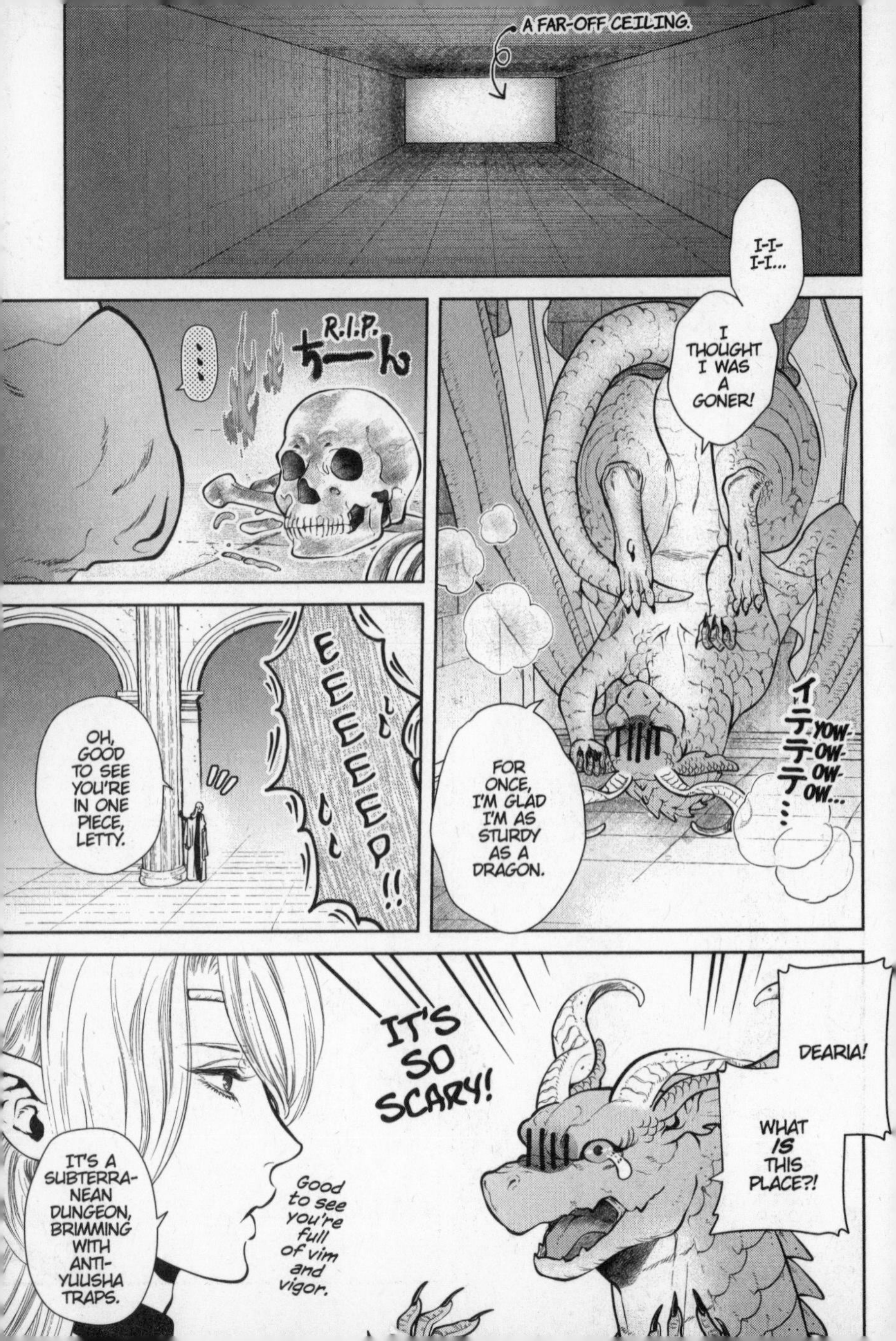
A FAR-OFF CEILING.
I-I-I-I...
I THOUGHT I WAS A GONER!
イテテテ…
YOW-OW-OW-OW...
FOR ONCE, I'M GLAD I'M AS STURDY AS A DRAGON.
...
R.I.P.
ち～ん
EEEEEEEP!!
OH, GOOD TO SEE YOU'RE IN ONE PIECE, LETTY.
DEARIA!
WHAT IS THIS PLACE?!
IT'S SO SCARY!
Good to see you're full of vim and vigor.
IT'S A SUBTERRANEAN DUNGEON, BRIMMING WITH ANTI-YUUSHA TRAPS.

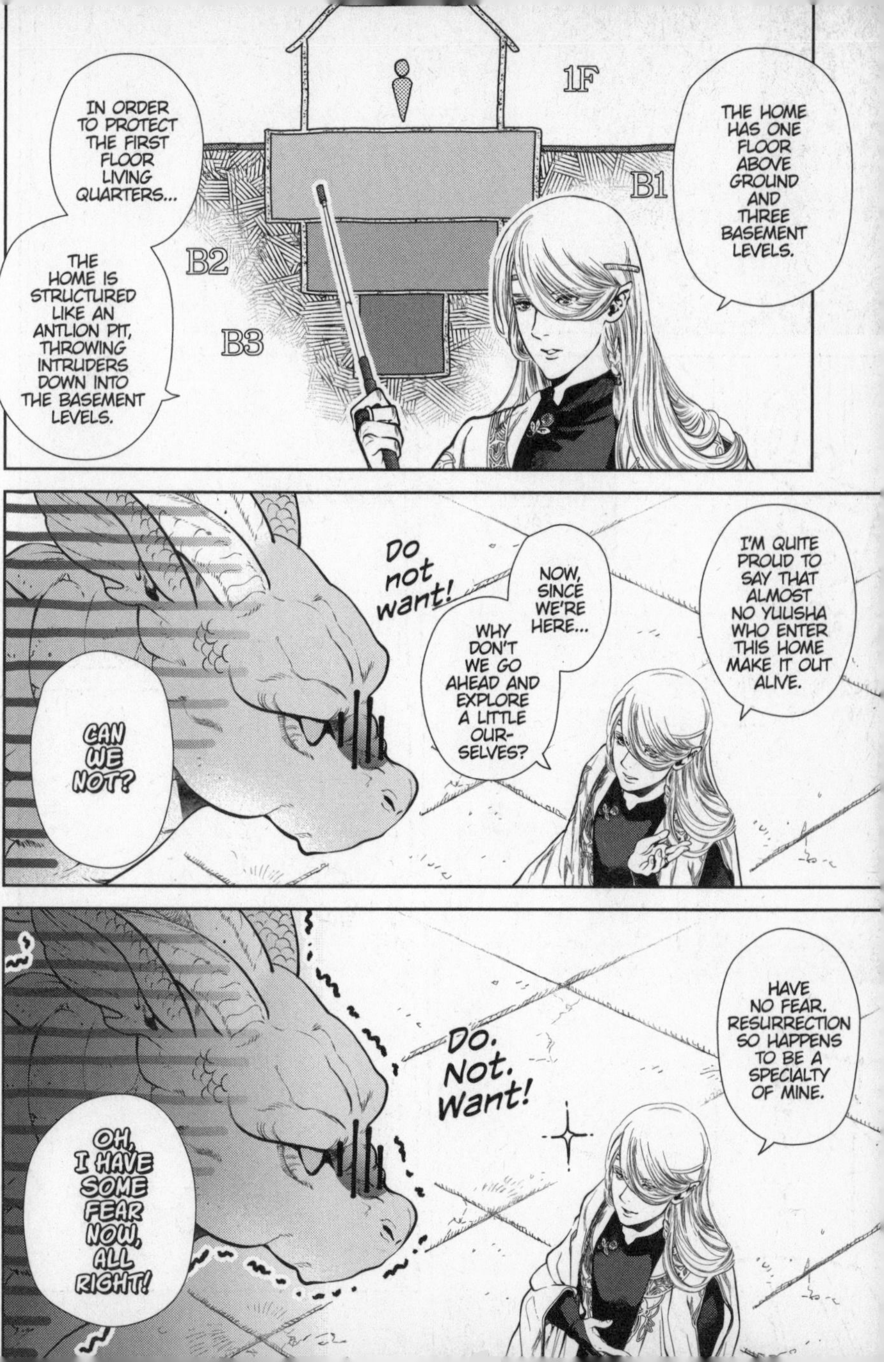
THE HOME HAS ONE FLOOR ABOVE GROUND AND THREE BASEMENT LEVELS.
1F
B1
B2
B3
IN ORDER TO PROTECT THE FIRST FLOOR LIVING QUARTERS...
THE HOME IS STRUCTURED LIKE AN ANTLION PIT, THROWING INTRUDERS DOWN INTO THE BASEMENT LEVELS.
I'M QUITE PROUD TO SAY THAT ALMOST NO YUUSHA WHO ENTER THIS HOME MAKE IT OUT ALIVE.
NOW, SINCE WE'RE HERE...
WHY DON'T WE GO AHEAD AND EXPLORE A LITTLE OUR-SELVES?
Do not want!
CAN WE NOT?
HAVE NO FEAR. RESURRECTION SO HAPPENS TO BE A SPECIALTY OF MINE.
Do. Not. Want!
OH, I HAVE SOME FEAR NOW, ALL RIGHT!

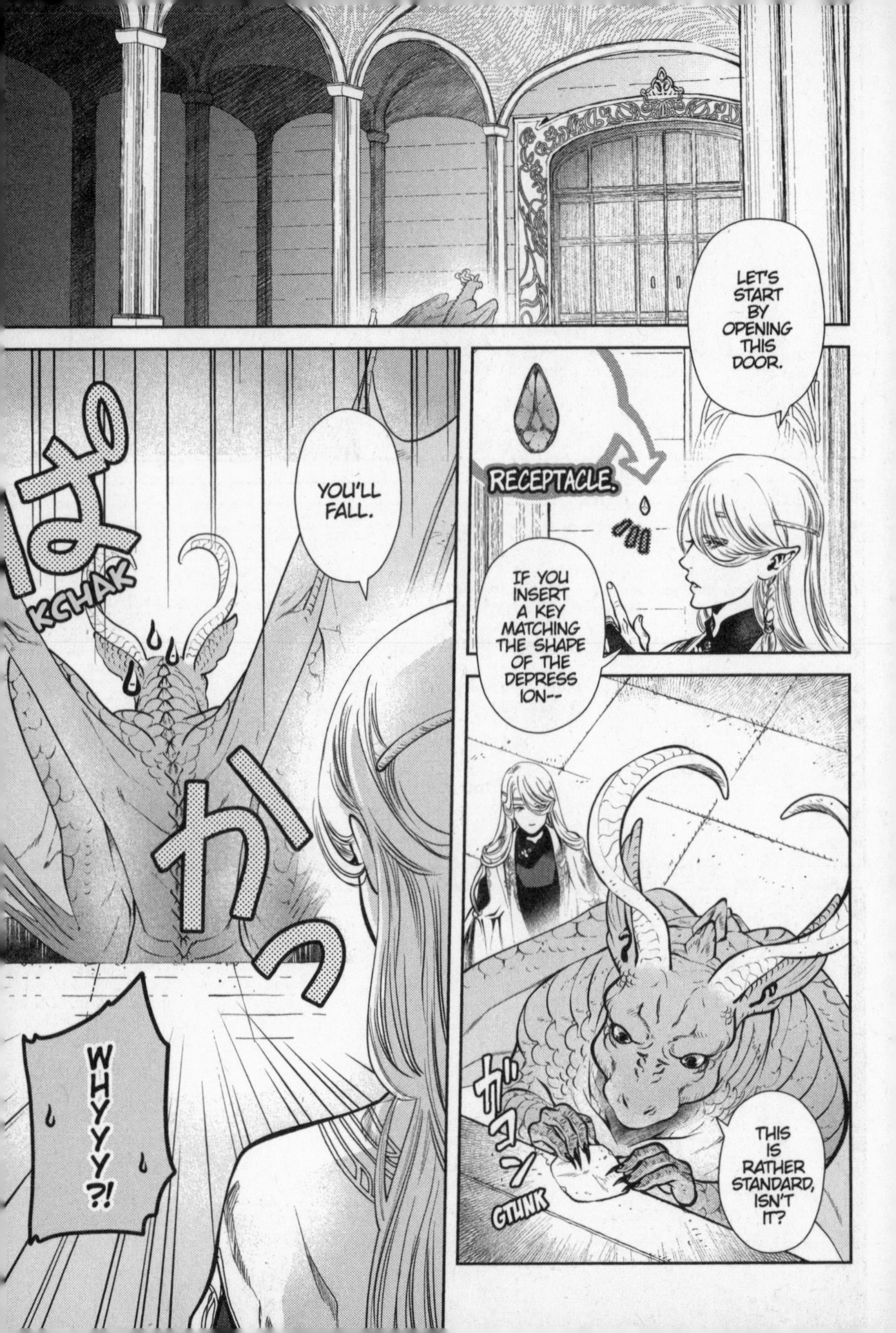
LET'S START BY OPENING THIS DOOR.
RECEPTACLE.
IF YOU INSERT A KEY MATCHING THE SHAPE OF THE DEPRESS ION--
GTUNK
THIS IS RATHER STANDARD, ISN'T IT?
KCHAK
YOU'LL FALL.
WHYYY?!

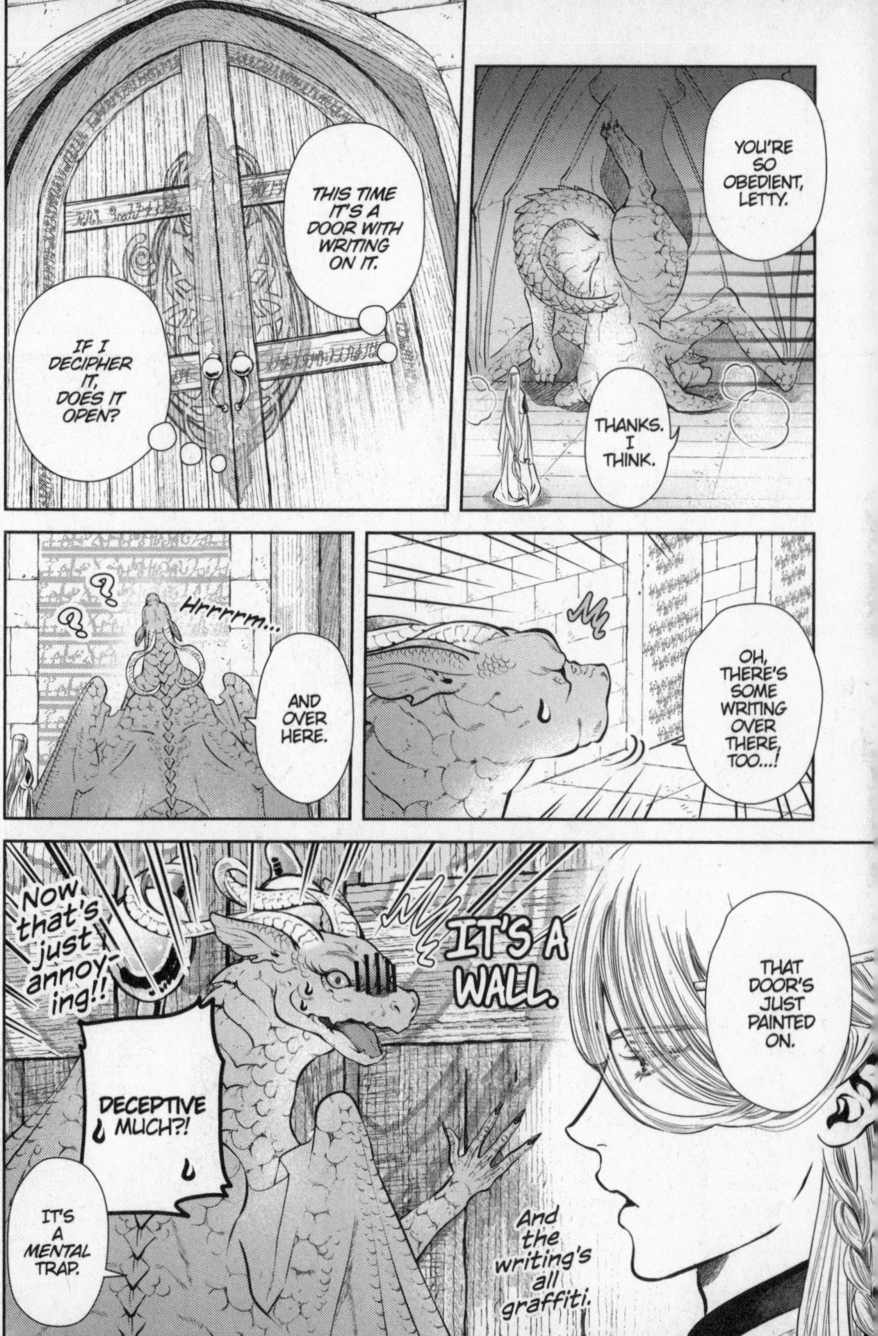
YOU'RE SO OBEDIENT, LETTY.
THANKS. I THINK.
THIS TIME IT'S A DOOR WITH WRITING ON IT.
IF I DECIPHER IT, DOES IT OPEN?
OH, THERE'S SOME WRITING OVER THERE, TOO...!
Hrrrrm...
AND OVER HERE.
THAT DOOR'S JUST PAINTED ON.
IT'S A WALL.
Now that's just annoying!!
DECEPTIVE MUCH?!
And the writing's all graffiti.
IT'S A MENTAL TRAP.

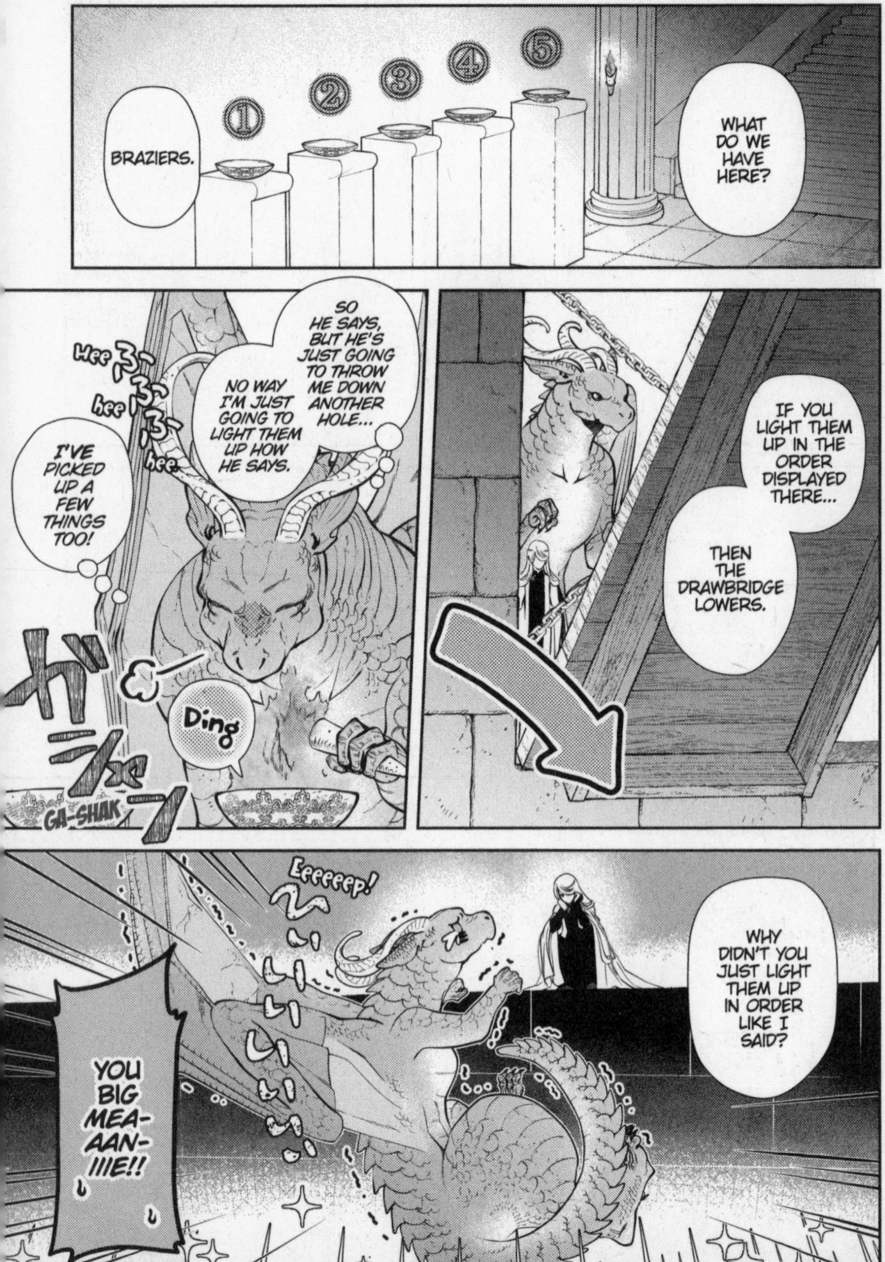
WHAT DO WE HAVE HERE?
5
4
3
2
1
BRAZIERS.
IF YOU LIGHT THEM UP IN THE ORDER DISPLAYED THERE...
THEN THE DRAWBRIDGE LOWERS.
SO HE SAYS, BUT HE'S JUST GOING TO THROW ME DOWN ANOTHER HOLE...
NO WAY I'M JUST GOING TO LIGHT THEM UP HOW HE SAYS.
Hee hee hee
I'VE PICKED UP A FEW THINGS TOO!
Ding
GA-SHAK
WHY DIDN'T YOU JUST LIGHT THEM UP IN ORDER LIKE I SAID?
Eeeeeep!
YOU BIG MEA-AAN-IIIIE!!

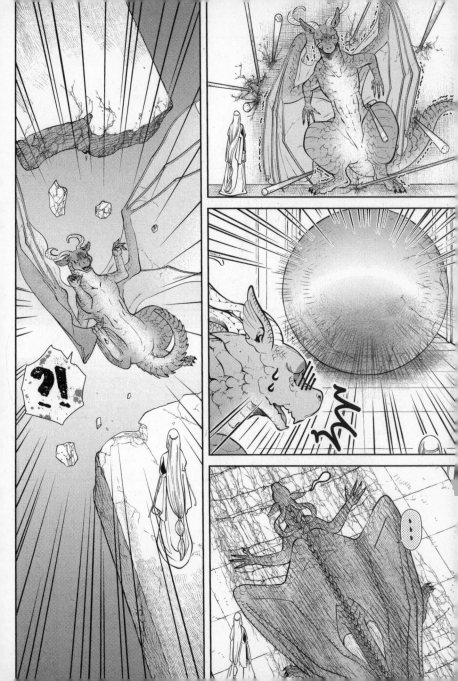

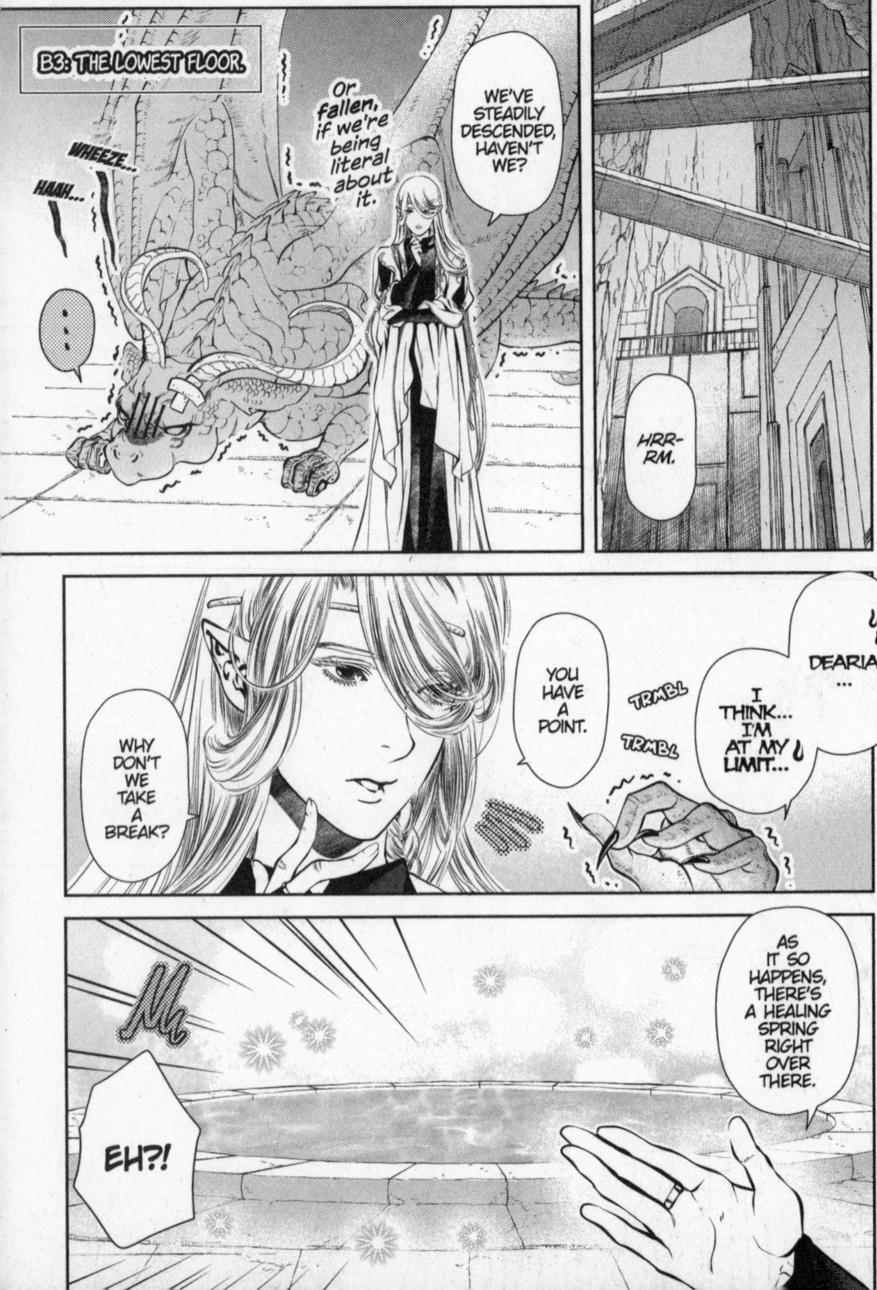
HRRR-RM.
WE'VE STEADILY DESCENDED, HAVEN'T WE?
Or fallen, if we're being literal about it.
B3: THE LOWEST FLOOR.
WHEEZE...
HAAH...
...
DEARIA...
I THINK... I'M AT MY LIMIT...
TRMBL
TRMBL
YOU HAVE A POINT.
WHY DON'T WE TAKE A BREAK?
AS IT SO HAPPENS, THERE'S A HEALING SPRING RIGHT OVER THERE.
EH?!

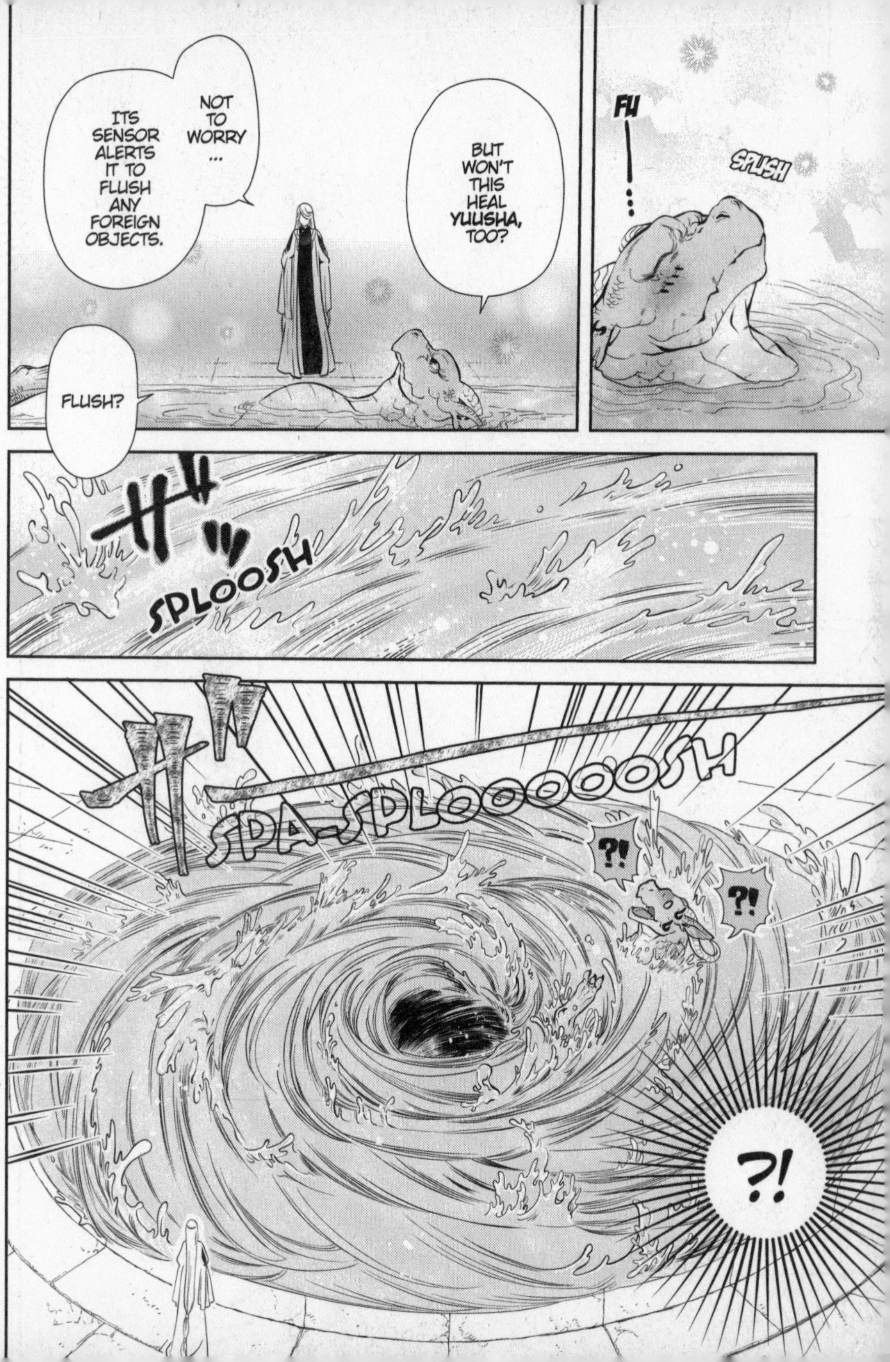
FU---...
SPLUSH
BUT WON'T THIS HEAL YUUSHA, TOO?
NOT TO WORRY...
ITS SENSOR ALERTS IT TO FLUSH ANY FOREIGN OBJECTS.
FLUSH?
SPLOOSH
SPA-SPLOOOOOOSH
?!
?!
?!

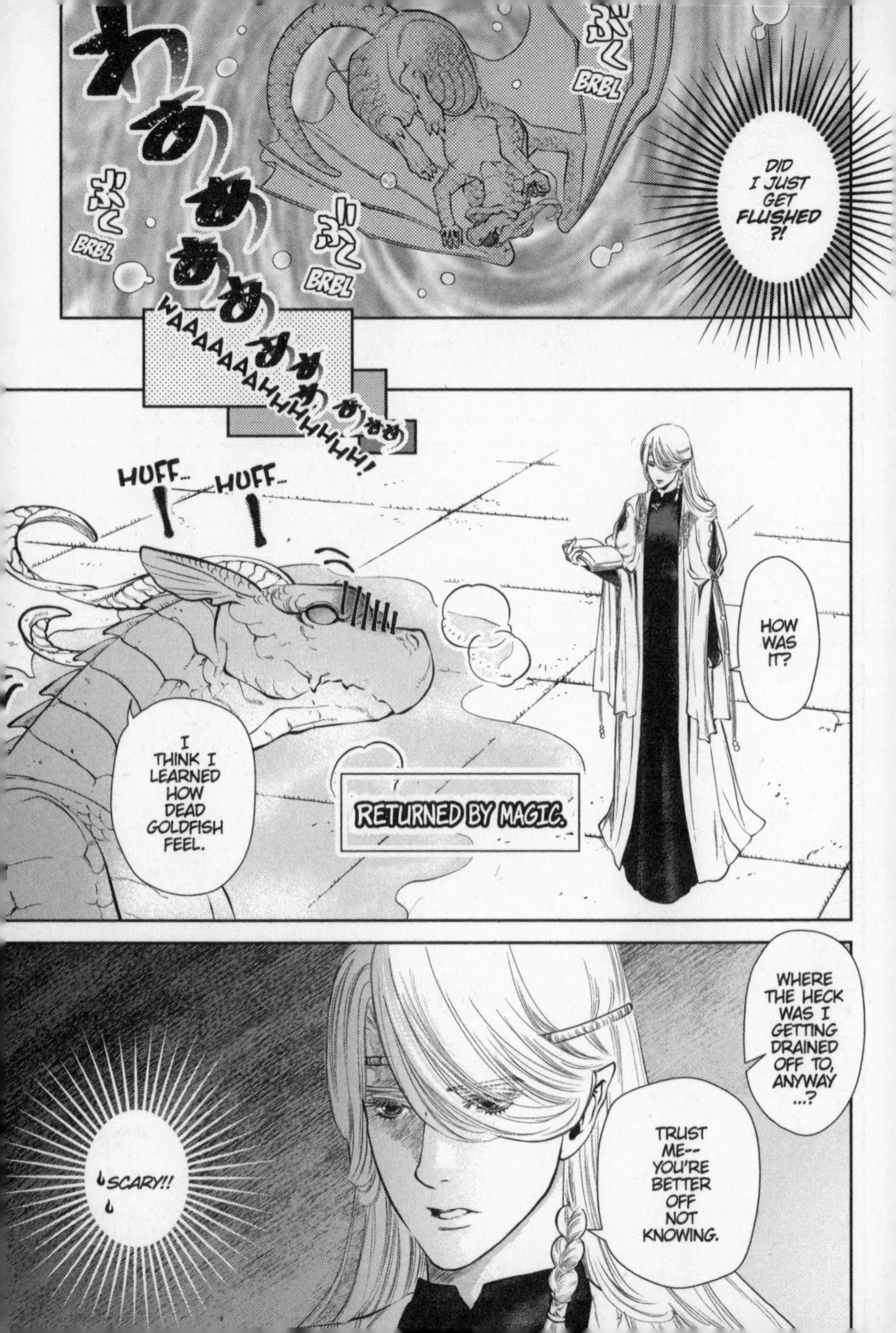
ぶく
BRBL
DID I JUST GET FLUSHED?!
ぶく
BRBL
ぶく
BRBL
WAAAAAAAHHHHHHH!
HOW WAS IT?
HUFF... HUFF...
I THINK I LEARNED HOW DEAD GOLDFISH FEEL.
RETURNED BY MAGIC.
WHERE THE HECK WAS I GETTING DRAINED OFF TO, ANYWAY...?
TRUST ME-- YOU'RE BETTER OFF NOT KNOWING.
SCARY!!

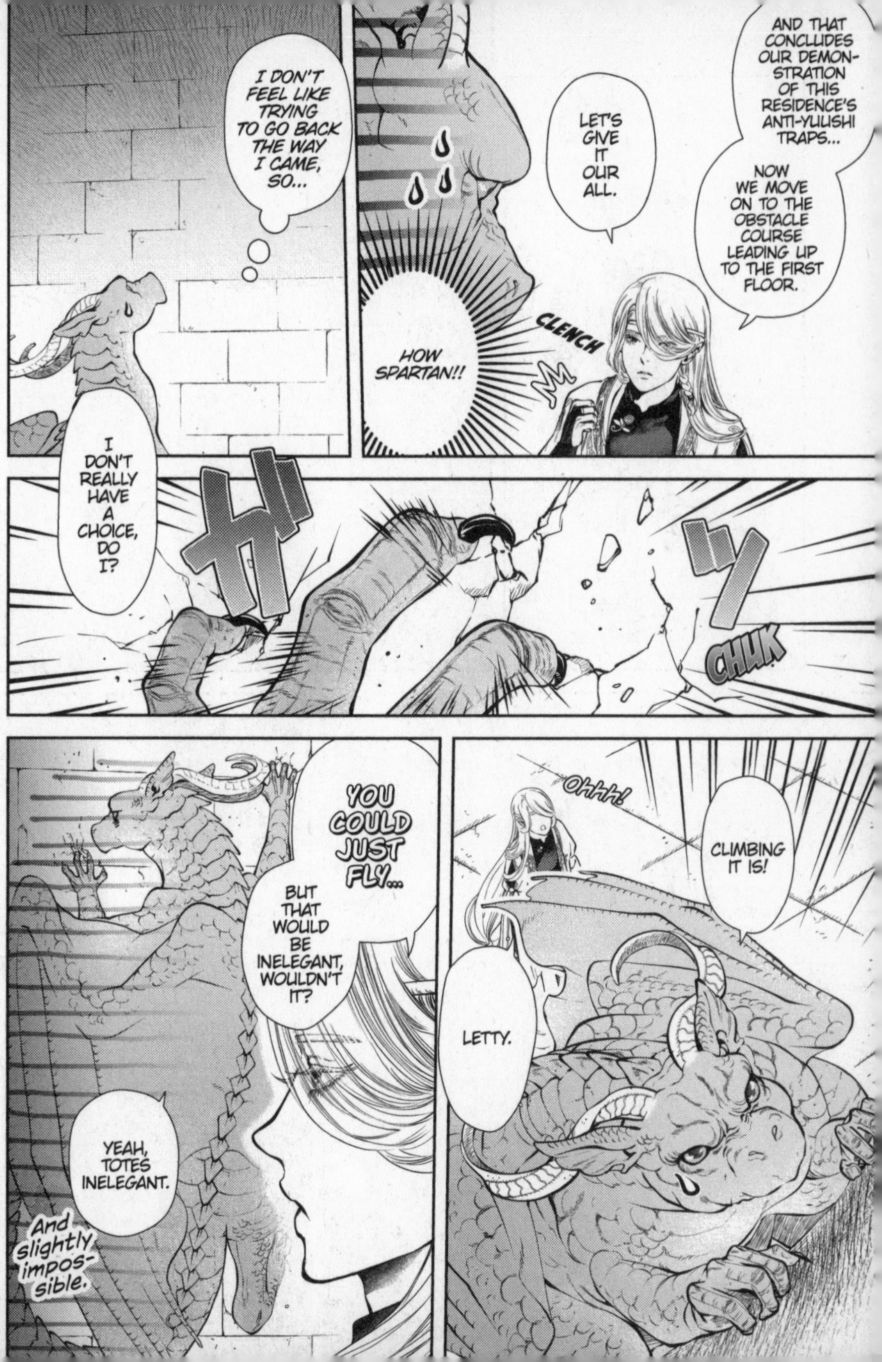

AND THAT CONCLUDES OUR DEMONSTRATION OF THIS RESIDENCE'S ANTI-YUUSHI TRAPS...
NOW WE MOVE ON TO THE OBSTACLE COURSE LEADING UP TO THE FIRST FLOOR.
LET'S GIVE IT OUR ALL.
CLENCH
HOW SPARTAN!!
I DON'T FEEL LIKE TRYING TO GO BACK THE WAY I CAME, SO...
I DON'T REALLY HAVE A CHOICE, DO I?
ガッ
CHUK
Ohhh!
CLIMBING IT IS!
LETTY.
YOU COULD JUST FLY...
BUT THAT WOULD BE INELEGANT, WOULDN'T IT?
YEAH, TOTES INELEGANT.
And slightly impossible.

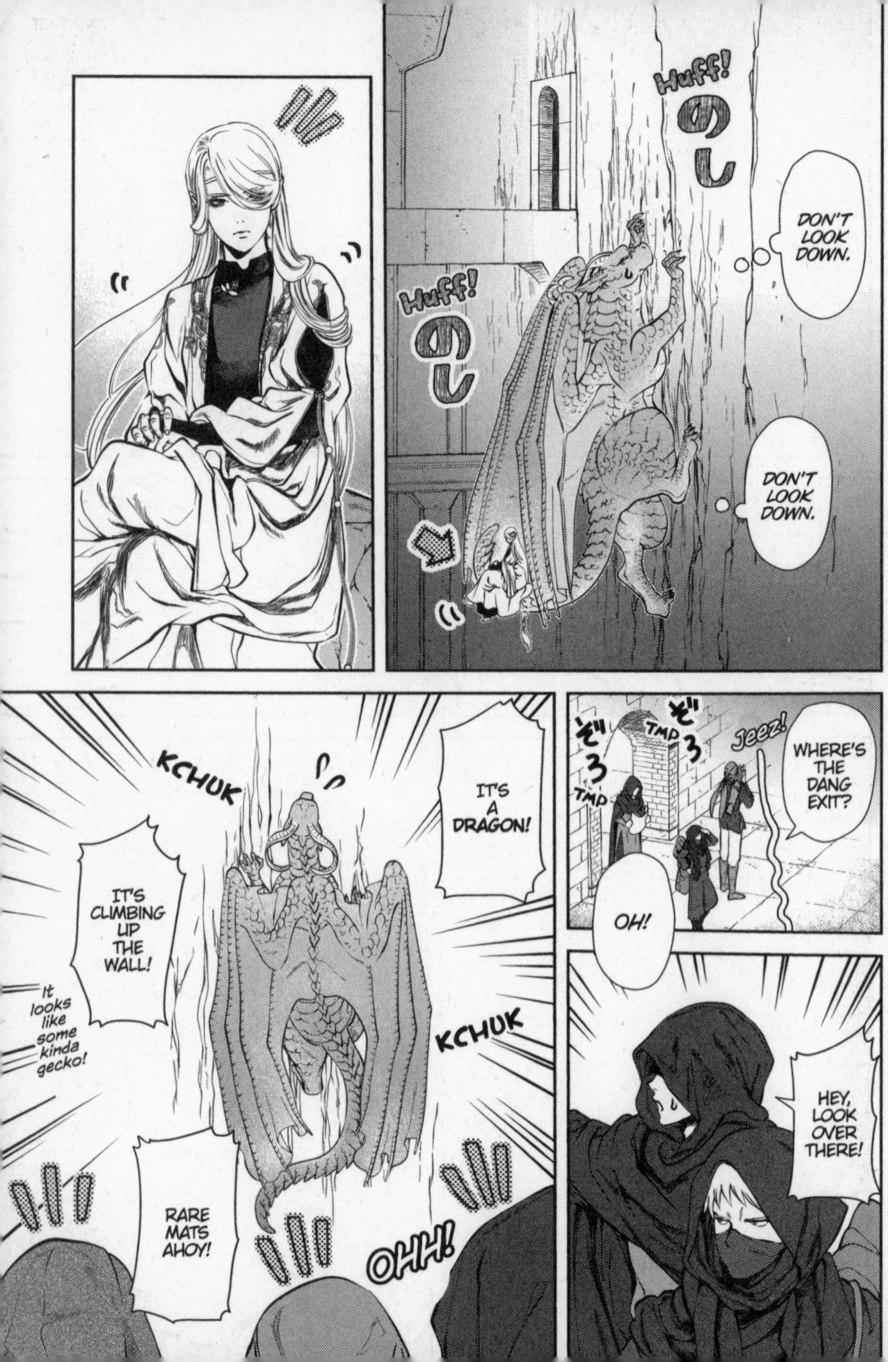
Huff!
のし
DON'T LOOK DOWN.
Huff!
のし
DON'T LOOK DOWN.
ぞろ
TMP
Jeez!
WHERE'S THE DANG EXIT?
ぞろ
TMP
OH!
HEY, LOOK OVER THERE!
IT'S A DRAGON!
KCHUK
IT'S CLIMBING UP THE WALL!
It looks like some kinda gecko!
KCHUK
OHH!
RARE MATS AHOY!

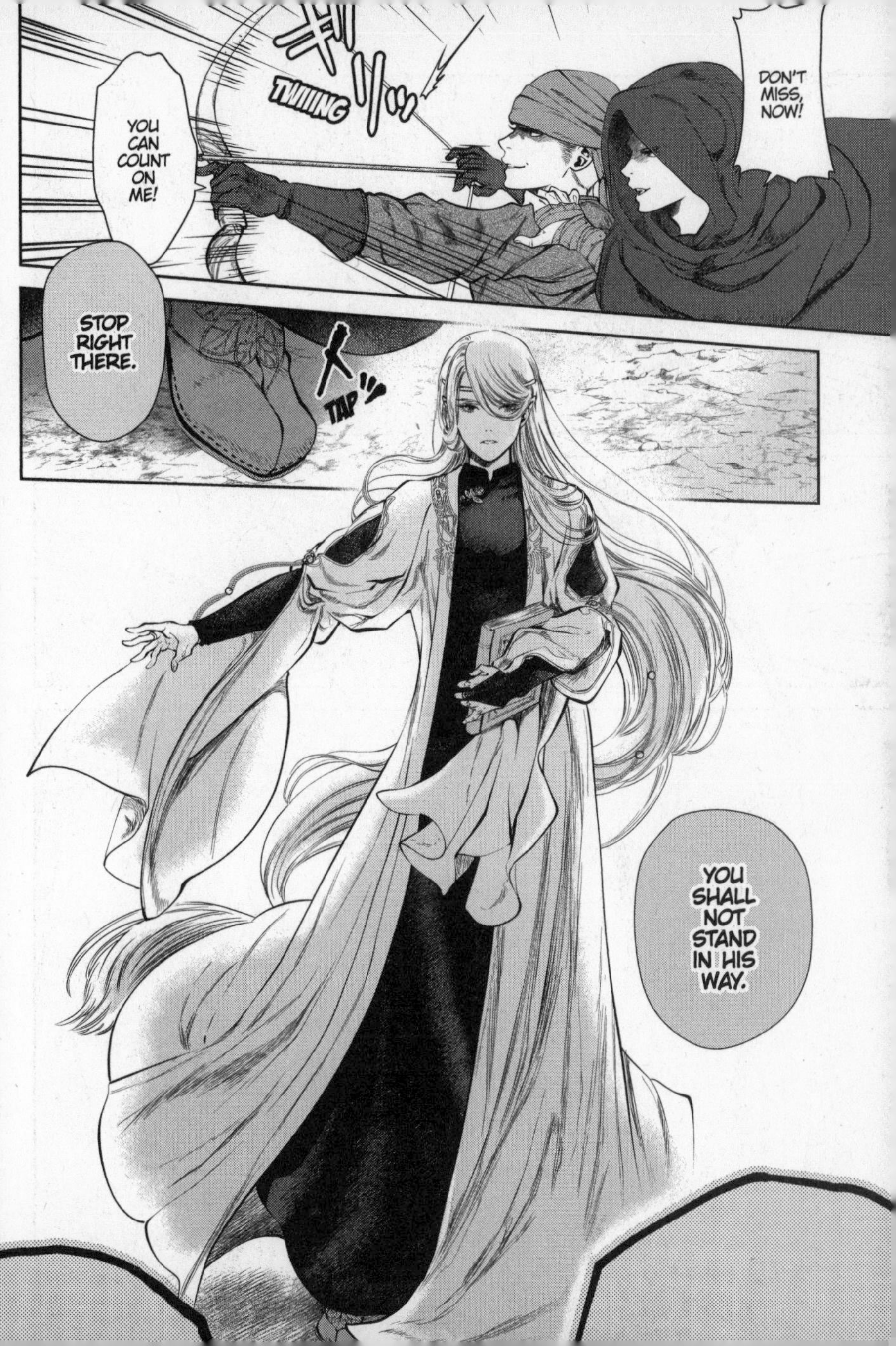
DON'T MISS, NOW!
TWIIING
YOU CAN COUNT ON ME!
TAP
STOP RIGHT THERE.
YOU SHALL NOT STAND IN HIS WAY.

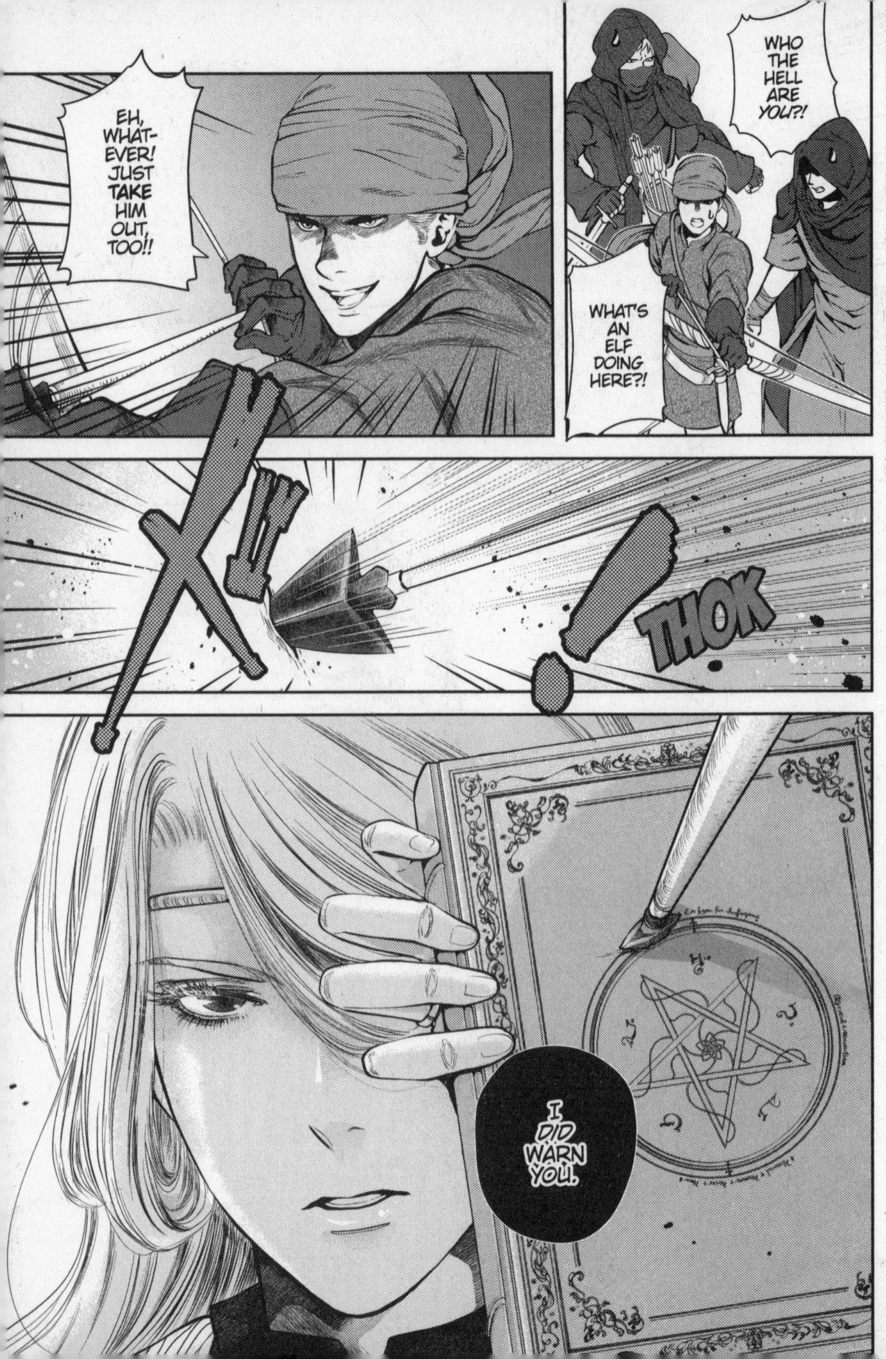
WHO THE HELL ARE YOU?!
WHAT'S AN ELF DOING HERE?!
EH, WHAT-EVER! JUST TAKE HIM OUT, TOO!!
THOK
I DID WARN YOU.

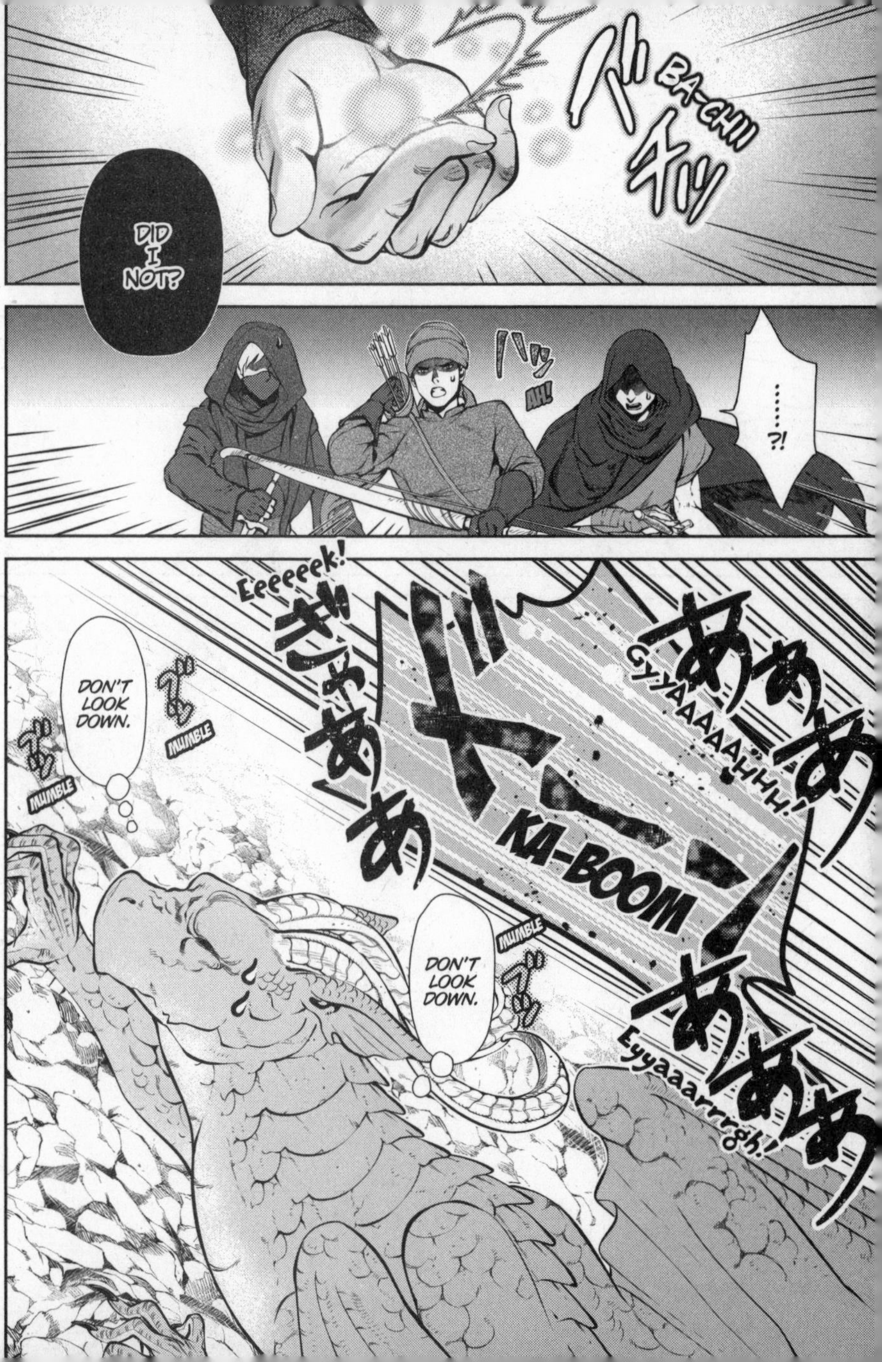
BA-CHII
DID I NOT?
……?!
AH!
GYYAAAAAHHH!
Eyyaaarrrgh!
KA-BOOM
Eeeeeek!
MUMBLE
DON'T LOOK DOWN.
MUMBLE
DON'T LOOK DOWN.
MUMBLE

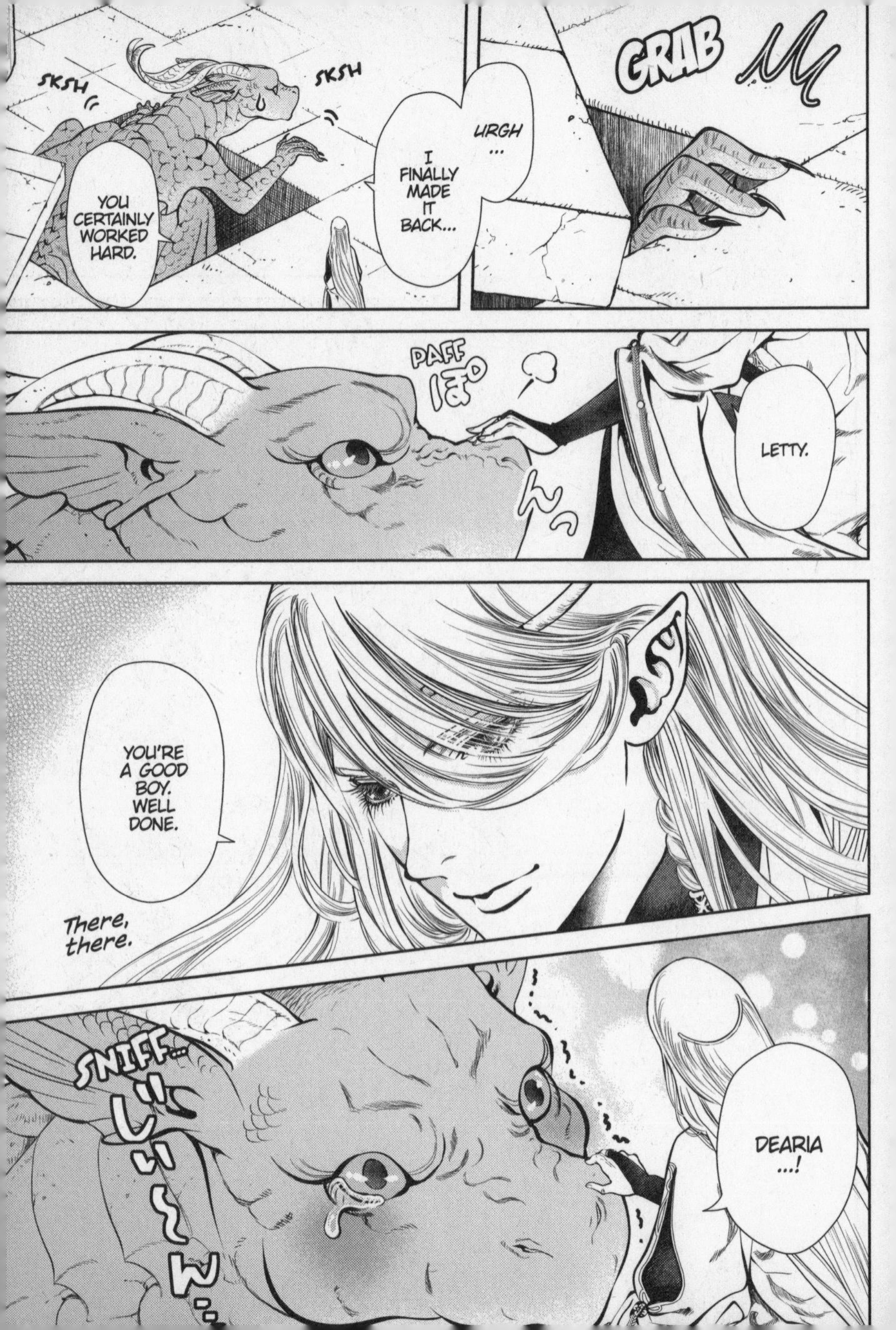
GRAB
SKSH
SKSH
URGH ... I FINALLY MADE IT BACK...
YOU CERTAINLY WORKED HARD.
LETTY.
PAFF
ぽ
んっ
YOU'RE A GOOD BOY. WELL DONE.
There, there.
DEARIA ...!
SNIFF...

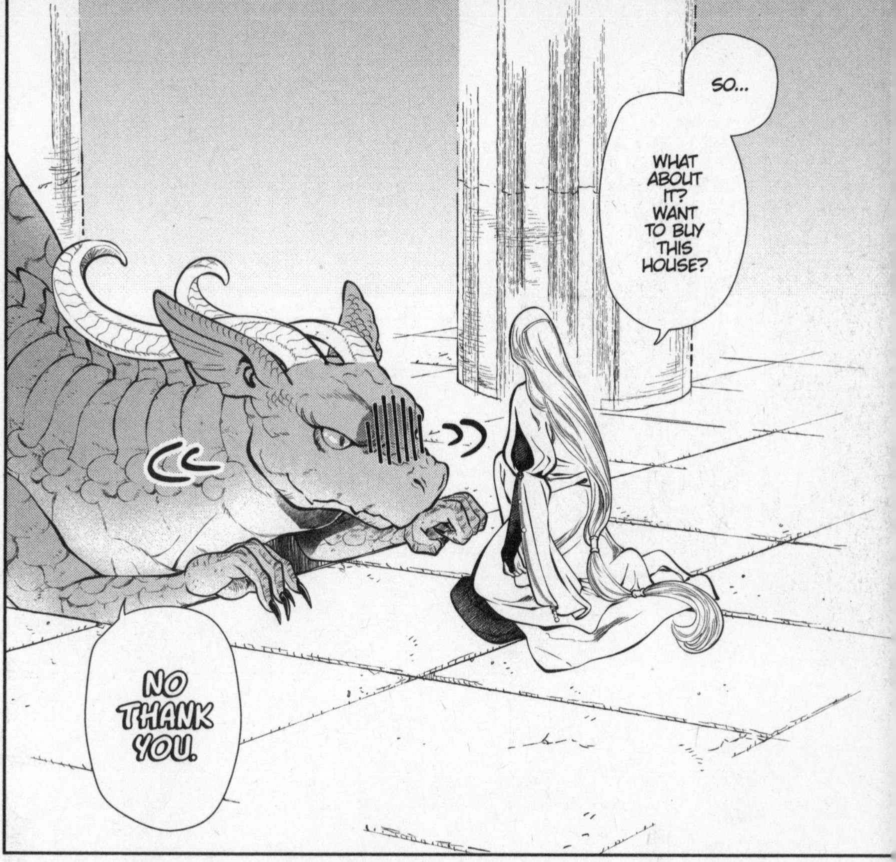
SO...
WHAT ABOUT IT? WANT TO BUY THIS HOUSE?
NO THANK YOU.

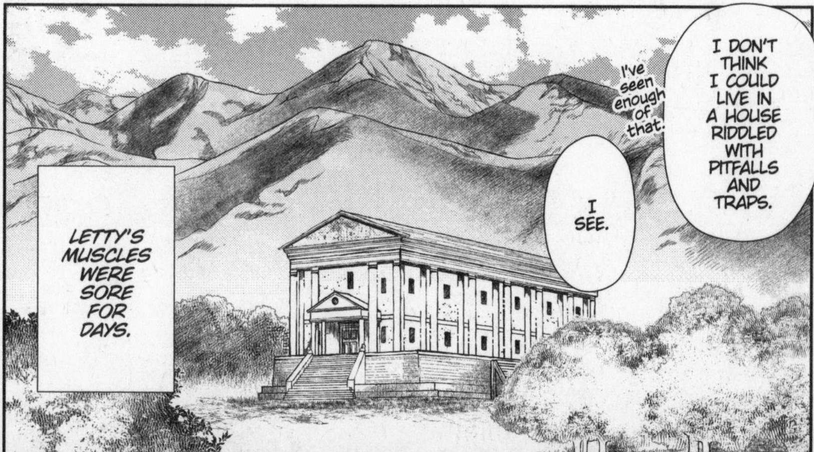
I DON'T THINK I COULD LIVE IN A HOUSE RIDDLED WITH PITFALLS AND TRAPS.
I've seen enough of that.
I SEE.
LETTY'S MUSCLES WERE SORE FOR DAYS.

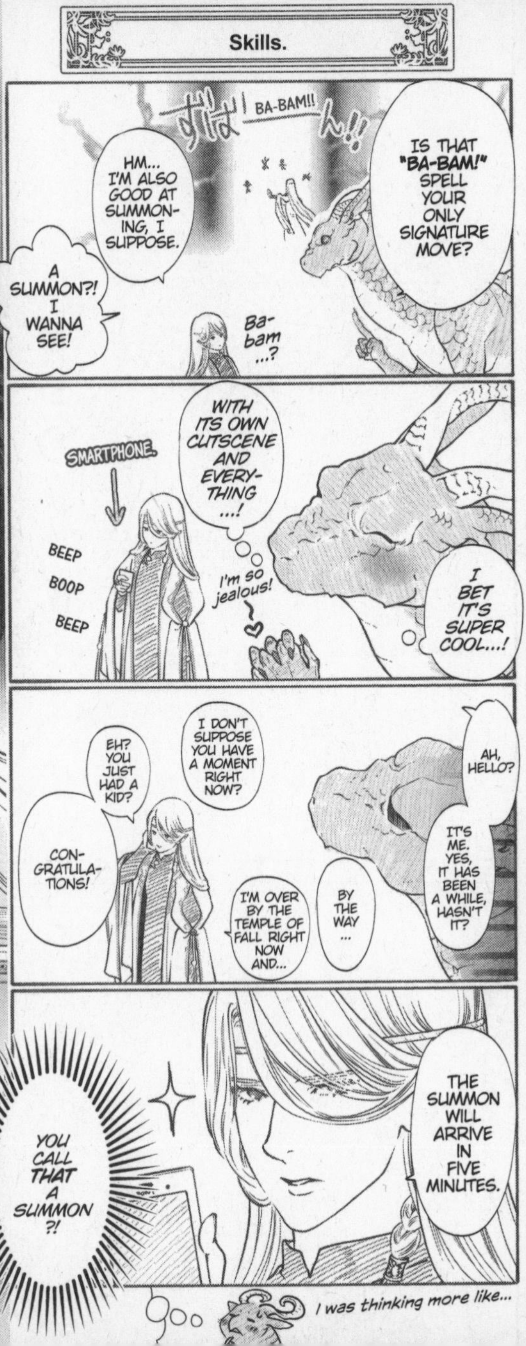
Skills.
ずば ん!!
BA-BAM!!
IS THAT "BA-BAM!" SPELL YOUR ONLY SIGNATURE MOVE?
HM... I'M ALSO GOOD AT SUMMONING, I SUPPOSE.
Ba-bam...?
A SUMMON?! I WANNA SEE!
WITH ITS OWN CUTSCENE AND EVERYTHING...!
I BET IT'S SUPER COOL...!
SMARTPHONE.
I'm so jealous!
BEEP
BOOP
BEEP
AH, HELLO?
IT'S ME. YES, IT HAS BEEN A WHILE, HASN'T IT?
I DON'T SUPPOSE YOU HAVE A MOMENT RIGHT NOW?
EH? YOU JUST HAD A KID?
BY THE WAY...
I'M OVER BY THE TEMPLE OF FALL RIGHT NOW AND...
CONGRATULATIONS!
THE SUMMON WILL ARRIVE IN FIVE MINUTES.
YOU CALL THAT A SUMMON?!
I was thinking more like...
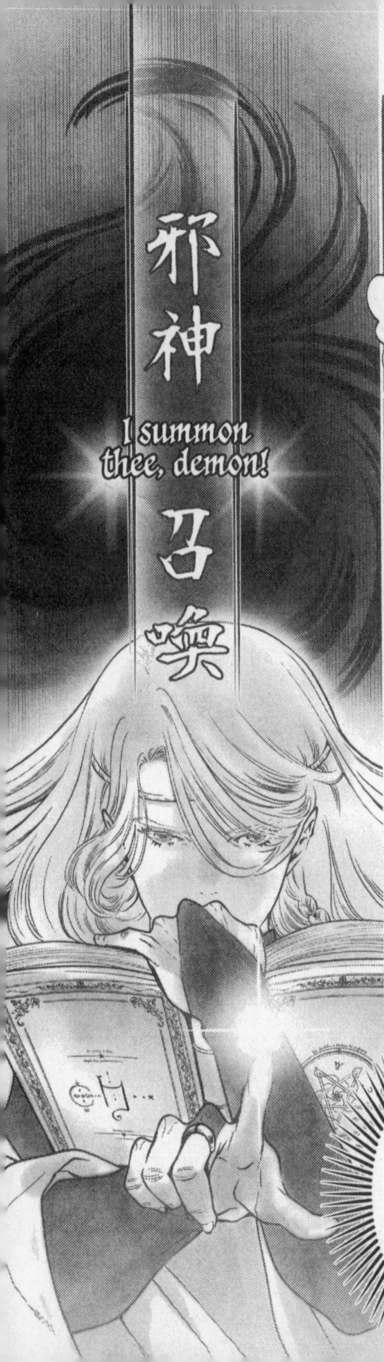
邪神召喚
I summon thee, demon!

Dragon Goes House-Hunting

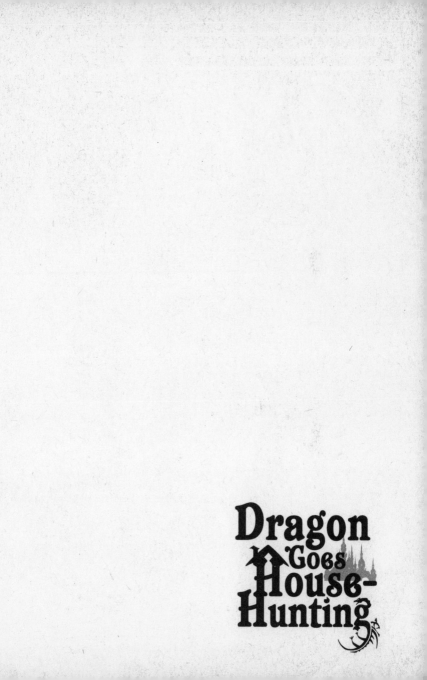

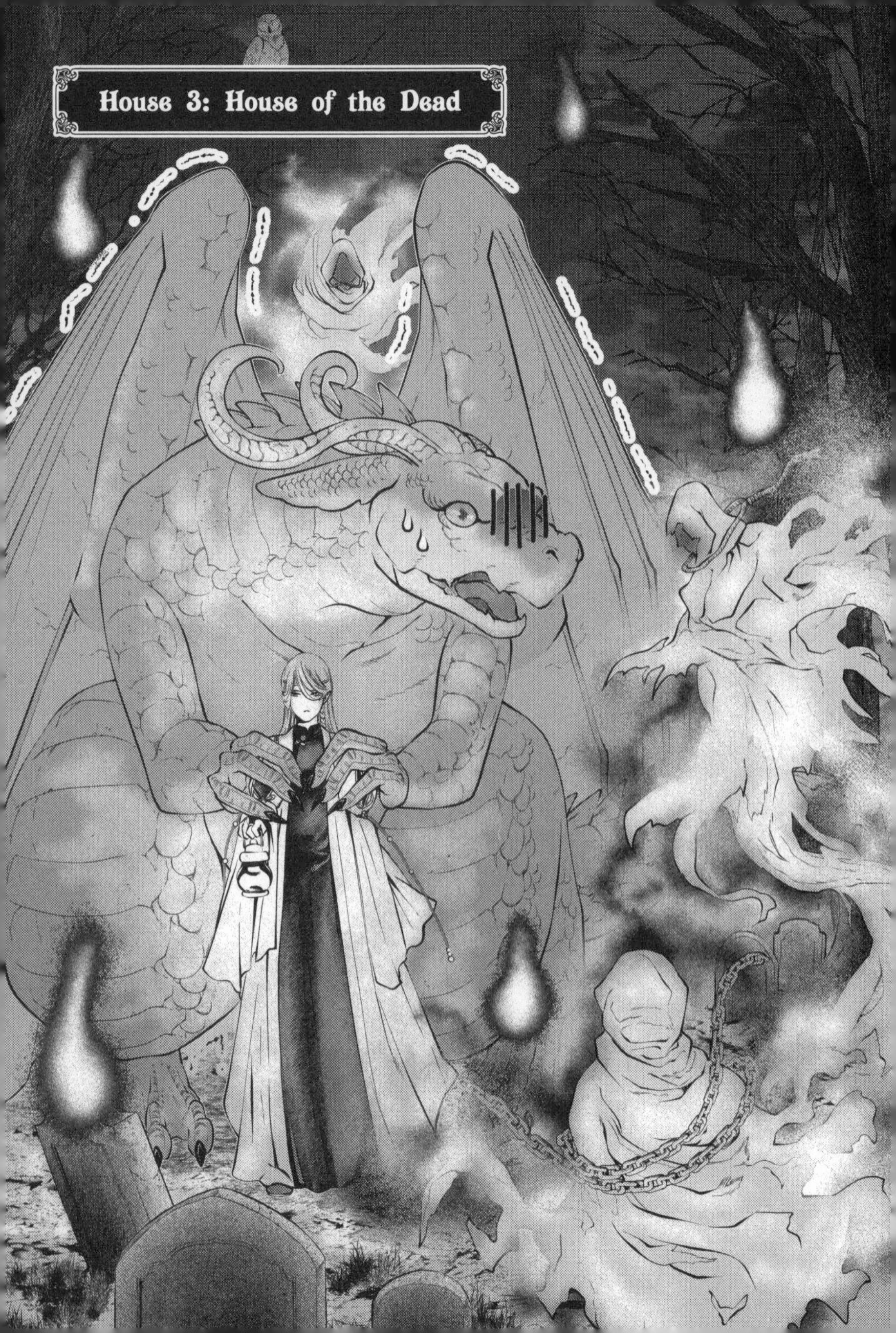
House 3: House of the Dead

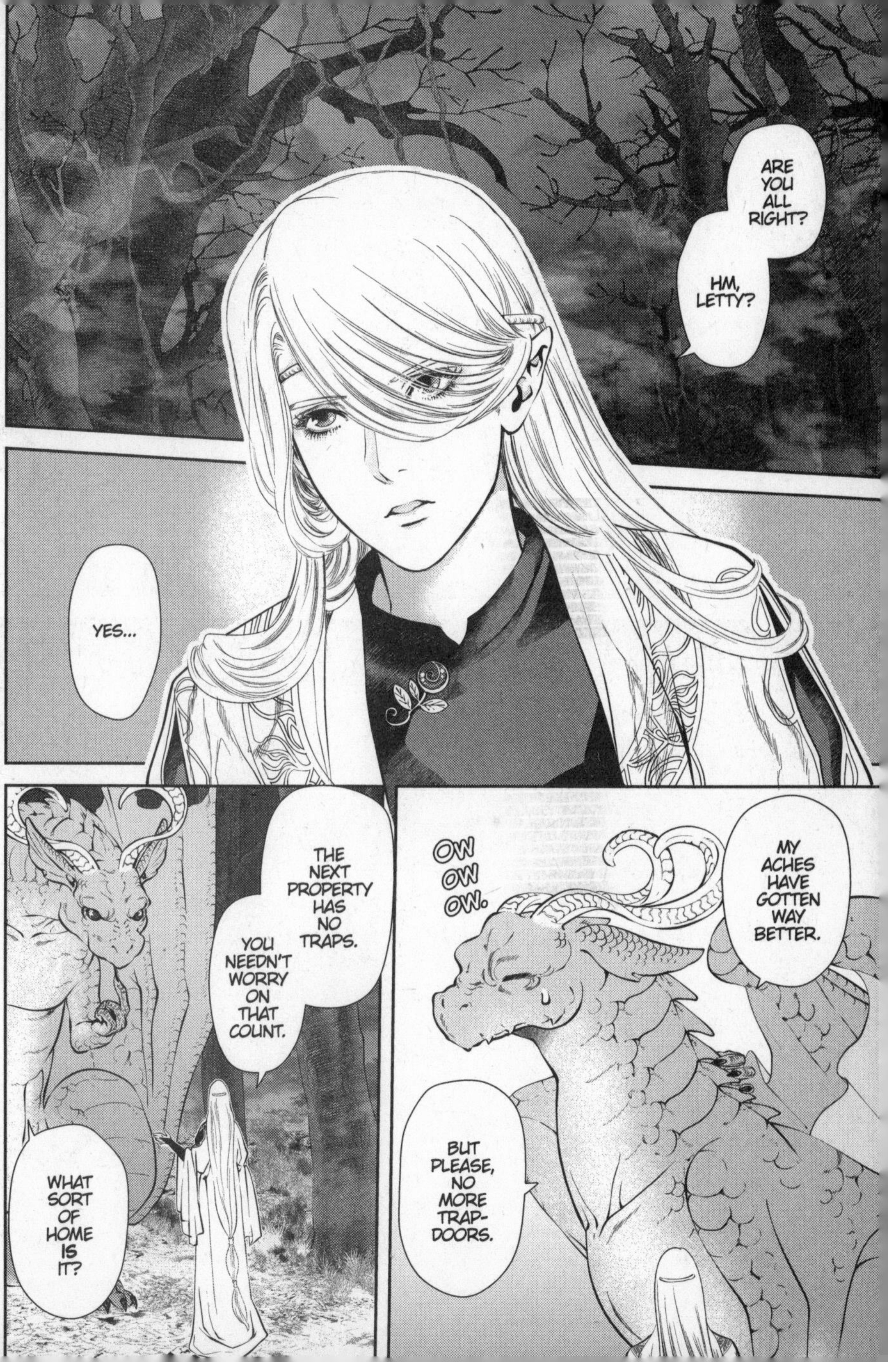
ARE YOU ALL RIGHT?
HM, LETTY?
YES...
MY ACHES HAVE GOTTEN WAY BETTER.
OW OW OW.
BUT PLEASE, NO MORE TRAP-DOORS.
THE NEXT PROPERTY HAS NO TRAPS.
YOU NEEDN'T WORRY ON THAT COUNT.
WHAT SORT OF HOME IS IT?

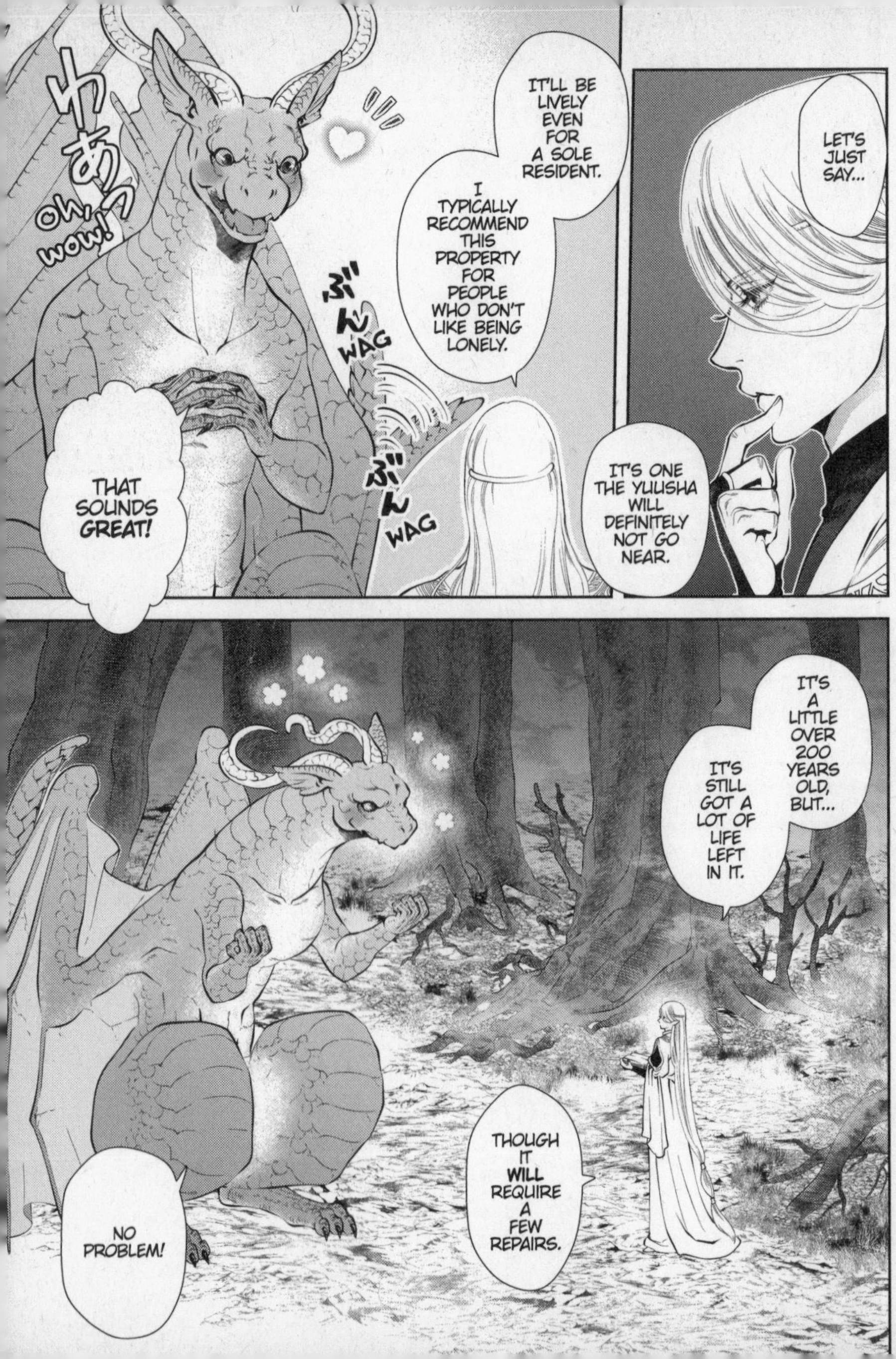
LET'S JUST SAY...
IT'S ONE THE YUUSHA WILL DEFINITELY NOT GO NEAR.
IT'LL BE LIVELY EVEN FOR A SOLE RESIDENT.
I TYPICALLY RECOMMEND THIS PROPERTY FOR PEOPLE WHO DON'T LIKE BEING LONELY.
ぶん WAG
ぶん WAG
わあっ
Oh, wow!
THAT SOUNDS GREAT!
IT'S A LITTLE OVER 200 YEARS OLD, BUT...
IT'S STILL GOT A LOT OF LIFE LEFT IN IT.
THOUGH IT WILL REQUIRE A FEW REPAIRS.
NO PROBLEM!

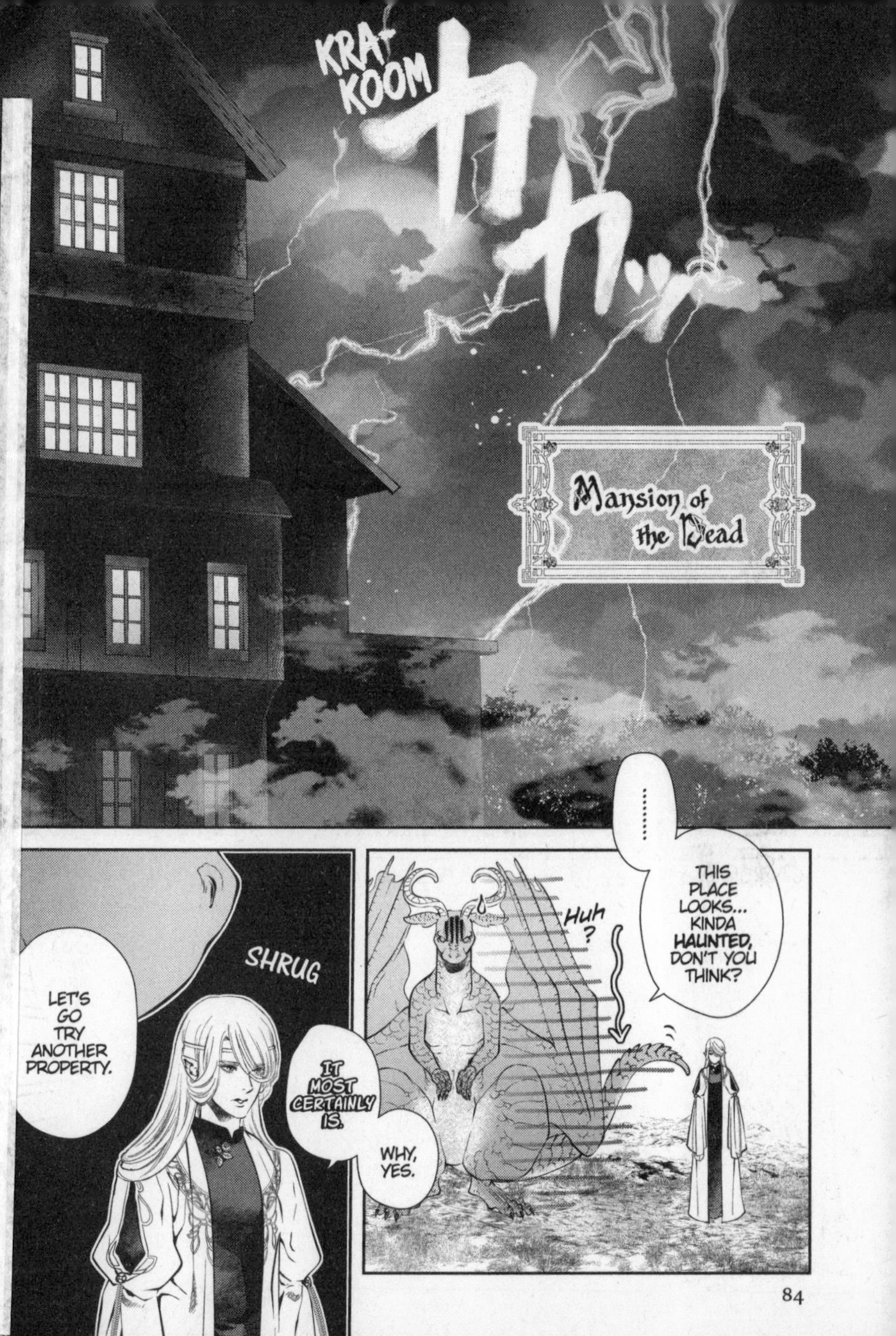
KRA-KOOM
Mansion of the Dead
......
THIS PLACE LOOKS... KINDA HAUNTED, DON'T YOU THINK?
Huh?
WHY, YES.
IT MOST CERTAINLY IS.
SHRUG
LET'S GO TRY ANOTHER PROPERTY.

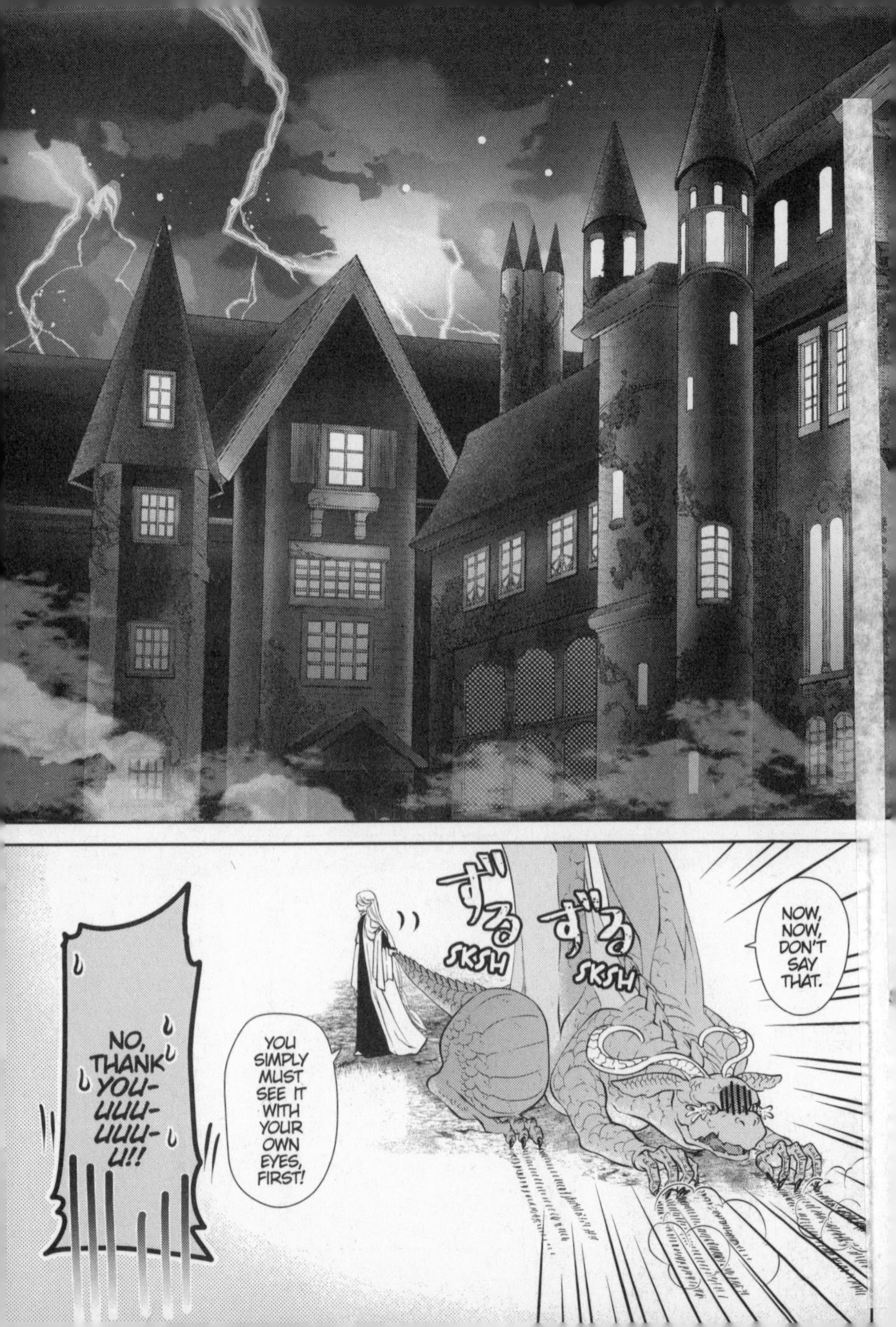
NOW, NOW, DON'T SAY THAT.
ずる
SKSH
ずる
SKSH
YOU SIMPLY MUST SEE IT WITH YOUR OWN EYES, FIRST!
NO, THANK YOU-UUU-UUUU-U!!

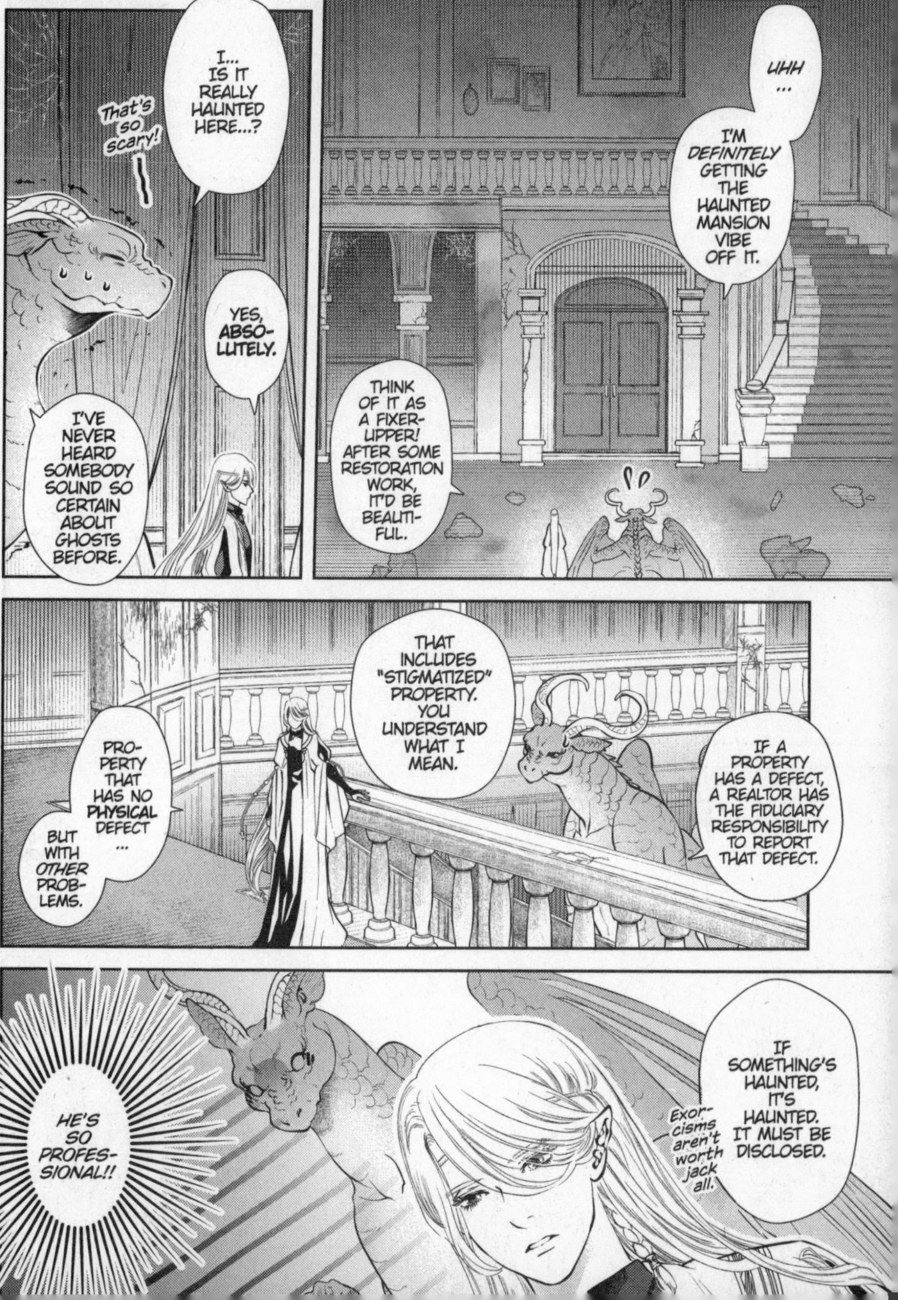
UHH ...
I'M DEFINITELY GETTING THE HAUNTED MANSION VIBE OFF IT.
THINK OF IT AS A FIXER-UPPER! AFTER SOME RESTORATION WORK, IT'D BE BEAUTIFUL.
I... IS IT REALLY HAUNTED HERE...?
That's so scary!
YES, ABSOLUTELY.
I'VE NEVER HEARD SOMEBODY SOUND SO CERTAIN ABOUT GHOSTS BEFORE.
IF A PROPERTY HAS A DEFECT, A REALTOR HAS THE FIDUCIARY RESPONSIBILITY TO REPORT THAT DEFECT.
THAT INCLUDES "STIGMATIZED" PROPERTY. YOU UNDERSTAND WHAT I MEAN.
PROPERTY THAT HAS NO PHYSICAL DEFECT ...
BUT WITH OTHER PROBLEMS.
IF SOMETHING'S HAUNTED, IT'S HAUNTED. IT MUST BE DISCLOSED.
Exorcisms aren't worth jack all.
HE'S SO PROFESSIONAL!!

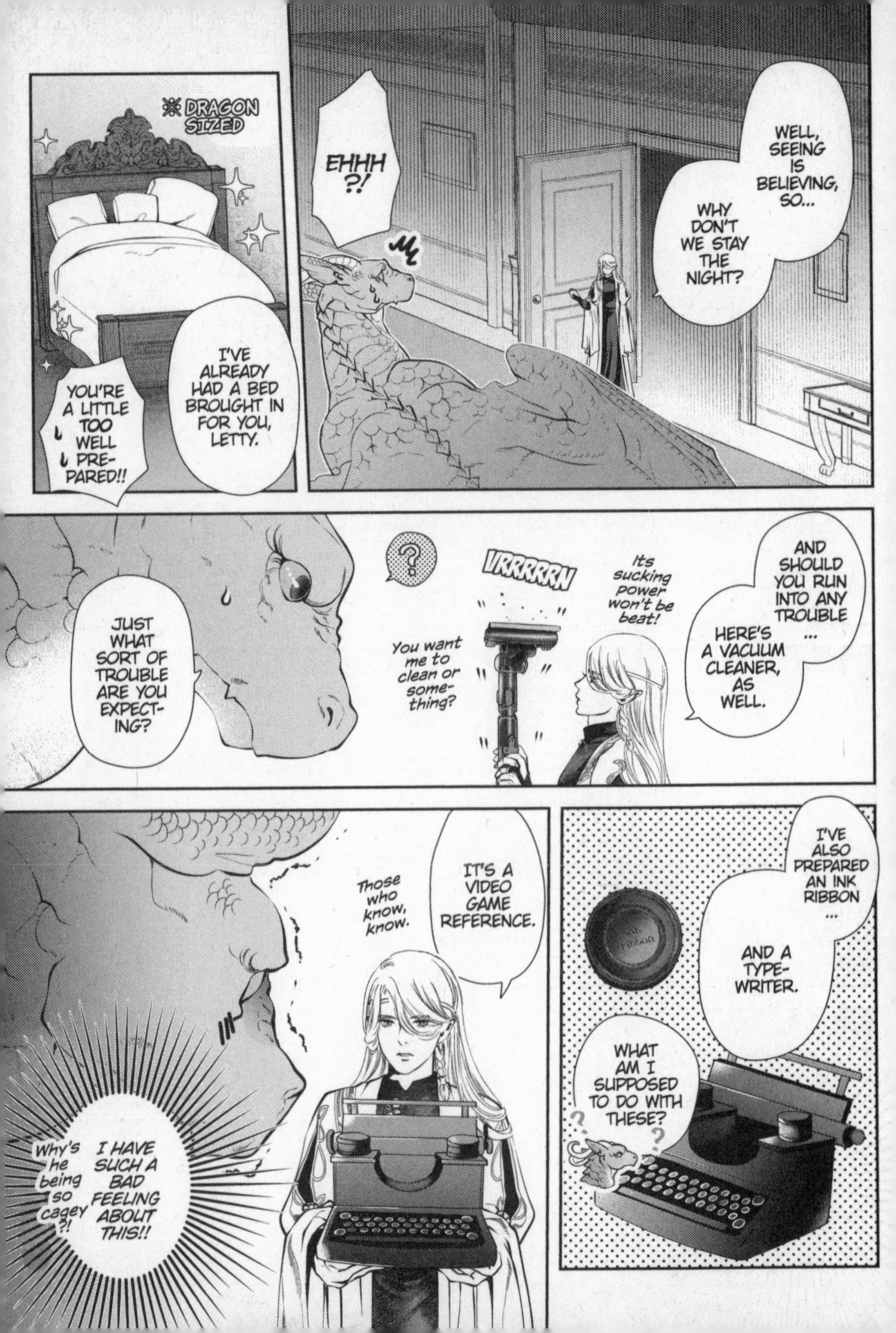
WELL, SEEING IS BELIEVING, SO...
WHY DON'T WE STAY THE NIGHT?
EHHH ?!
I'VE ALREADY HAD A BED BROUGHT IN FOR YOU, LETTY.
※DRAGON SIZED
YOU'RE A LITTLE TOO WELL PRE-PARED!!
AND SHOULD YOU RUN INTO ANY TROUBLE ...
HERE'S A VACUUM CLEANER, AS WELL.
Its sucking power won't be beat!
VRRRRRN
You want me to clean or some-thing?
JUST WHAT SORT OF TROUBLE ARE YOU EXPECT-ING?
I'VE ALSO PREPARED AN INK RIBBON ...
AND A TYPE-WRITER.
WHAT AM I SUPPOSED TO DO WITH THESE?
IT'S A VIDEO GAME REFERENCE.
Those who know, know.
I HAVE SUCH A BAD FEELING ABOUT THIS!!
Why's he being so cagey ?!

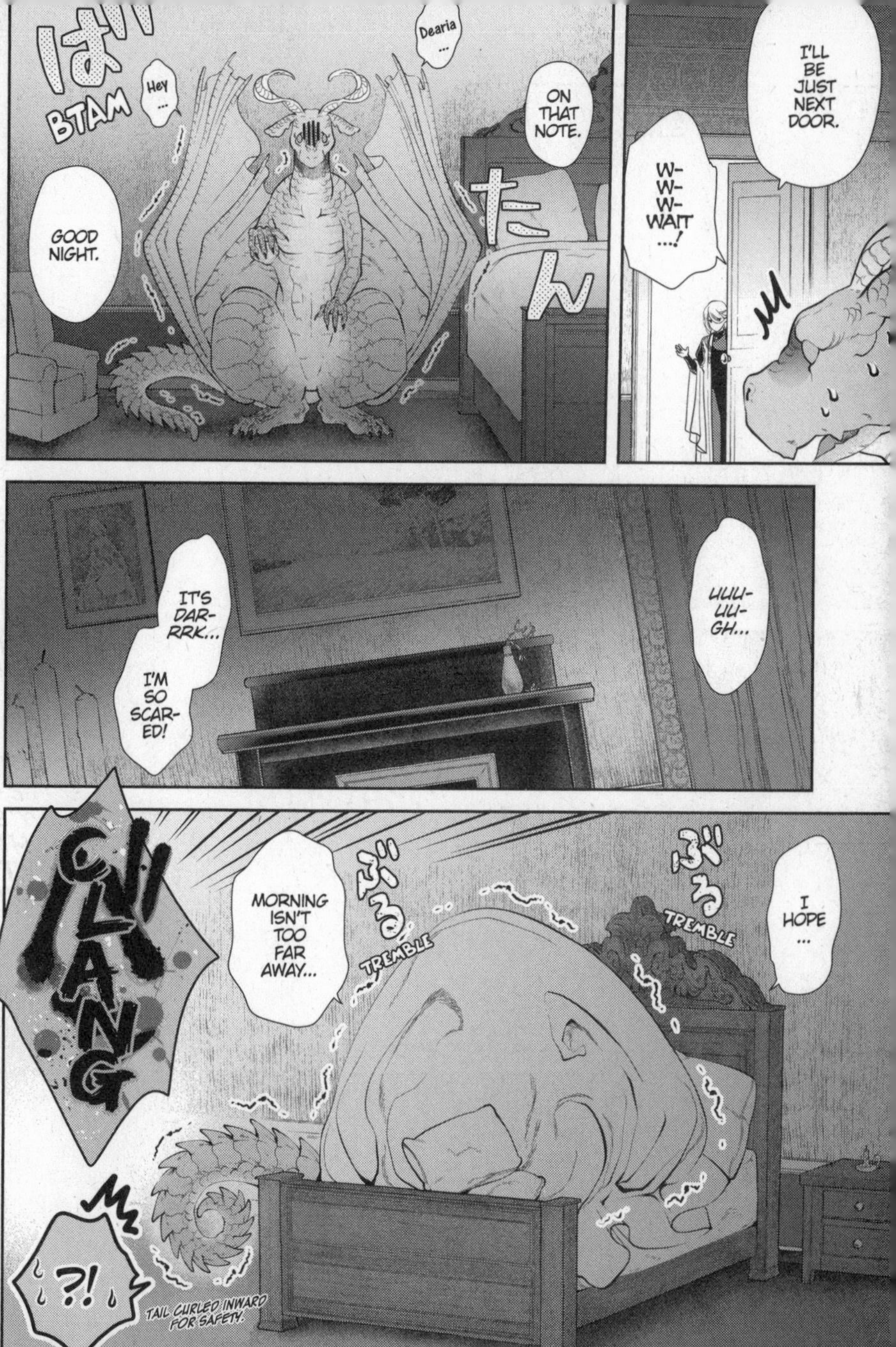

I'LL BE JUST NEXT DOOR.
W-W-W-WAIT ...!
ON THAT NOTE.
たん
Dearia ...
Hey ...
BTAM
GOOD NIGHT.
UUUU-UUGH...
IT'S DARRRK...
I'M SO SCARED!
I HOPE ...
ぶる
TREMBLE
MORNING ISN'T TOO FAR AWAY...
ぶる
TREMBLE
CLANG
?!
TAIL CURLED INWARD FOR SAFETY.

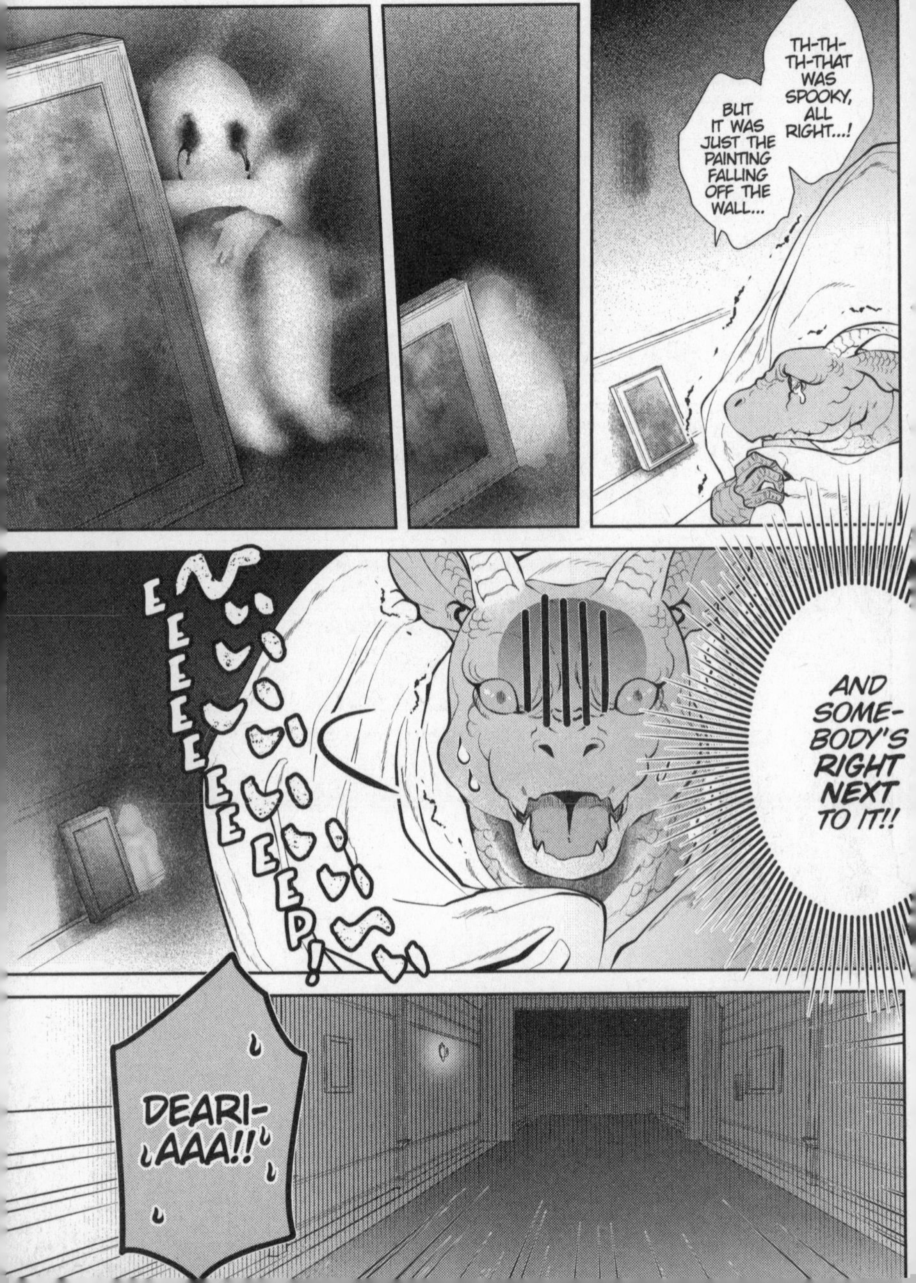
TH-TH-TH-THAT WAS SPOOKY, ALL RIGHT...!
BUT IT WAS JUST THE PAINTING FALLING OFF THE WALL...
AND SOMEBODY'S RIGHT NEXT TO IT!!
EEEEEEEEEP!
DEARI-AAA!!

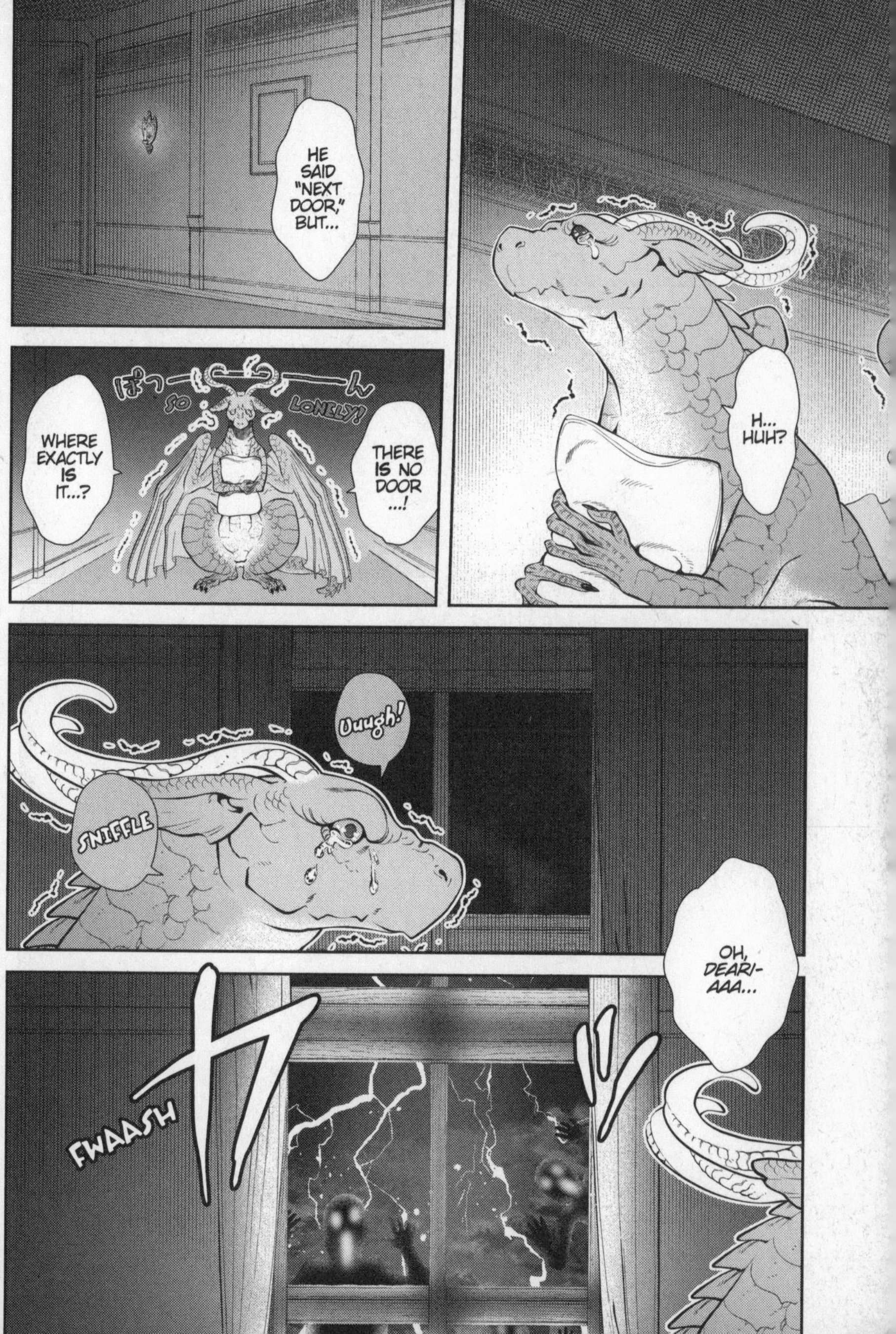
H... HUH?
HE SAID "NEXT DOOR," BUT...
THERE IS NO DOOR ...!
SO LONELY!
WHERE EXACTLY IS IT...?
OH, DEARI-AAA...
Uuugh!
SNIFFLE
FWAASH

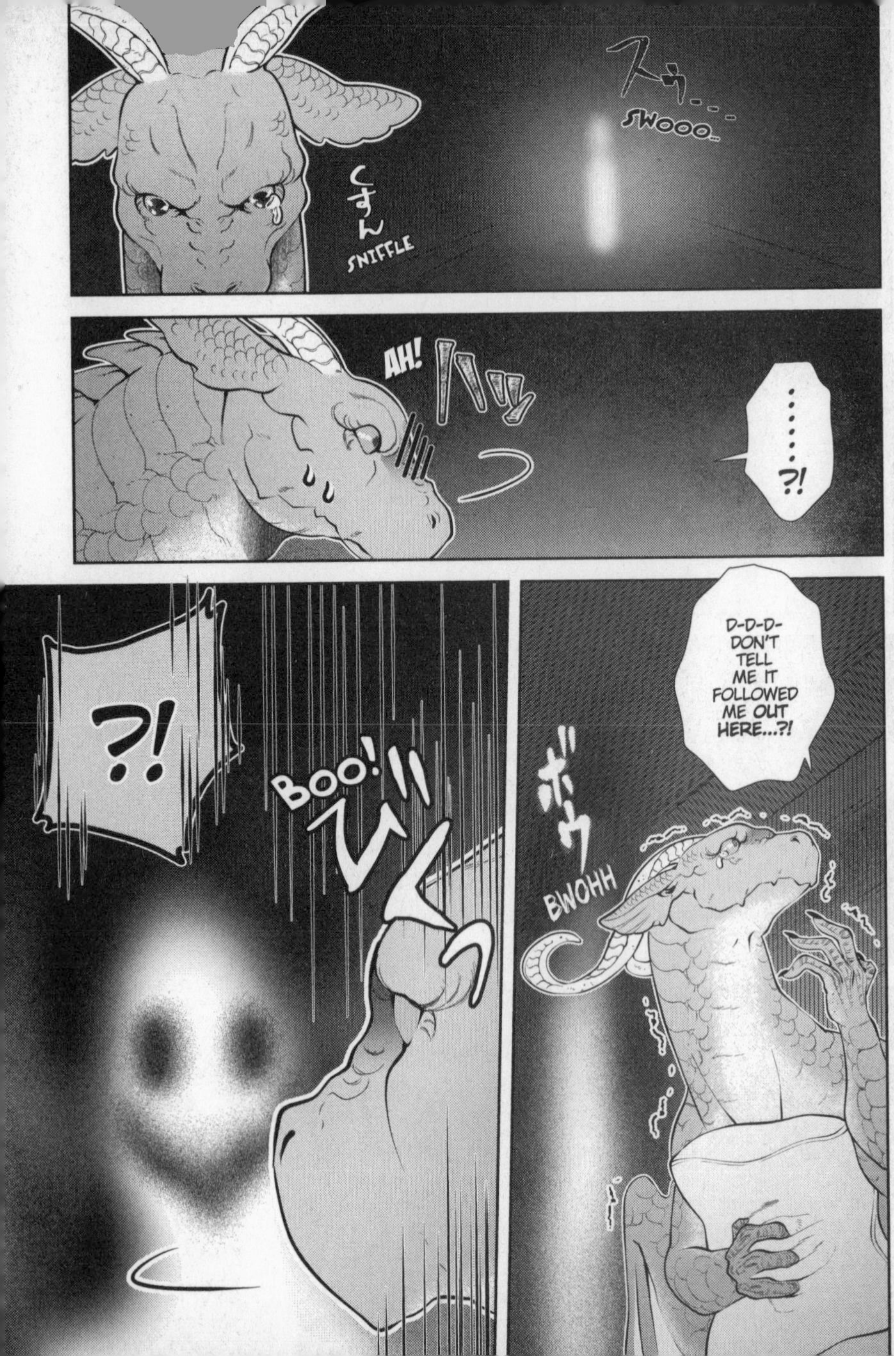
スゥ...
SWOOO...
くすん
SNIFFLE
......?!
ハッ
AH!
つ
D-D-D-DON'T TELL ME IT FOLLOWED ME OUT HERE...?!
ボウ
BWOHH
?!
びく
BOO!

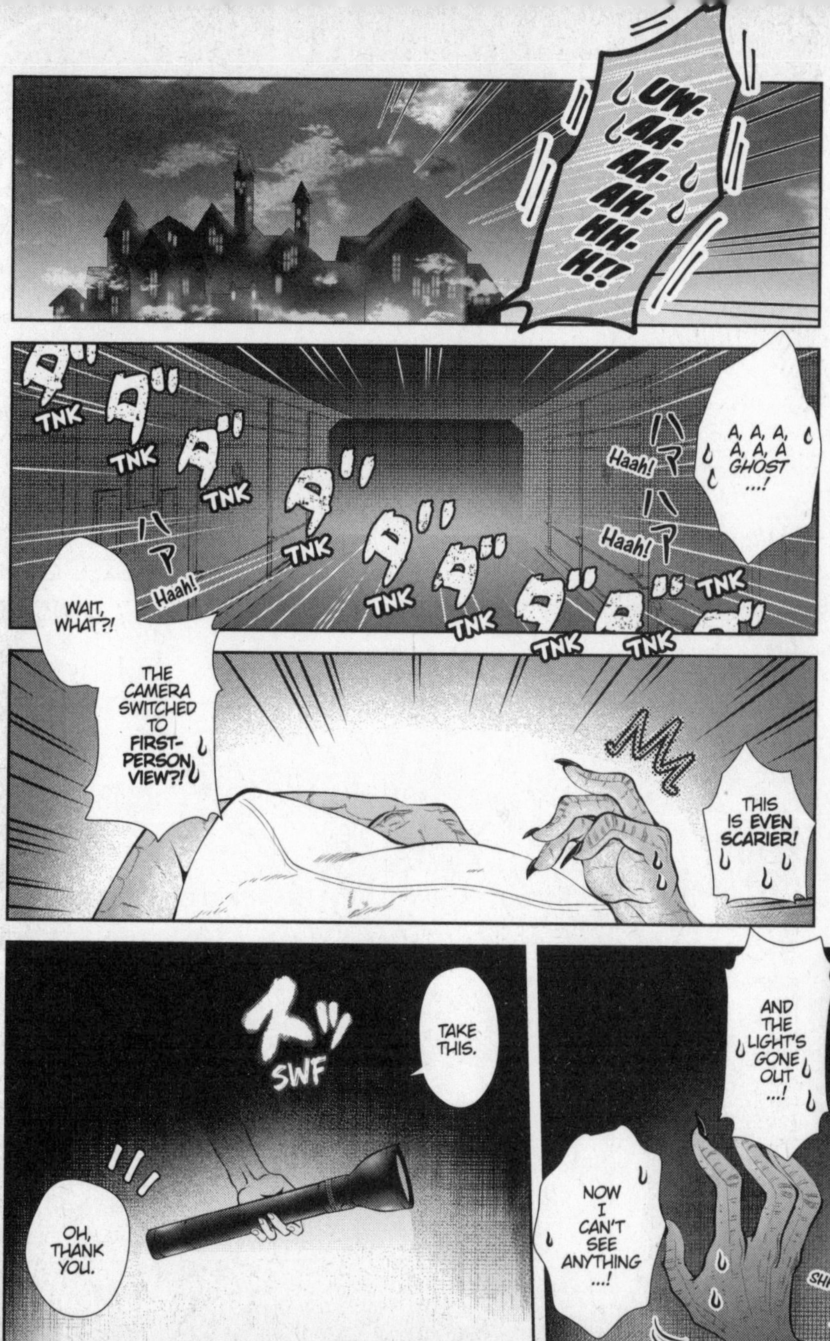
UW-AA-AA-AH-HH-H!?!
A, A, A, A, A, A GHOST ...!
ハァハァ
Haah!
Haah!
ダッ ダッ ダッ ダッ ダッ ダッ ダッ ダッ
TNK TNK TNK TNK TNK TNK TNK TNK TNK
ハァ
Haah!
WAIT, WHAT?!
THE CAMERA SWITCHED TO FIRST-PERSON VIEW?!
THIS IS EVEN SCARIER!
AND THE LIGHT'S GONE OUT ...!
NOW I CAN'T SEE ANYTHING ...!
カベ
SHF
TAKE THIS.
スッ
SWF
OH, THANK YOU.

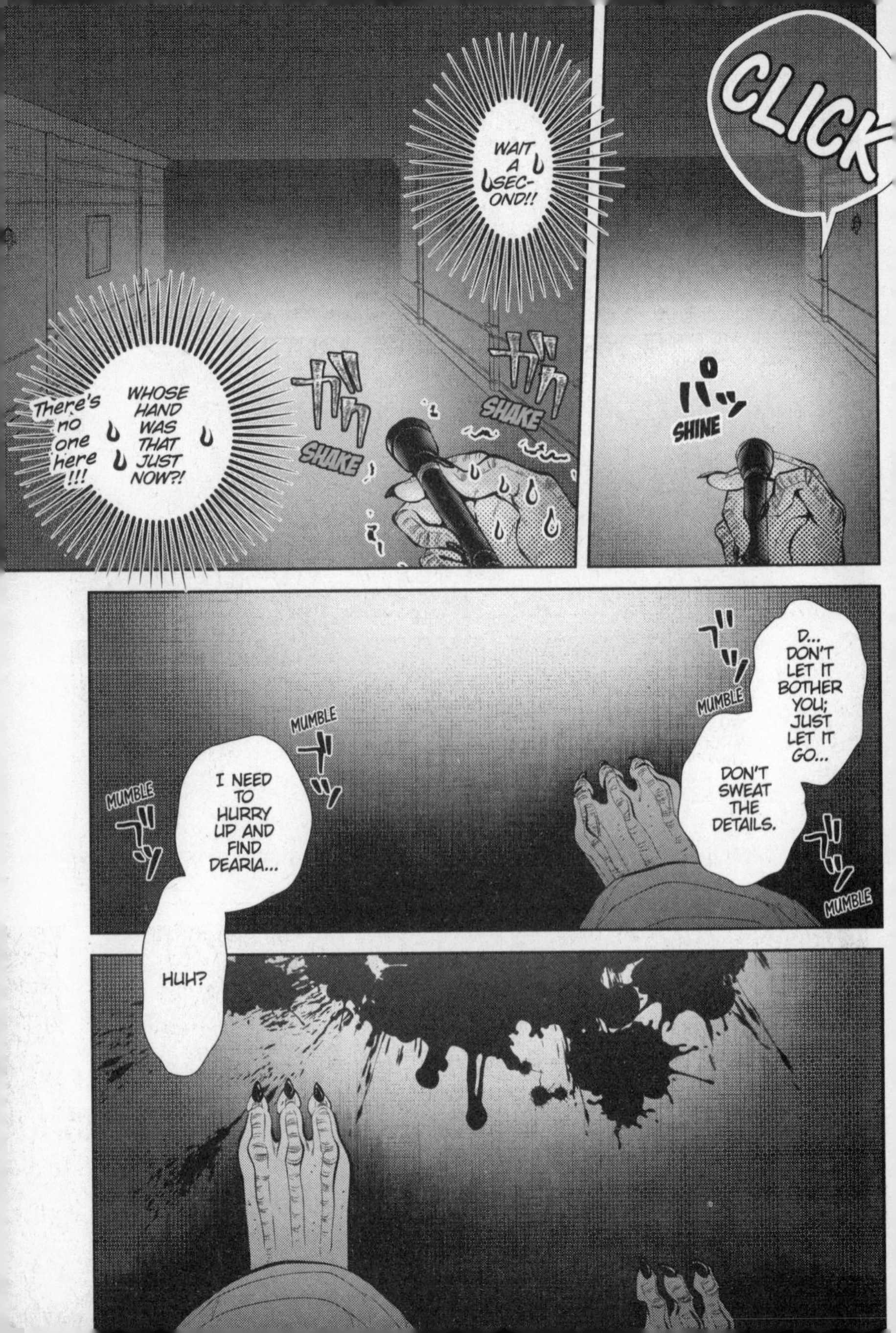
CLICK
パッ
SHINE
WAIT A SEC-OND!!
WHOSE HAND WAS THAT JUST NOW?!
There's no one here!!!
SHAKE
SHAKE
D... DON'T LET IT BOTHER YOU; JUST LET IT GO...
MUMBLE
DON'T SWEAT THE DETAILS.
MUMBLE
MUMBLE
I NEED TO HURRY UP AND FIND DEARIA...
MUMBLE
HUH?

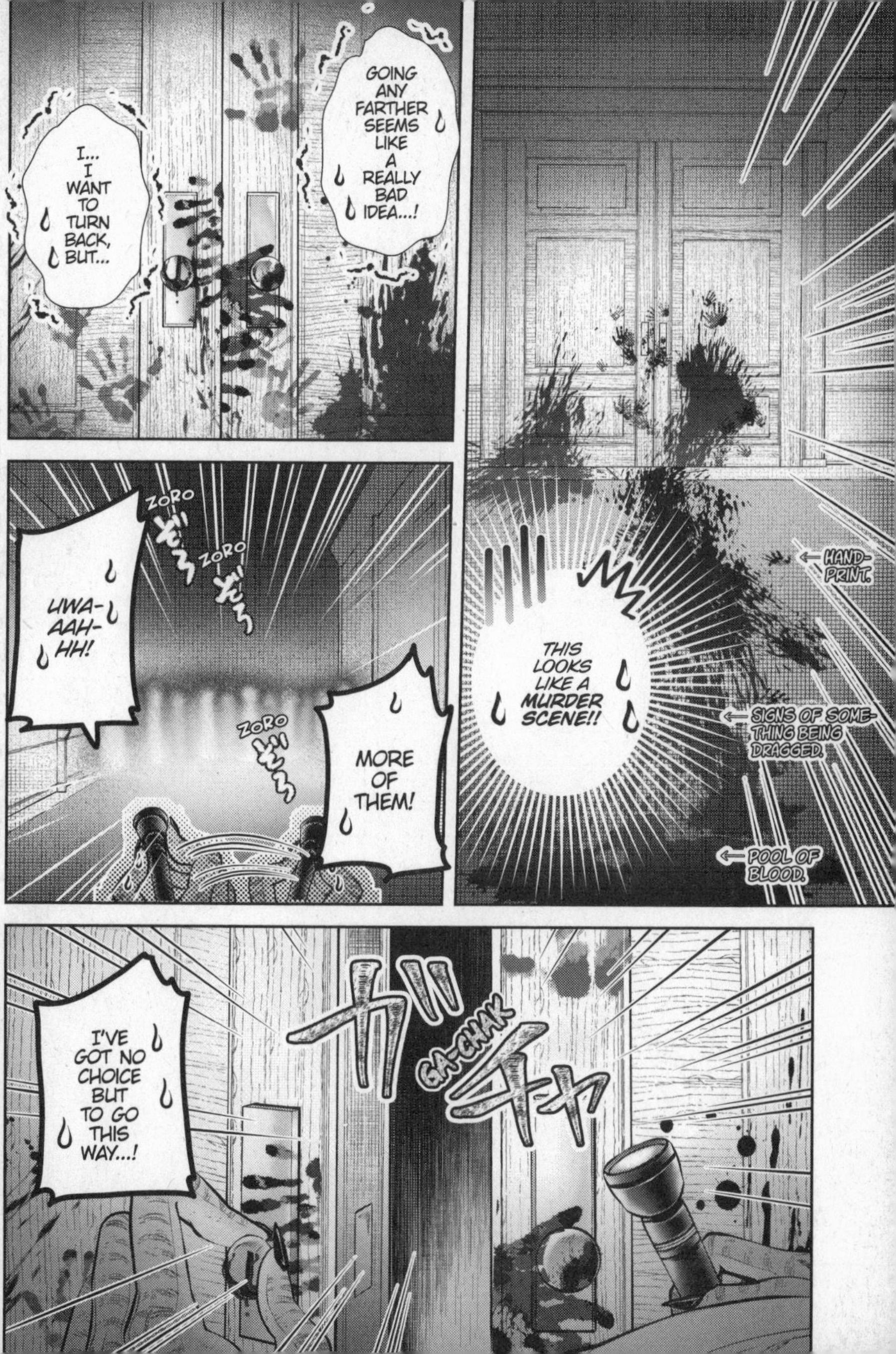
HAND-PRINT.
THIS LOOKS LIKE A MURDER SCENE!!
SIGNS OF SOME-THING BEING DRAGGED.
POOL OF BLOOD.
GOING ANY FARTHER SEEMS LIKE A REALLY BAD IDEA...!
I... I WANT TO TURN BACK, BUT...
ZORO
ZORO
UWA-AAH-HH!
ZORO
MORE OF THEM!
GA-CHAK
I'VE GOT NO CHOICE BUT TO GO THIS WAY...!

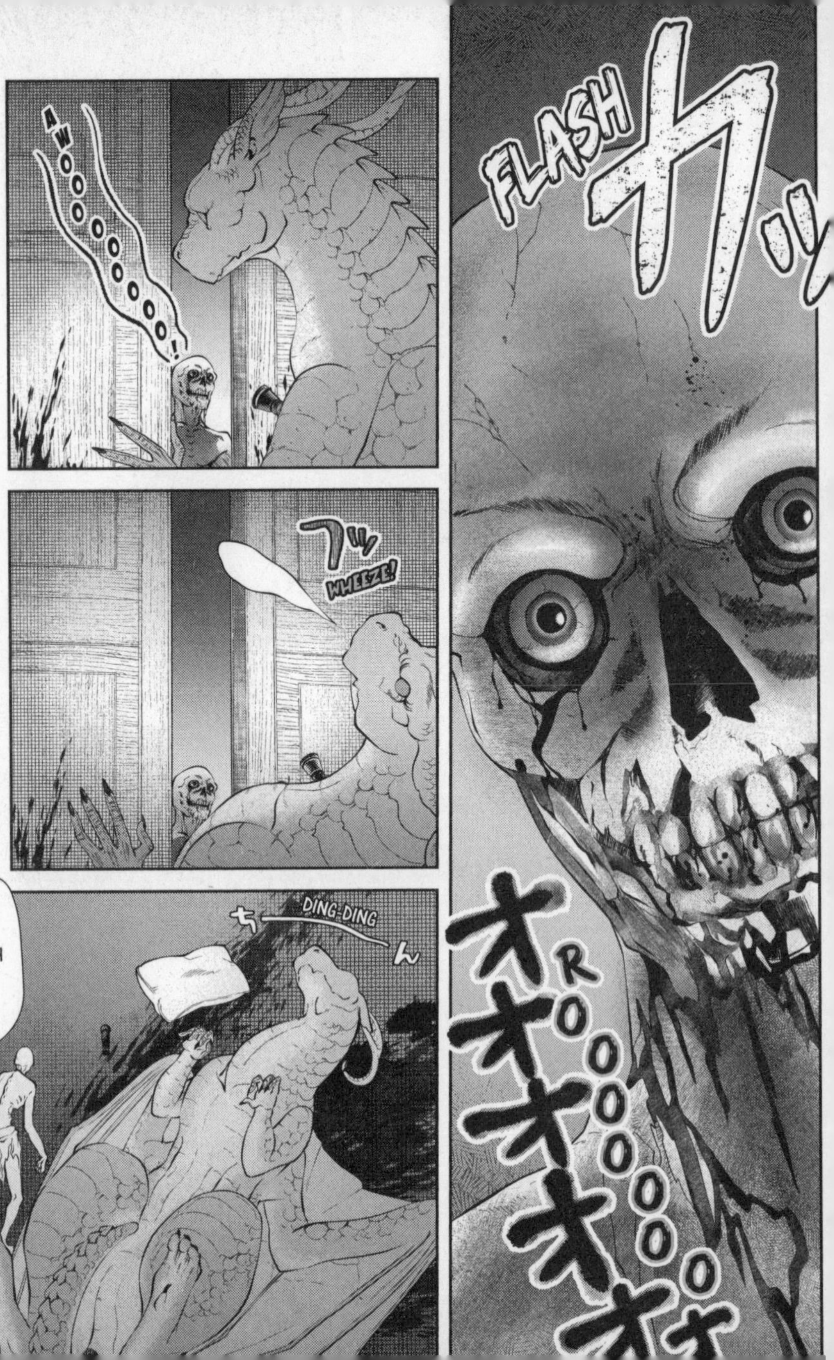
FLASH
ROOOOOOOOO
AWOOOOOOOOO!
WHEEZE!
DING-DING
HUH ...?

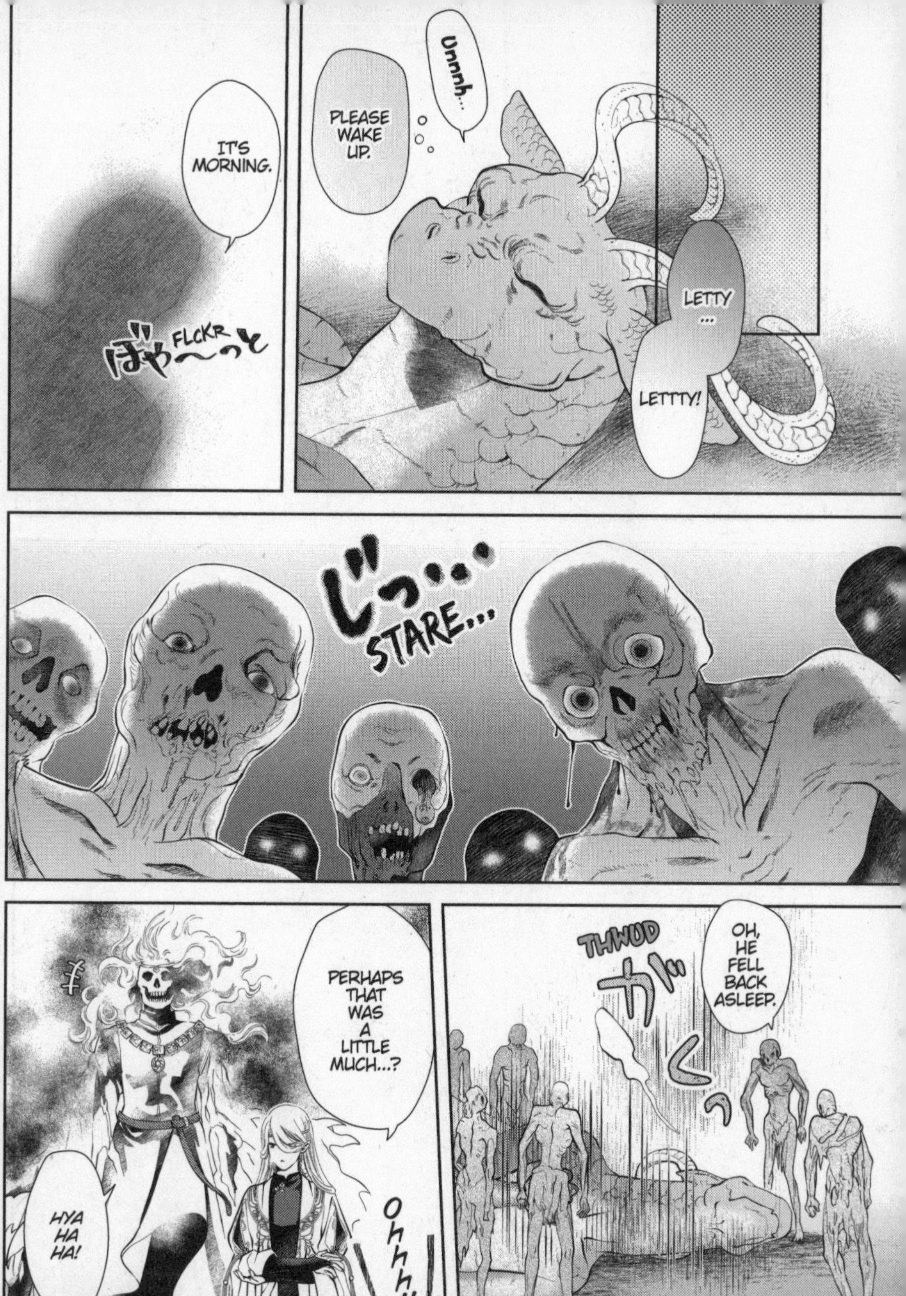
LETTY ...
LETTTY!
PLEASE WAKE UP.
Unnnh...
IT'S MORNING.
FLCKR
ぼや〜っと
じっ…
STARE...
OH, HE FELL BACK ASLEEP.
THWUD
がくっ
PERHAPS THAT WAS A LITTLE MUCH...?
ギ
HYA HA HA!
Ohhhh!!

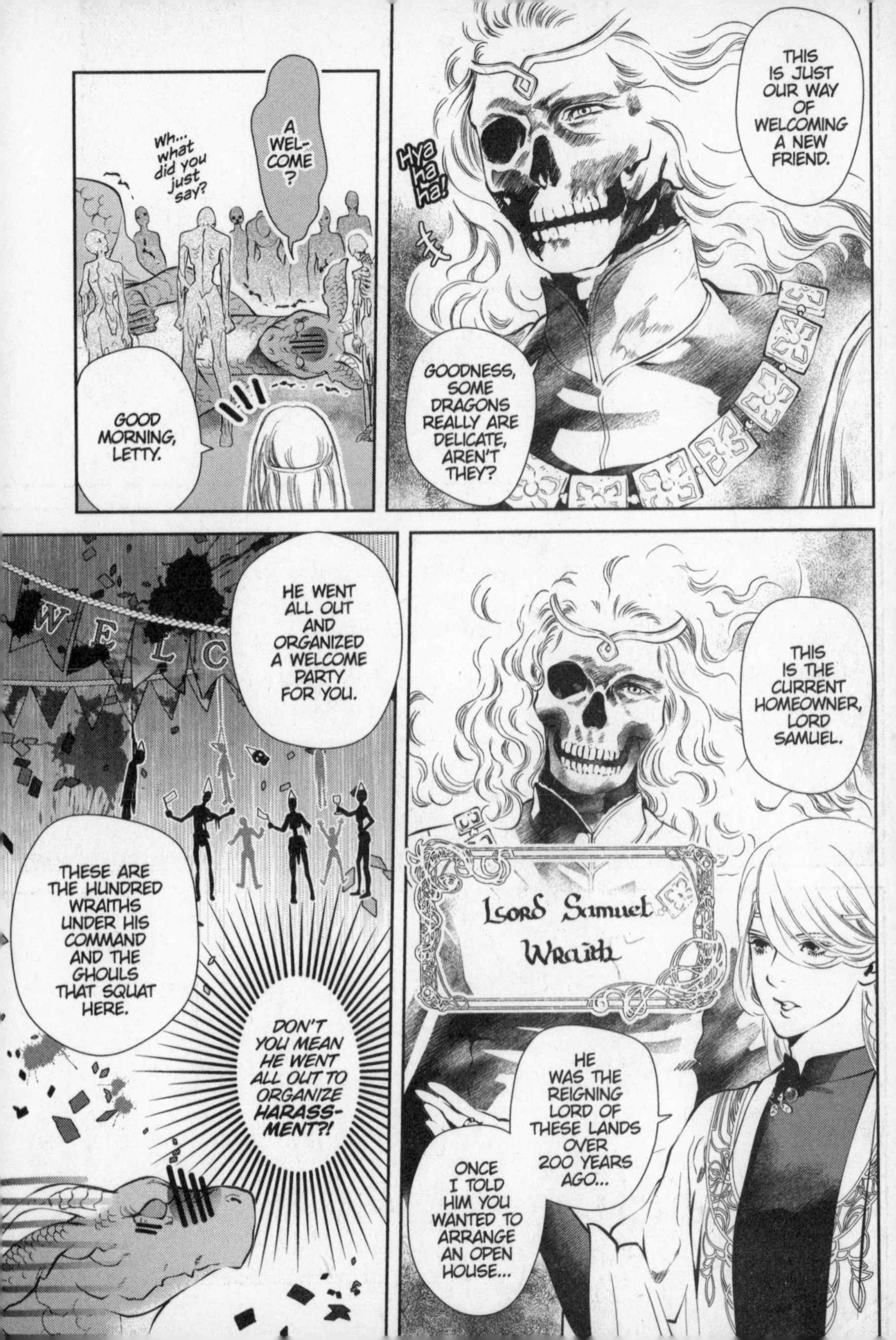
THIS IS JUST OUR WAY OF WELCOMING A NEW FRIEND.
Hya ha ha!
GOODNESS, SOME DRAGONS REALLY ARE DELICATE, AREN'T THEY?
A WEL-COME?
Wh... what did you just say?
GOOD MORNING, LETTY.
THIS IS THE CURRENT HOMEOWNER, LORD SAMUEL.
Lord Samuel
Wraith
HE WAS THE REIGNING LORD OF THESE LANDS OVER 200 YEARS AGO...
ONCE I TOLD HIM YOU WANTED TO ARRANGE AN OPEN HOUSE...
HE WENT ALL OUT AND ORGANIZED A WELCOME PARTY FOR YOU.
W E L C
THESE ARE THE HUNDRED WRAITHS UNDER HIS COMMAND AND THE GHOULS THAT SQUAT HERE.
DON'T YOU MEAN HE WENT ALL OUT TO ORGANIZE **HARASS-MENT?!**

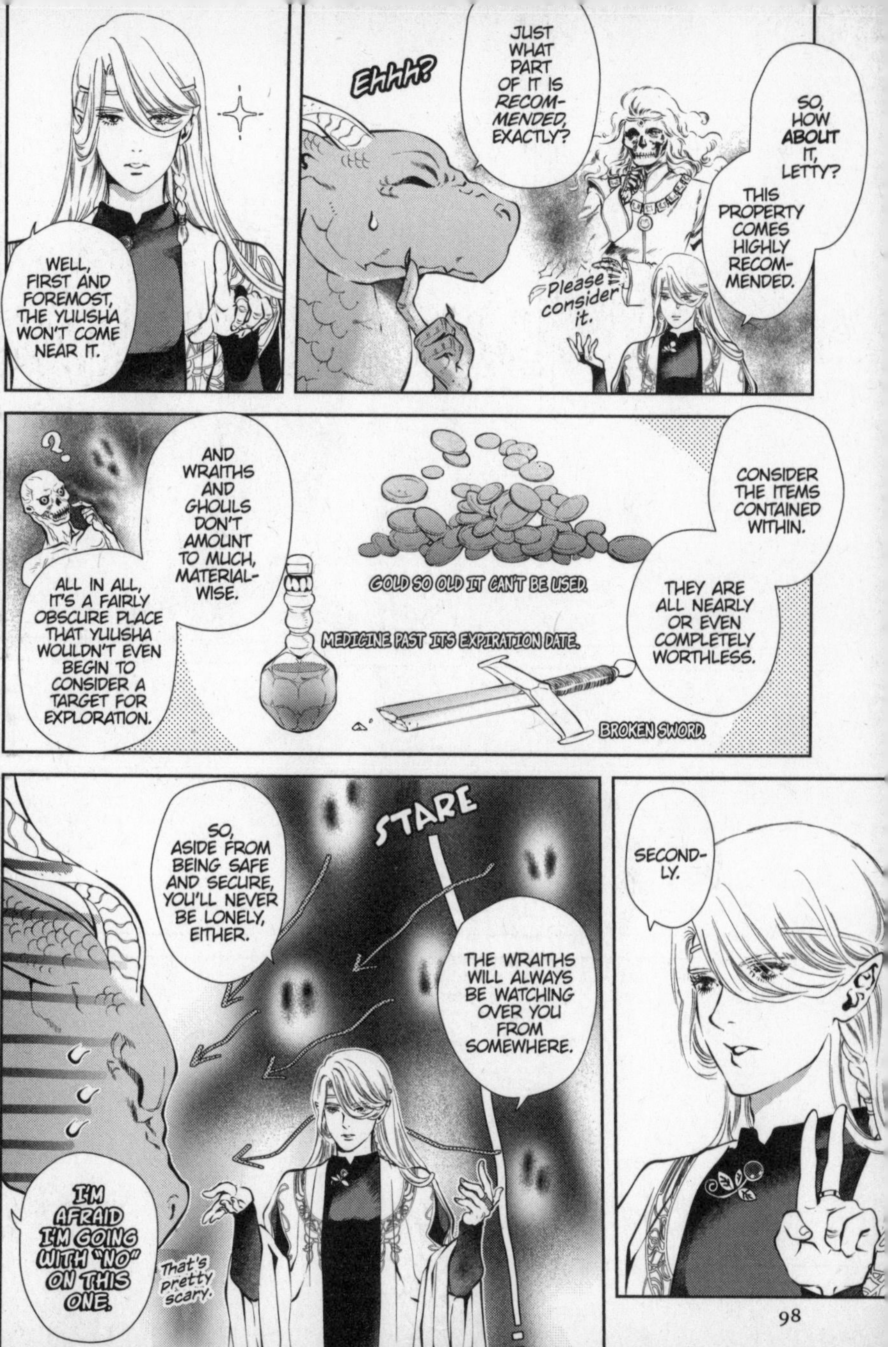
SO, HOW ABOUT IT, LETTY?
THIS PROPERTY COMES HIGHLY RECOMMENDED.
Please consider it.
JUST WHAT PART OF IT IS RECOMMENDED, EXACTLY?
Ehhh?
WELL, FIRST AND FOREMOST, THE YUUSHA WON'T COME NEAR IT.
CONSIDER THE ITEMS CONTAINED WITHIN.
THEY ARE ALL NEARLY OR EVEN COMPLETELY WORTHLESS.
GOLD SO OLD IT CAN'T BE USED.
MEDICINE PAST ITS EXPIRATION DATE.
BROKEN SWORD.
AND WRAITHS AND GHOULS DON'T AMOUNT TO MUCH, MATERIAL-WISE.
ALL IN ALL, IT'S A FAIRLY OBSCURE PLACE THAT YUUSHA WOULDN'T EVEN BEGIN TO CONSIDER A TARGET FOR EXPLORATION.
?
SECONDLY.
STARE
SO, ASIDE FROM BEING SAFE AND SECURE, YOU'LL NEVER BE LONELY, EITHER.
THE WRAITHS WILL ALWAYS BE WATCHING OVER YOU FROM SOMEWHERE.
I'M AFRAID I'M GOING WITH "NO" ON THIS ONE.
That's pretty scary.

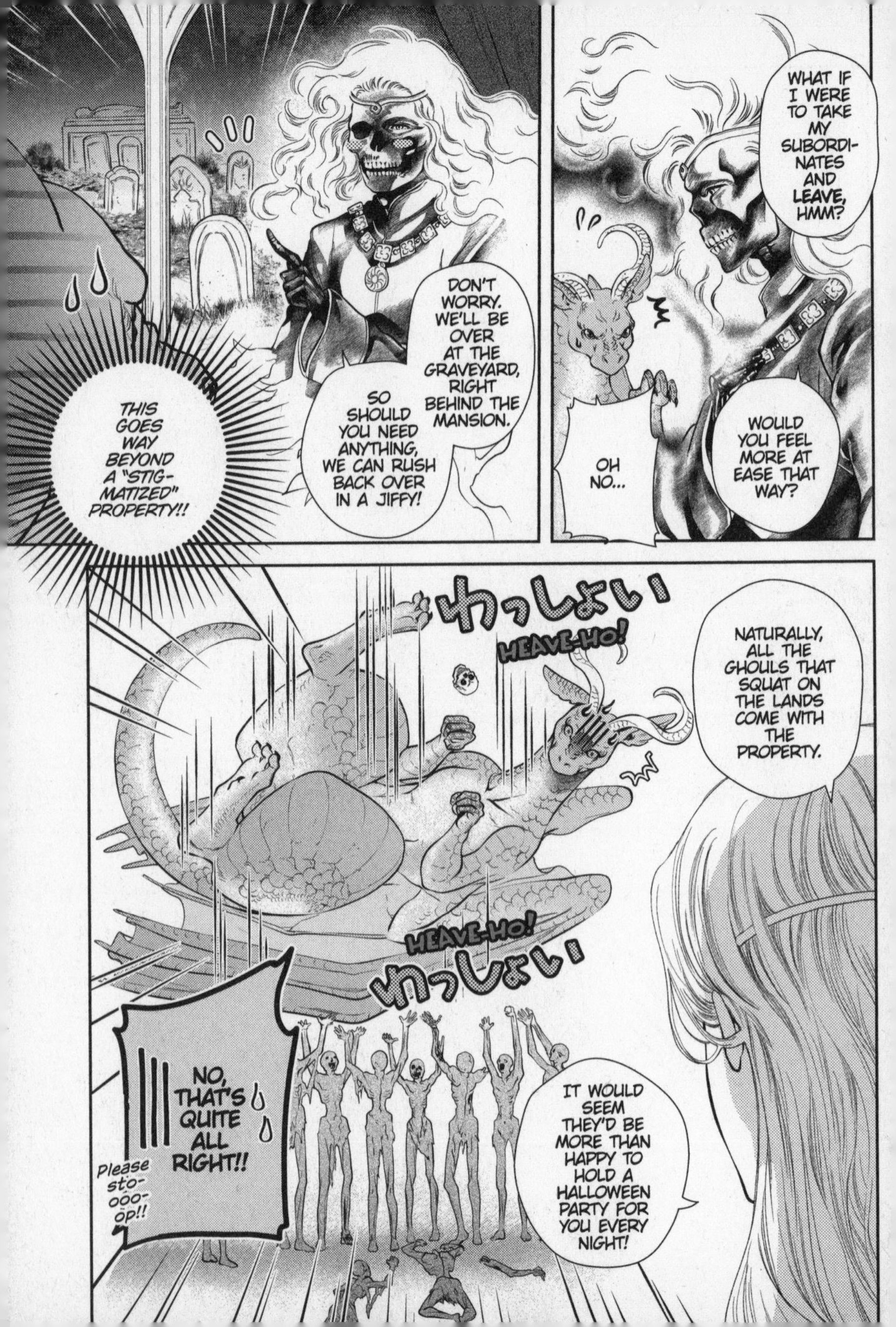
WHAT IF I WERE TO TAKE MY SUBORDINATES AND LEAVE, HMM?
WOULD YOU FEEL MORE AT EASE THAT WAY?
OH NO...
DON'T WORRY. WE'LL BE OVER AT THE GRAVEYARD, RIGHT BEHIND THE MANSION.
SO SHOULD YOU NEED ANYTHING, WE CAN RUSH BACK OVER IN A JIFFY!
THIS GOES WAY BEYOND A "STIG-MATIZED" PROPERTY!!
NATURALLY, ALL THE GHOULS THAT SQUAT ON THE LANDS COME WITH THE PROPERTY.
わっしょい
HEAVE-HO!
IT WOULD SEEM THEY'D BE MORE THAN HAPPY TO HOLD A HALLOWEEN PARTY FOR YOU EVERY NIGHT!
HEAVE-HO!
わっしょい
NO, THAT'S QUITE ALL RIGHT!!
Please sto-ooo-op!!

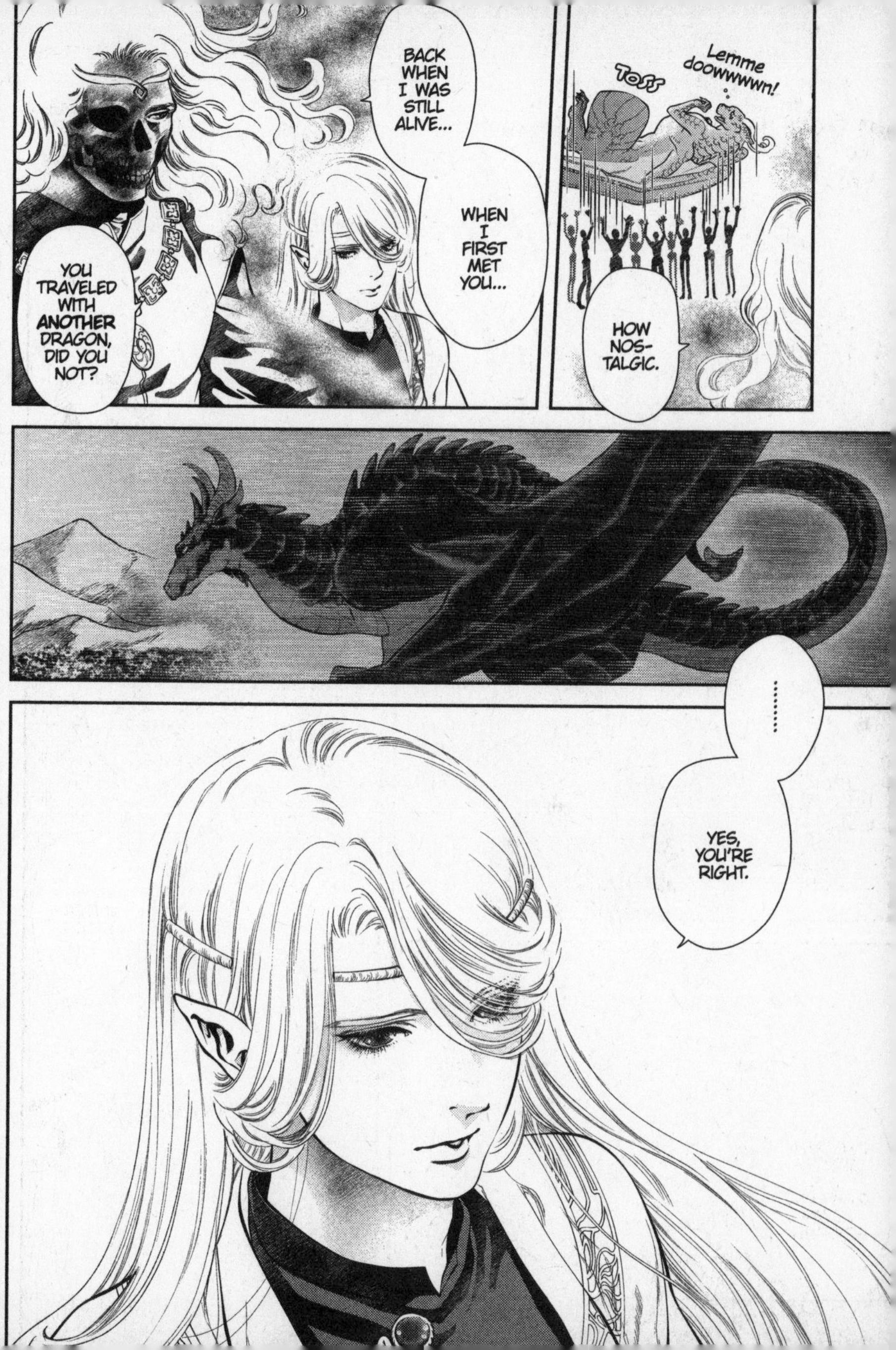
Lemme doowwwwn!
TOSS
HOW NOS-TALGIC.
BACK WHEN I WAS STILL ALIVE...
WHEN I FIRST MET YOU...
YOU TRAVELED WITH ANOTHER DRAGON, DID YOU NOT?
......
YES, YOU'RE RIGHT.

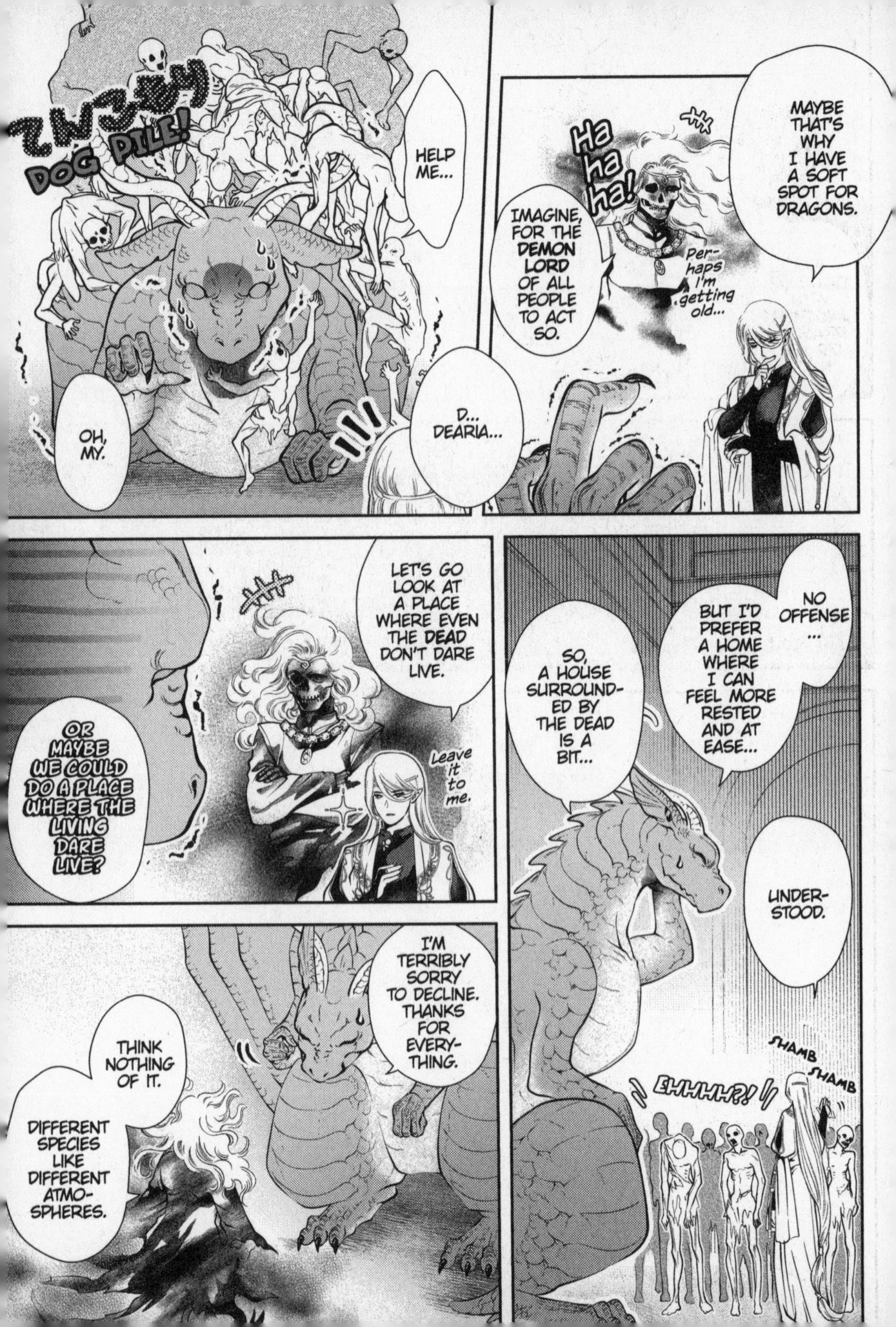
MAYBE THAT'S WHY I HAVE A SOFT SPOT FOR DRAGONS.
Ha ha ha!
IMAGINE, FOR THE DEMON LORD OF ALL PEOPLE TO ACT SO.
Perhaps I'm getting old...
HELP ME...
D... DEARIA...
DOG PILE!
OH, MY.
NO OFFENSE...
BUT I'D PREFER A HOME WHERE I CAN FEEL MORE RESTED AND AT EASE...
SO, A HOUSE SURROUNDED BY THE DEAD IS A BIT...
UNDERSTOOD.
SHAMB
SHAMB
EHHHH?!
LET'S GO LOOK AT A PLACE WHERE EVEN THE DEAD DON'T DARE LIVE.
Leave it to me.
OR MAYBE WE COULD DO A PLACE WHERE THE LIVING DARE LIVE?
I'M TERRIBLY SORRY TO DECLINE. THANKS FOR EVERYTHING.
THINK NOTHING OF IT.
DIFFERENT SPECIES LIKE DIFFERENT ATMOSPHERES.

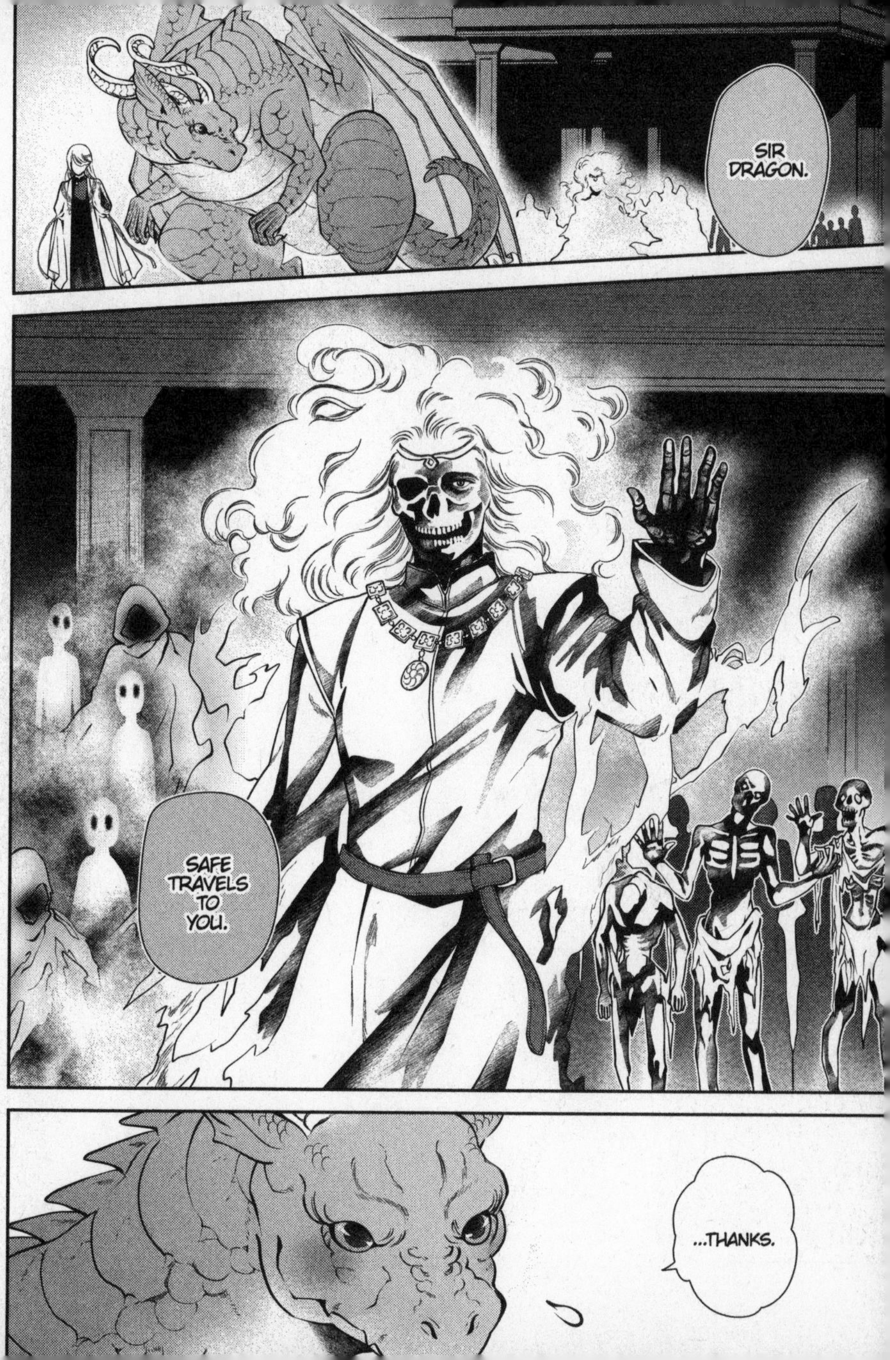
SIR DRAGON.
SAFE TRAVELS TO YOU.
...THANKS.

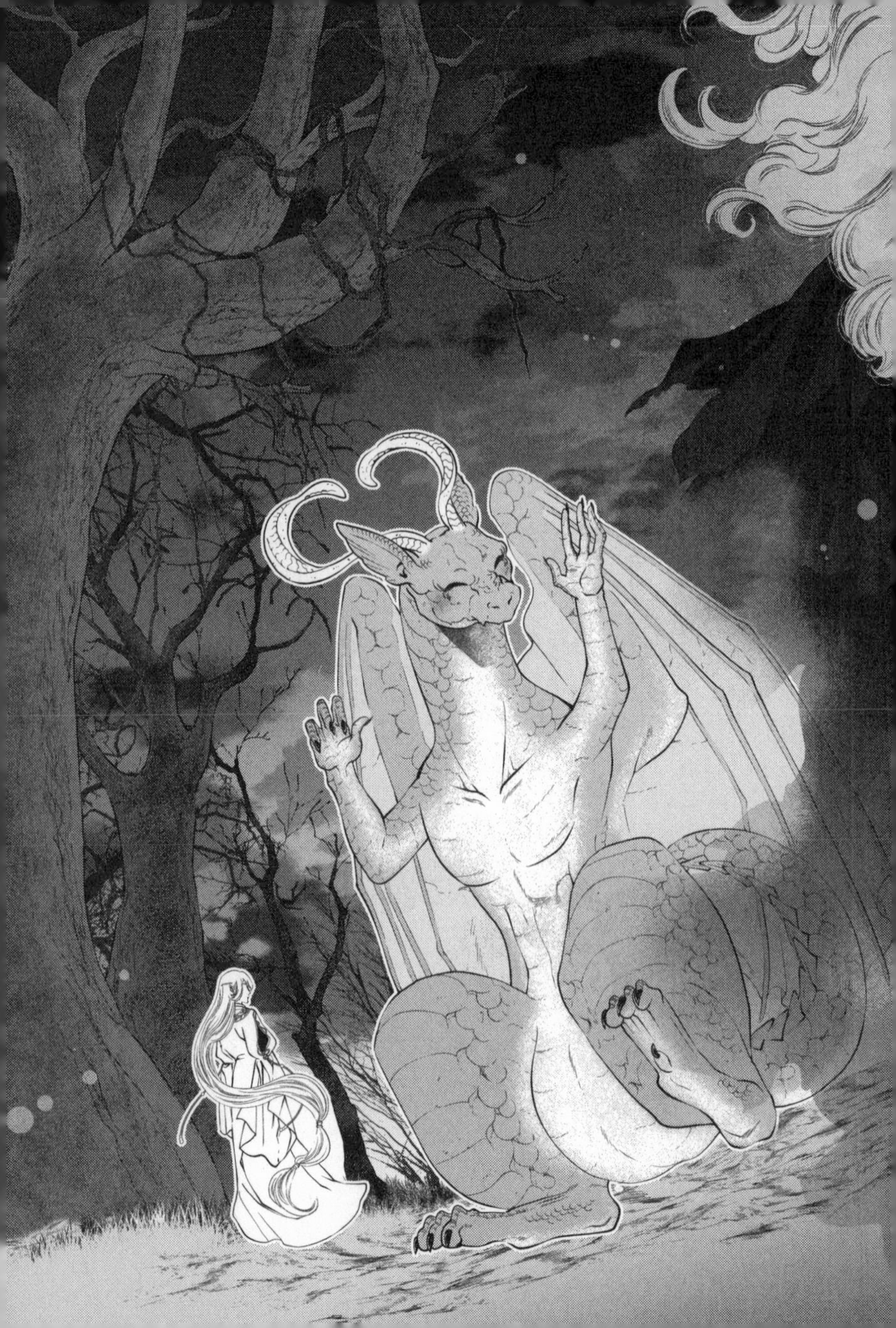

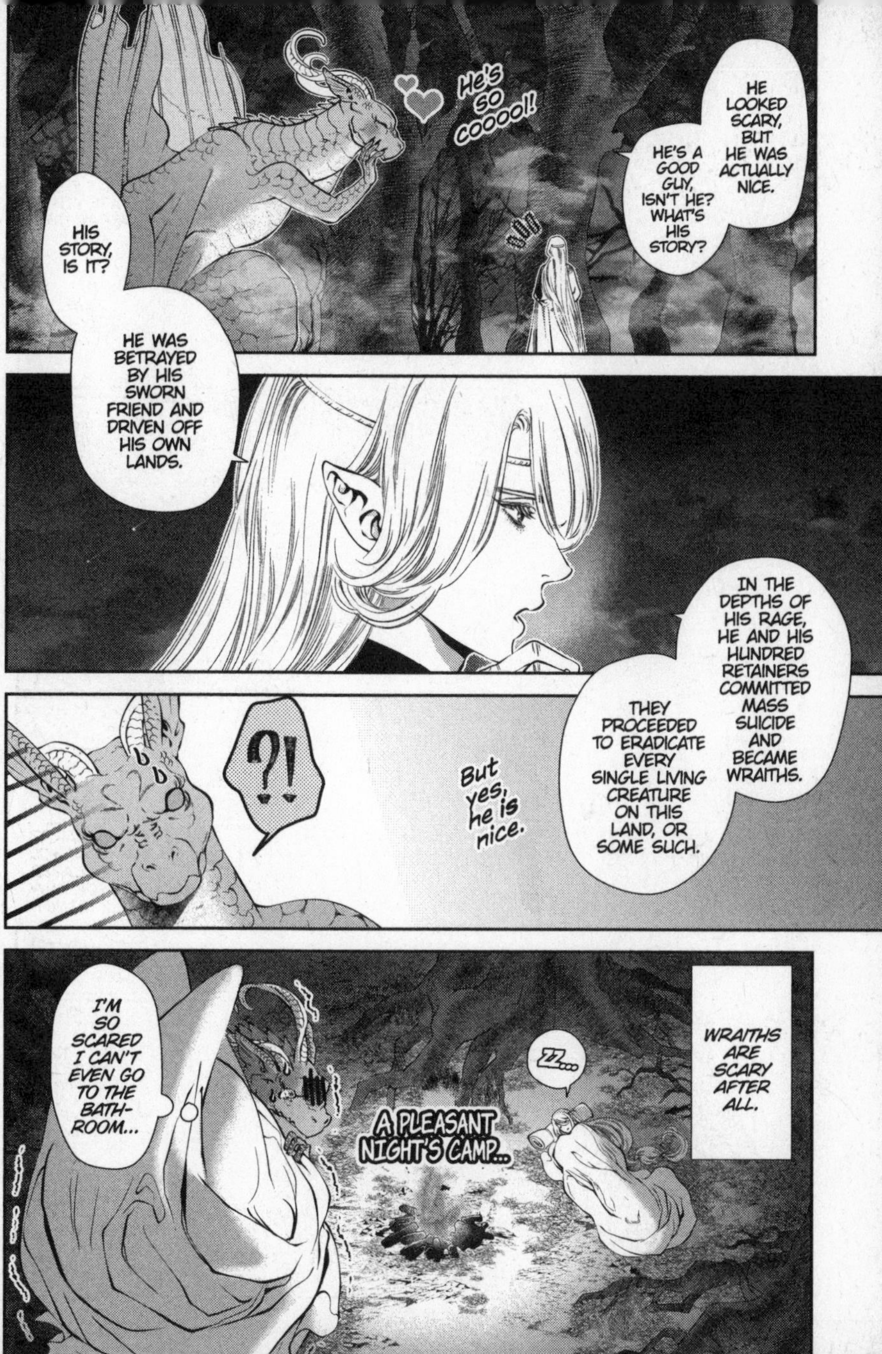
HE LOOKED SCARY, BUT HE WAS ACTUALLY NICE.
HE'S A GOOD GUY, ISN'T HE? WHAT'S HIS STORY?
He's so cooool!
HIS STORY, IS IT?
HE WAS BETRAYED BY HIS SWORN FRIEND AND DRIVEN OFF HIS OWN LANDS.
IN THE DEPTHS OF HIS RAGE, HE AND HIS HUNDRED RETAINERS COMMITTED MASS SUICIDE AND BECAME WRAITHS.
THEY PROCEEDED TO ERADICATE EVERY SINGLE LIVING CREATURE ON THIS LAND, OR SOME SUCH.
But yes, he is nice.
?!
WRAITHS ARE SCARY AFTER ALL.
Zz...
A PLEASANT NIGHT'S CAMP...
I'M SO SCARED I CAN'T EVEN GO TO THE BATH-ROOM...

What Are You Scared Of?

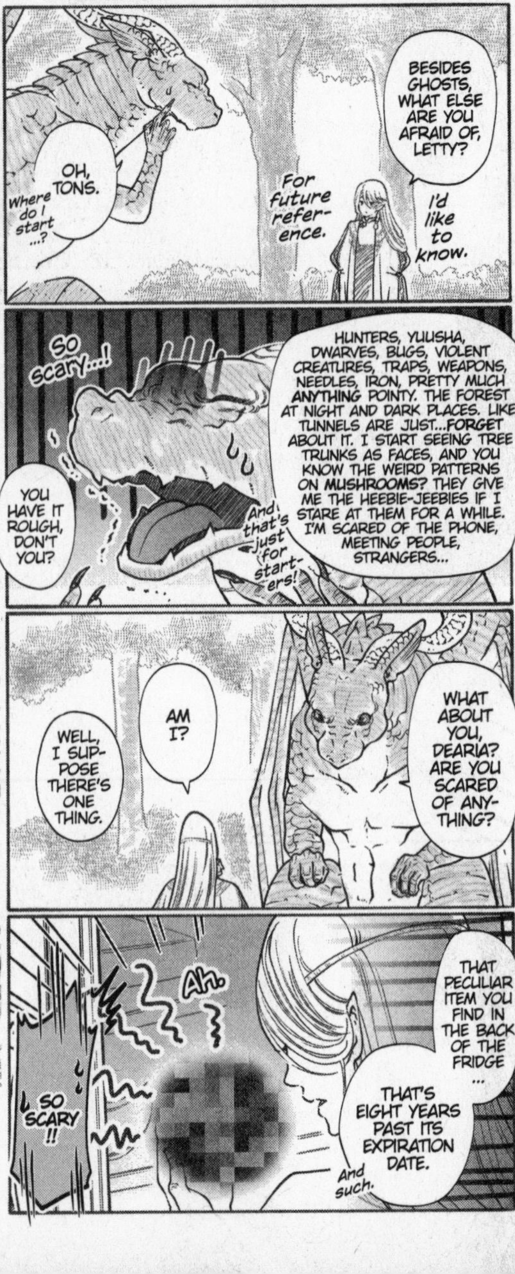
BESIDES GHOSTS, WHAT ELSE ARE YOU AFRAID OF, LETTY?
I'd like to know.
For future reference.
OH, TONS.
Where do I start ...?
HUNTERS, YUUSHA, DWARVES, BUGS, VIOLENT CREATURES, TRAPS, WEAPONS, NEEDLES, IRON, PRETTY MUCH ANYTHING POINTY. THE FOREST AT NIGHT AND DARK PLACES. LIKE, TUNNELS ARE JUST...FORGET ABOUT IT. I START SEEING TREE TRUNKS AS FACES, AND YOU KNOW THE WEIRD PATTERNS ON MUSHROOMS? THEY GIVE ME THE HEEBIE-JEEBIES IF I STARE AT THEM FOR A WHILE. I'M SCARED OF THE PHONE, MEETING PEOPLE, STRANGERS...
And that's just for start-ers!
So scary...!
YOU HAVE IT ROUGH, DON'T YOU?
WHAT ABOUT YOU, DEARIA? ARE YOU SCARED OF ANY-THING?
AM I?
WELL, I SUP-POSE THERE'S ONE THING.
THAT PECULIAR ITEM YOU FIND IN THE BACK OF THE FRIDGE ...
THAT'S EIGHT YEARS PAST ITS EXPIRATION DATE.
And such.
Ah.
SO SCARY !!

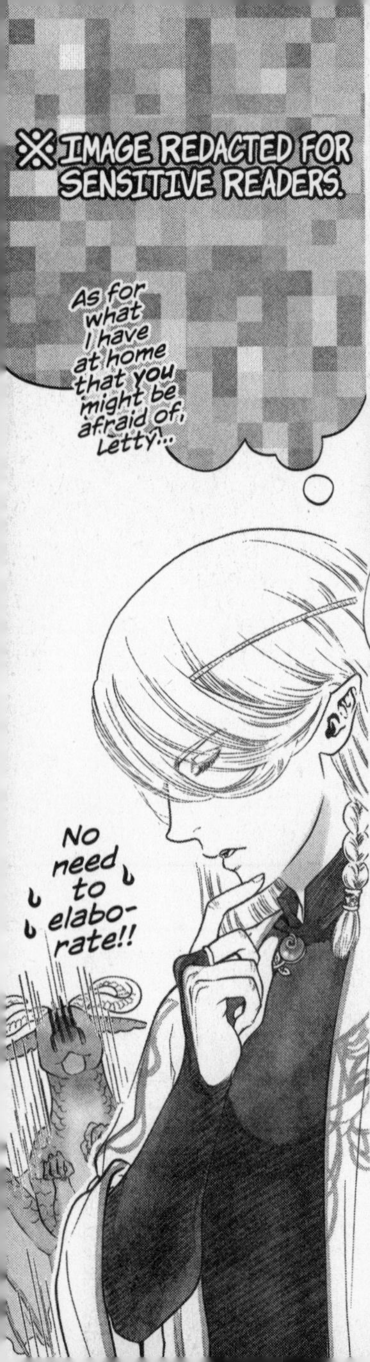
※IMAGE REDACTED FOR SENSITIVE READERS.
As for what I have at home that you might be afraid of, Letty...
No need to elaborate!!

Dragon Goes House-Hunting

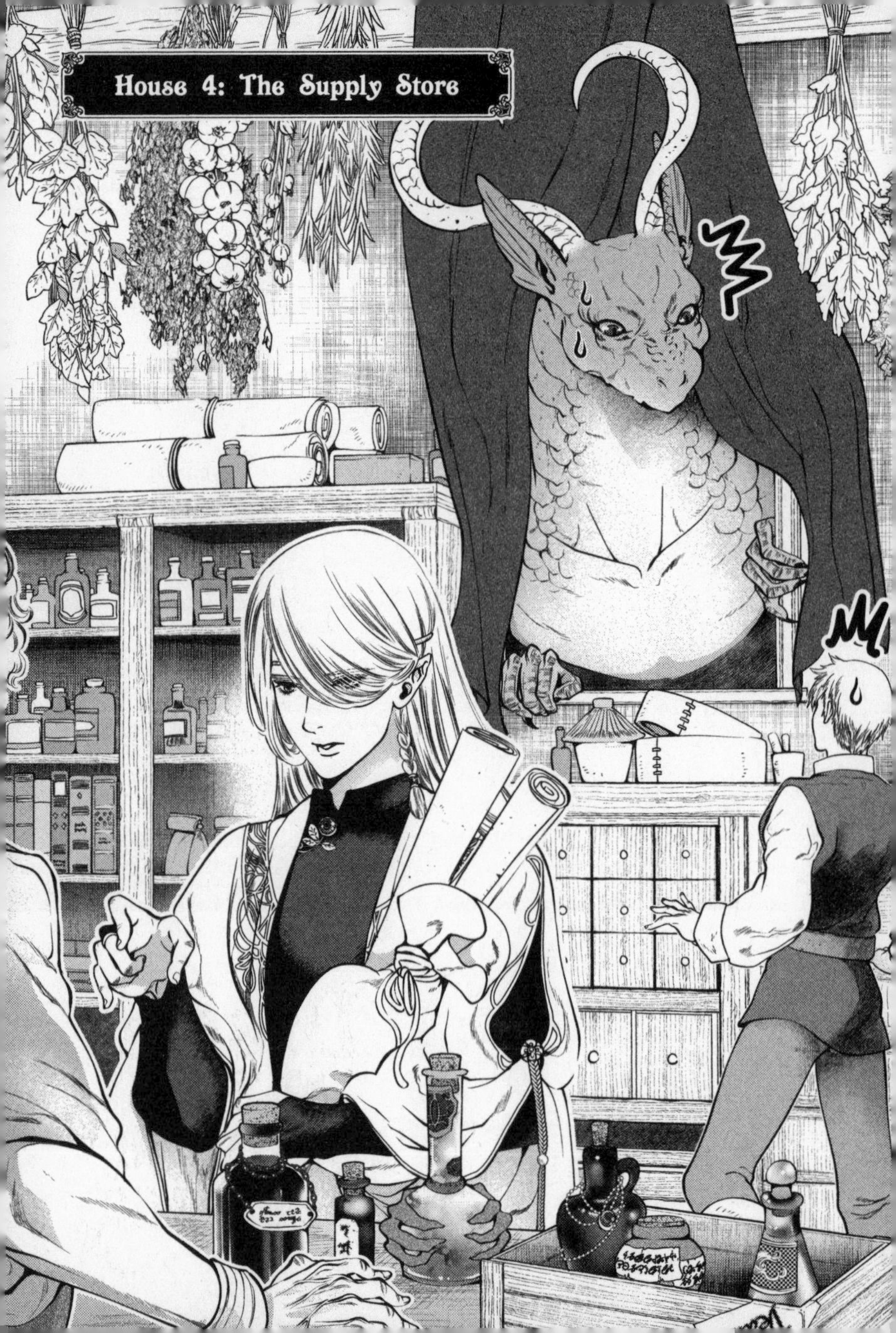
House 4: The Supply Store

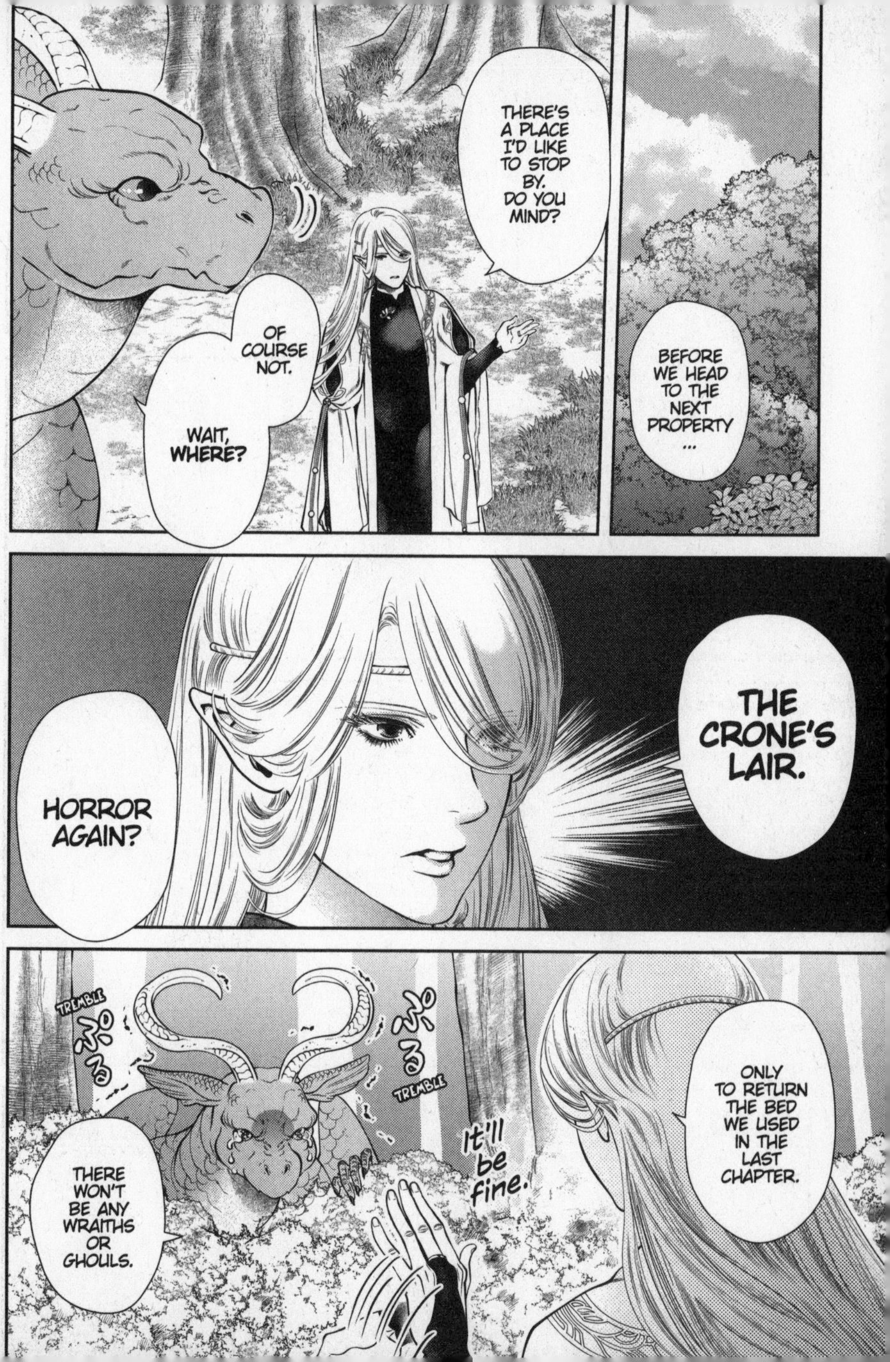
BEFORE WE HEAD TO THE NEXT PROPERTY ...
THERE'S A PLACE I'D LIKE TO STOP BY. DO YOU MIND?
OF COURSE NOT.
WAIT, WHERE?
THE CRONE'S LAIR.
HORROR AGAIN?
ONLY TO RETURN THE BED WE USED IN THE LAST CHAPTER.
ぷる TREMBLE
It'll be fine.
TREMBLE ぷる
THERE WON'T BE ANY WRAITHS OR GHOULS.

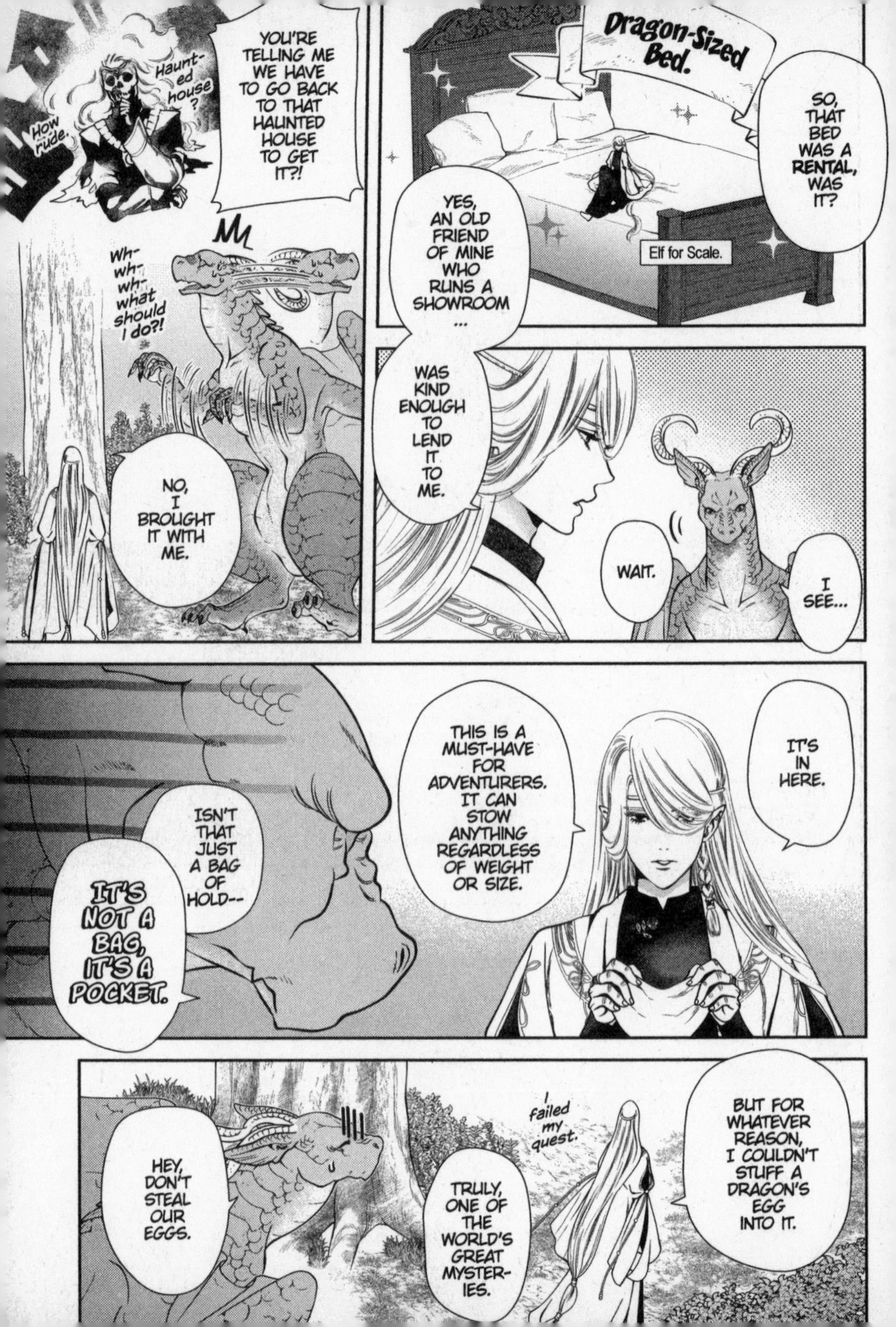
Dragon-Sized Bed.
SO, THAT BED WAS A RENTAL, WAS IT?
Elf for Scale.
YES, AN OLD FRIEND OF MINE WHO RUNS A SHOWROOM ...
WAS KIND ENOUGH TO LEND IT TO ME.
I SEE...
WAIT.
YOU'RE TELLING ME WE HAVE TO GO BACK TO THAT HAUNTED HOUSE TO GET IT?!
Haunt-ed house?
How rude.
Wh-wh-wh-what should I do?!
NO, I BROUGHT IT WITH ME.
IT'S IN HERE.
THIS IS A MUST-HAVE FOR ADVENTURERS. IT CAN STOW ANYTHING REGARDLESS OF WEIGHT OR SIZE.
ISN'T THAT JUST A BAG OF HOLD--
IT'S NOT A BAG, IT'S A POCKET.
BUT FOR WHATEVER REASON, I COULDN'T STUFF A DRAGON'S EGG INTO IT.
I failed my quest.
TRULY, ONE OF THE WORLD'S GREAT MYSTER-IES.
HEY, DON'T STEAL OUR EGGS.

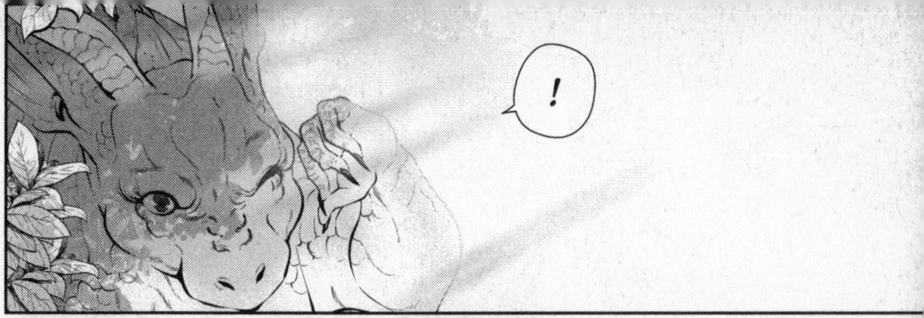
!

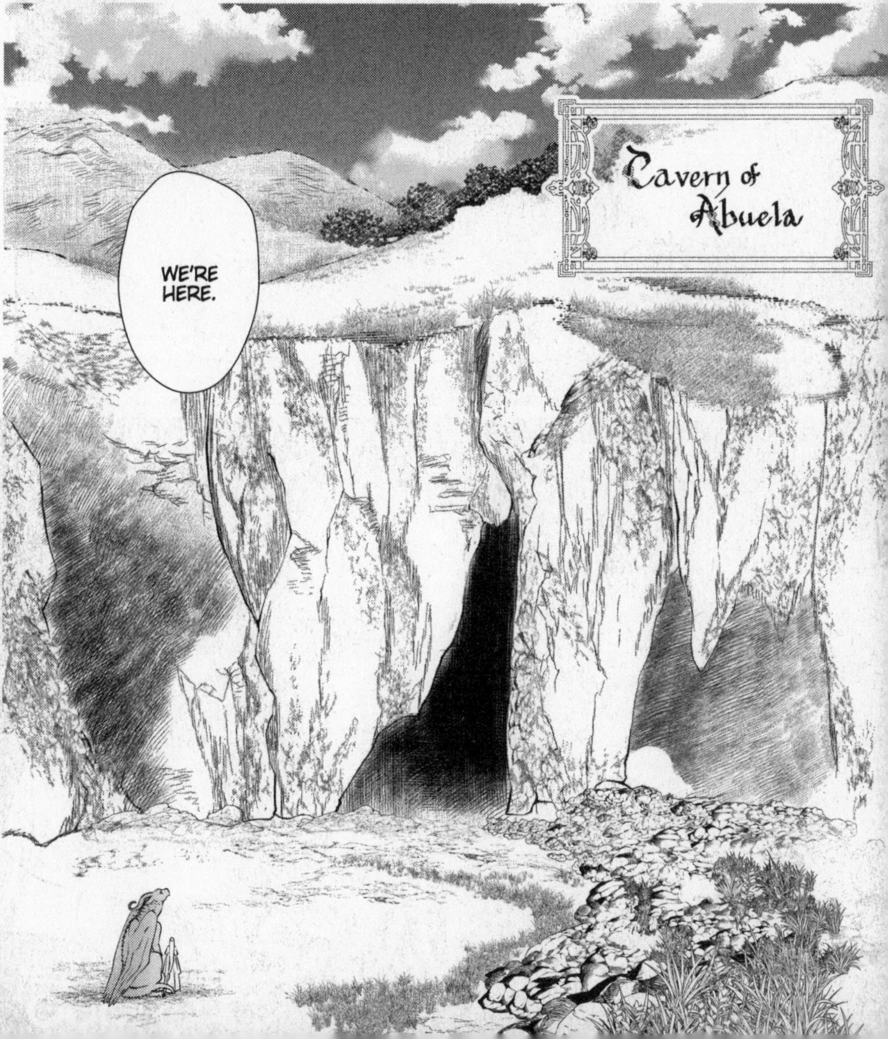
Cavern of Abuela
WE'RE HERE.

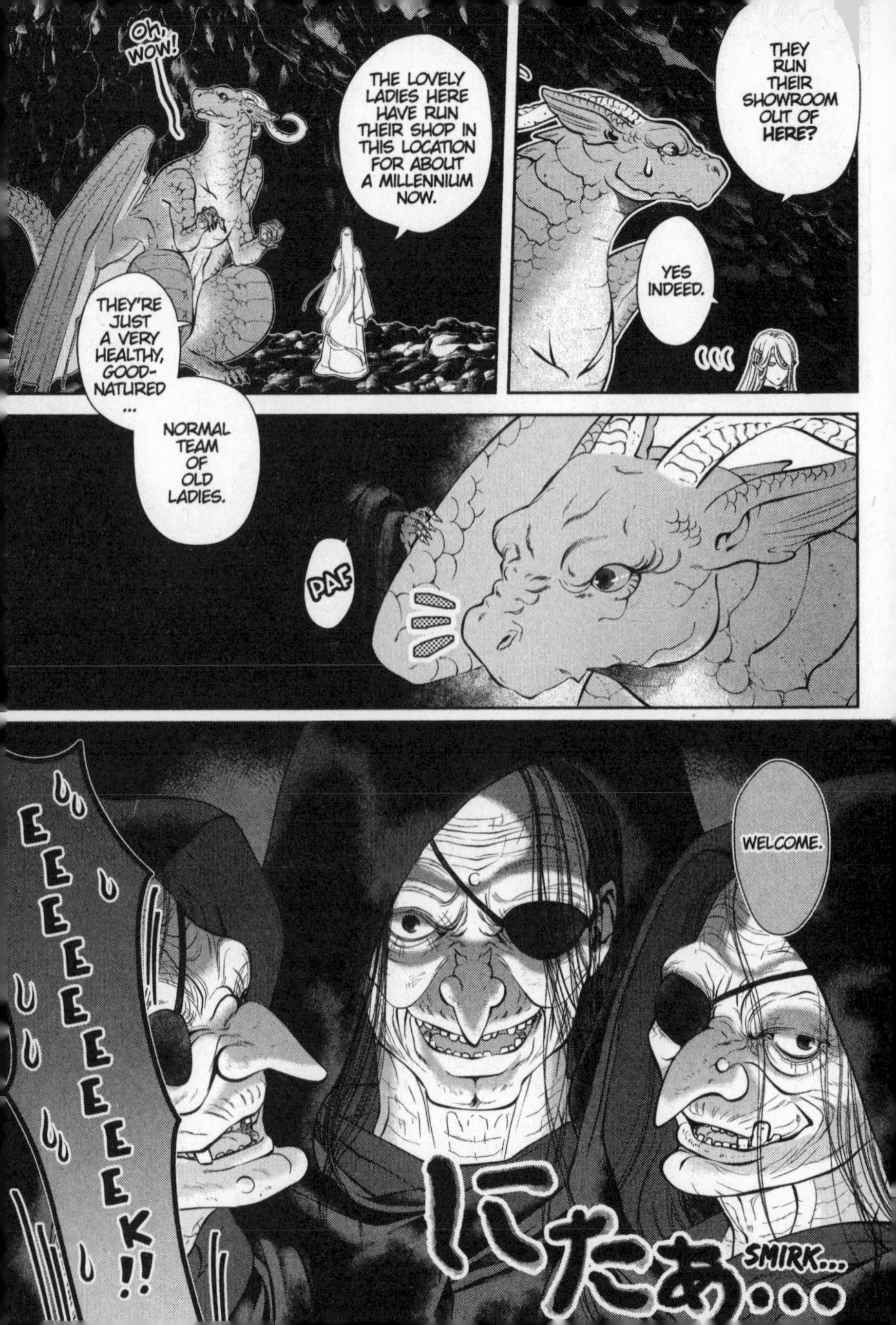
THEY RUN THEIR SHOWROOM OUT OF HERE?
YES INDEED.
Oh, WOW!
THE LOVELY LADIES HERE HAVE RUN THEIR SHOP IN THIS LOCATION FOR ABOUT A MILLENNIUM NOW.
THEY'RE JUST A VERY HEALTHY, GOOD-NATURED ...
NORMAL TEAM OF OLD LADIES.
PAF
WELCOME.
EEEEEEEEEEK!!
にたあ…
SMIRK...

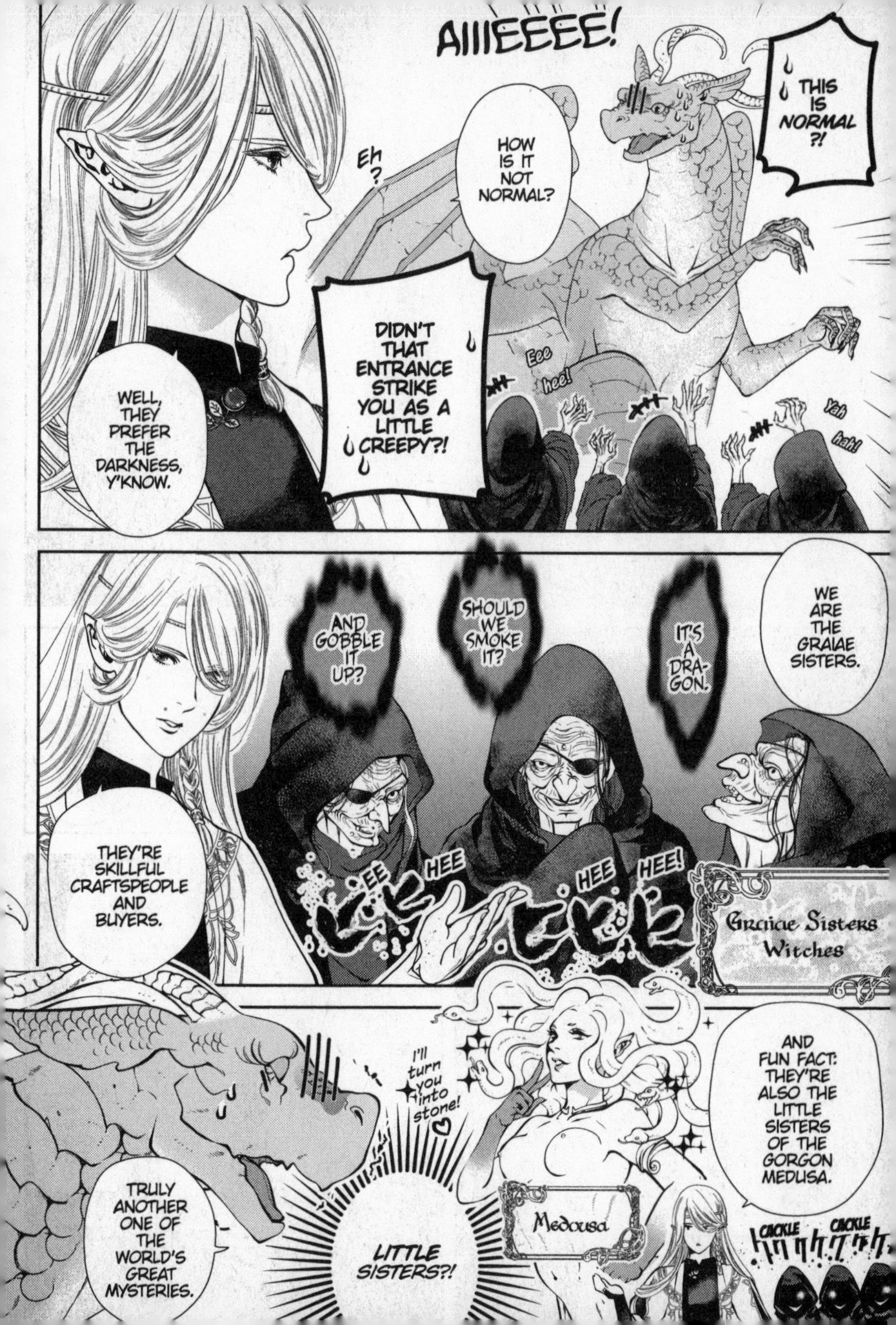
AIIIEEEE!
THIS IS NORMAL?!
Eh?
HOW IS IT NOT NORMAL?
DIDN'T THAT ENTRANCE STRIKE YOU AS A LITTLE CREEPY?!
Yah hah!
Eee hee!
WELL, THEY PREFER THE DARKNESS, Y'KNOW.
WE ARE THE GRAIAE SISTERS.
IT'S A DRA-GON.
SHOULD WE SMOKE IT?
AND GOBBLE IT UP?
Graiae Sisters
Witches
HEE HEE!
EE HEE
THEY'RE SKILLFUL CRAFTSPEOPLE AND BUYERS.
AND FUN FACT: THEY'RE ALSO THE LITTLE SISTERS OF THE GORGON MEDUSA.
CACKLE CACKLE
I'll turn you into stone! ♡
Medusa
LITTLE SISTERS?!
TRULY ANOTHER ONE OF THE WORLD'S GREAT MYSTERIES.

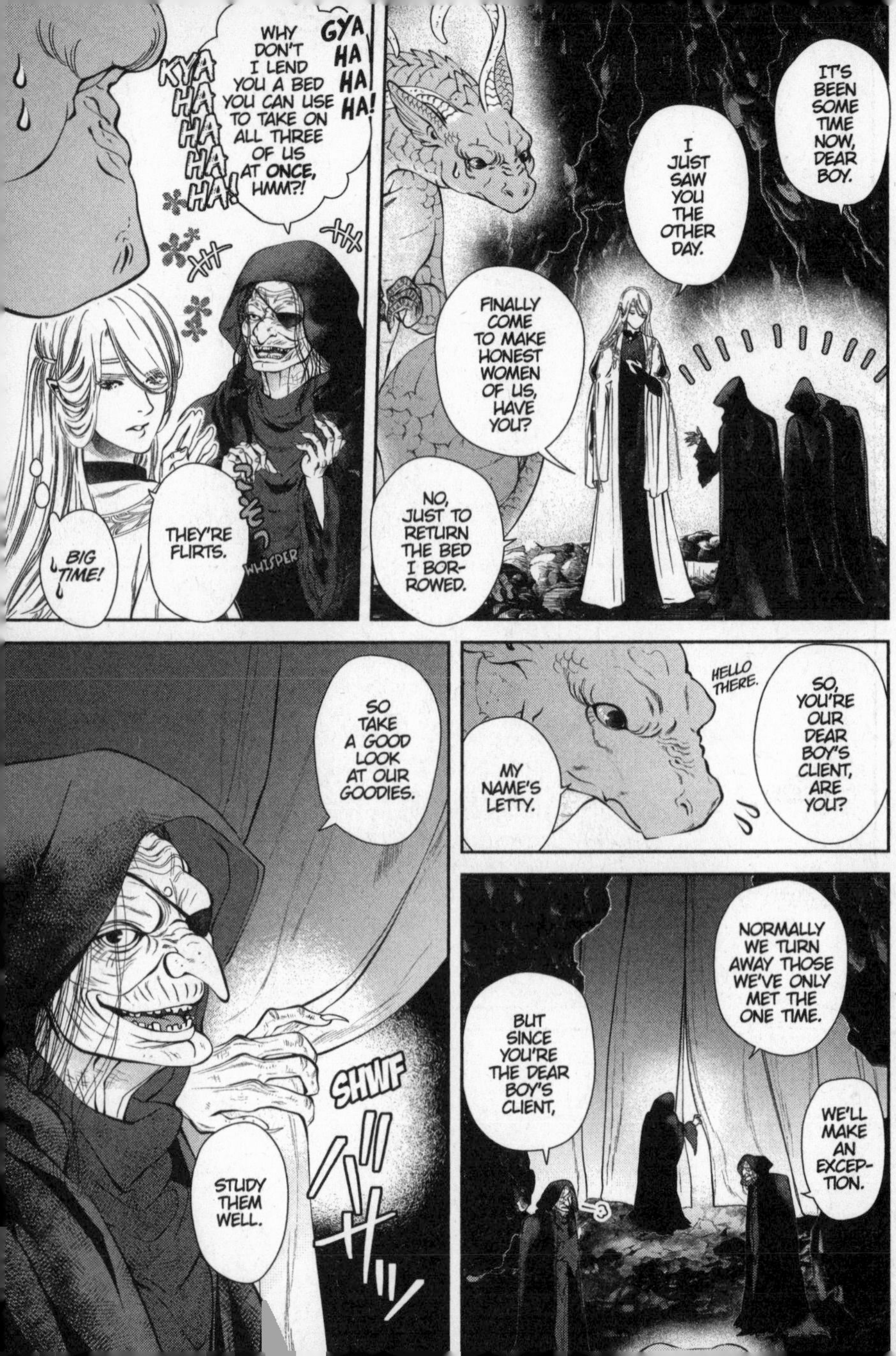
IT'S BEEN SOME TIME NOW, DEAR BOY.
I JUST SAW YOU THE OTHER DAY.
FINALLY COME TO MAKE HONEST WOMEN OF US, HAVE YOU?
NO, JUST TO RETURN THE BED I BOR-ROWED.
GYA HA HA HA HA!
WHY DON'T I LEND YOU A BED YOU CAN USE TO TAKE ON ALL THREE OF US AT ONCE, HMM?!
KYA HA HA HA HA HA!
WHISPER
THEY'RE FLIRTS.
BIG TIME!
SO, YOU'RE OUR DEAR BOY'S CLIENT, ARE YOU?
HELLO THERE.
MY NAME'S LETTY.
NORMALLY WE TURN AWAY THOSE WE'VE ONLY MET THE ONE TIME.
BUT SINCE YOU'RE THE DEAR BOY'S CLIENT,
WE'LL MAKE AN EXCEP-TION.
SO TAKE A GOOD LOOK AT OUR GOODIES.
SHWF
STUDY THEM WELL.

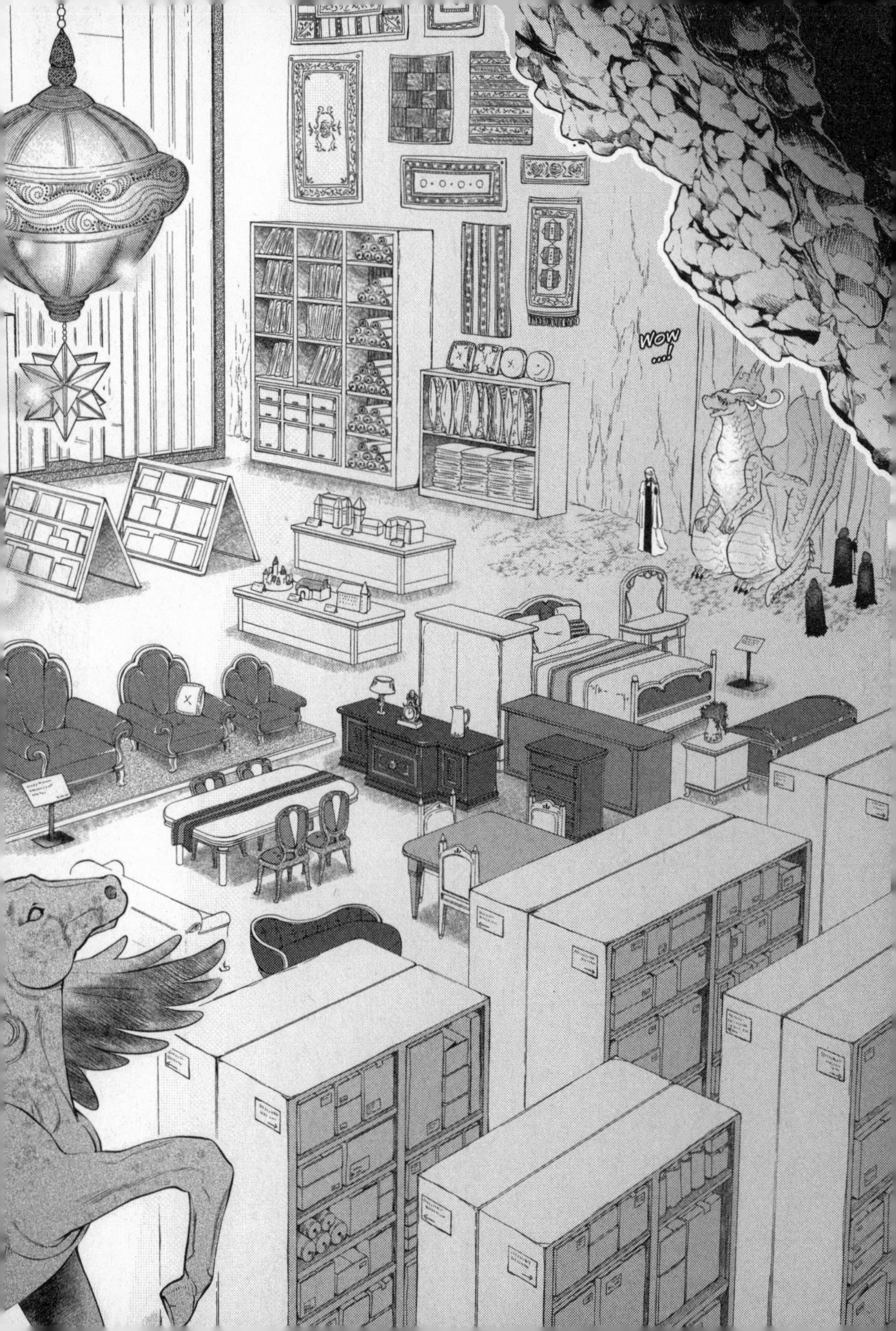
WOW ...!

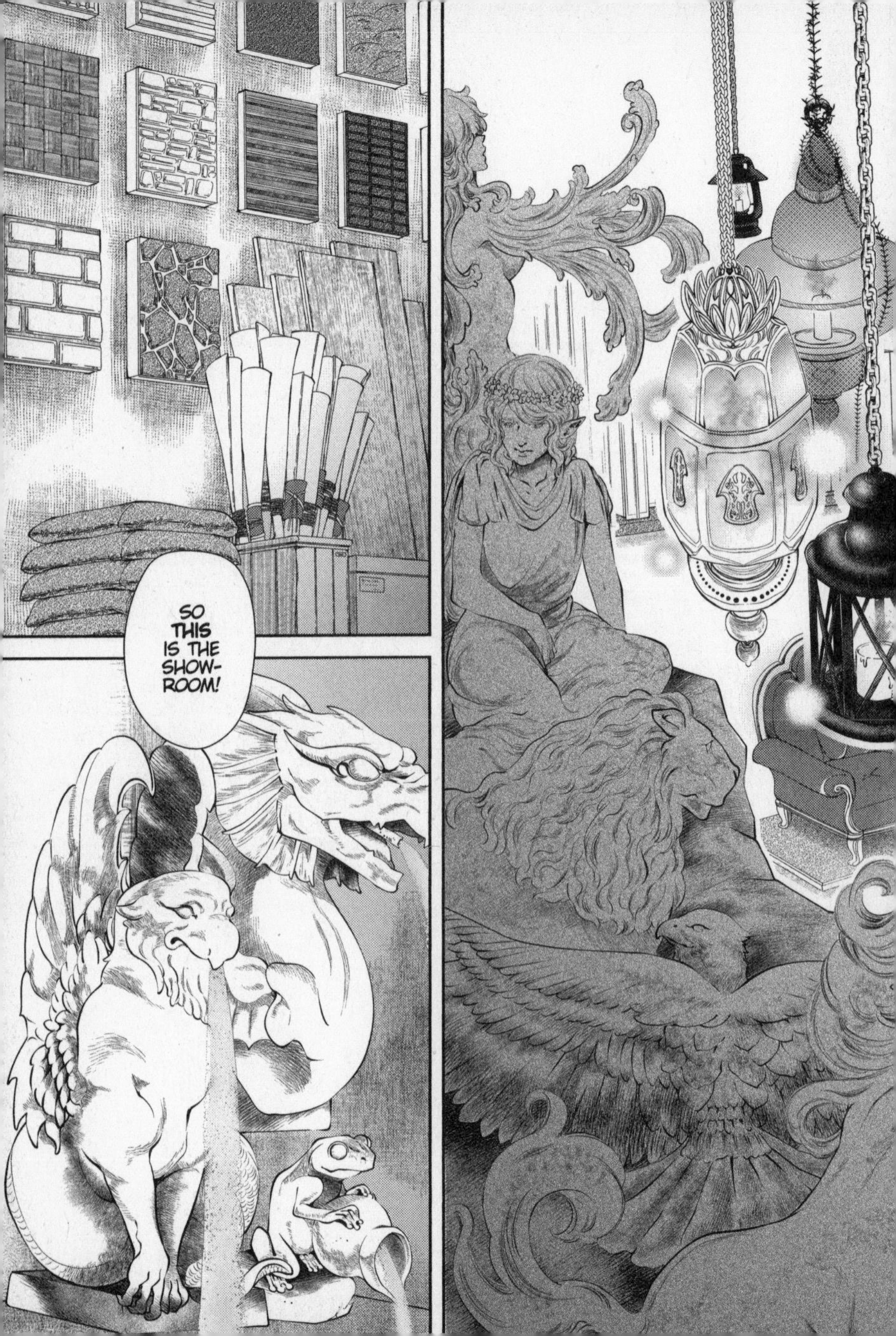
SO THIS IS THE SHOW-ROOM!

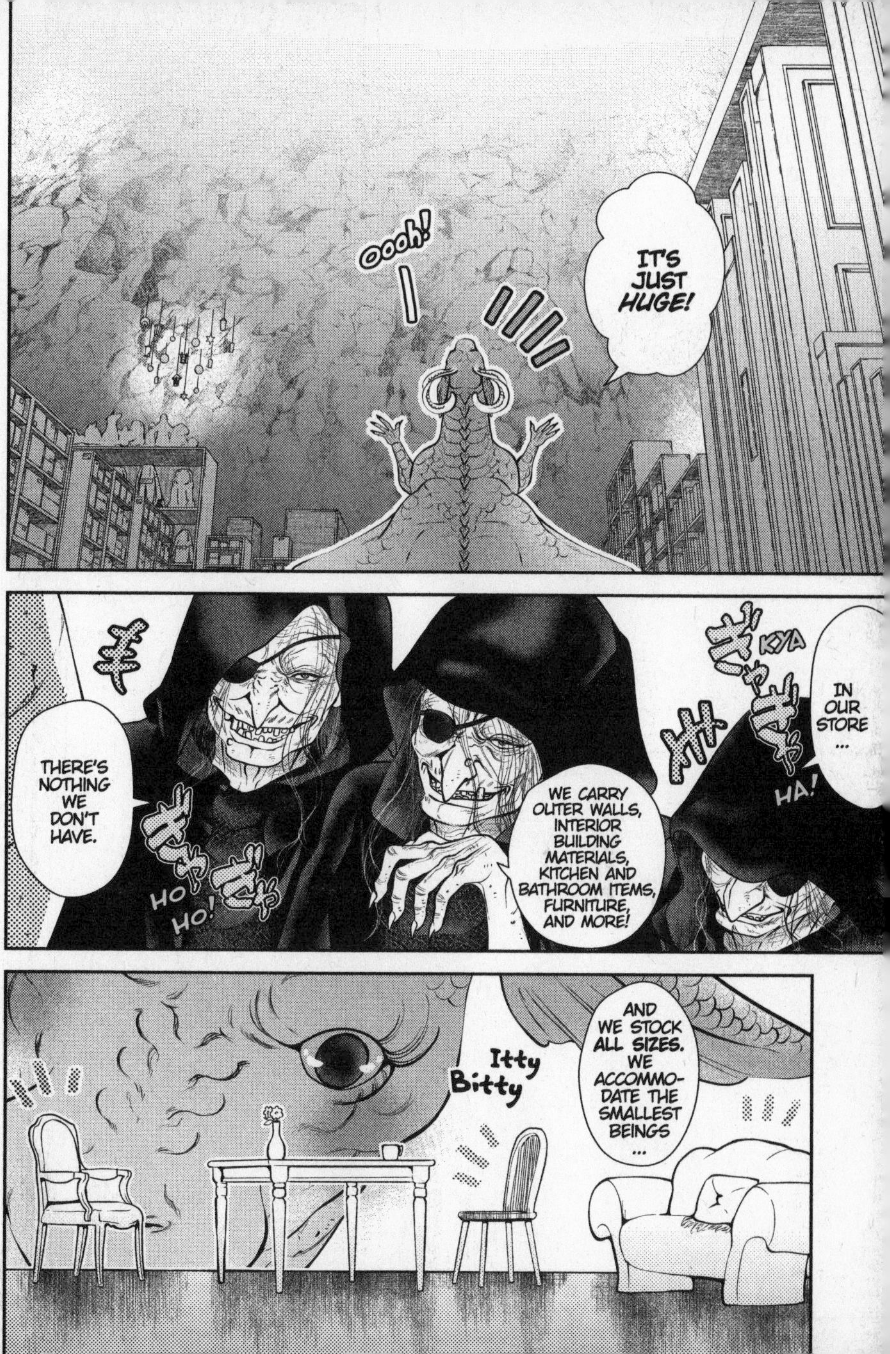
IT'S JUST HUGE!
Oooh!
IN OUR STORE ...
KYA HA!
WE CARRY OUTER WALLS, INTERIOR BUILDING MATERIALS, KITCHEN AND BATHROOM ITEMS, FURNITURE, AND MORE!
THERE'S NOTHING WE DON'T HAVE.
HO HO!
AND WE STOCK ALL SIZES. WE ACCOMMODATE THE SMALLEST BEINGS ...
Itty Bitty

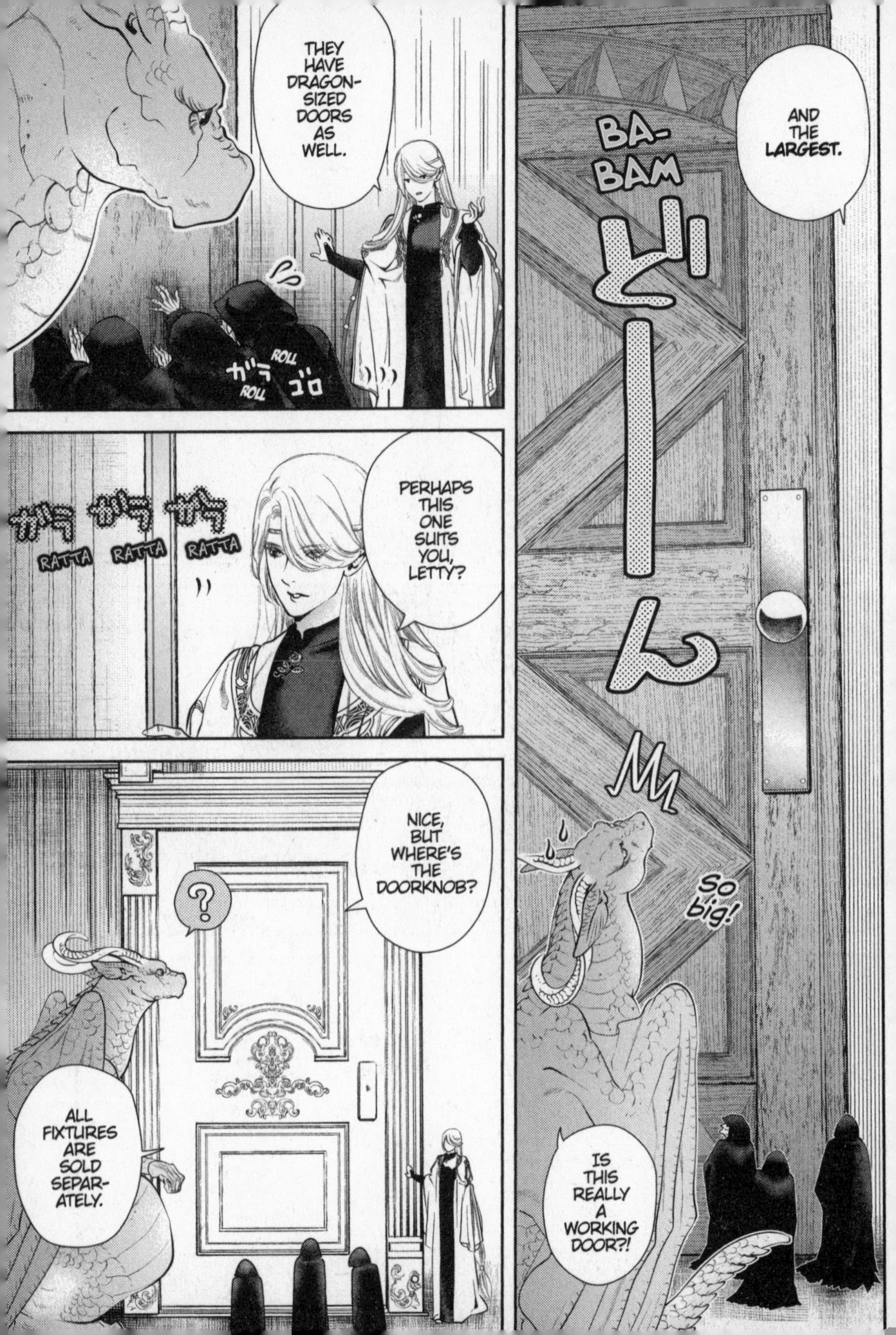
AND THE LARGEST.
BA-BAM
どーん
So big!
IS THIS REALLY A WORKING DOOR?!
THEY HAVE DRAGON-SIZED DOORS AS WELL.
ROLL ROLL
ガラ ゴロ
ガタ ガタ ガタ
RATTA RATTA RATTA
PERHAPS THIS ONE SUITS YOU, LETTY?
NICE, BUT WHERE'S THE DOORKNOB?
?
ALL FIXTURES ARE SOLD SEPARATELY.

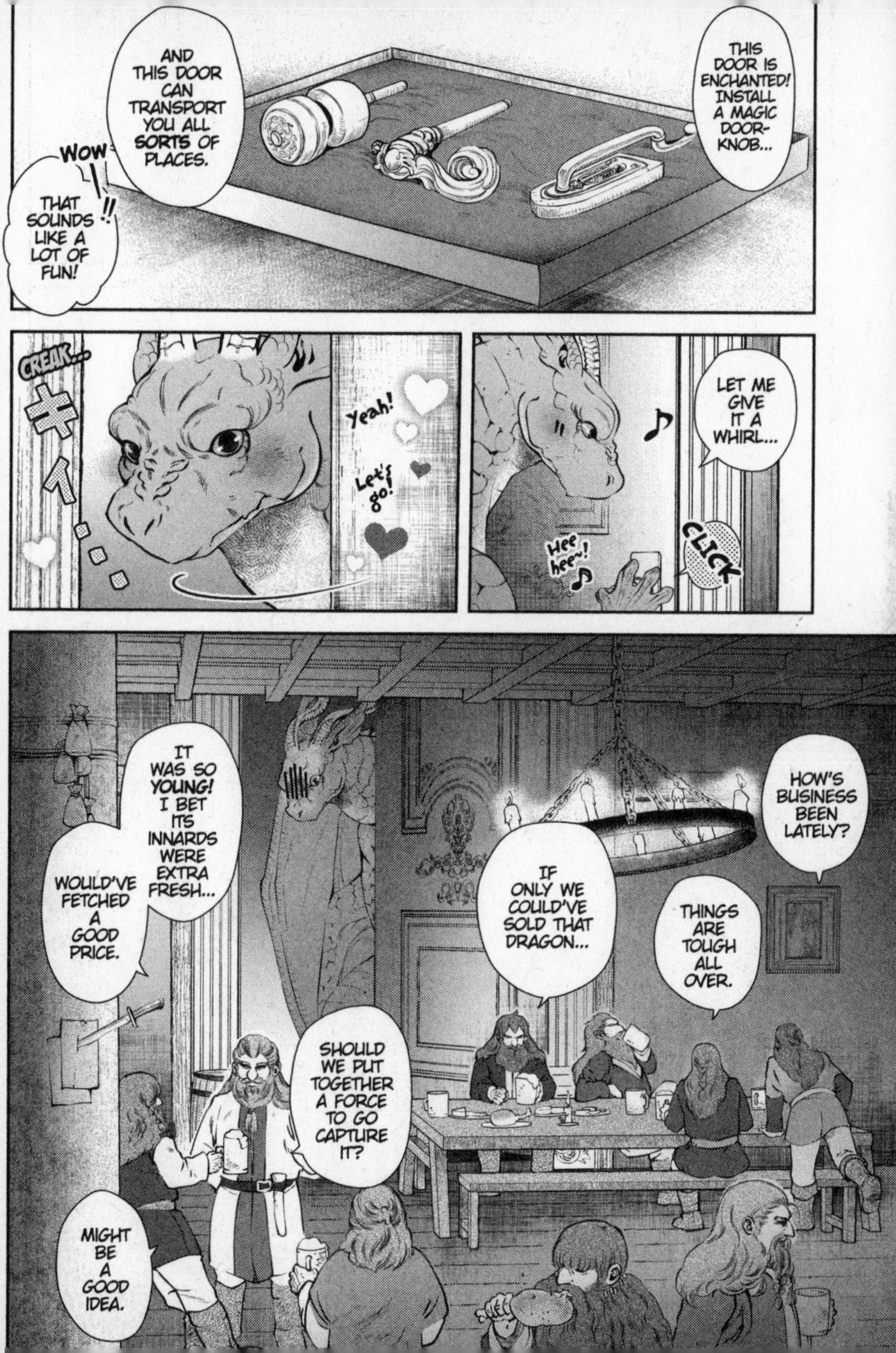
THIS DOOR IS ENCHANTED! INSTALL A MAGIC DOOR-KNOB...
AND THIS DOOR CAN TRANSPORT YOU ALL SORTS OF PLACES.
WOW!!
THAT SOUNDS LIKE A LOT OF FUN!
LET ME GIVE IT A WHIRL...
CLICK
Hee hee~!
Yeah!
Let's go!
CREAK...
キイ
HOW'S BUSINESS BEEN LATELY?
THINGS ARE TOUGH ALL OVER.
IF ONLY WE COULD'VE SOLD THAT DRAGON...
IT WAS SO YOUNG! I BET ITS INNARDS WERE EXTRA FRESH...
WOULD'VE FETCHED A GOOD PRICE.
SHOULD WE PUT TOGETHER A FORCE TO GO CAPTURE IT?
MIGHT BE A GOOD IDEA.

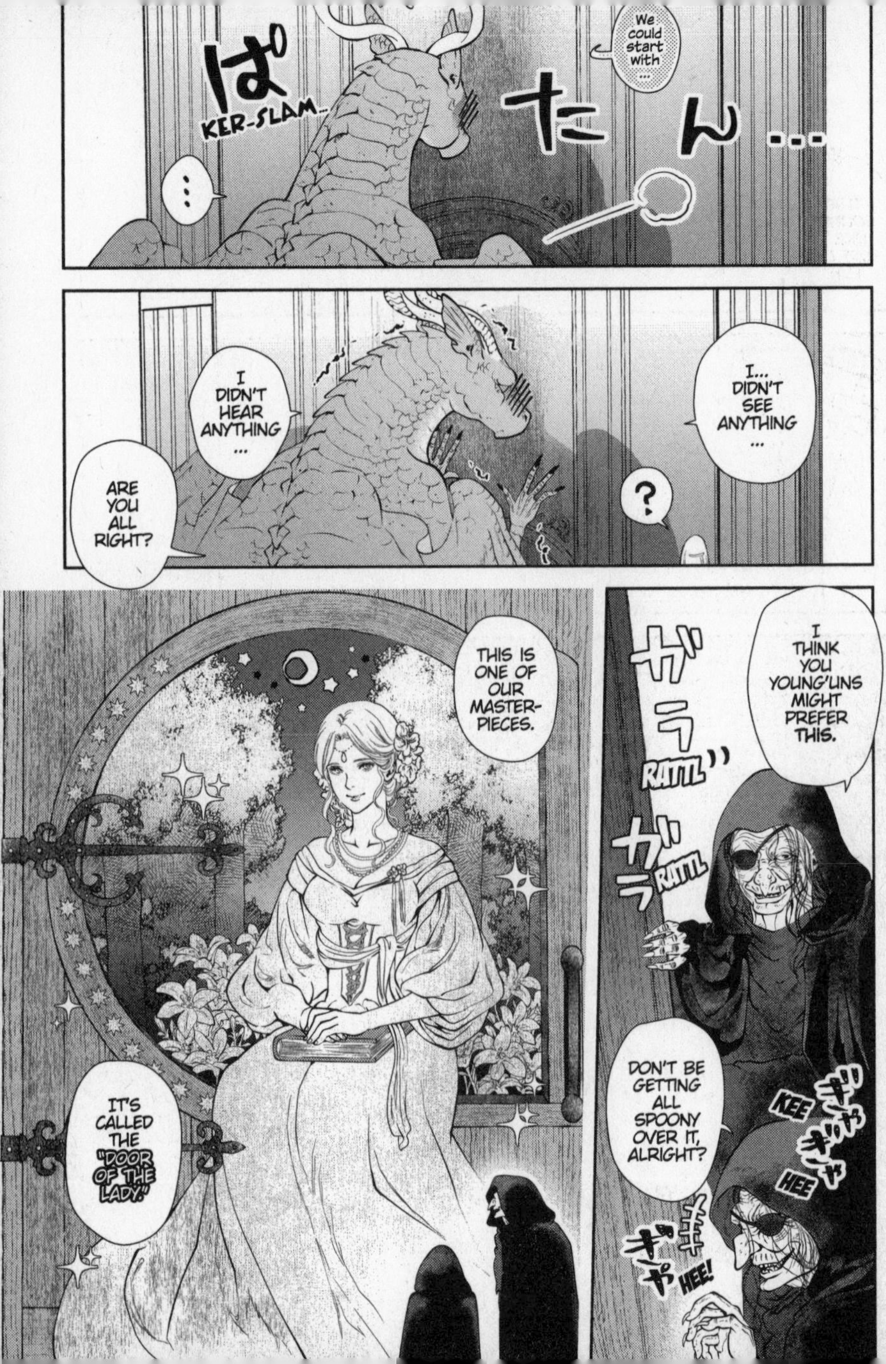

We could start with ...
ぱたん...
KER-SLAM...
...
I... DIDN'T SEE ANYTHING ...
?
I DIDN'T HEAR ANYTHING ...
ARE YOU ALL RIGHT?
I THINK YOU YOUNG'UNS MIGHT PREFER THIS.
ガラ
RATTL
ガラ
RATTL
DON'T BE GETTING ALL SPOONY OVER IT, ALRIGHT?
KEE
HEE
HEE!
THIS IS ONE OF OUR MASTER-PIECES.
IT'S CALLED THE "DOOR OF THE LADY."

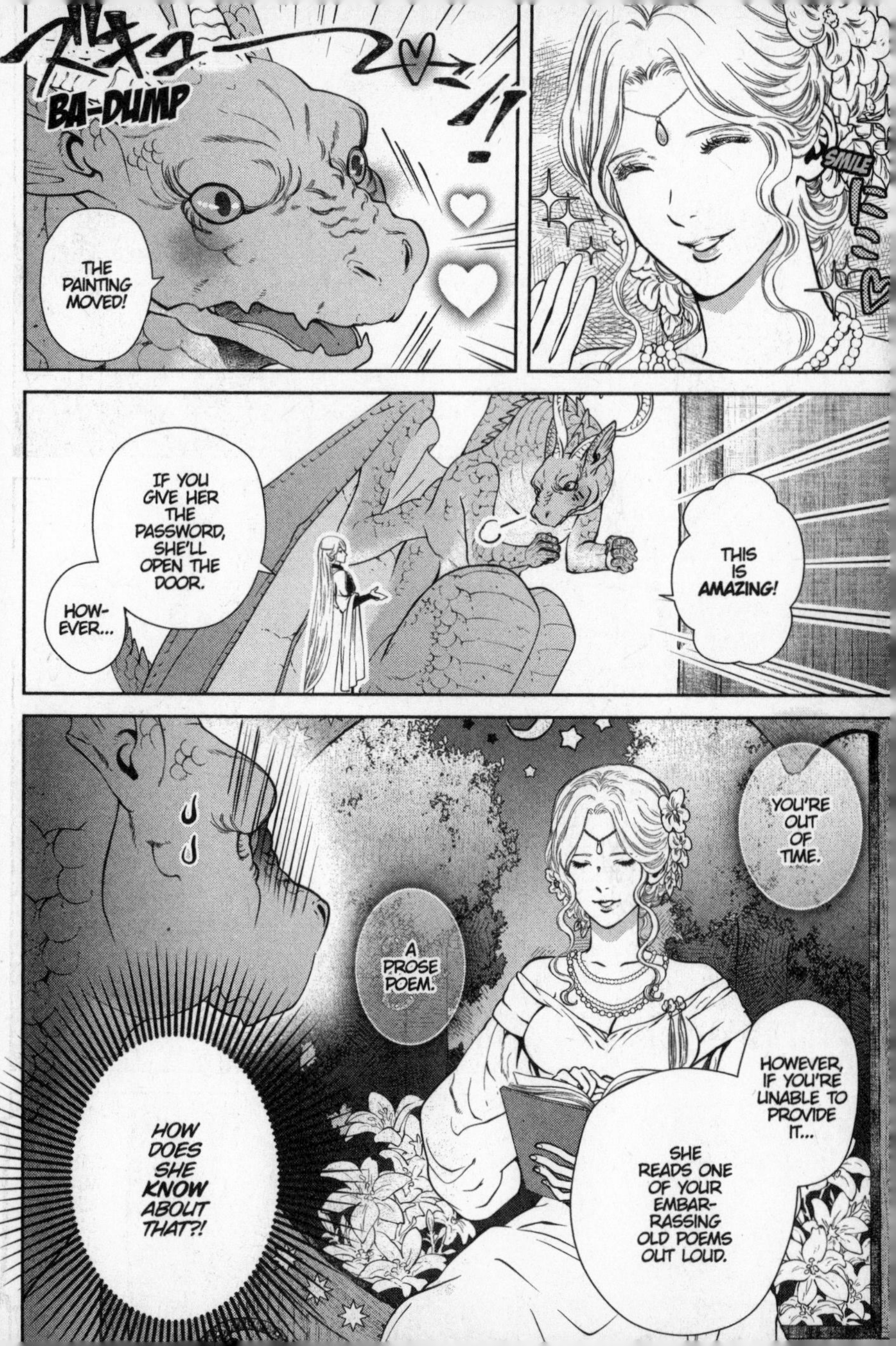
SMILE
BA-DUMP
THE PAINTING MOVED!
THIS IS AMAZING!
IF YOU GIVE HER THE PASSWORD, SHE'LL OPEN THE DOOR.
HOW-EVER...
YOU'RE OUT OF TIME.
A PROSE POEM.
HOWEVER, IF YOU'RE UNABLE TO PROVIDE IT...
SHE READS ONE OF YOUR EMBAR-RASSING OLD POEMS OUT LOUD.
HOW DOES SHE KNOW ABOUT THAT?!

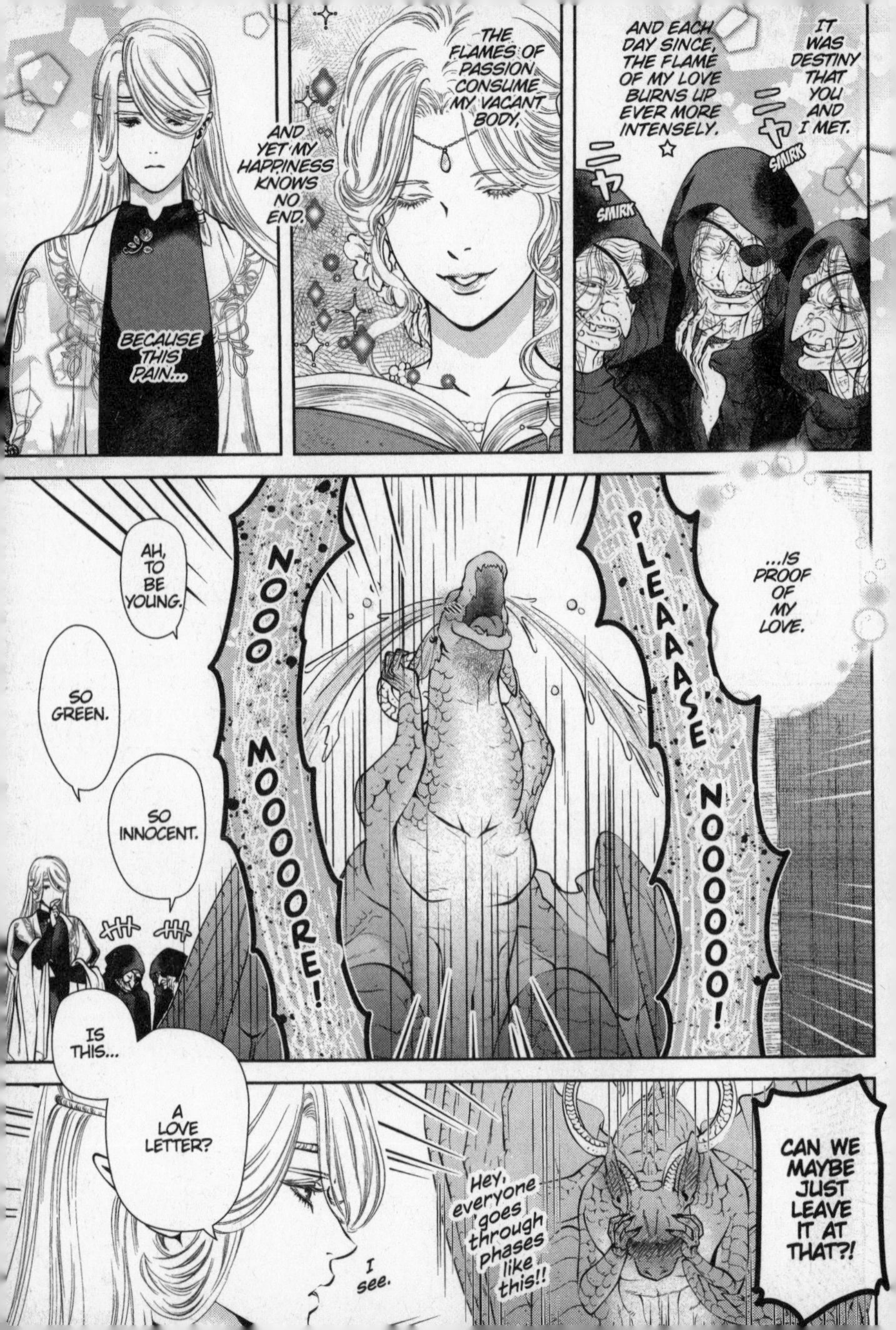
IT WAS DESTINY THAT YOU AND I MET.
AND EACH DAY SINCE, THE FLAME OF MY LOVE BURNS UP EVER MORE INTENSELY.
SMIRK
SMIRK
THE FLAMES OF PASSION CONSUME MY VACANT BODY,
AND YET MY HAPPINESS KNOWS NO END.
BECAUSE THIS PAIN...
...IS PROOF OF MY LOVE.
PLEAAAASE, NOOOOOO!
NOOO MOOOOOORE!
AH, TO BE YOUNG.
SO GREEN.
SO INNOCENT.
IS THIS...
CAN WE MAYBE JUST LEAVE IT AT THAT?!
Hey, everyone goes through phases like this!!
I see.
A LOVE LETTER?

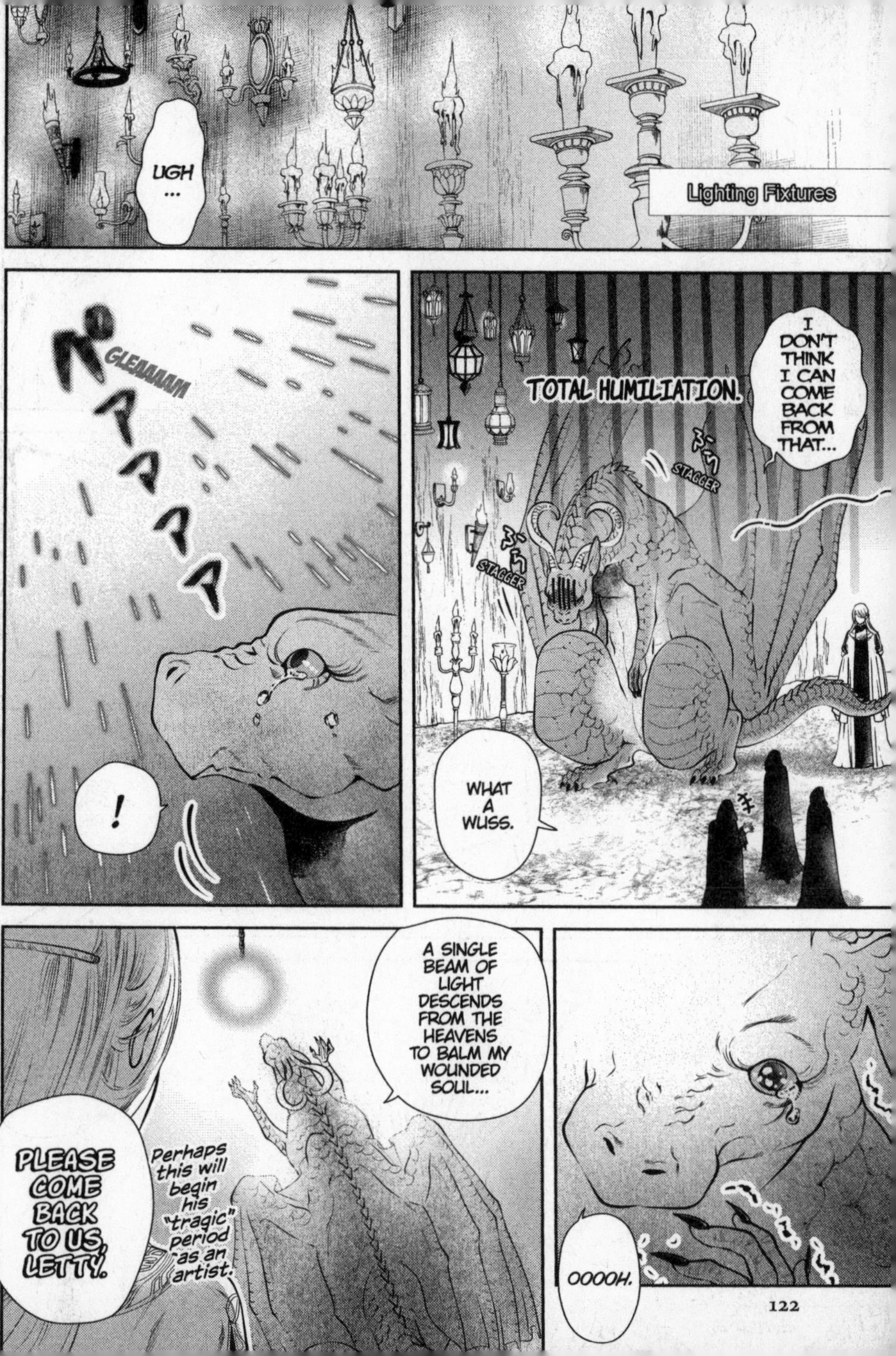
Lighting Fixtures
UGH ...
I DON'T THINK I CAN COME BACK FROM THAT...
TOTAL HUMILIATION.
STAGGER
STAGGER
WHAT A WUSS.
GLEAAAAM
!
OOOOH.
A SINGLE BEAM OF LIGHT DESCENDS FROM THE HEAVENS TO BALM MY WOUNDED SOUL...
Perhaps this will begin his "tragic" period as an artist.
PLEASE COME BACK TO US, LETTY.

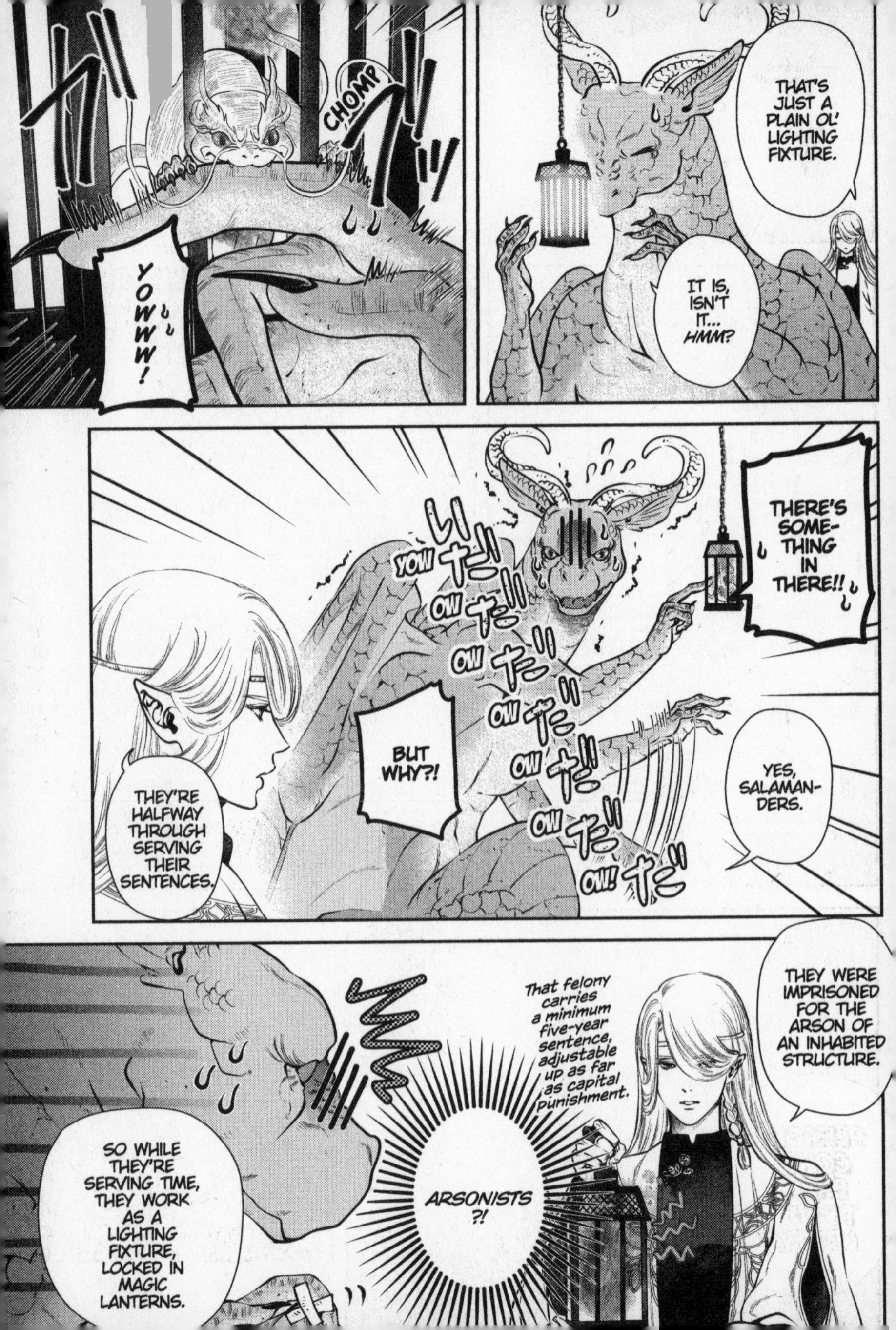
THAT'S JUST A PLAIN OL' LIGHTING FIXTURE.
IT IS, ISN'T IT... HMM?
CHOMP
YOWWW!
THERE'S SOME-THING IN THERE!!
YOW OW OW OW OW OW OW!
BUT WHY?!
YES, SALAMAN-DERS.
THEY'RE HALFWAY THROUGH SERVING THEIR SENTENCES.
THEY WERE IMPRISONED FOR THE ARSON OF AN INHABITED STRUCTURE.
That felony carries a minimum five-year sentence, adjustable up as far as capital punishment.
ARSONISTS?!
SO WHILE THEY'RE SERVING TIME, THEY WORK AS A LIGHTING FIXTURE, LOCKED IN MAGIC LANTERNS.

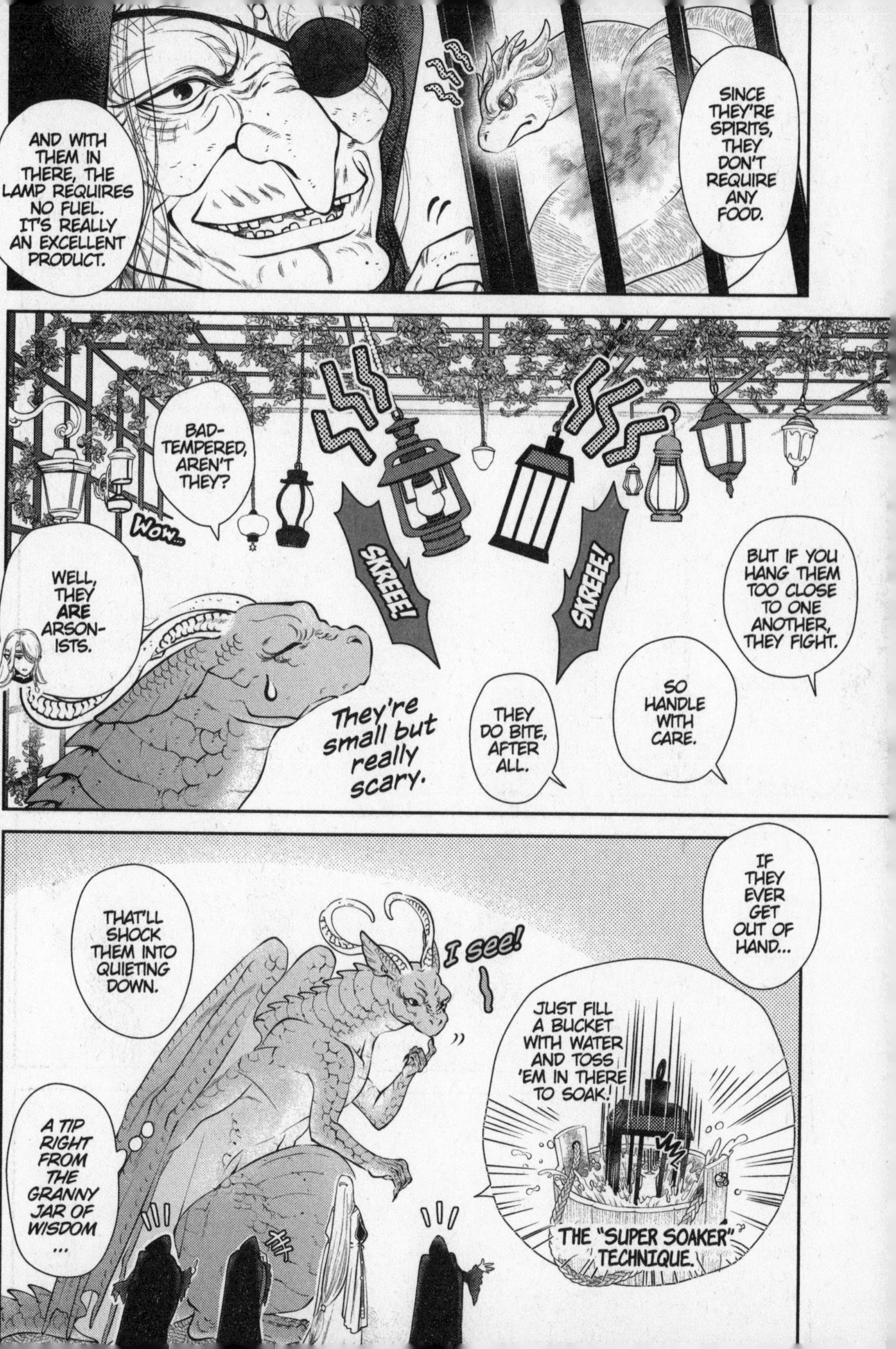
SINCE THEY'RE SPIRITS, THEY DON'T REQUIRE ANY FOOD.
AND WITH THEM IN THERE, THE LAMP REQUIRES NO FUEL. IT'S REALLY AN EXCELLENT PRODUCT.
BUT IF YOU HANG THEM TOO CLOSE TO ONE ANOTHER, THEY FIGHT.
SKREEE!
SKREEE!
SO HANDLE WITH CARE.
THEY DO BITE, AFTER ALL.
BAD-TEMPERED, AREN'T THEY?
Wow...
WELL, THEY ARE ARSONISTS.
They're small but really scary.
IF THEY EVER GET OUT OF HAND...
JUST FILL A BUCKET WITH WATER AND TOSS 'EM IN THERE TO SOAK!
THE "SUPER SOAKER" TECHNIQUE.
I see!
THAT'LL SHOCK THEM INTO QUIETING DOWN.
A TIP RIGHT FROM THE GRANNY JAR OF WISDOM...

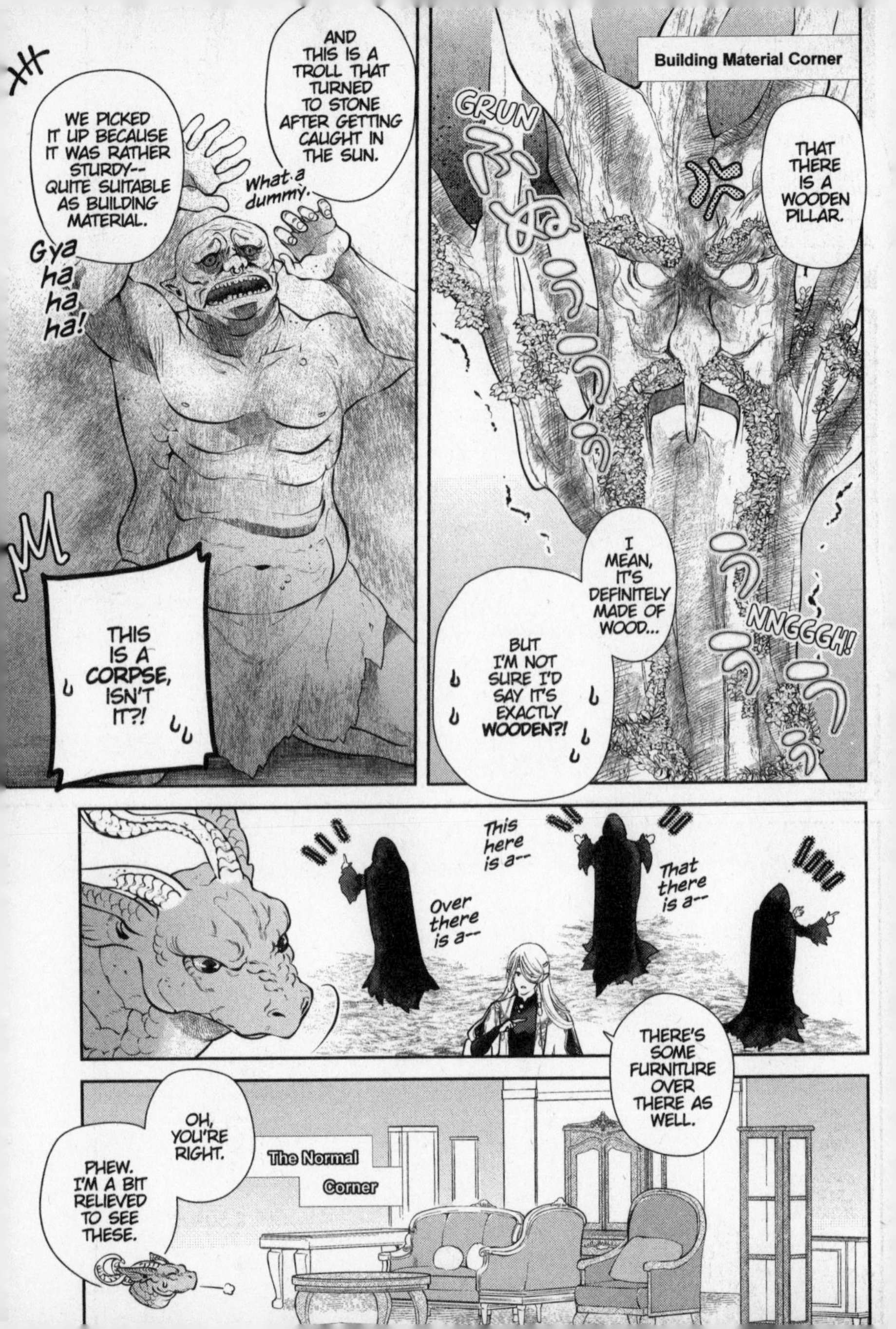

Building Material Corner
THAT THERE IS A WOODEN PILLAR.
GRUN
NNGGGH!
I MEAN, IT'S DEFINITELY MADE OF WOOD...
BUT I'M NOT SURE I'D SAY IT'S EXACTLY WOODEN?!
AND THIS IS A TROLL THAT TURNED TO STONE AFTER GETTING CAUGHT IN THE SUN.
WE PICKED IT UP BECAUSE IT WAS RATHER STURDY-- QUITE SUITABLE AS BUILDING MATERIAL.
What a dummy.
Gya ha ha ha!
THIS IS A CORPSE, ISN'T IT?!
That there is a--
This here is a--
Over there is a--
THERE'S SOME FURNITURE OVER THERE AS WELL.
The Normal Corner
OH, YOU'RE RIGHT.
PHEW. I'M A BIT RELIEVED TO SEE THESE.

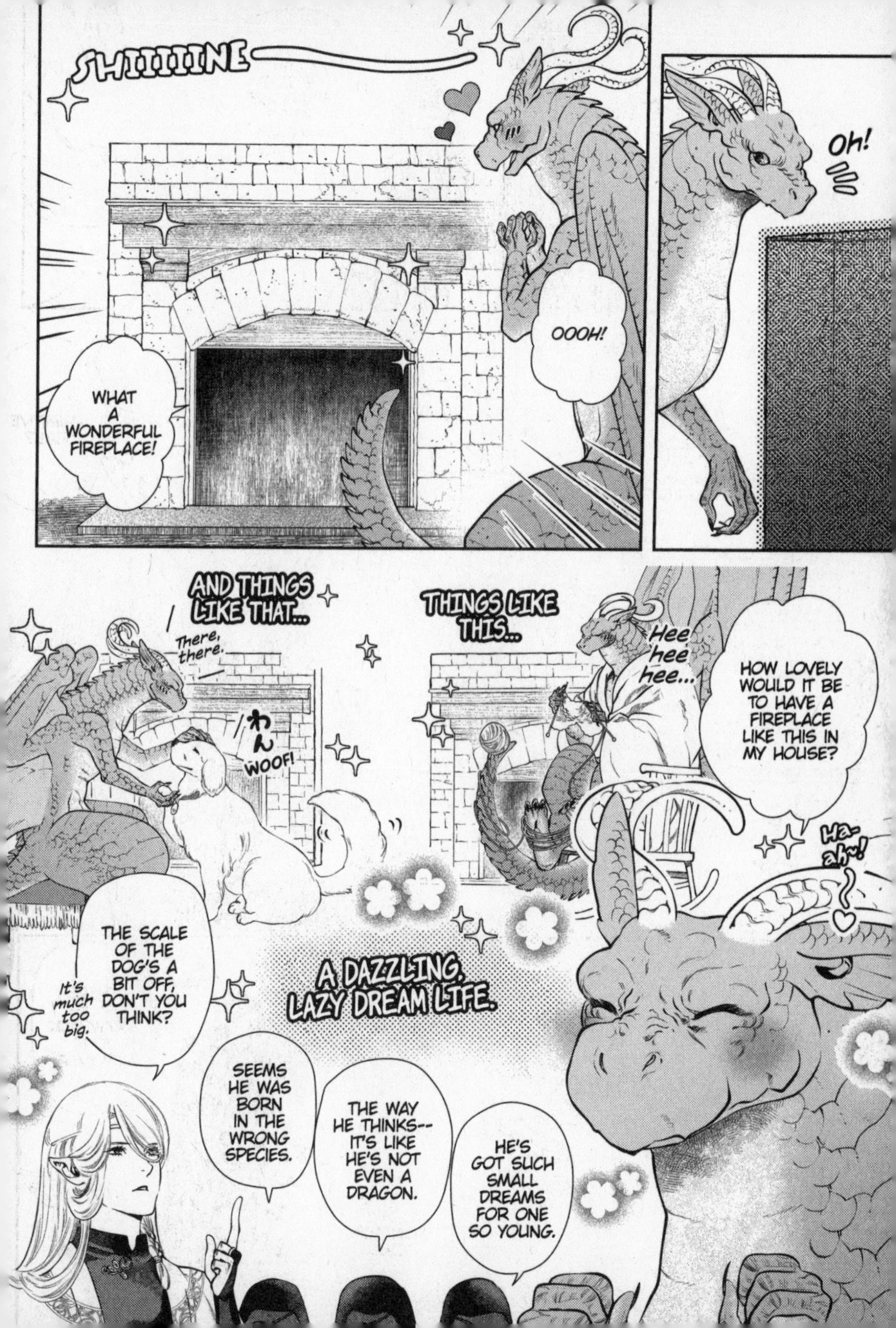
Oh!
SHIIIIINE
OOOH!
WHAT A WONDERFUL FIREPLACE!
THINGS LIKE THIS...
Hee hee hee...
HOW LOVELY WOULD IT BE TO HAVE A FIREPLACE LIKE THIS IN MY HOUSE?
Ha-ah~!
AND THINGS LIKE THAT...
There, there.
わん
WOOF!
A DAZZLING, LAZY DREAM LIFE.
THE SCALE OF THE DOG'S A BIT OFF, DON'T YOU THINK?
It's much too big.
HE'S GOT SUCH SMALL DREAMS FOR ONE SO YOUNG.
THE WAY HE THINKS-- IT'S LIKE HE'S NOT EVEN A DRAGON.
SEEMS HE WAS BORN IN THE WRONG SPECIES.

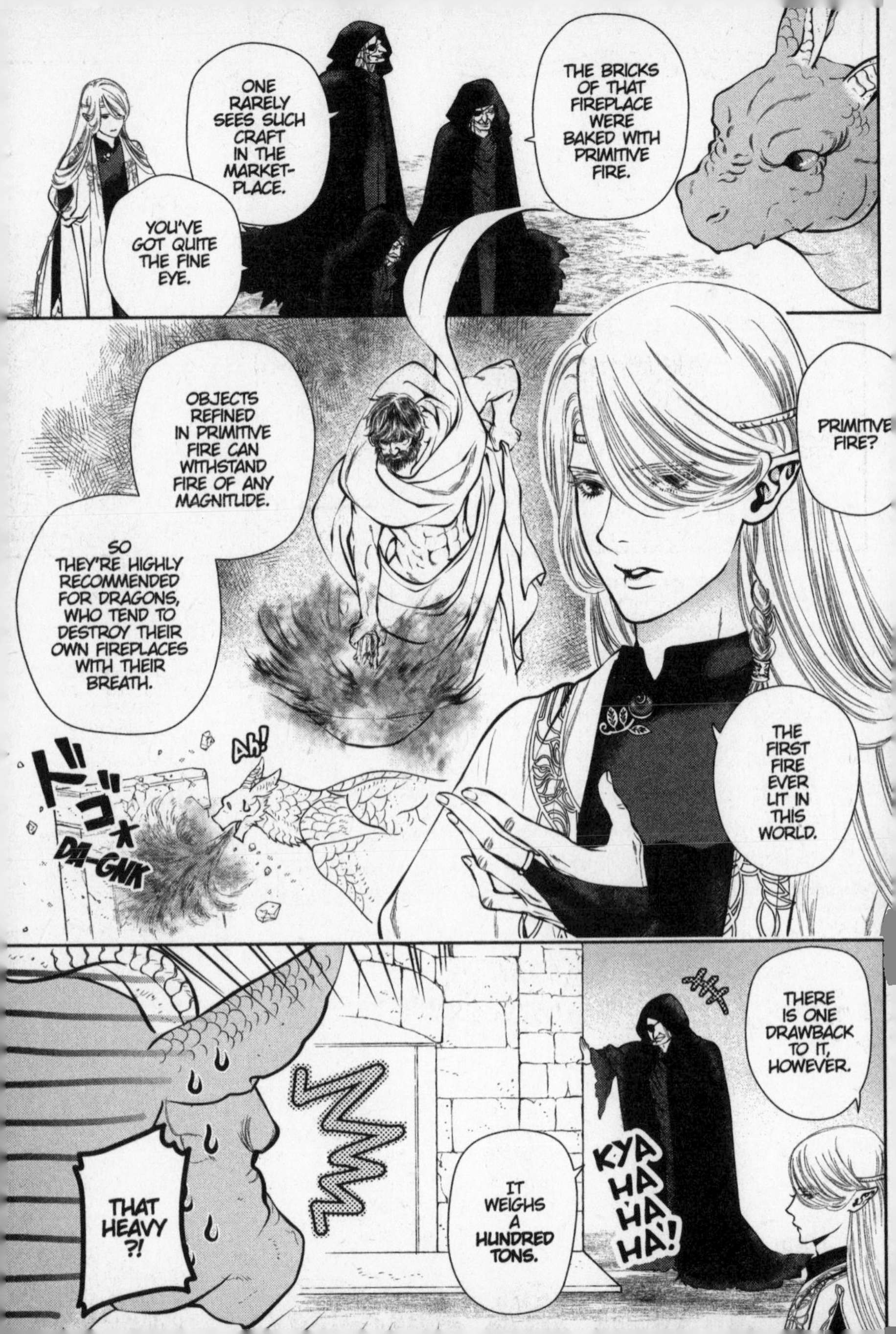

THE BRICKS OF THAT FIREPLACE WERE BAKED WITH PRIMITIVE FIRE.
ONE RARELY SEES SUCH CRAFT IN THE MARKETPLACE.
YOU'VE GOT QUITE THE FINE EYE.
PRIMITIVE FIRE?
THE FIRST FIRE EVER LIT IN THIS WORLD.
OBJECTS REFINED IN PRIMITIVE FIRE CAN WITHSTAND FIRE OF ANY MAGNITUDE.
SO THEY'RE HIGHLY RECOMMENDED FOR DRAGONS, WHO TEND TO DESTROY THEIR OWN FIREPLACES WITH THEIR BREATH.
Ah!
DA-GNK
THERE IS ONE DRAWBACK TO IT, HOWEVER.
KYA HA HA HA!
IT WEIGHS A HUNDRED TONS.
THAT HEAVY?!

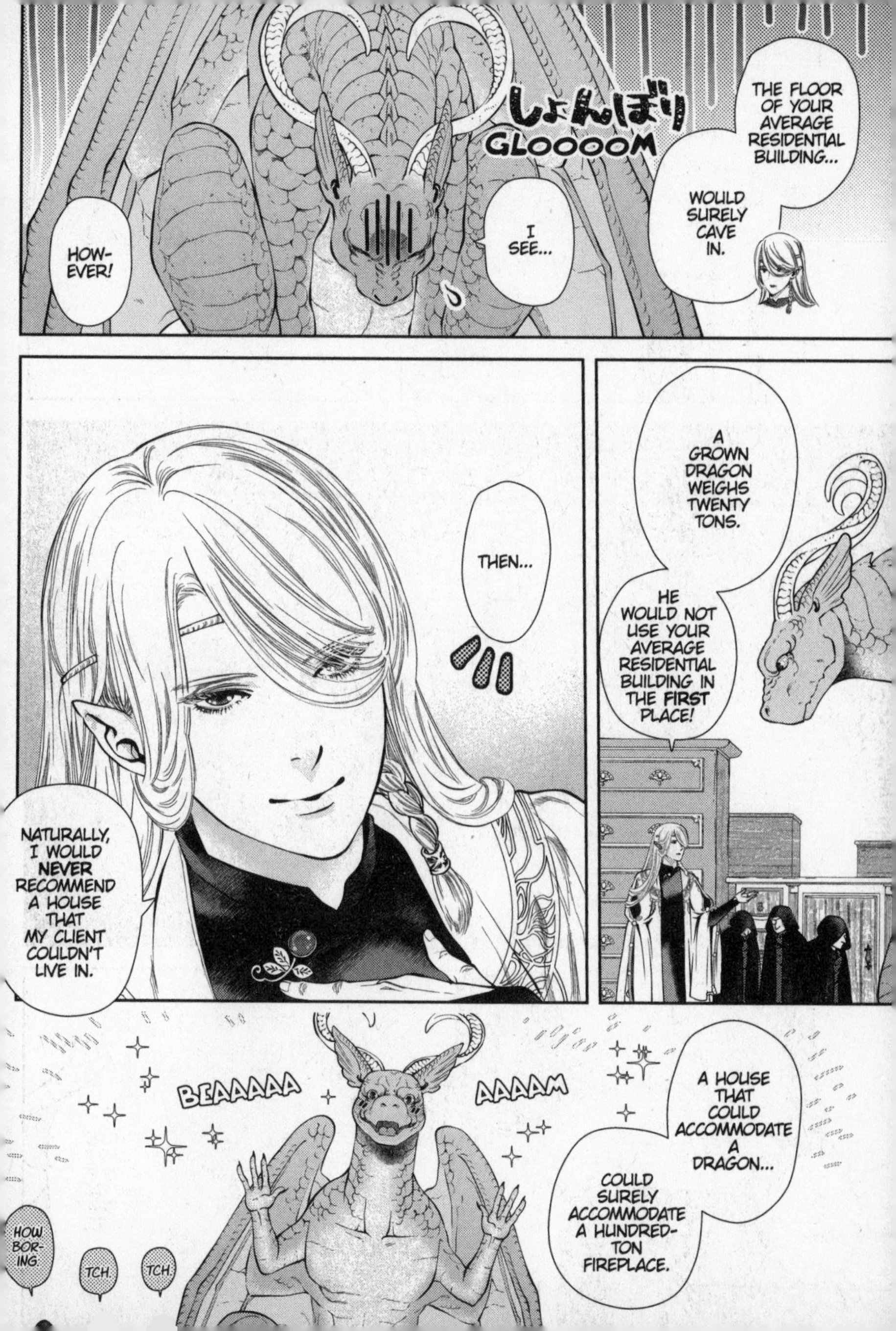
THE FLOOR OF YOUR AVERAGE RESIDENTIAL BUILDING...
WOULD SURELY CAVE IN.
しょんぼり
GLOOOOM
I SEE...
HOW-EVER!
A GROWN DRAGON WEIGHS TWENTY TONS.
HE WOULD NOT USE YOUR AVERAGE RESIDENTIAL BUILDING IN THE FIRST PLACE!
THEN...
NATURALLY, I WOULD NEVER RECOMMEND A HOUSE THAT MY CLIENT COULDN'T LIVE IN.
A HOUSE THAT COULD ACCOMMODATE A DRAGON...
COULD SURELY ACCOMMODATE A HUNDRED-TON FIREPLACE.
BEAAAAA
AAAAM
TCH.
TCH.
HOW BORING.

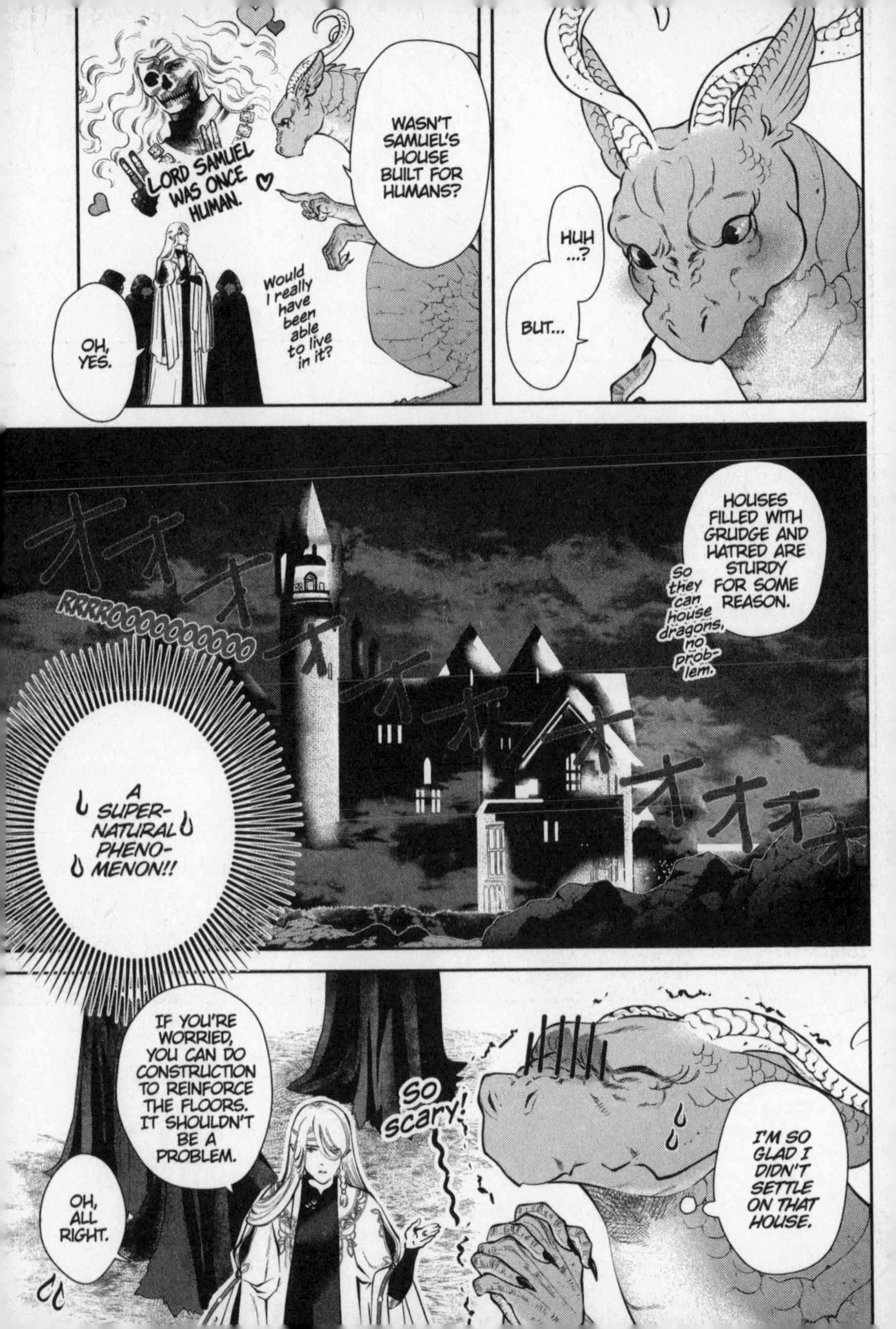
HUH ...?
BUT...
WASN'T SAMUEL'S HOUSE BUILT FOR HUMANS?
Would I really have been able to live in it?
LORD SAMUEL WAS ONCE HUMAN.
OH, YES.
HOUSES FILLED WITH GRUDGE AND HATRED ARE STURDY FOR SOME REASON.
So they can house dragons, no prob-lem.
RRRRROOOOOOOOOO
A SUPER-NATURAL PHENO-MENON!!
I'M SO GLAD I DIDN'T SETTLE ON THAT HOUSE.
So scary!
IF YOU'RE WORRIED, YOU CAN DO CONSTRUCTION TO REINFORCE THE FLOORS. IT SHOULDN'T BE A PROBLEM.
OH, ALL RIGHT.

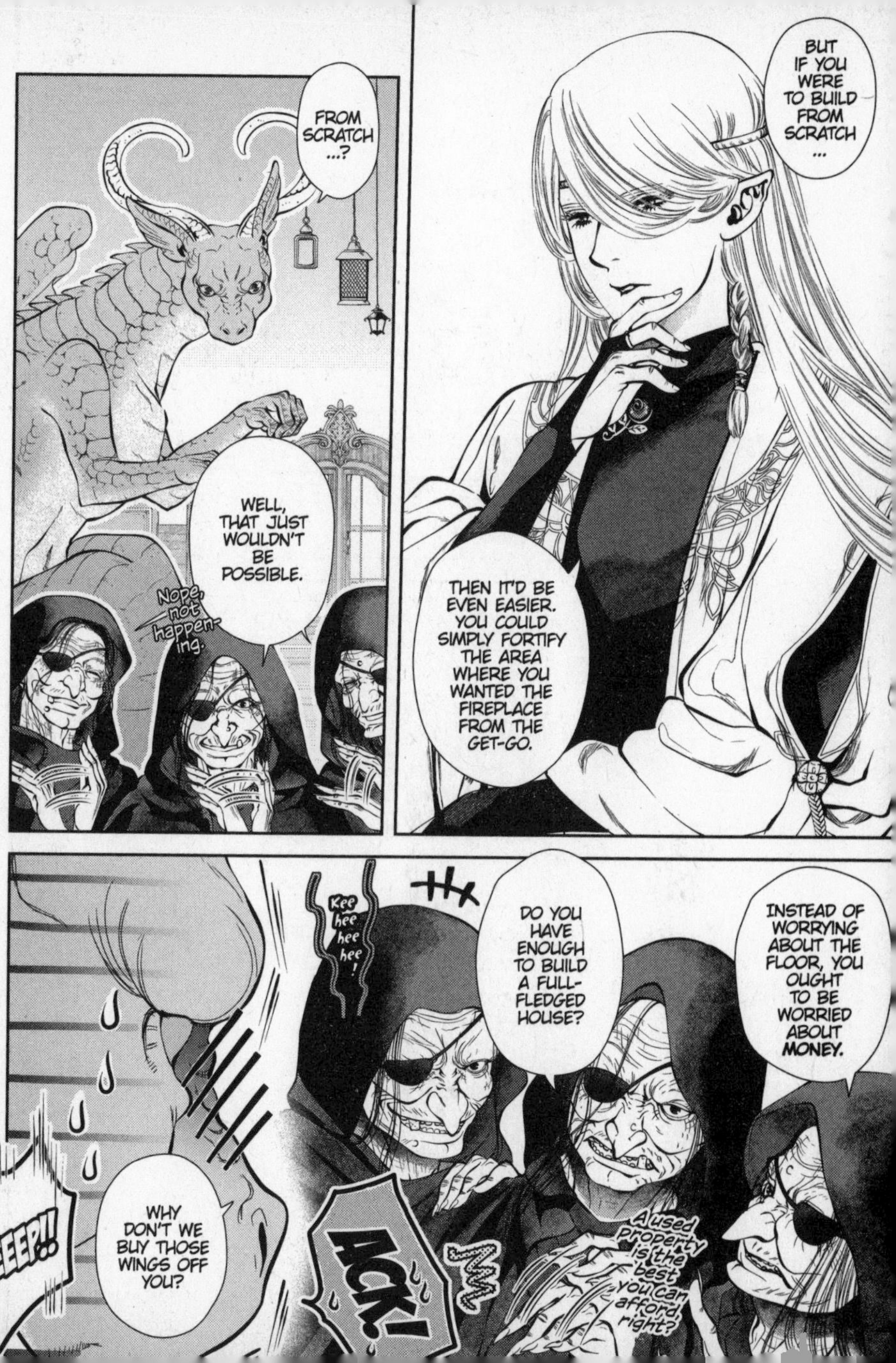
BUT IF YOU WERE TO BUILD FROM SCRATCH ...
THEN IT'D BE EVEN EASIER. YOU COULD SIMPLY FORTIFY THE AREA WHERE YOU WANTED THE FIREPLACE FROM THE GET-GO.
FROM SCRATCH ...?
WELL, THAT JUST WOULDN'T BE POSSIBLE.
Nope, not happen-ing.
INSTEAD OF WORRYING ABOUT THE FLOOR, YOU OUGHT TO BE WORRIED ABOUT MONEY.
DO YOU HAVE ENOUGH TO BUILD A FULL-FLEDGED HOUSE?
Kee hee hee hee!
A used property is the best you can afford, right?
ACK!
WHY DON'T WE BUY THOSE WINGS OFF YOU?
EEEP!!

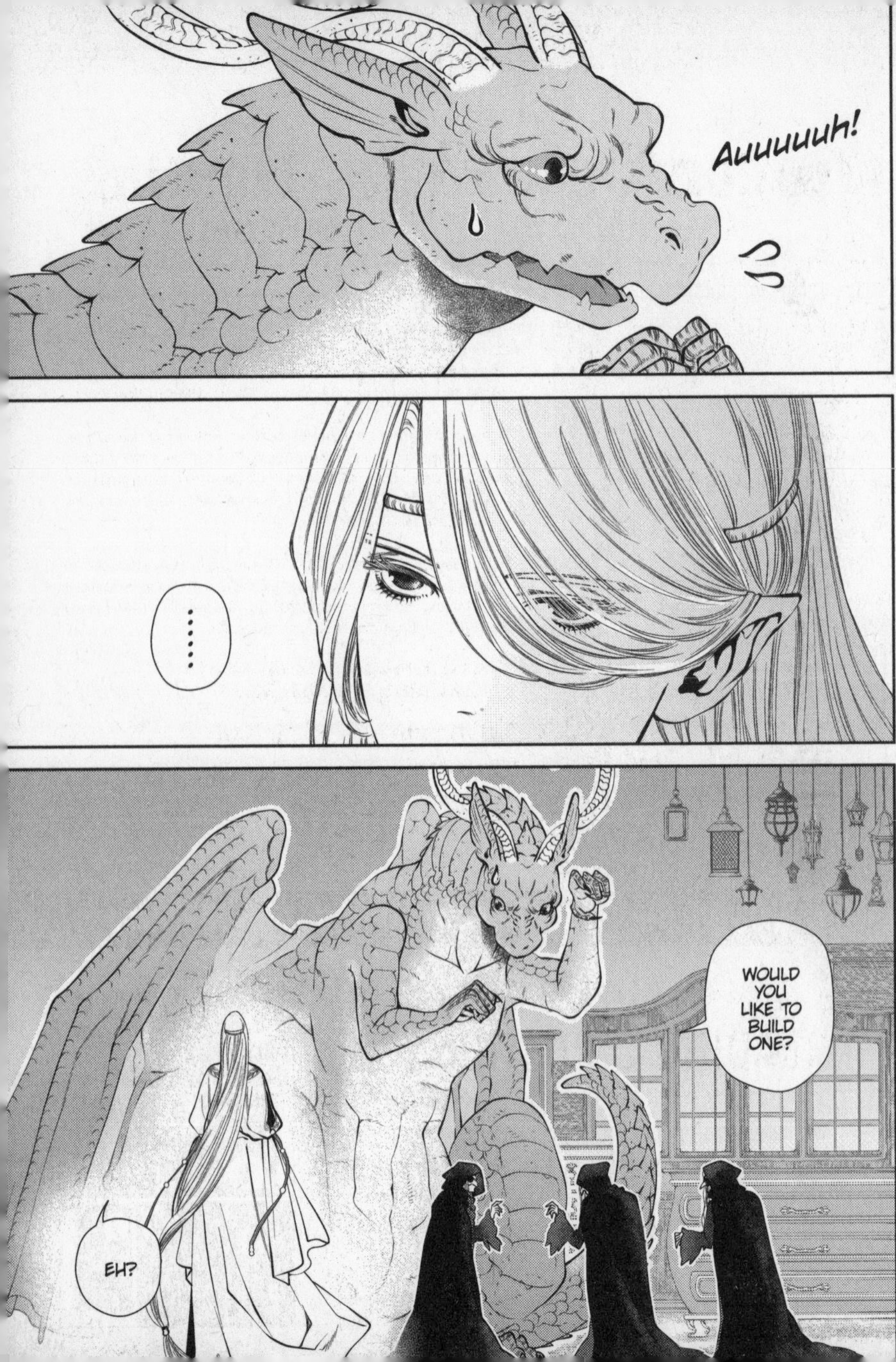
Auuuuuh!
......
WOULD YOU LIKE TO BUILD ONE?
EH?

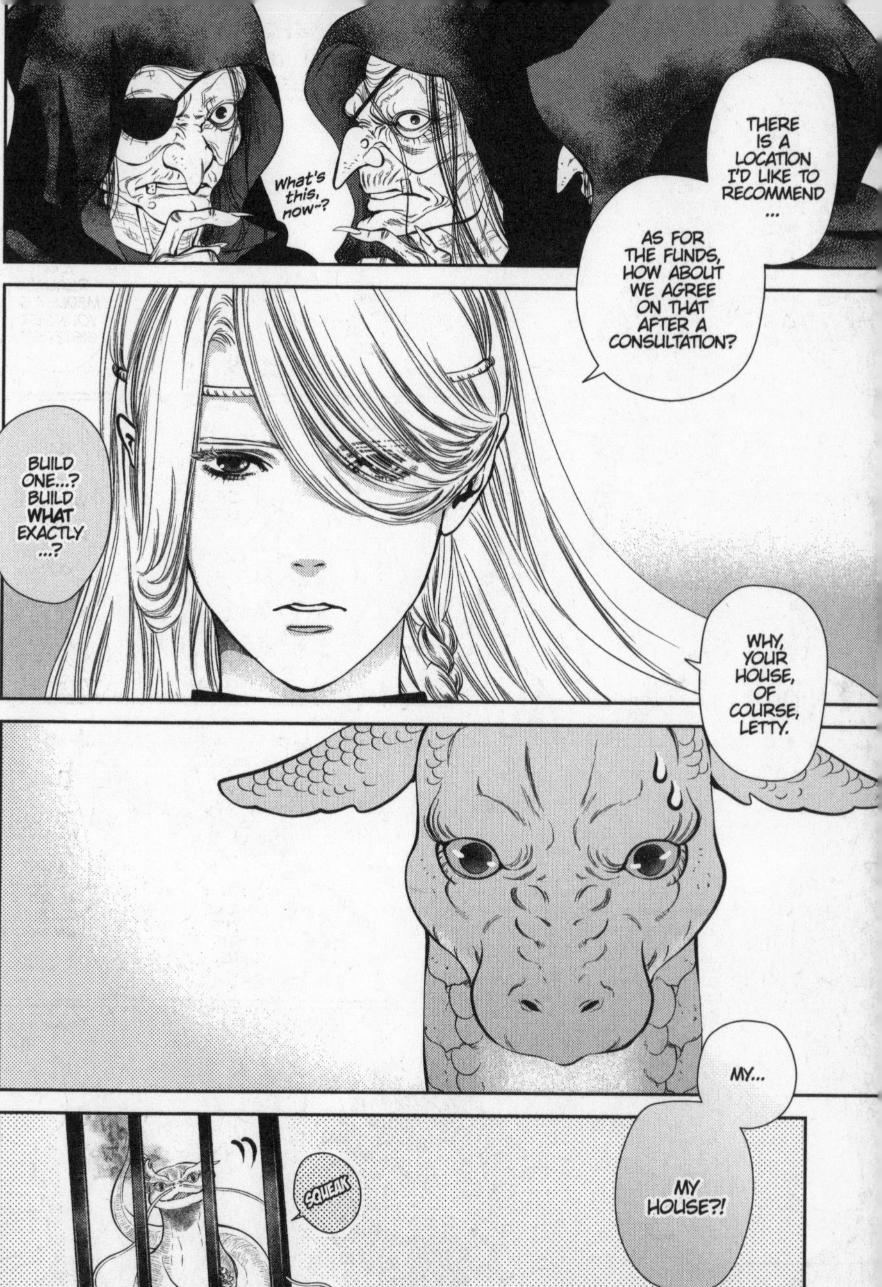
THERE IS A LOCATION I'D LIKE TO RECOMMEND ...
What's this, now~?
AS FOR THE FUNDS, HOW ABOUT WE AGREE ON THAT AFTER A CONSULTATION?
BUILD ONE...? BUILD WHAT EXACTLY ...?
WHY, YOUR HOUSE, OF COURSE, LETTY.
MY...
MY HOUSE?!
SQUEAK

Back in the Day

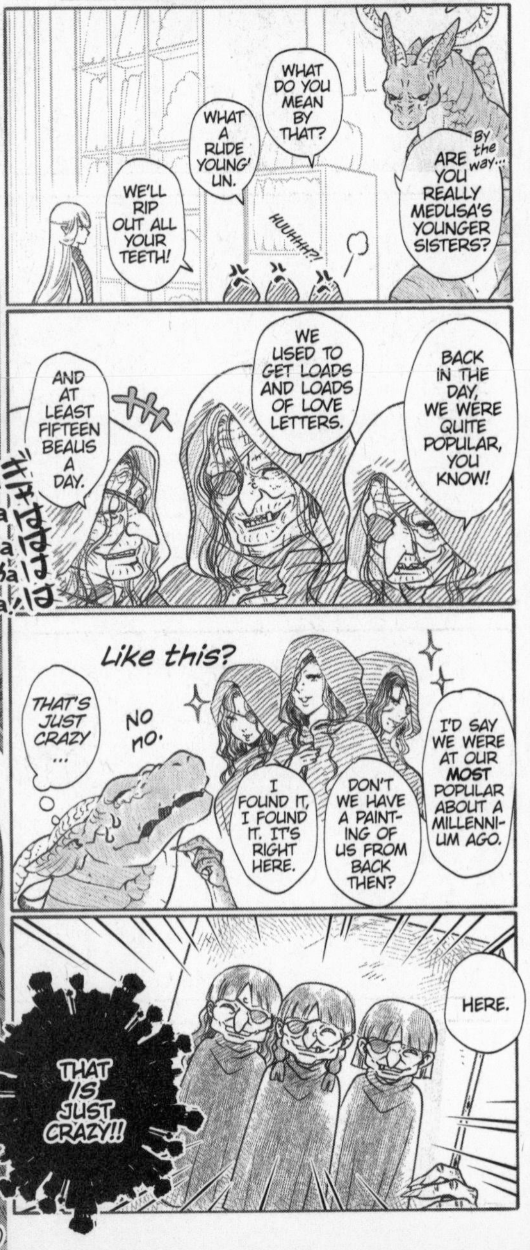
By the way...
ARE YOU REALLY MEDUSA'S YOUNGER SISTERS?
HUUHHH?!
WHAT DO YOU MEAN BY THAT?
WHAT A RUDE YOUNG' UN.
WE'LL RIP OUT ALL YOUR TEETH!
BACK IN THE DAY, WE WERE QUITE POPULAR, YOU KNOW!
WE USED TO GET LOADS AND LOADS OF LOVE LETTERS.
AND AT LEAST FIFTEEN BEAUS A DAY.
Kya ha ha ha ha!!
I'D SAY WE WERE AT OUR MOST POPULAR ABOUT A MILLENNIUM AGO.
DON'T WE HAVE A PAINTING OF US FROM BACK THEN?
I FOUND IT, I FOUND IT. IT'S RIGHT HERE.
Like this?
NO no.
THAT'S JUST CRAZY...
HERE.
THAT IS JUST CRAZY!!

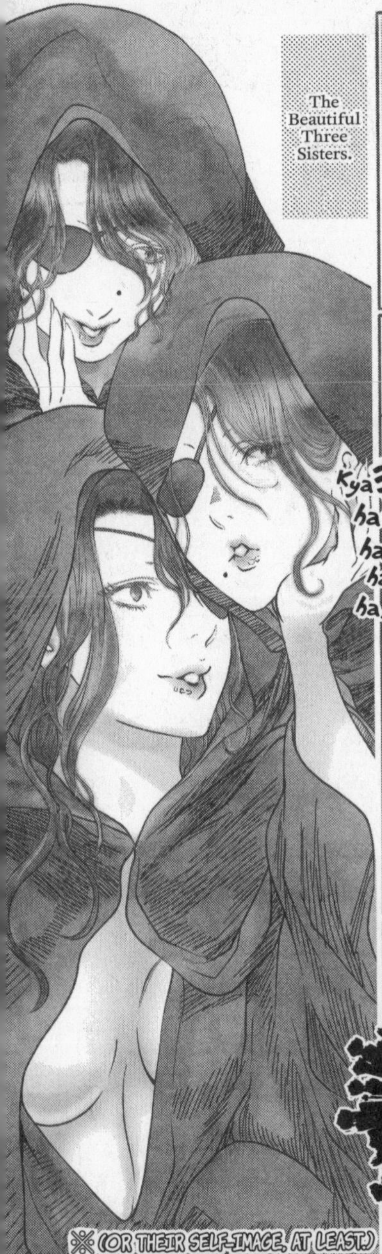
The Beautiful Three Sisters.
※(OR THEIR SELF-IMAGE, AT LEAST.)

Dragon Goes House-Hunting

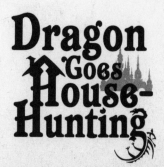

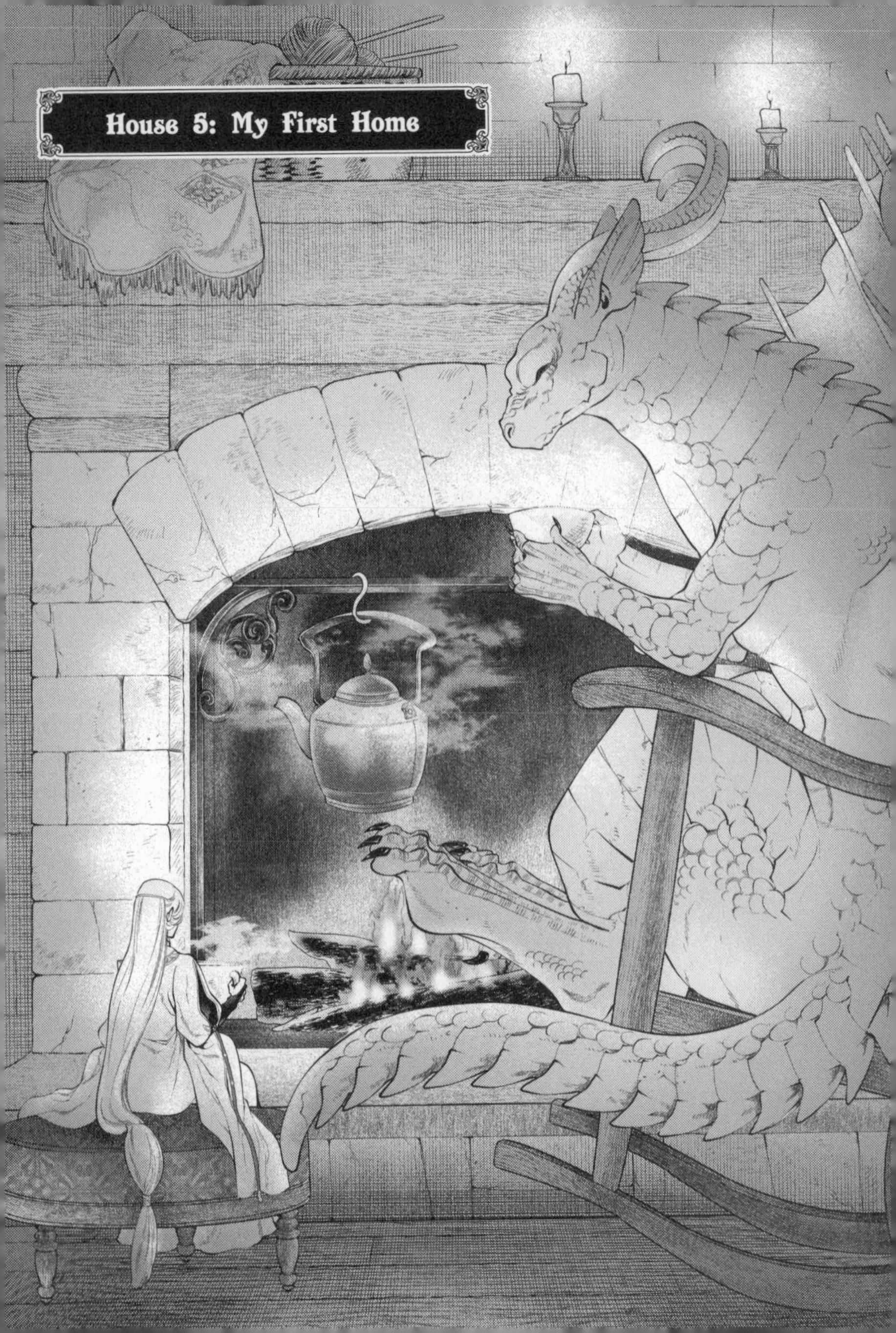
House 5: My First Home

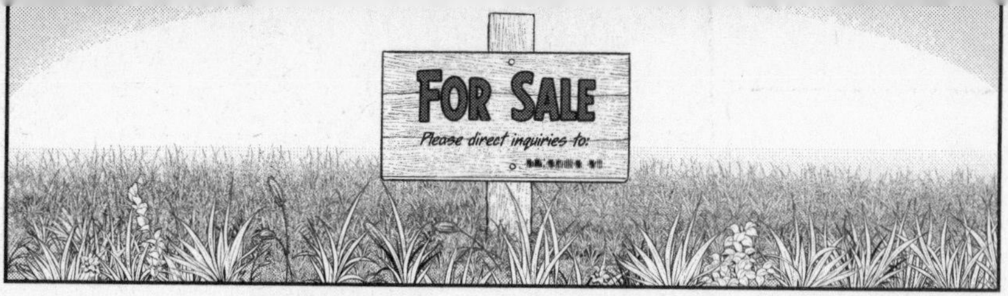
FOR SALE
Please direct inquiries to:

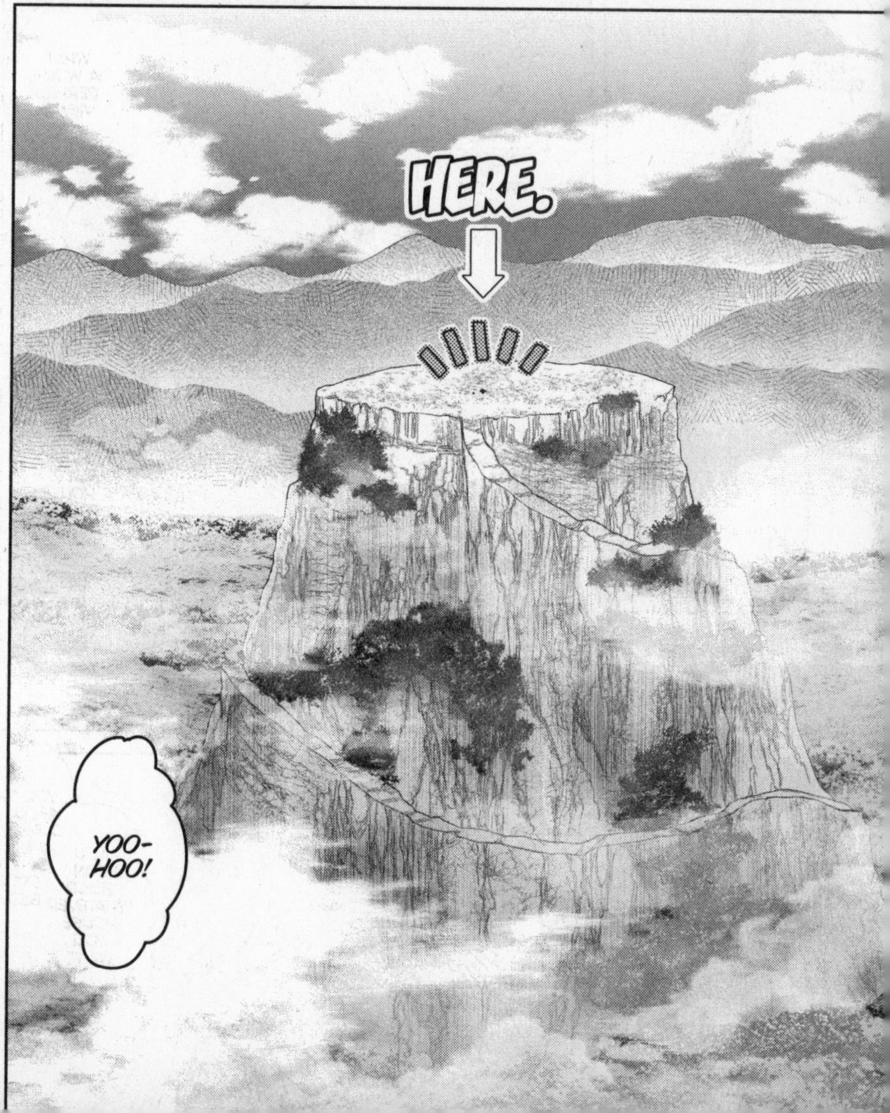
HERE.
YOO-HOO!

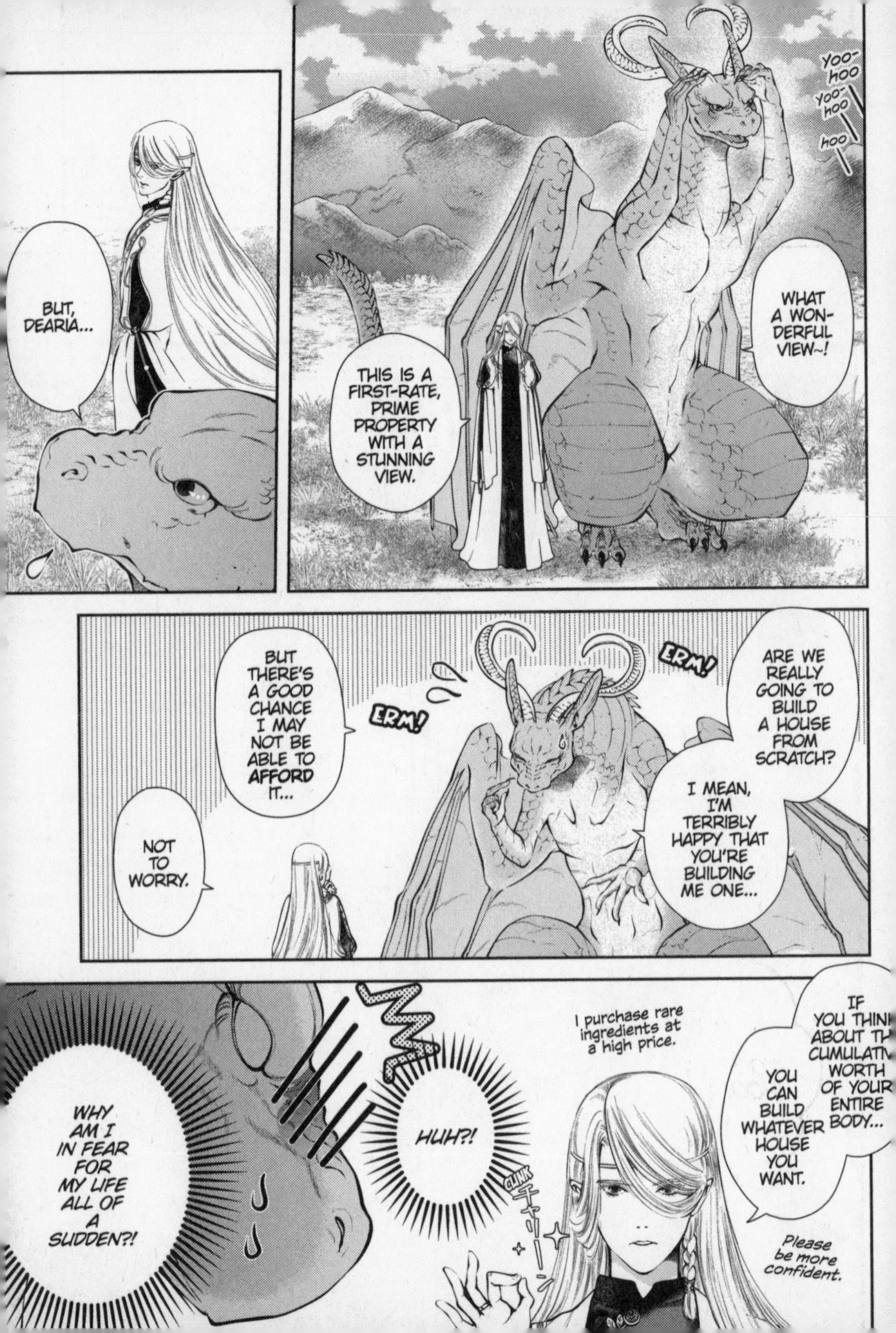
Yoo-hoo
Yoo-hoo
hoo
WHAT A WONDERFUL VIEW~!
THIS IS A FIRST-RATE, PRIME PROPERTY WITH A STUNNING VIEW.
BUT, DEARIA...
ARE WE REALLY GOING TO BUILD A HOUSE FROM SCRATCH?
I MEAN, I'M TERRIBLY HAPPY THAT YOU'RE BUILDING ME ONE...
ERM!
ERM!
BUT THERE'S A GOOD CHANCE I MAY NOT BE ABLE TO **AFFORD** IT...
NOT TO WORRY.
IF YOU THIN ABOUT TH CUMULATIV WORTH OF YOUR ENTIRE BODY...
YOU CAN BUILD WHATEVER HOUSE YOU WANT.
I purchase rare ingredients at a high price.
Please be more confident.
CLINK
HUH?!
WHY AM I IN FEAR FOR MY LIFE ALL OF A SUDDEN?!

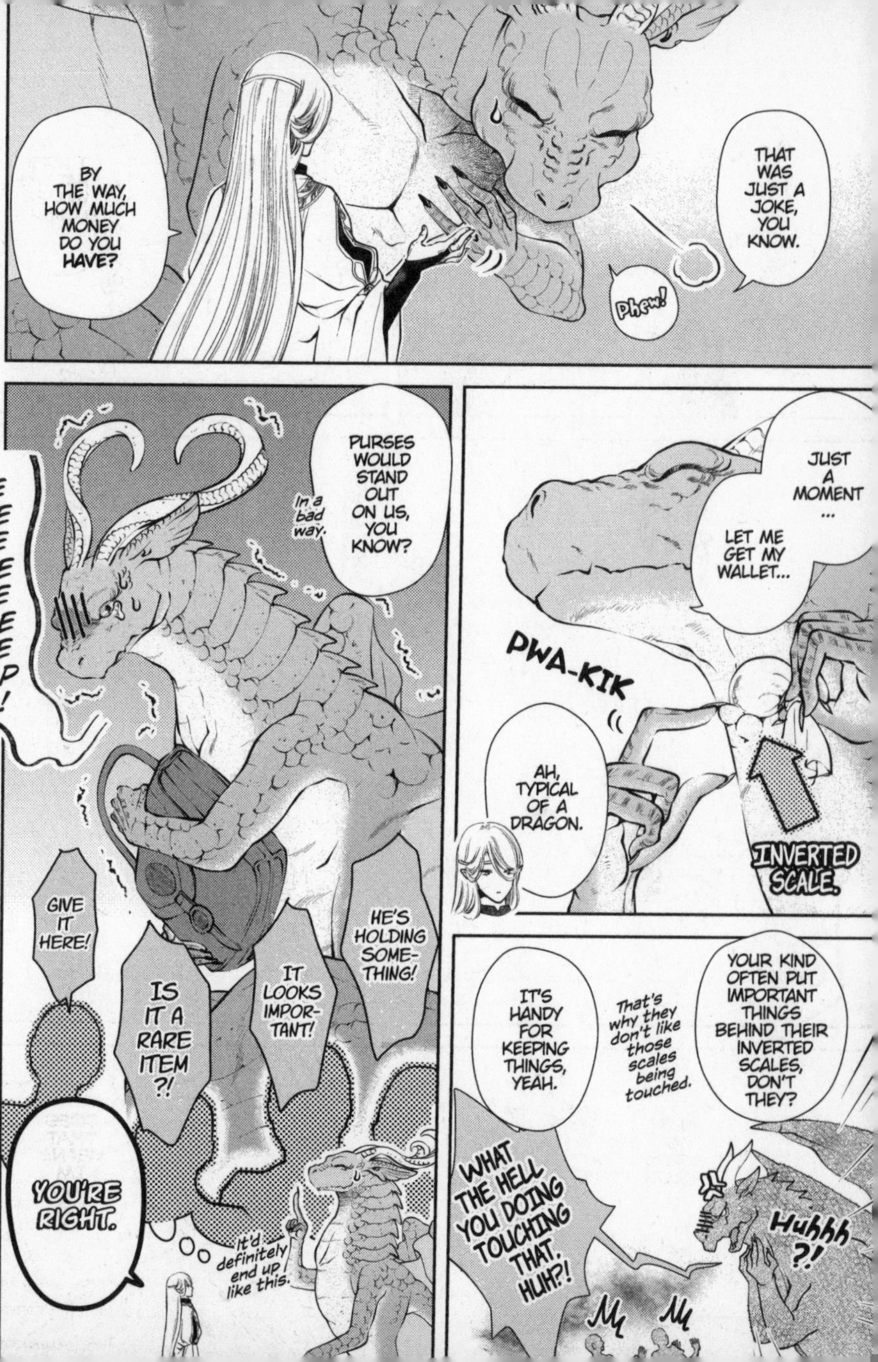
THAT WAS JUST A JOKE, YOU KNOW.
Phew!
BY THE WAY, HOW MUCH MONEY DO YOU HAVE?
JUST A MOMENT... LET ME GET MY WALLET...
PWA-KIK
INVERTED SCALE.
AH, TYPICAL OF A DRAGON.
YOUR KIND OFTEN PUT IMPORTANT THINGS BEHIND THEIR INVERTED SCALES, DON'T THEY?
That's why they don't like those scales being touched.
IT'S HANDY FOR KEEPING THINGS, YEAH.
Huhhh?!
WHAT THE HELL YOU DOING TOUCHING THAT, HUH?!
PURSES WOULD STAND OUT ON US, YOU KNOW?
In a bad way.
EEEEEEEEP!
HE'S HOLDING SOMETHING!
IT LOOKS IMPORTANT!
IS IT A RARE ITEM?!
GIVE IT HERE!
YOU'RE RIGHT.
It'd definitely end up like this.

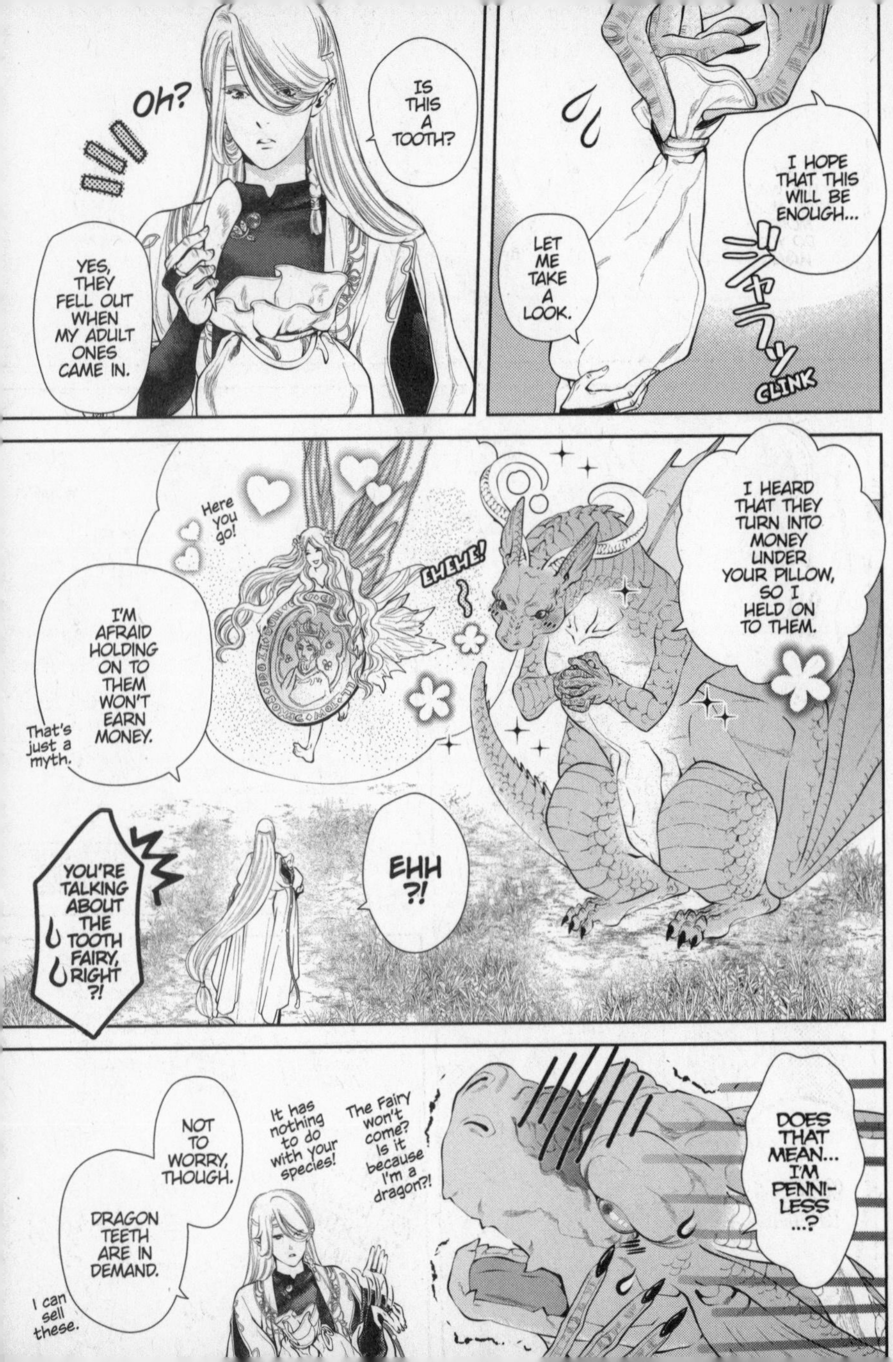
I HOPE THAT THIS WILL BE ENOUGH...
ジャラッ
CLINK
LET ME TAKE A LOOK.
IS THIS A TOOTH?
Oh?
YES, THEY FELL OUT WHEN MY ADULT ONES CAME IN.
I HEARD THAT THEY TURN INTO MONEY UNDER YOUR PILLOW, SO I HELD ON TO THEM.
EHEHE!
Here you go!
I'M AFRAID HOLDING ON TO THEM WON'T EARN MONEY.
That's just a myth.
EHH ?!
YOU'RE TALKING ABOUT THE TOOTH FAIRY, RIGHT ?!
DOES THAT MEAN... I'M PENNI-LESS ...?
The Fairy won't come? Is it because I'm a dragon?!
It has nothing to do with your species!
NOT TO WORRY, THOUGH.
DRAGON TEETH ARE IN DEMAND.
I can sell these.

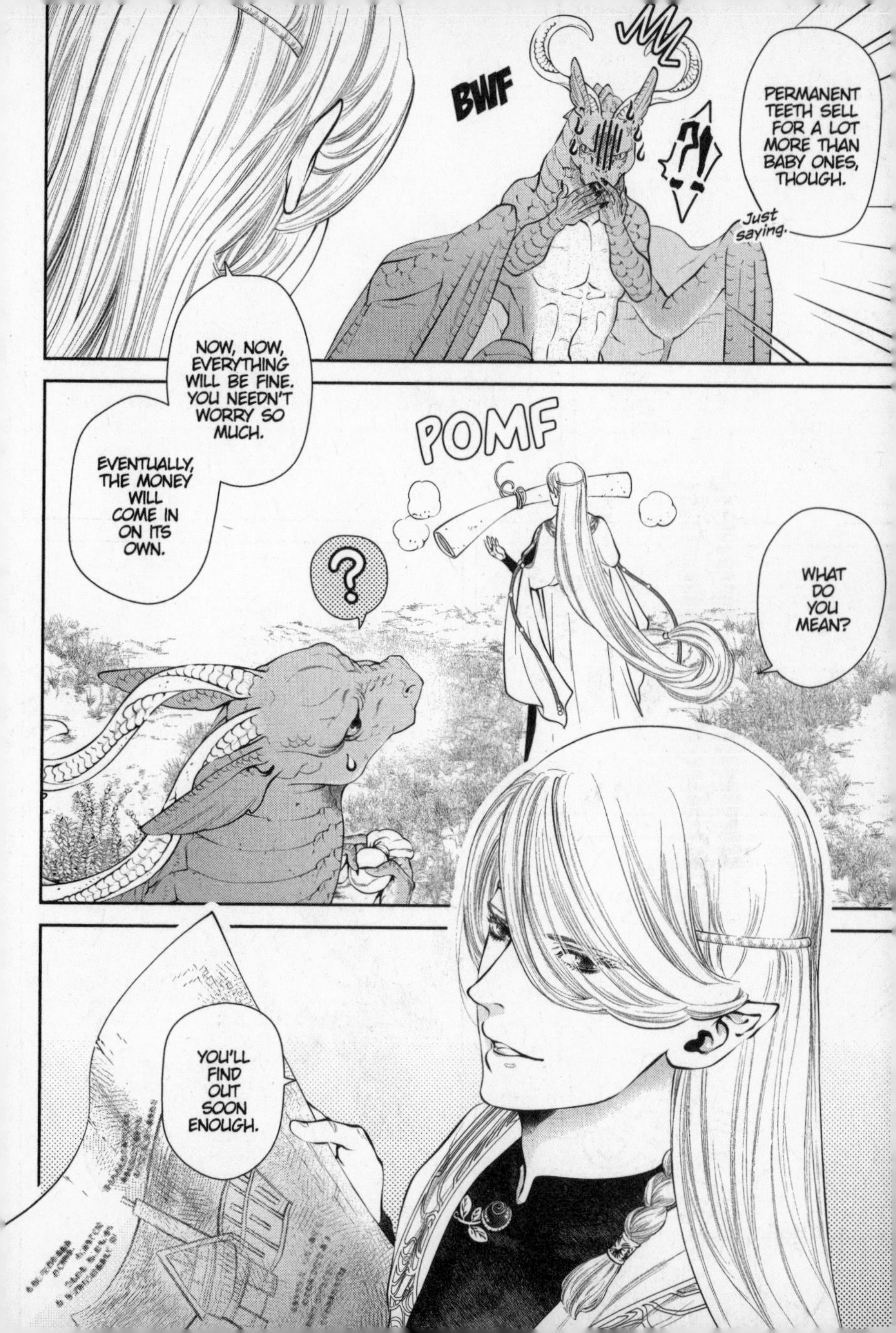
PERMANENT TEETH SELL FOR A LOT MORE THAN BABY ONES, THOUGH.
Just saying.
?!
BWF
NOW, NOW, EVERYTHING WILL BE FINE. YOU NEEDN'T WORRY SO MUCH.
EVENTUALLY, THE MONEY WILL COME IN ON ITS OWN.
POMF
?
WHAT DO YOU MEAN?
YOU'LL FIND OUT SOON ENOUGH.

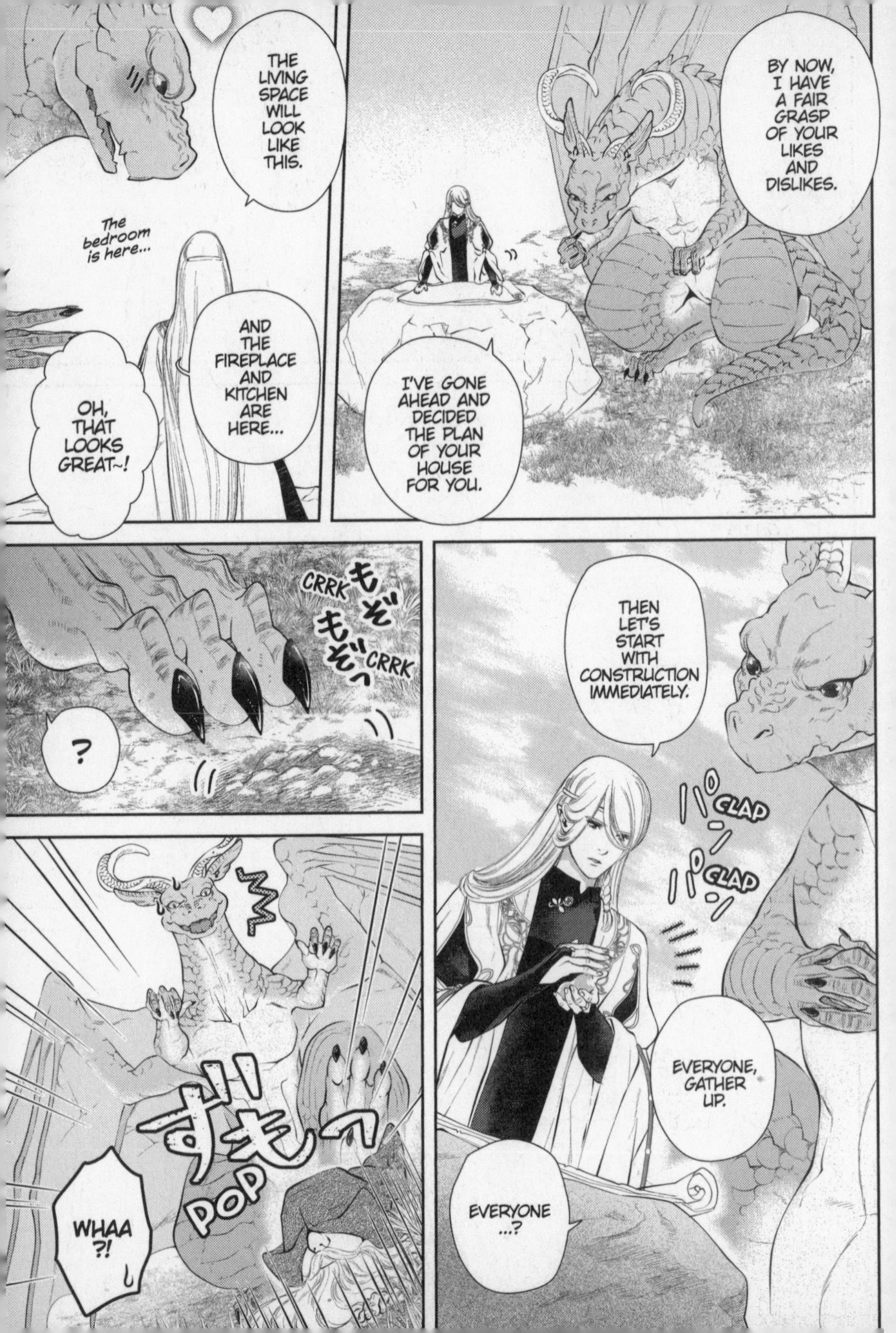

BY NOW, I HAVE A FAIR GRASP OF YOUR LIKES AND DISLIKES.
I'VE GONE AHEAD AND DECIDED THE PLAN OF YOUR HOUSE FOR YOU.
THE LIVING SPACE WILL LOOK LIKE THIS.
The bedroom is here...
AND THE FIREPLACE AND KITCHEN ARE HERE...
OH, THAT LOOKS GREAT~!
THEN LET'S START WITH CONSTRUCTION IMMEDIATELY.
CLAP
CLAP
EVERYONE, GATHER UP.
EVERYONE ...?
CRRK
もぞもぞ
CRRK
?
POP
WHAA ?!

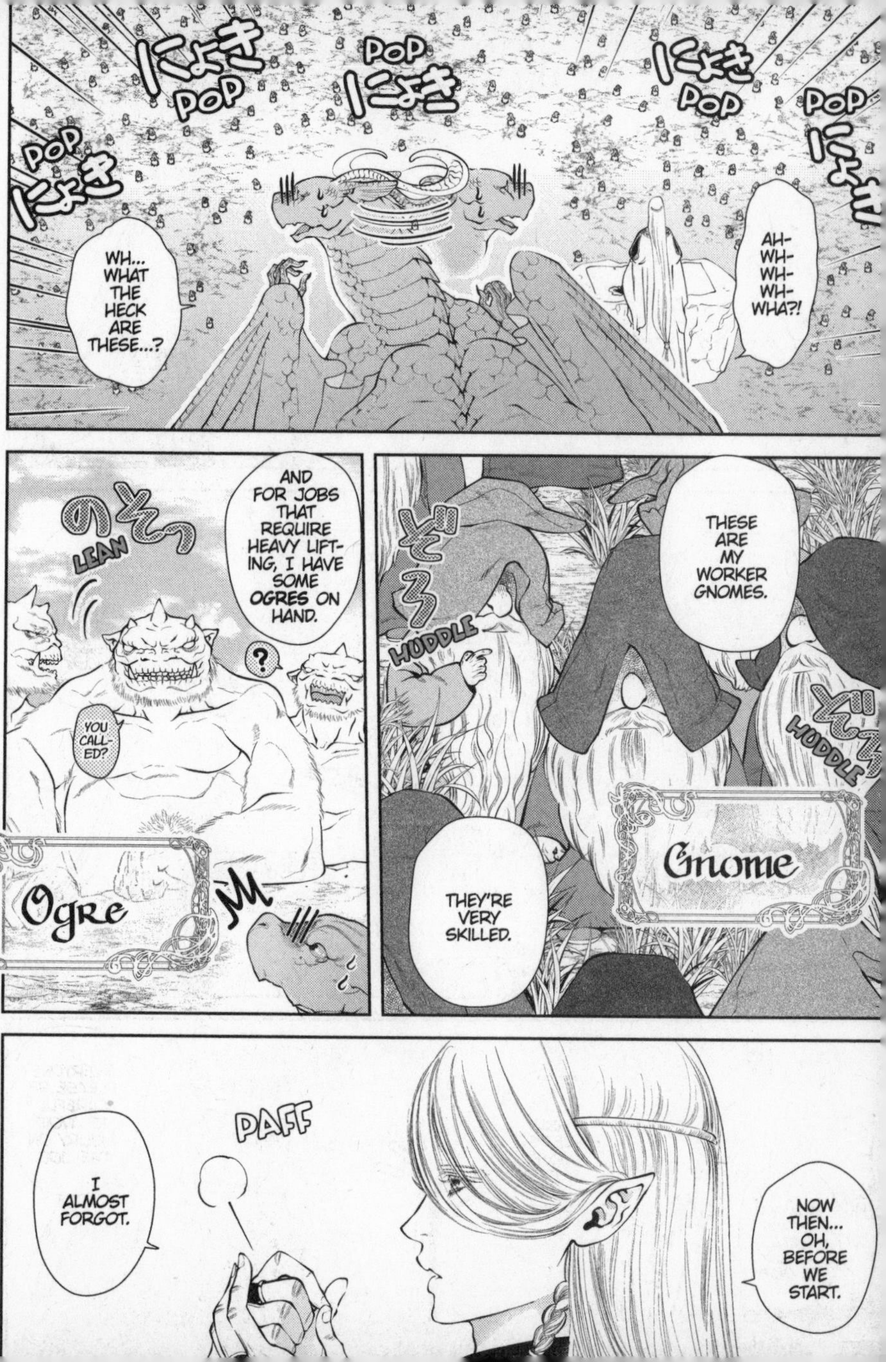
POP
にょき
にょき
POP
POP
にょき
にょき
POP
POP
にょき
AH-WH-WH-WH-WHA?!
WH... WHAT THE HECK ARE THESE...?
THESE ARE MY WORKER GNOMES.
ぞろ
HUDDLE
ぞろ
HUDDLE
Gnome
THEY'RE VERY SKILLED.
AND FOR JOBS THAT REQUIRE HEAVY LIFTING, I HAVE SOME OGRES ON HAND.
のそっ
LEAN
?
YOU CALLED?
Ogre
NOW THEN... OH, BEFORE WE START.
PAFF
I ALMOST FORGOT.

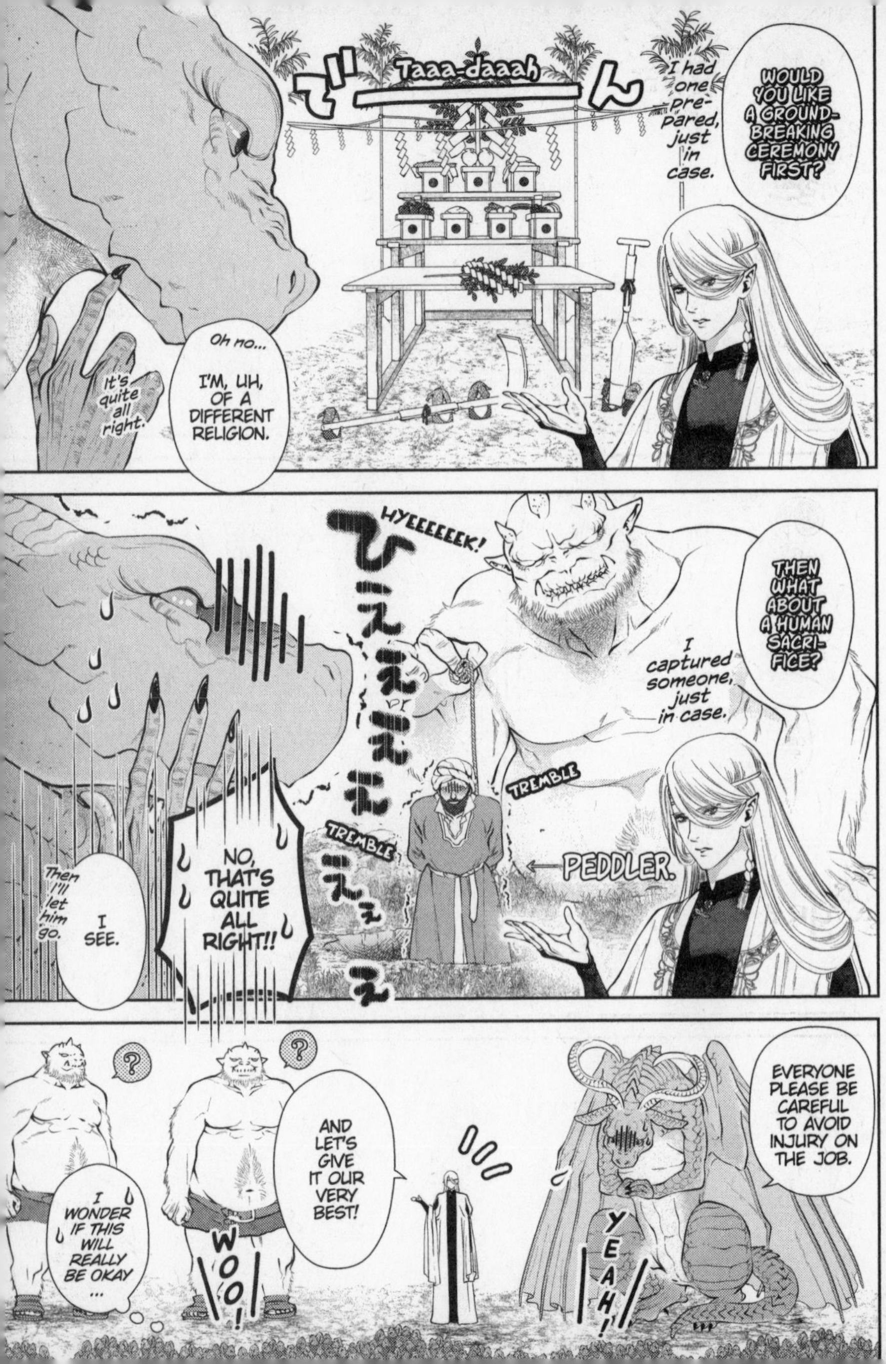
WOULD YOU LIKE A GROUND-BREAKING CEREMONY FIRST?
I had one prepared, just in case.
でーん
Taaa-daaah
Oh no...
I'M, UH, OF A DIFFERENT RELIGION.
It's quite all right.
THEN WHAT ABOUT A HUMAN SACRIFICE?
I captured someone, just in case.
PEDDLER.
HYEEEEEEK!
ひえええええぇぇ
TREMBLE
TREMBLE
NO, THAT'S QUITE ALL RIGHT!!
I SEE.
Then I'll let him go.
EVERYONE PLEASE BE CAREFUL TO AVOID INJURY ON THE JOB.
YEAH!
AND LET'S GIVE IT OUR VERY BEST!
WOO!
?
?
I WONDER IF THIS WILL REALLY BE OKAY...

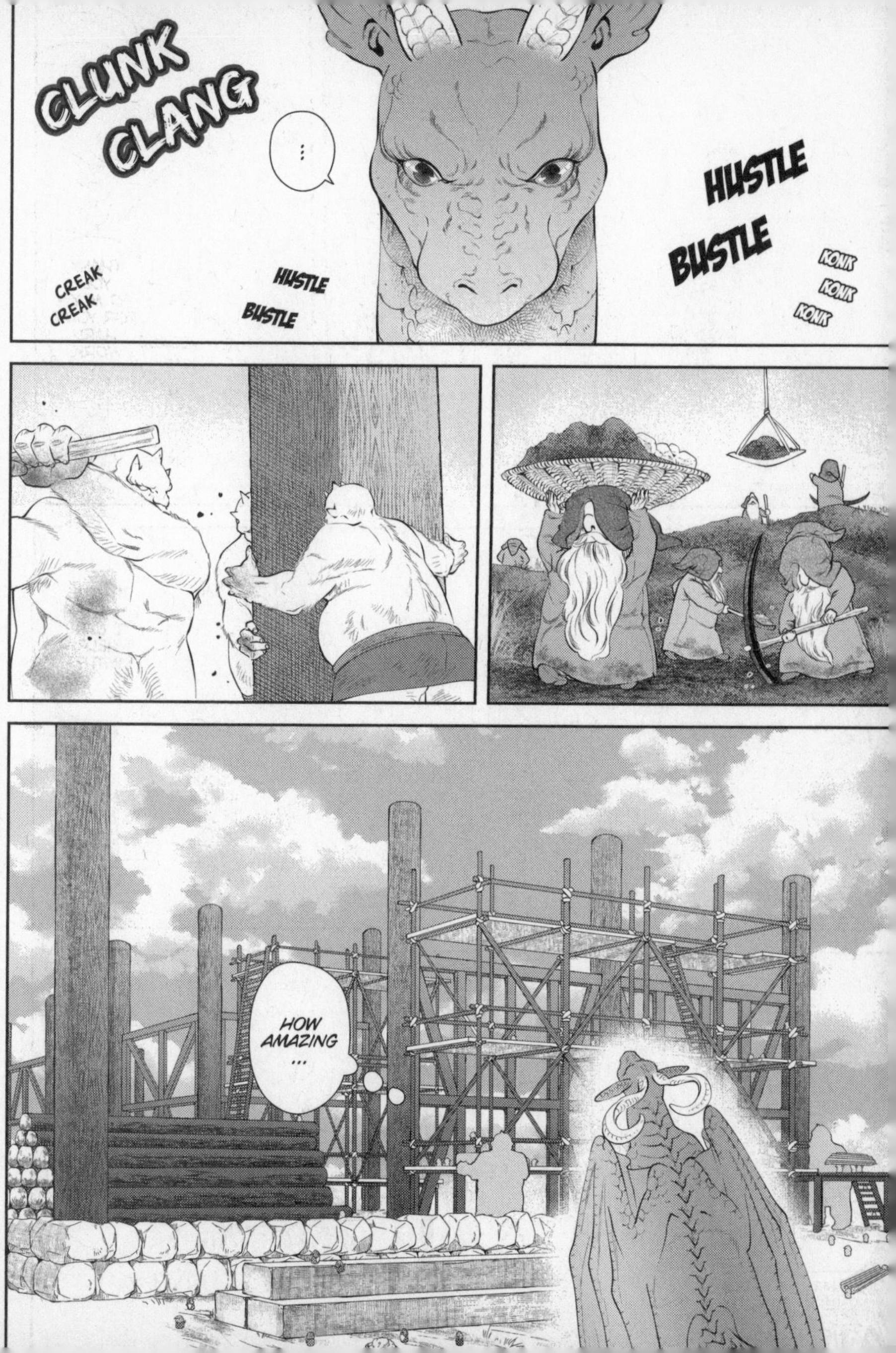
HUSTLE
BUSTLE
KONK
KONK
KONK
...
CLUNK
CLANG
HUSTLE
BUSTLE
CREAK
CREAK
HOW AMAZING ...

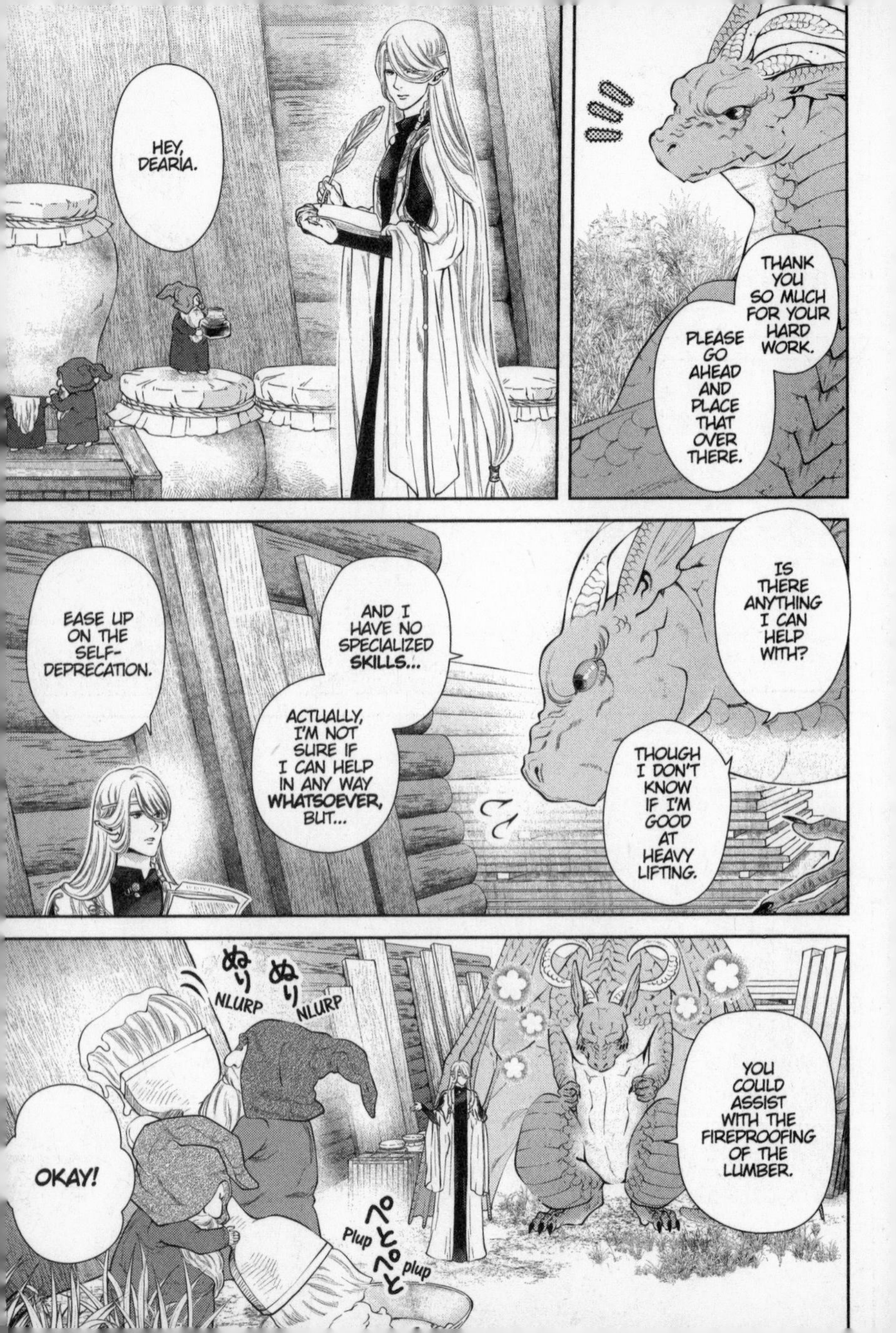
THANK YOU SO MUCH FOR YOUR HARD WORK.
PLEASE GO AHEAD AND PLACE THAT OVER THERE.
HEY, DEARIA.
IS THERE ANYTHING I CAN HELP WITH?
THOUGH I DON'T KNOW IF I'M GOOD AT HEAVY LIFTING.
ACTUALLY, I'M NOT SURE IF I CAN HELP IN ANY WAY WHATSOEVER, BUT...
AND I HAVE NO SPECIALIZED SKILLS...
EASE UP ON THE SELF-DEPRECATION.
YOU COULD ASSIST WITH THE FIREPROOFING OF THE LUMBER.
ぬり NLURP
ぬり NLURP
OKAY!
ぺと Plup
ぺと plup

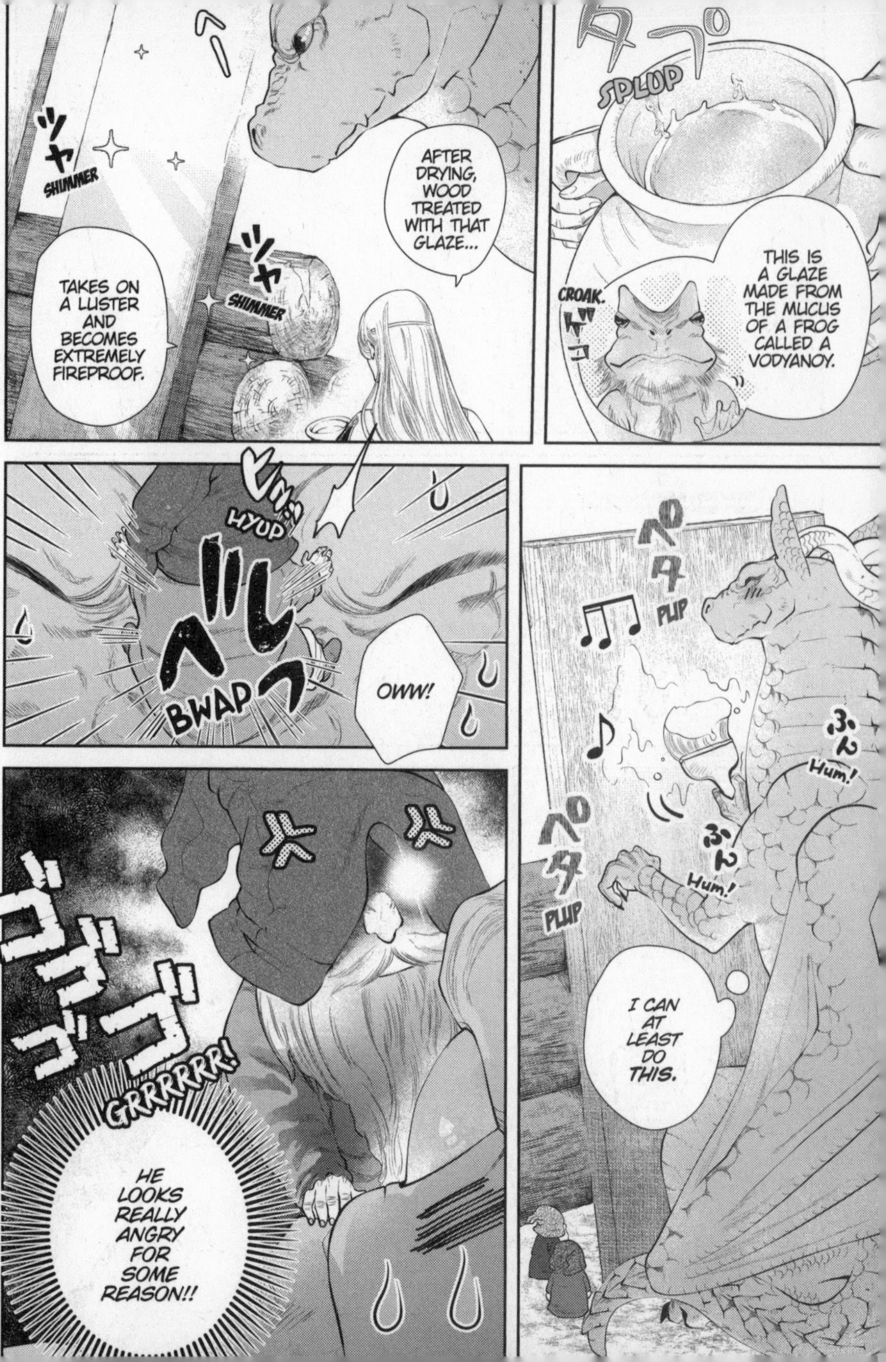

SPLUP
THIS IS A GLAZE MADE FROM THE MUCUS OF A FROG CALLED A VODYANOY.
CROAK.
ツヤ
SHIMMER
AFTER DRYING, WOOD TREATED WITH THAT GLAZE...
ツヤ
SHIMMER
TAKES ON A LUSTER AND BECOMES EXTREMELY FIREPROOF.
ペタ
PLUP
ふん
Hum!
ふん
Hum!
ペタ
PLUP
I CAN AT LEAST DO THIS.
HYUP
BWAP
OWW!
GRRRRRR!
HE LOOKS REALLY ANGRY FOR SOME REASON!!

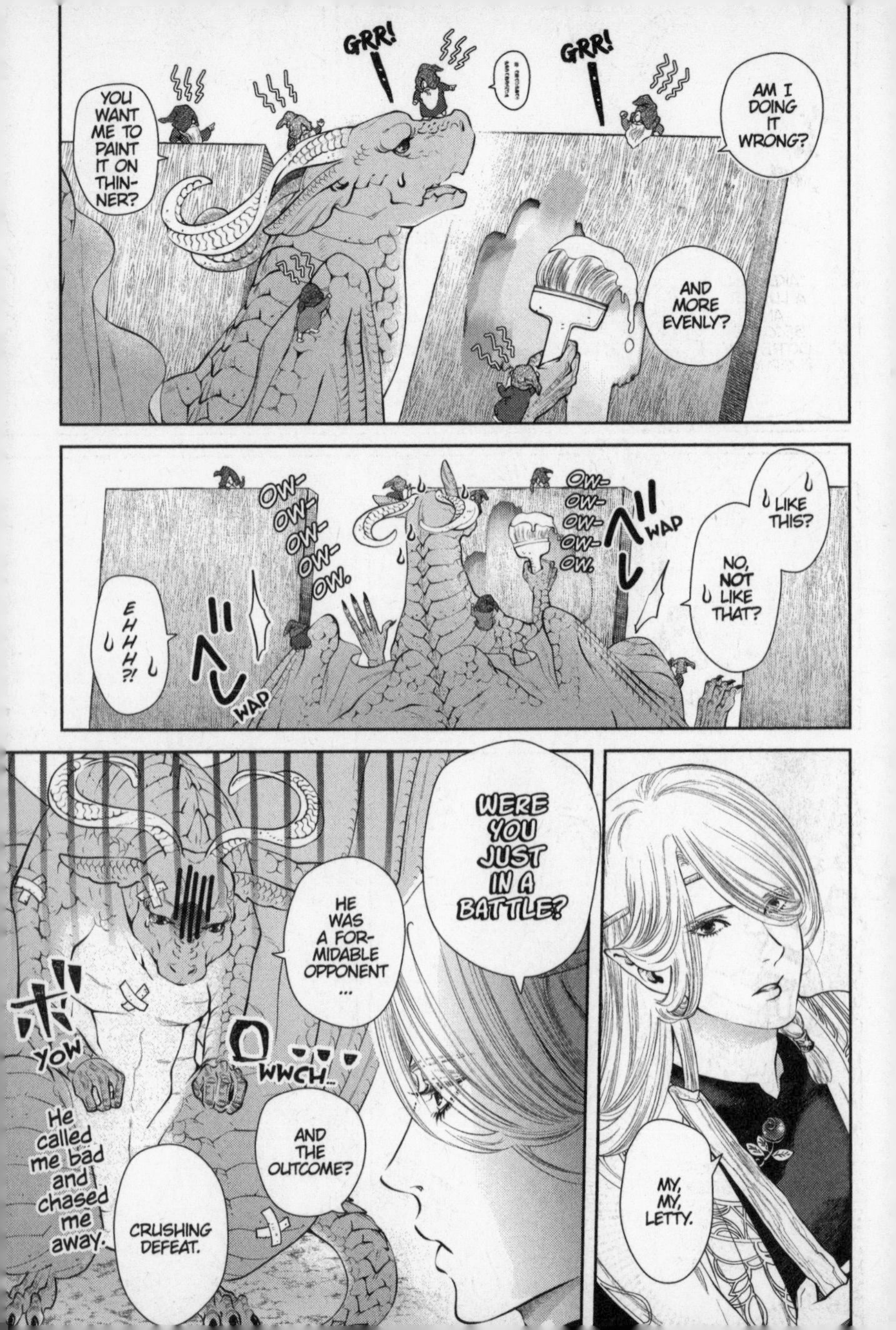
AM I DOING IT WRONG?
GRR!
GRR!
YOU WANT ME TO PAINT IT ON THIN-NER?
AND MORE EVENLY?
LIKE THIS?
NO, NOT LIKE THAT?
OW-OW-OW-OW-OW.
WAP
OW-OW-OW-OW-OW.
EHHH?!
WAP
MY, MY, LETTY.
WERE YOU JUST IN A BATTLE?
HE WAS A FOR-MIDABLE OPPONENT...
AND THE OUTCOME?
CRUSHING DEFEAT.
OWWCH...
YOW
He called me bad and chased me away.

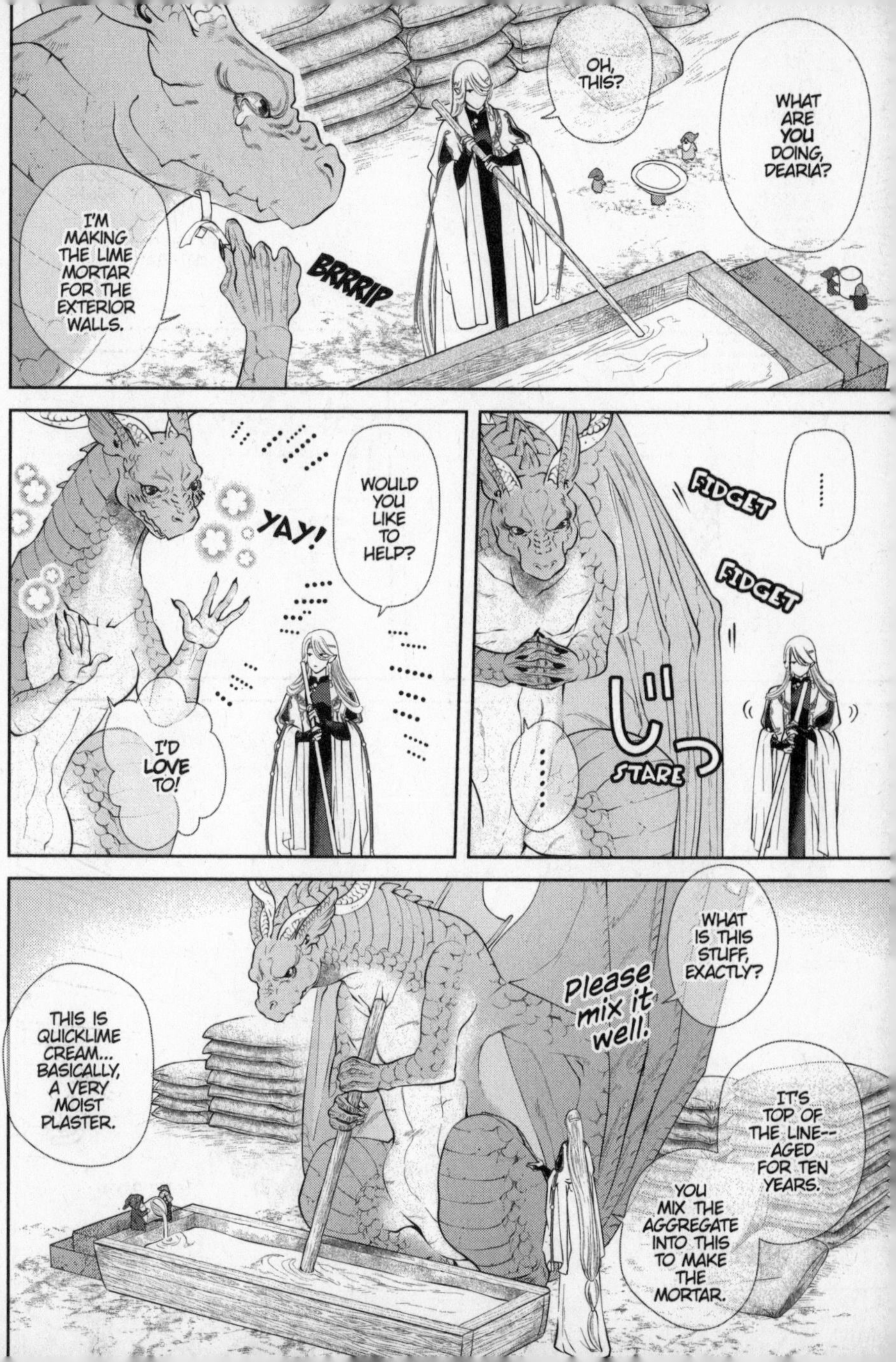

WHAT ARE YOU DOING, DEARIA?
OH, THIS?
BRRRRIP
I'M MAKING THE LIME MORTAR FOR THE EXTERIOR WALLS.
......
FIDGET
FIDGET
じっ
STARE
......
WOULD YOU LIKE TO HELP?
YAY!
I'D LOVE TO!
WHAT IS THIS STUFF, EXACTLY?
IT'S TOP OF THE LINE--AGED FOR TEN YEARS.
YOU MIX THE AGGREGATE INTO THIS TO MAKE THE MORTAR.
Please mix it well.
THIS IS QUICKLIME CREAM... BASICALLY, A VERY MOIST PLASTER.

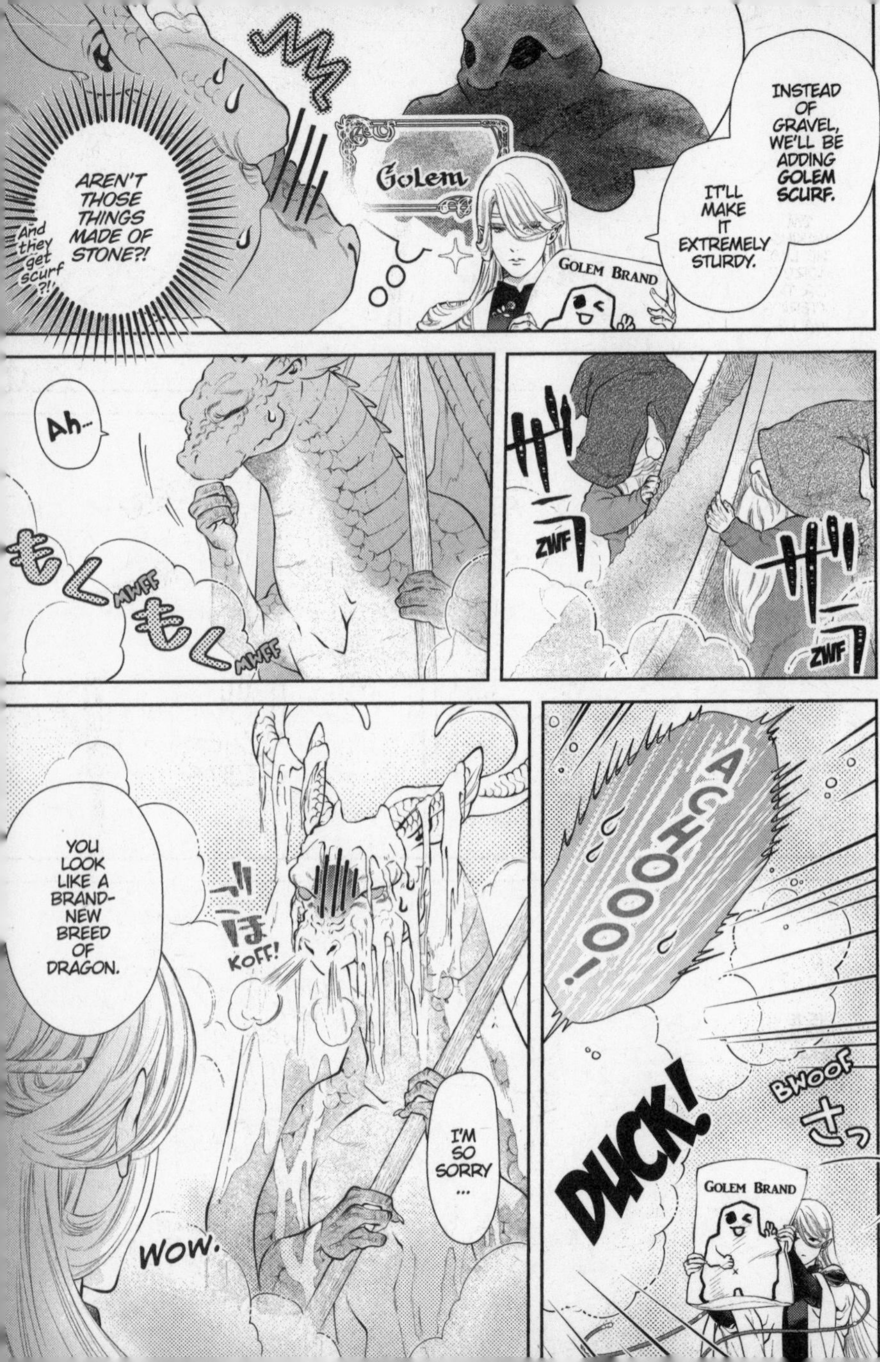

INSTEAD OF GRAVEL, WE'LL BE ADDING GOLEM SCURF.
IT'LL MAKE IT EXTREMELY STURDY.
Golem
GOLEM BRAND
AREN'T THOSE THINGS MADE OF STONE?!
And they get scurf?!
ザーッ
ZWF
ザーッ
ZWF
Ah...
もくもく
MWFF
もくもく
MWFF
ACHOOOO!
BWOOF
さっ
DUCK!
GOLEM BRAND
ごほ
KOFF!
YOU LOOK LIKE A BRAND-NEW BREED OF DRAGON.
I'M SO SORRY...
WOW.

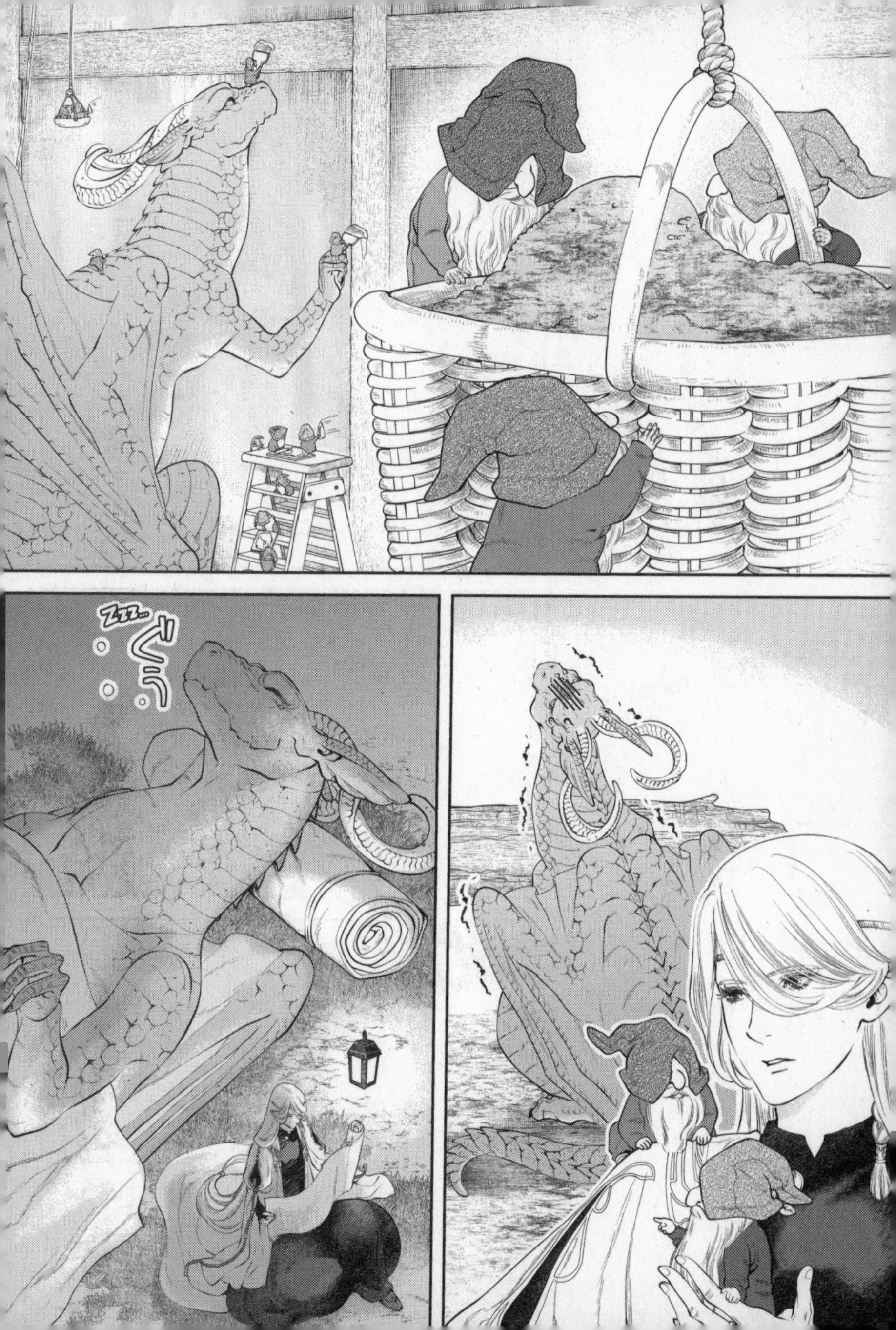
ZZZ...
ぐーー

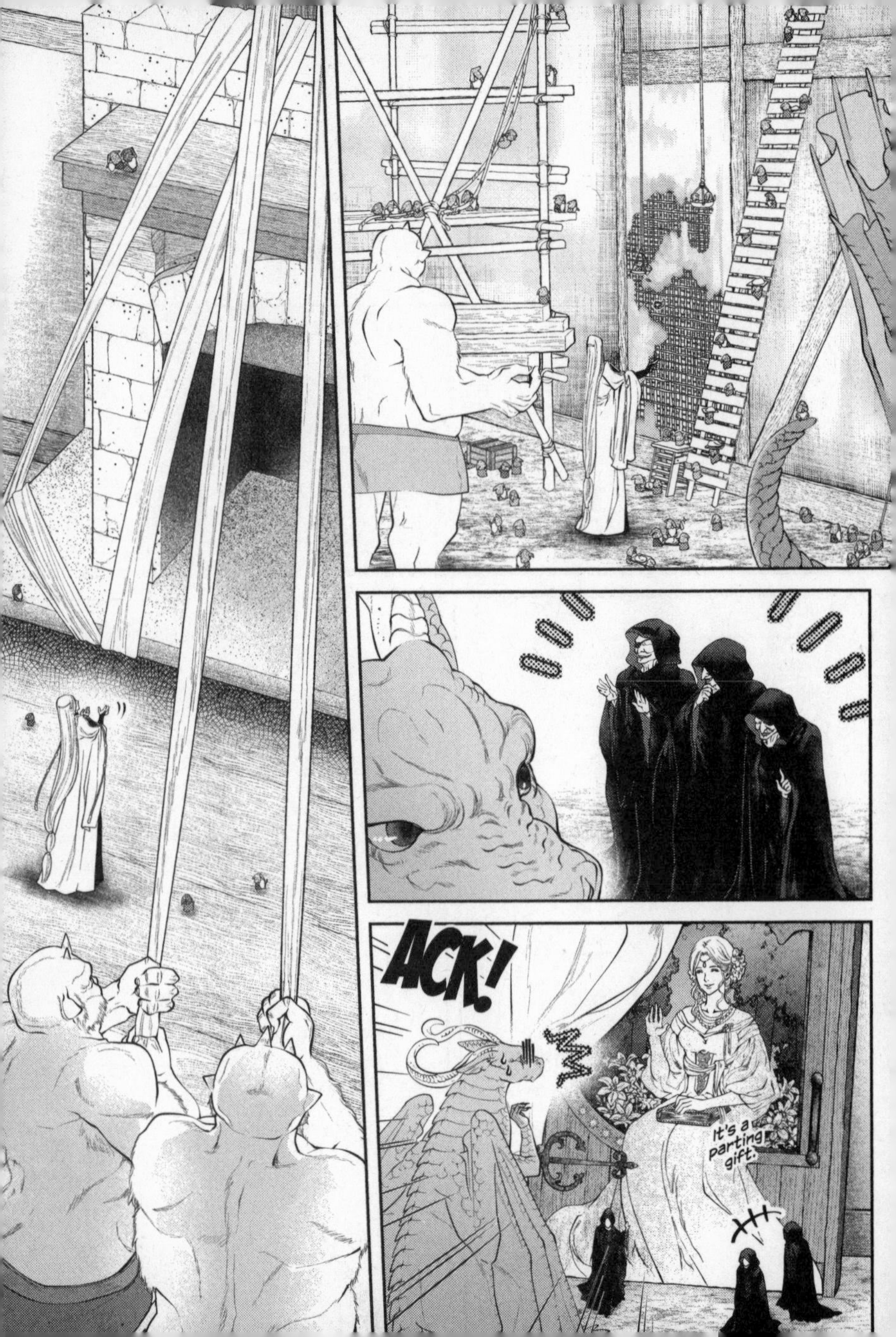
ACK!
MM
It's a parting gift.

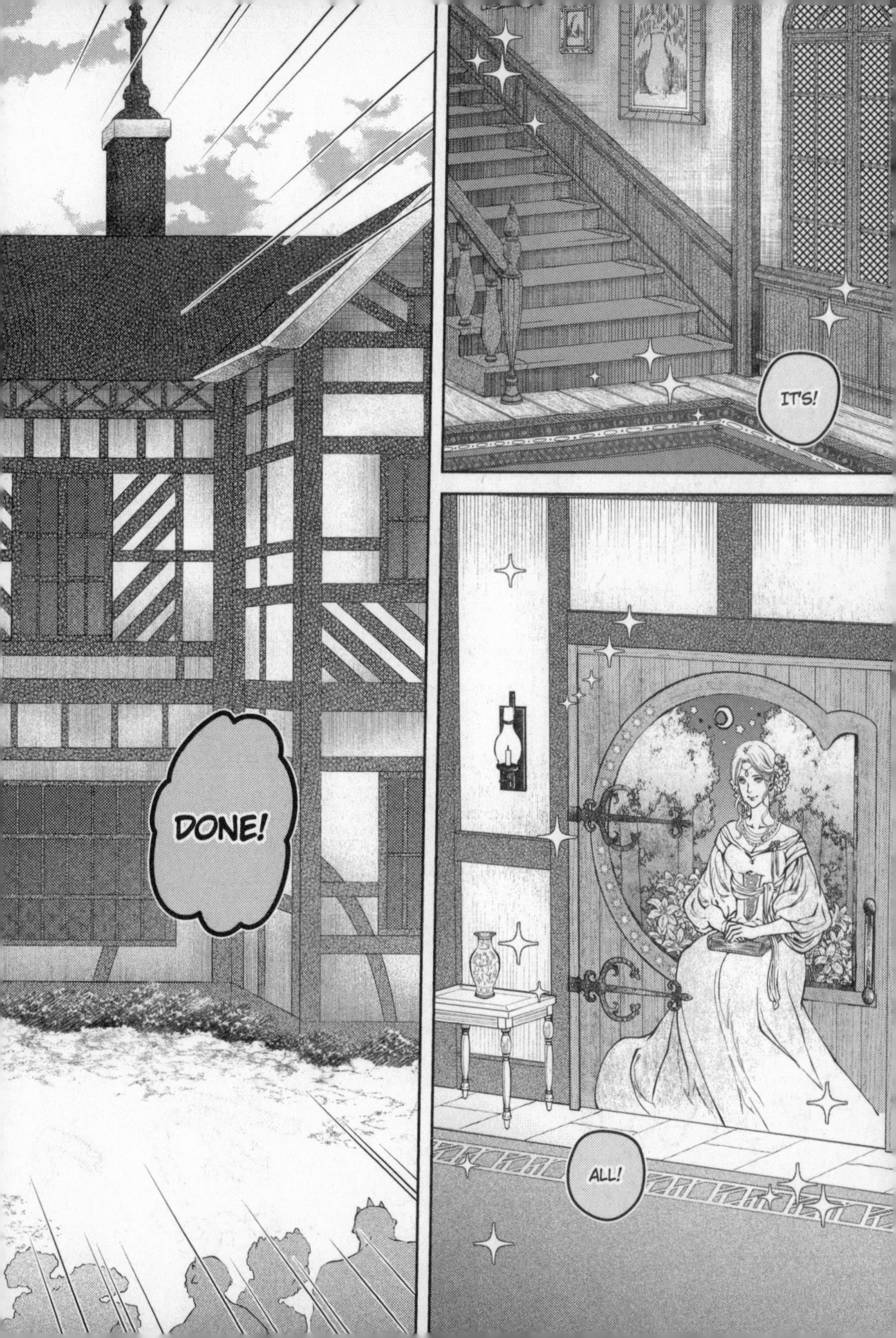
IT'S!
ALL!
DONE!

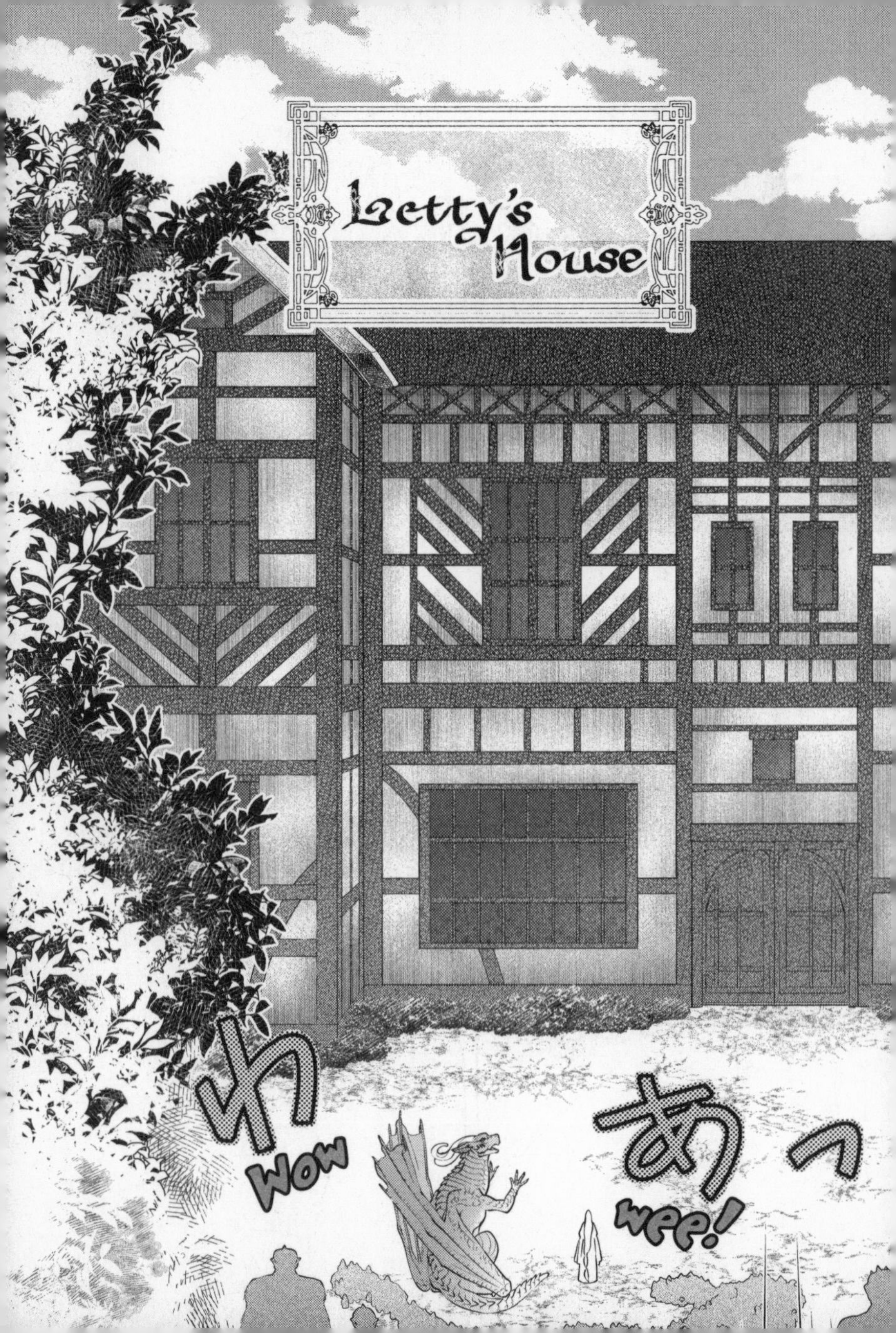
Letty's House
わあっ
WOW
WEE!

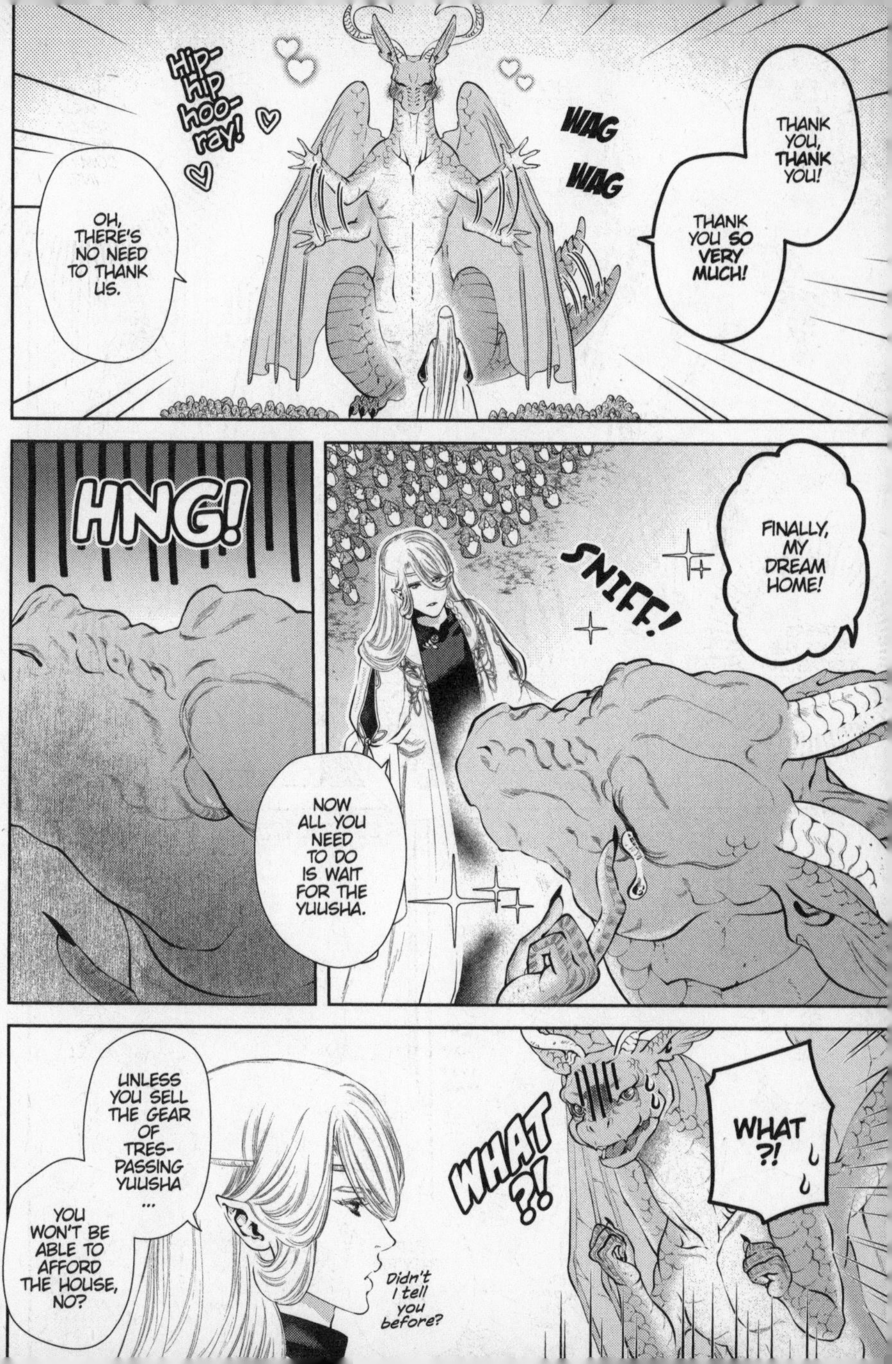
THANK YOU, THANK YOU!
THANK YOU SO VERY MUCH!
WAG
WAG
Hip-hip hoo-ray! ♡
OH, THERE'S NO NEED TO THANK US.
FINALLY, MY DREAM HOME!
SNIFF!
NOW ALL YOU NEED TO DO IS WAIT FOR THE YUUSHA.
HNG!
WHAT ?!
WHAT ?!
UNLESS YOU SELL THE GEAR OF TRES-PASSING YUUSHA ...
YOU WON'T BE ABLE TO AFFORD THE HOUSE, NO?
Didn't I tell you before?

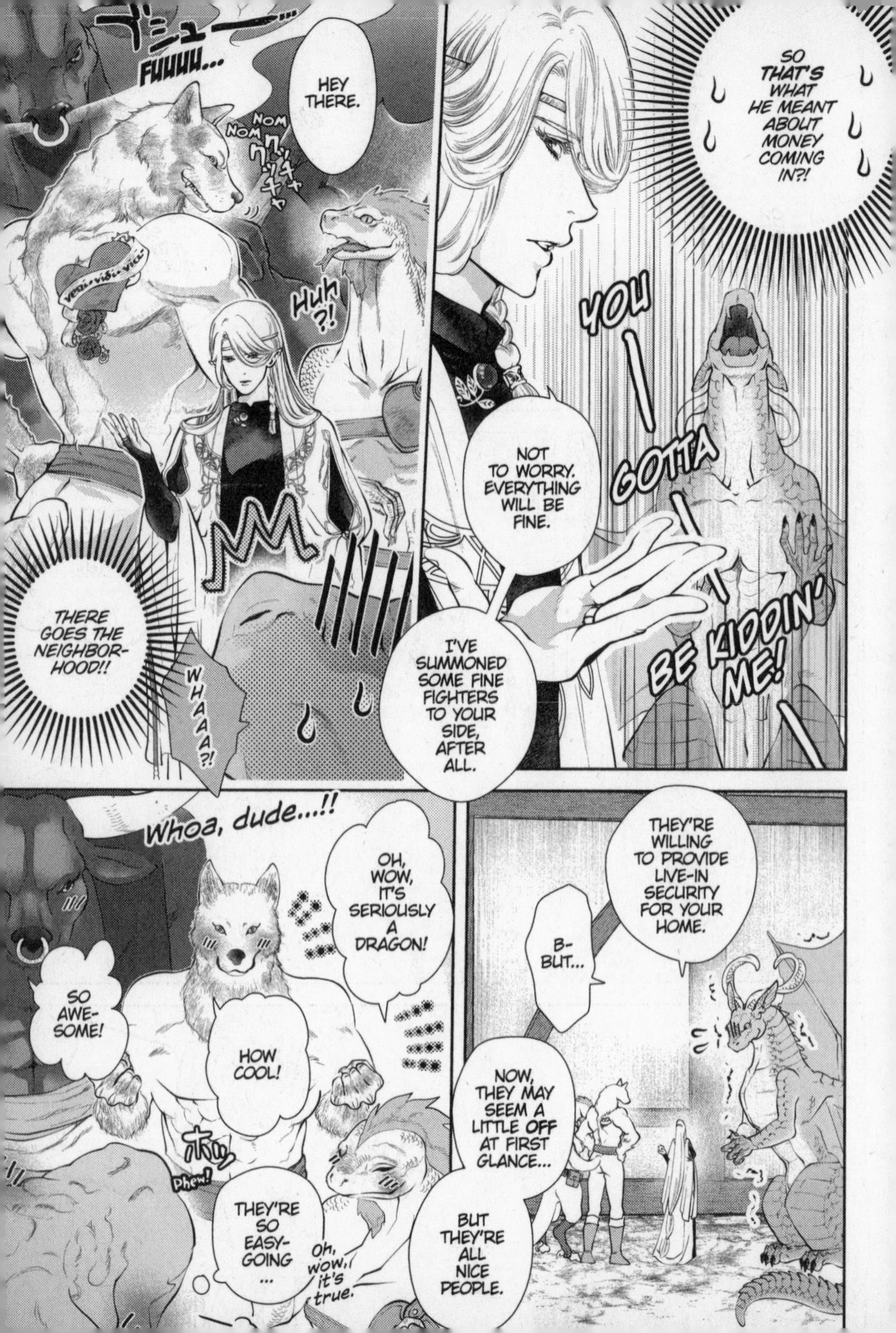
SO THAT'S WHAT HE MEANT ABOUT MONEY COMING IN?!
YOU GOTTA BE KIDDIN' ME!
NOT TO WORRY. EVERYTHING WILL BE FINE.
I'VE SUMMONED SOME FINE FIGHTERS TO YOUR SIDE, AFTER ALL.
FUUUU...
HEY THERE.
NOM NOM
Huh ?!
THERE GOES THE NEIGHBORHOOD!!
WHAAAA?!
THEY'RE WILLING TO PROVIDE LIVE-IN SECURITY FOR YOUR HOME.
B-BUT...
NOW, THEY MAY SEEM A LITTLE OFF AT FIRST GLANCE...
BUT THEY'RE ALL NICE PEOPLE.
Whoa, dude...!!
OH, WOW, IT'S SERIOUSLY A DRAGON!
SO AWE-SOME!
HOW COOL!
Phew!
THEY'RE SO EASY-GOING ...
Oh, wow, it's true.

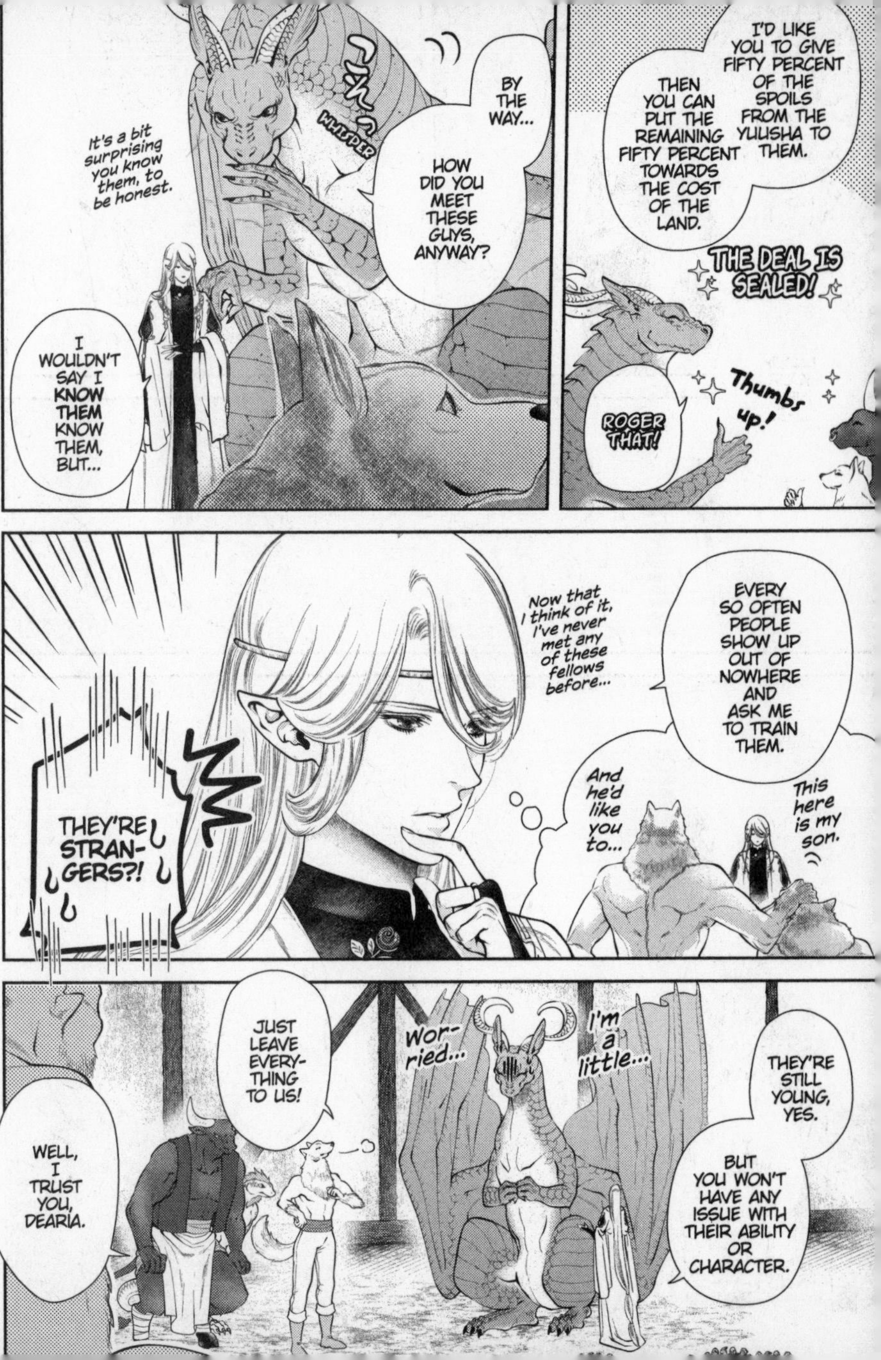
I'D LIKE YOU TO GIVE FIFTY PERCENT OF THE SPOILS FROM THE YUUSHA TO THEM.
THEN YOU CAN PUT THE REMAINING FIFTY PERCENT TOWARDS THE COST OF THE LAND.
THE DEAL IS SEALED!
Thumbs up!
ROGER THAT!
BY THE WAY...
HOW DID YOU MEET THESE GUYS, ANYWAY?
WHISPER
It's a bit surprising you know them, to be honest.
I WOULDN'T SAY I KNOW THEM KNOW THEM, BUT...
EVERY SO OFTEN PEOPLE SHOW UP OUT OF NOWHERE AND ASK ME TO TRAIN THEM.
Now that I think of it, I've never met any of these fellows before...
This here is my son.
And he'd like you to...
THEY'RE STRANGERS?!
THEY'RE STILL YOUNG, YES.
BUT YOU WON'T HAVE ANY ISSUE WITH THEIR ABILITY OR CHARACTER.
I'm a little...
Wor-ried...
JUST LEAVE EVERY-THING TO US!
WELL, I TRUST YOU, DEARIA.

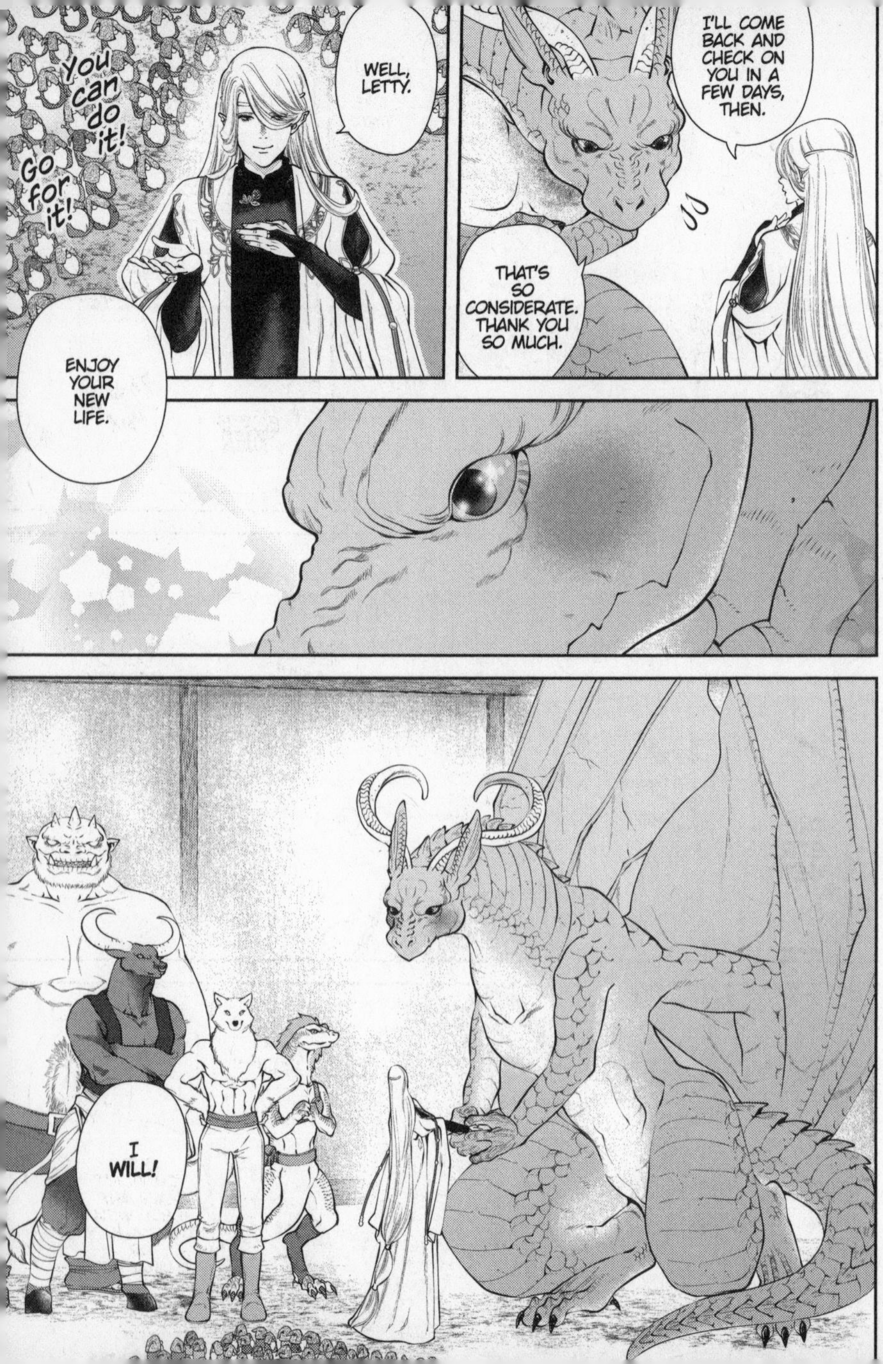
I'LL COME BACK AND CHECK ON YOU IN A FEW DAYS, THEN.
THAT'S SO CONSIDERATE. THANK YOU SO MUCH.
WELL, LETTY.
You can do it!
Go for it!
ENJOY YOUR NEW LIFE.
I WILL!

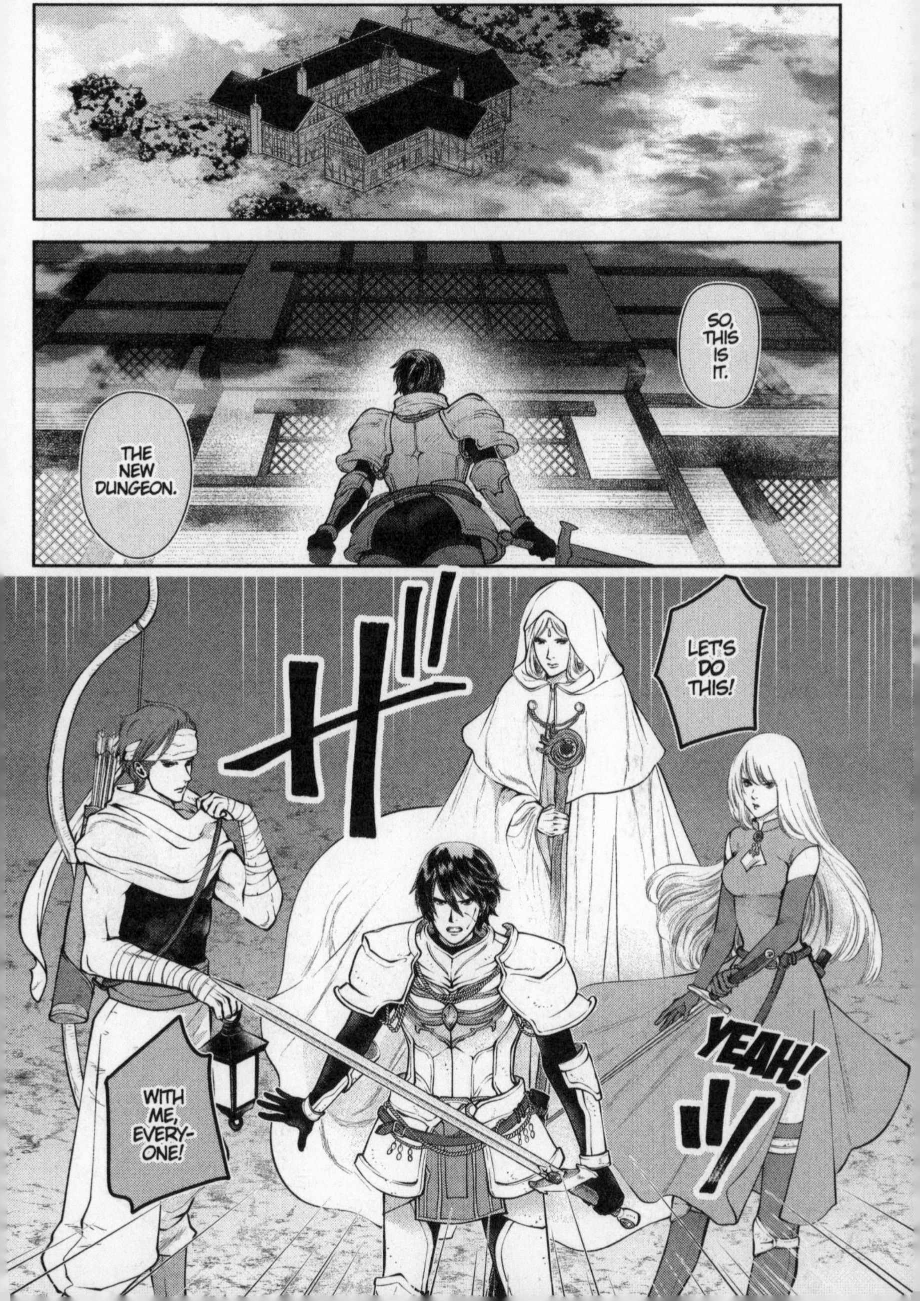
SO, THIS IS IT.
THE NEW DUNGEON.
LET'S DO THIS!
YEAH!
WITH ME, EVERY-ONE!

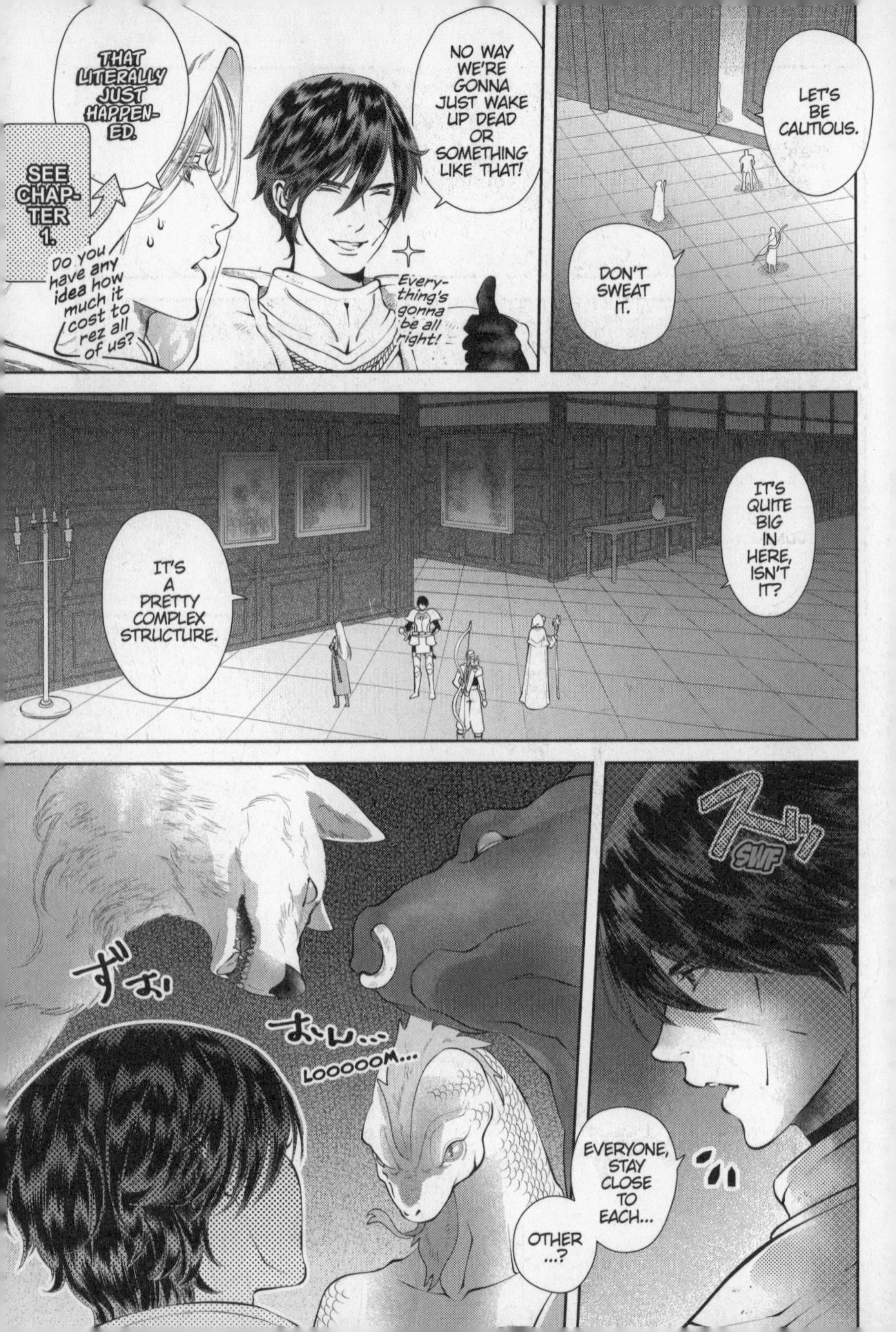
LET'S BE CAUTIOUS.
DON'T SWEAT IT.
NO WAY WE'RE GONNA JUST WAKE UP DEAD OR SOMETHING LIKE THAT!
THAT LITERALLY JUST HAPPEN-ED.
SEE CHAP-TER 1.
Every-thing's gonna be all right!
Do you have any idea how much it cost to rez all of us?
IT'S QUITE BIG IN HERE, ISN'T IT?
IT'S A PRETTY COMPLEX STRUCTURE.
SWF
EVERYONE, STAY CLOSE TO EACH...
OTHER ...?
LOOOOOM...

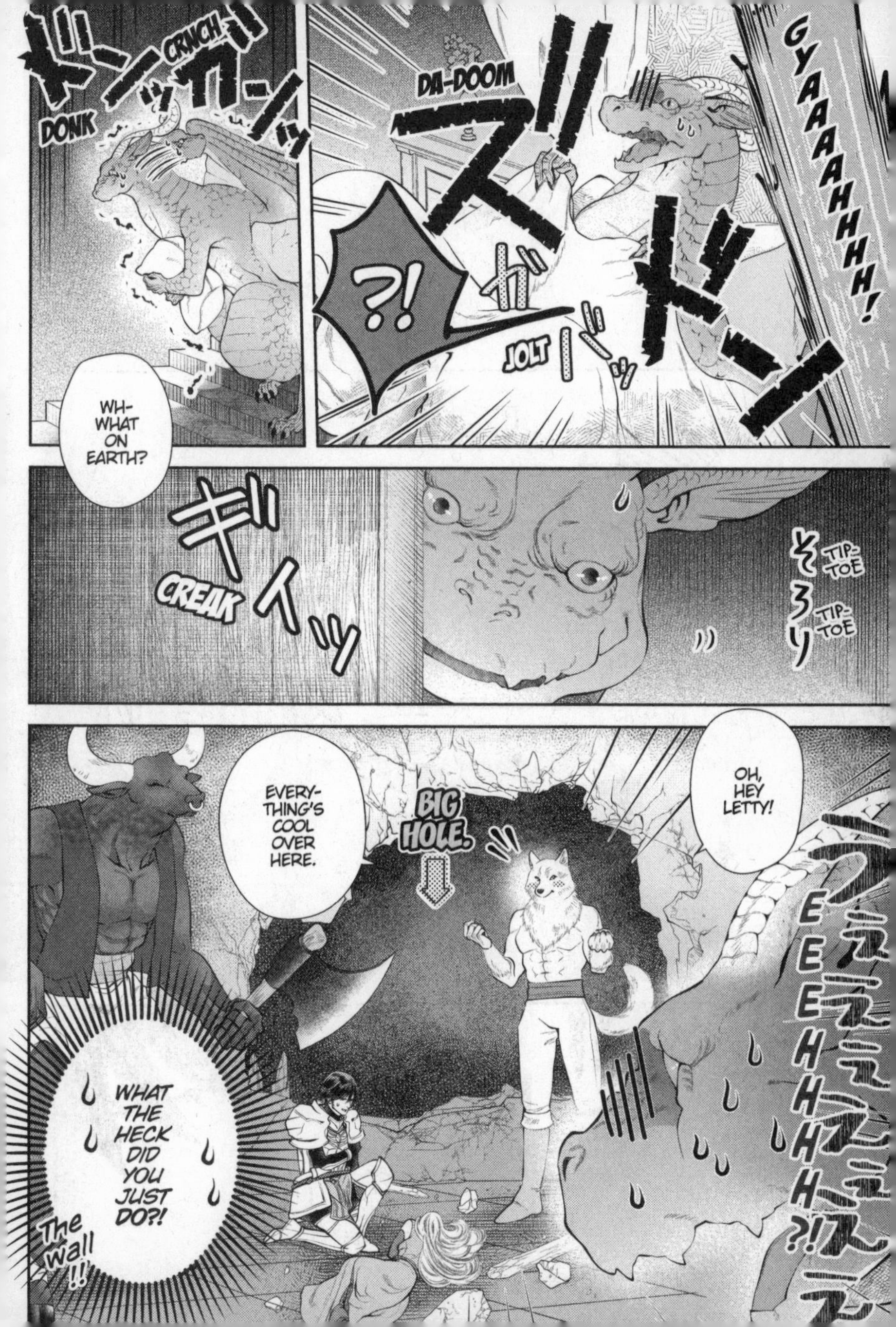
GYAAAAHHHHH!
DA-DOOM
?!
JOLT
CRNCH
DONK
WH-WHAT ON EARTH?
TIP-TOE
TIP-TOE
CREAK
OH, HEY LETTY!
EEEEHHHHH?!
EVERYTHING'S COOL OVER HERE.
BIG HOLE.
WHAT THE HECK DID YOU JUST DO?!
The wall!!

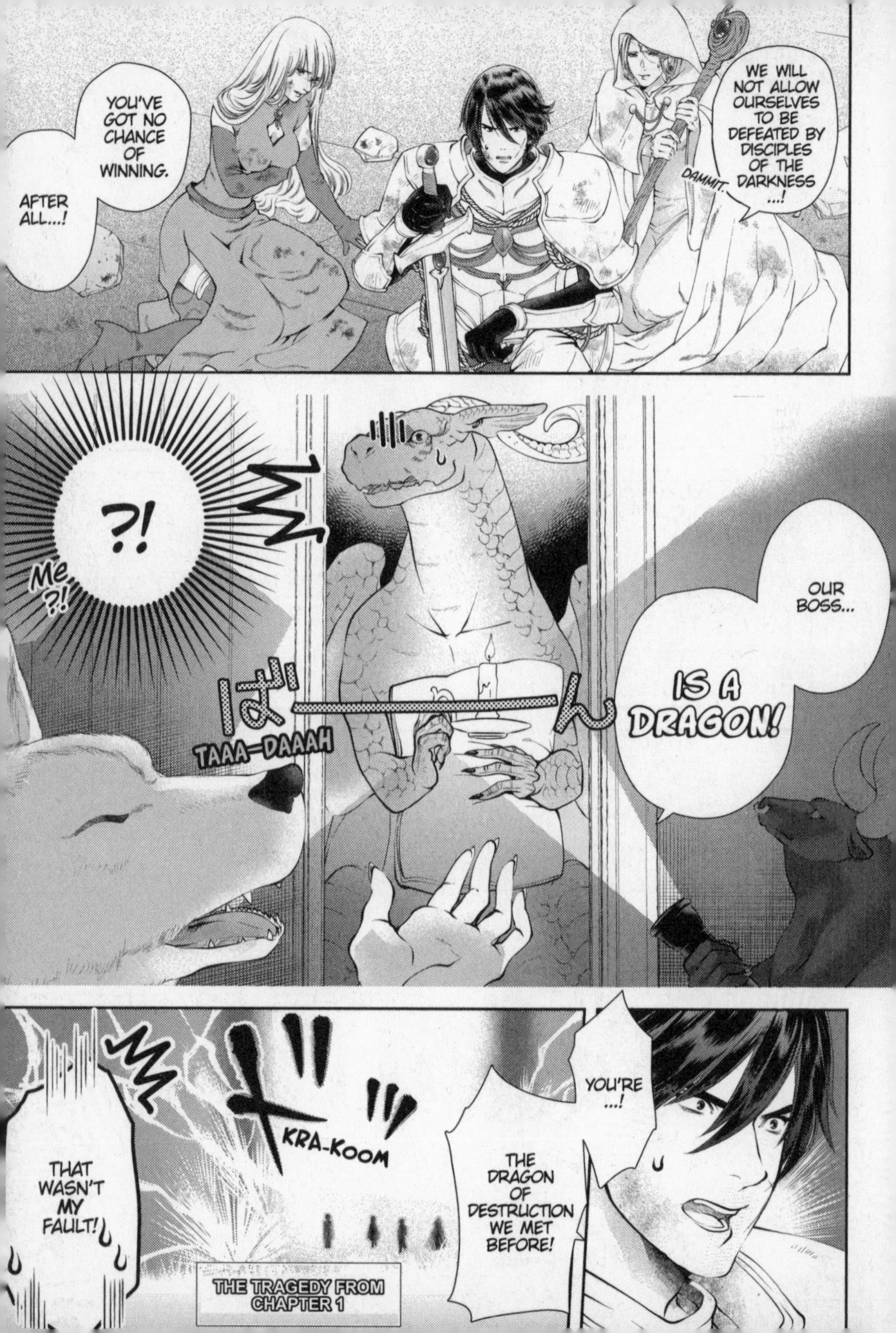
WE WILL NOT ALLOW OURSELVES TO BE DEFEATED BY DISCIPLES OF THE DARKNESS ...!
DAMMIT.
YOU'VE GOT NO CHANCE OF WINNING.
AFTER ALL...!
OUR BOSS...
IS A DRAGON!
ば———ん
TAAA-DAAAH
?!
Me ?!
YOU'RE ...!
THE DRAGON OF DESTRUCTION WE MET BEFORE!
KRA-KOOM
THAT WASN'T MY FAULT!
THE TRAGEDY FROM CHAPTER 1

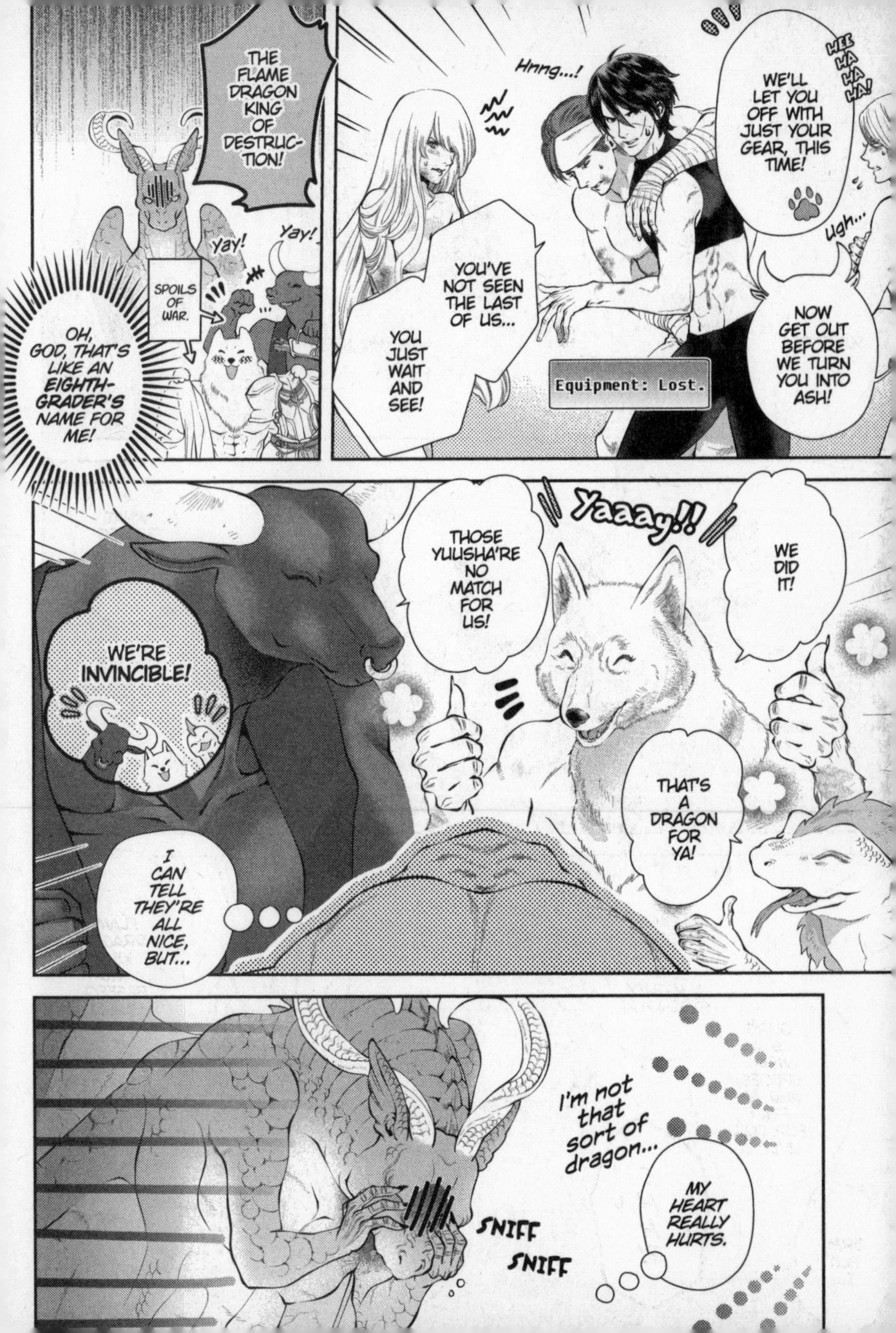
HEE HA HA HA!
WE'LL LET YOU OFF WITH JUST YOUR GEAR, THIS TIME!
Hnng...!
Ugh...
NOW GET OUT BEFORE WE TURN YOU INTO ASH!
Equipment: Lost.
YOU'VE NOT SEEN THE LAST OF US...
YOU JUST WAIT AND SEE!
THE FLAME DRAGON KING OF DESTRUCTION!
Yay!
Yay!
SPOILS OF WAR.
OH, GOD, THAT'S LIKE AN EIGHTH-GRADER'S NAME FOR ME!
WE DID IT!
Yaaay!!
THOSE YUUSHA'RE NO MATCH FOR US!
THAT'S A DRAGON FOR YA!
WE'RE INVINCIBLE!
I CAN TELL THEY'RE ALL NICE, BUT...
I'm not that sort of dragon...
MY HEART REALLY HURTS.
SNIFF
SNIFF

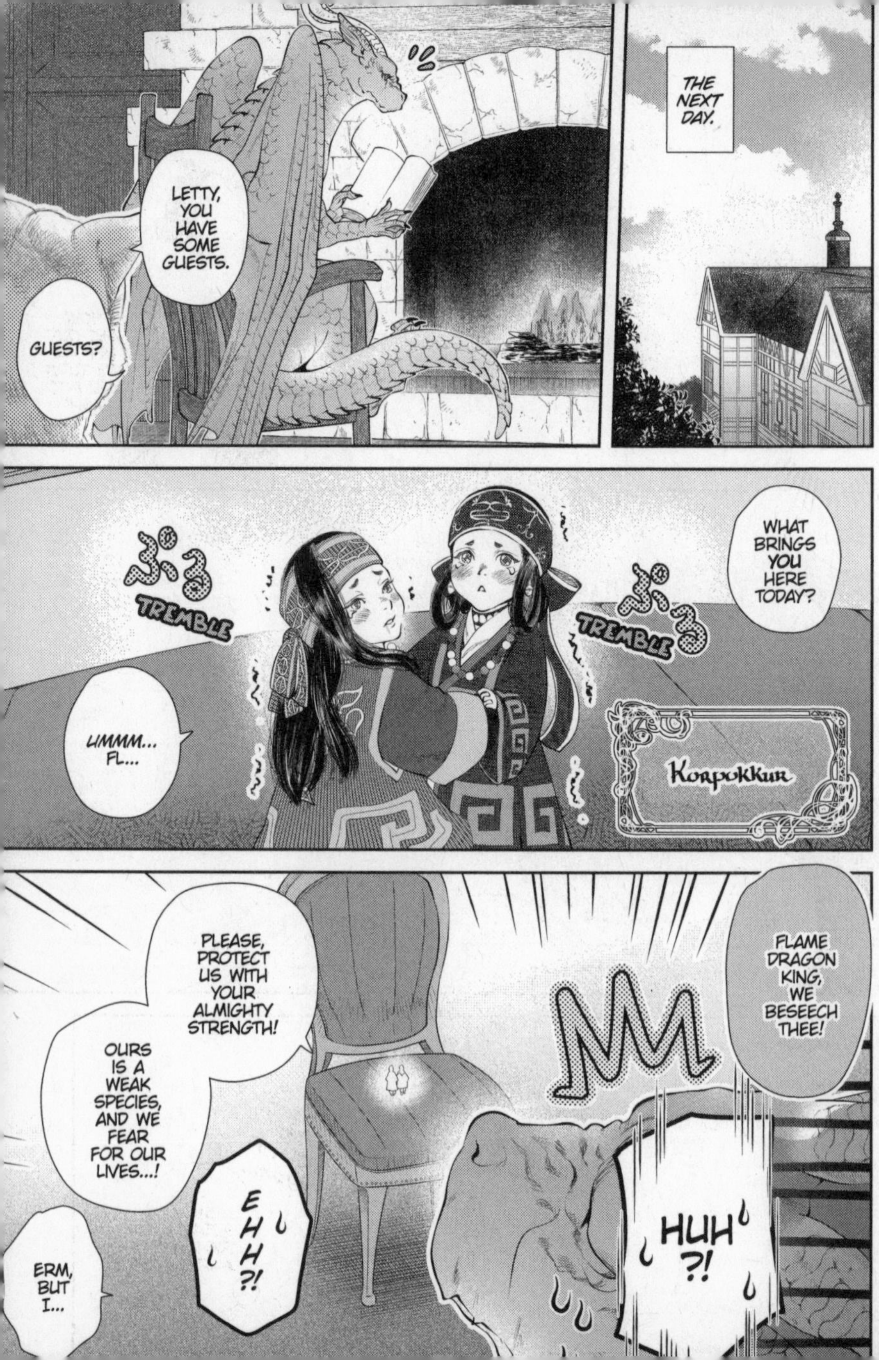
THE NEXT DAY.
LETTY, YOU HAVE SOME GUESTS.
GUESTS?
WHAT BRINGS YOU HERE TODAY?
ぷる TREMBLE
ぷる TREMBLE
Korpokkur
UMMM... FL...
FLAME DRAGON KING, WE BESEECH THEE!
MM
PLEASE, PROTECT US WITH YOUR ALMIGHTY STRENGTH!
OURS IS A WEAK SPECIES, AND WE FEAR FOR OUR LIVES...!
HUH?!
EHH?!
ERM, BUT I...

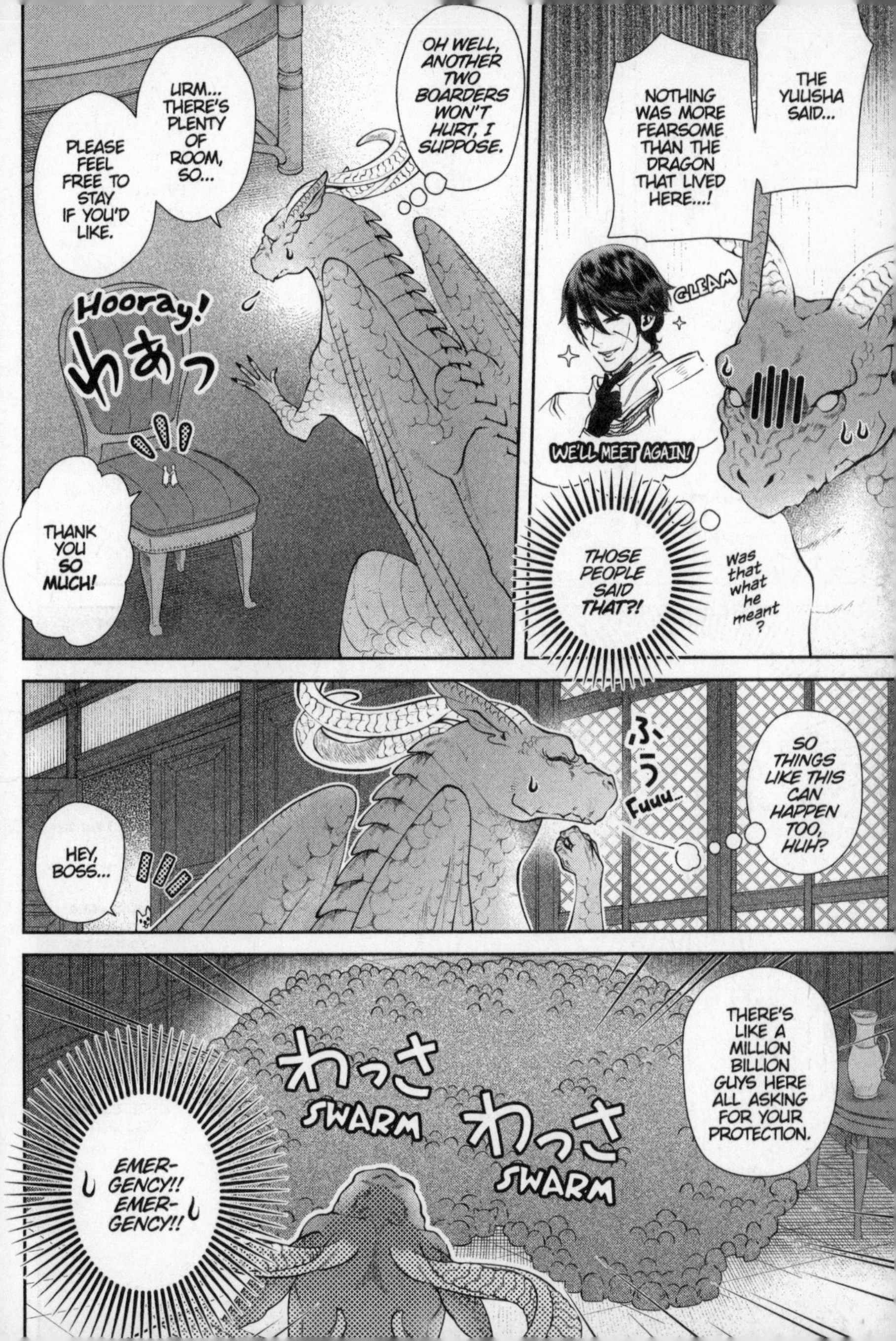
THE YUUSHA SAID...
NOTHING WAS MORE FEARSOME THAN THE DRAGON THAT LIVED HERE...!
GLEAM
WE'LL MEET AGAIN!
THOSE PEOPLE SAID THAT?!
Was that what he meant?
OH WELL, ANOTHER TWO BOARDERS WON'T HURT, I SUPPOSE.
URM... THERE'S PLENTY OF ROOM, SO...
PLEASE FEEL FREE TO STAY IF YOU'D LIKE.
Hooray!
わあっ
THANK YOU SO MUCH!
SO THINGS LIKE THIS CAN HAPPEN TOO, HUH?
ふう
Fuuu..
HEY, BOSS...
THERE'S LIKE A MILLION BILLION GUYS HERE ALL ASKING FOR YOUR PROTECTION.
わっさ
SWARM
わっさ
SWARM
EMERGENCY!! EMERGENCY!!

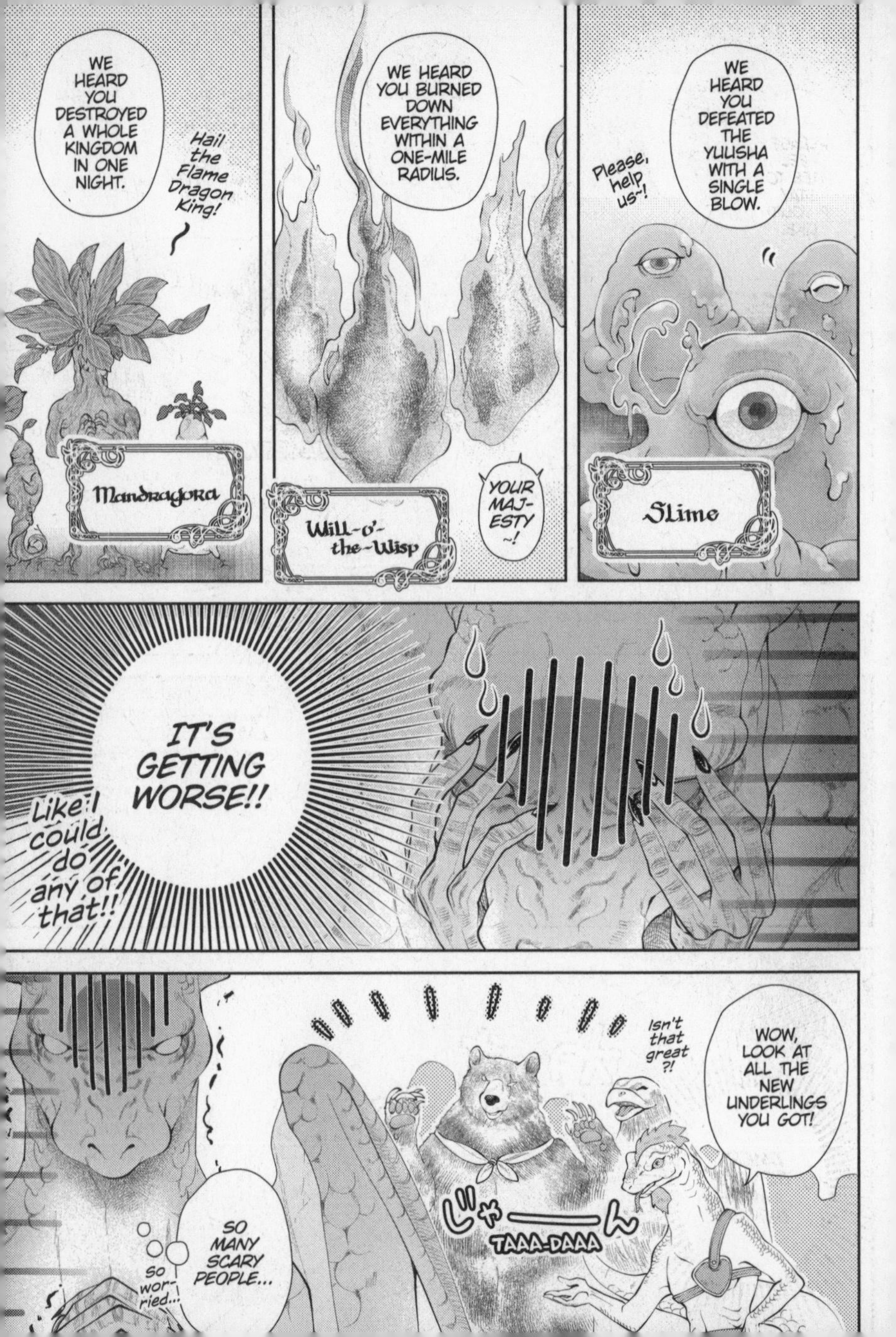
WE HEARD YOU DEFEATED THE YUUSHA WITH A SINGLE BLOW.
Please, help us~!
Slime
WE HEARD YOU BURNED DOWN EVERYTHING WITHIN A ONE-MILE RADIUS.
YOUR MAJ-ESTY~!
Will-o'-the-Wisp
WE HEARD YOU DESTROYED A WHOLE KINGDOM IN ONE NIGHT.
Hail the Flame Dragon King!
Mandragora
IT'S GETTING WORSE!!
Like I could do any of that!!
WOW, LOOK AT ALL THE NEW UNDERLINGS YOU GOT!
Isn't that great?!
じゃーーん
TAAA-DAAA
SO MANY SCARY PEOPLE...
So wor-ried...!

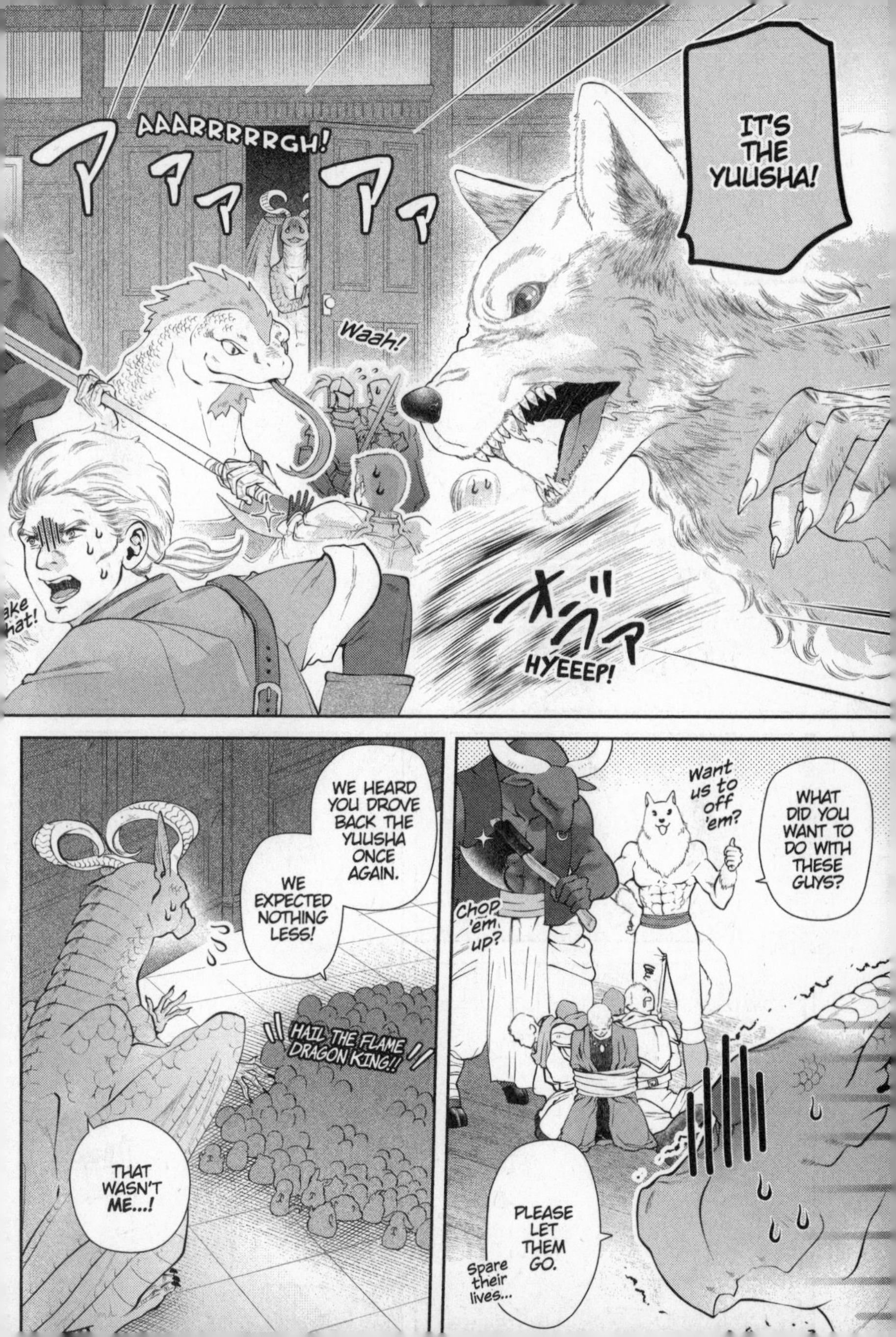
IT'S THE YUUSHA!
AAARRRRRGH!
Waah!
HYEEEP!
WHAT DID YOU WANT TO DO WITH THESE GUYS?
Want us to off 'em?
Chop 'em up?
PLEASE LET THEM GO.
Spare their lives...
WE HEARD YOU DROVE BACK THE YUUSHA ONCE AGAIN.
WE EXPECTED NOTHING LESS!
HAIL THE FLAME DRAGON KING!!
THAT WASN'T ME...!

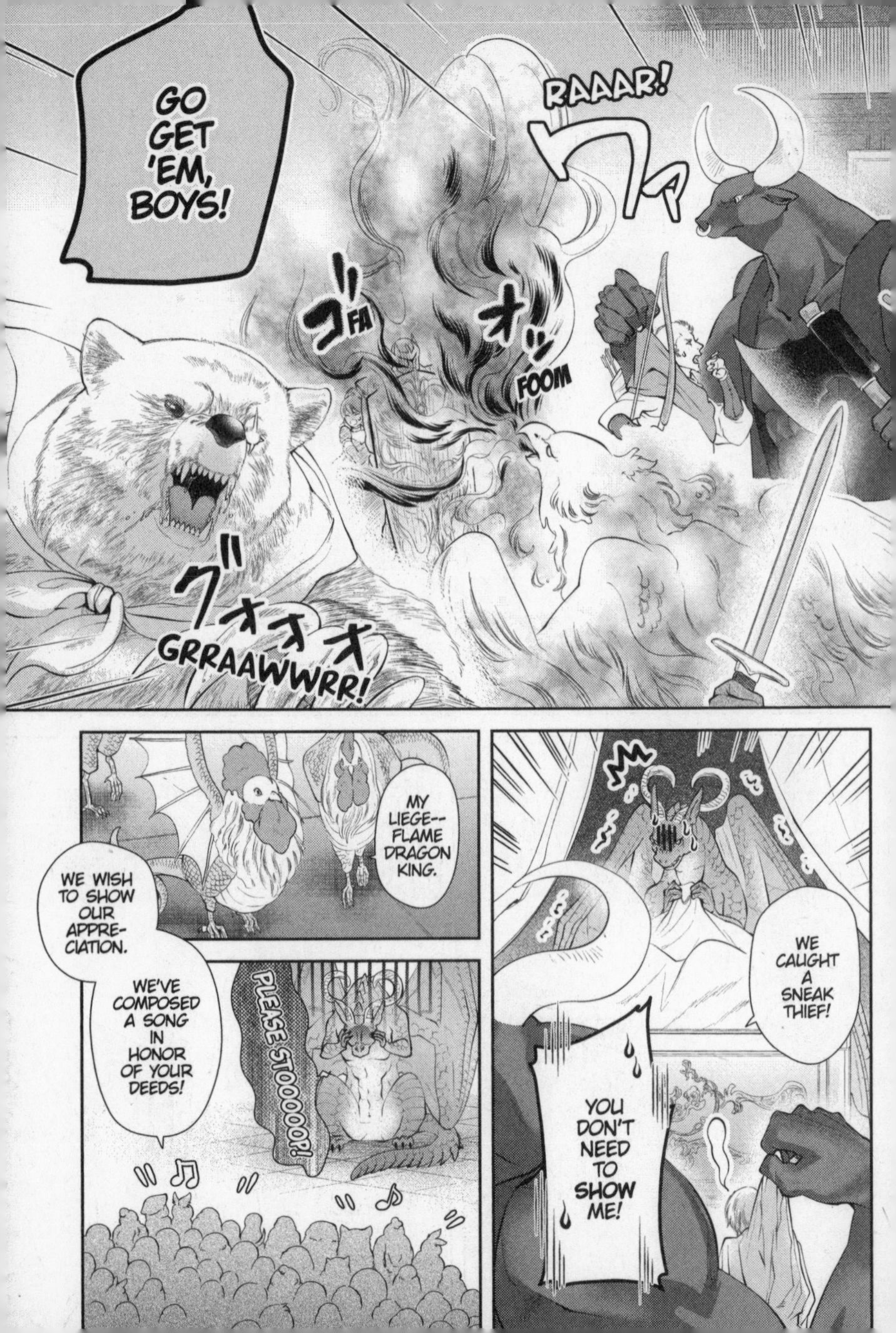
RAAAR!
GO GET 'EM, BOYS!
FA
FOOM
GRRAAWWRR!
WE CAUGHT A SNEAK THIEF!
YOU DON'T NEED TO SHOW ME!
MY LIEGE-- FLAME DRAGON KING.
WE WISH TO SHOW OUR APPRE-CIATION.
WE'VE COMPOSED A SONG IN HONOR OF YOUR DEEDS!
PLEASE STOOOOOP!

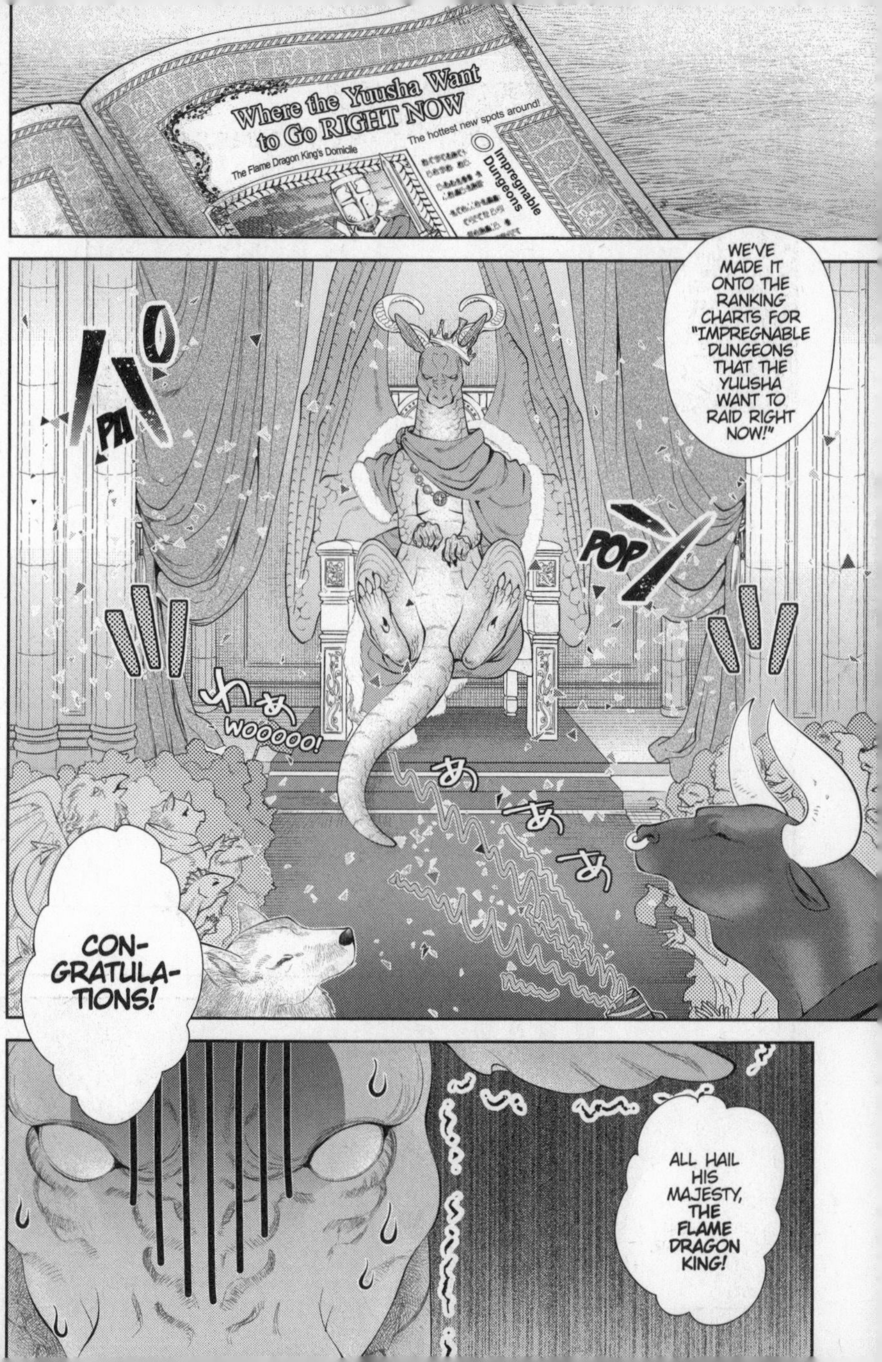
Where the Yuusha Want to Go RIGHT NOW
The hottest new spots around!
Impregnable Dungeons
The Flame Dragon King's Domicile
WE'VE MADE IT ONTO THE RANKING CHARTS FOR "IMPREGNABLE DUNGEONS THAT THE YUUSHA WANT TO RAID RIGHT NOW!"
POP
PA
わあ
WOOOOOO!
あ あ あ
CON-GRATULA-TIONS!
ALL HAIL HIS MAJESTY, THE FLAME DRAGON KING!

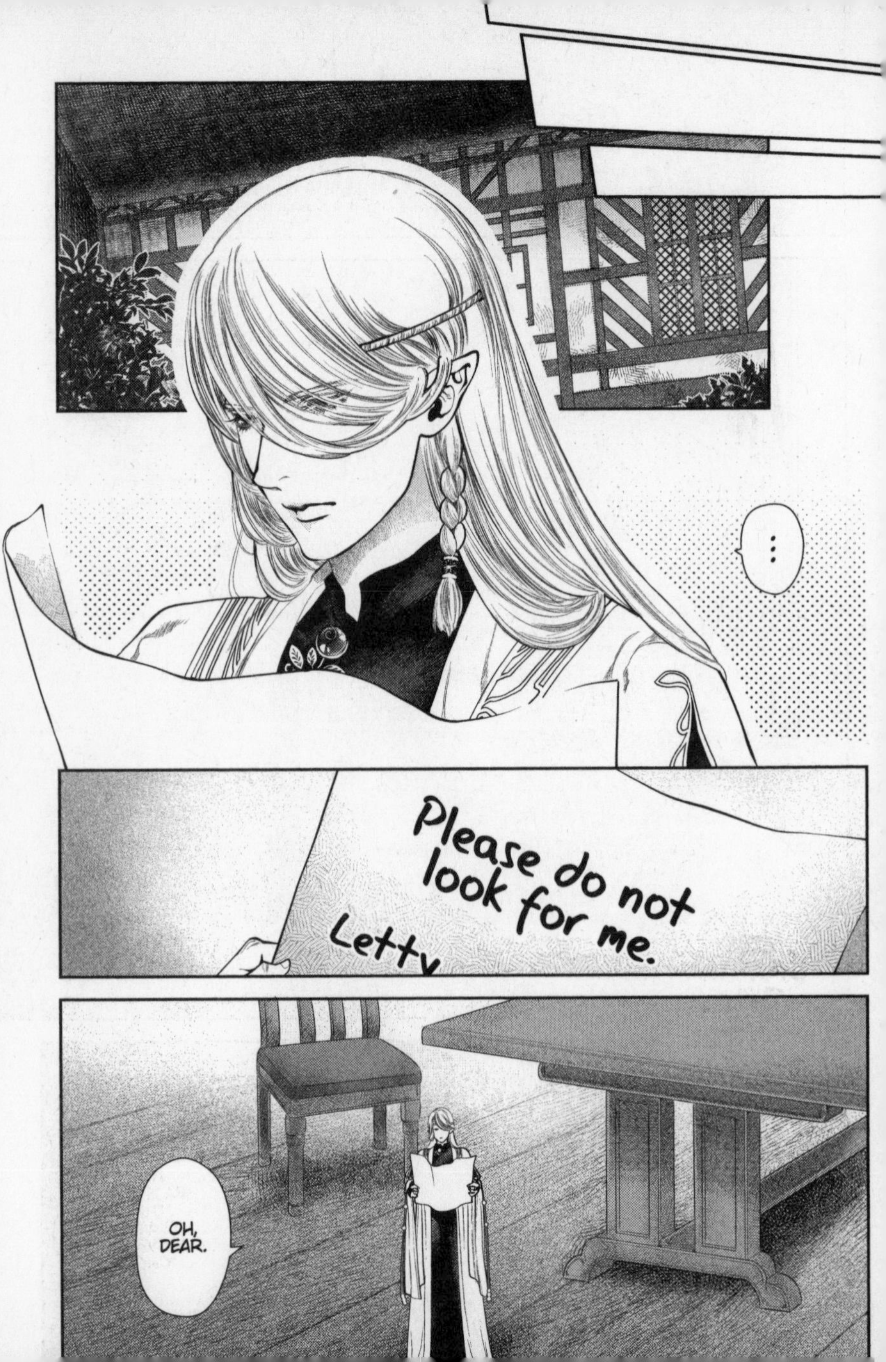
...
Please do not look for me.
Letty
OH, DEAR.

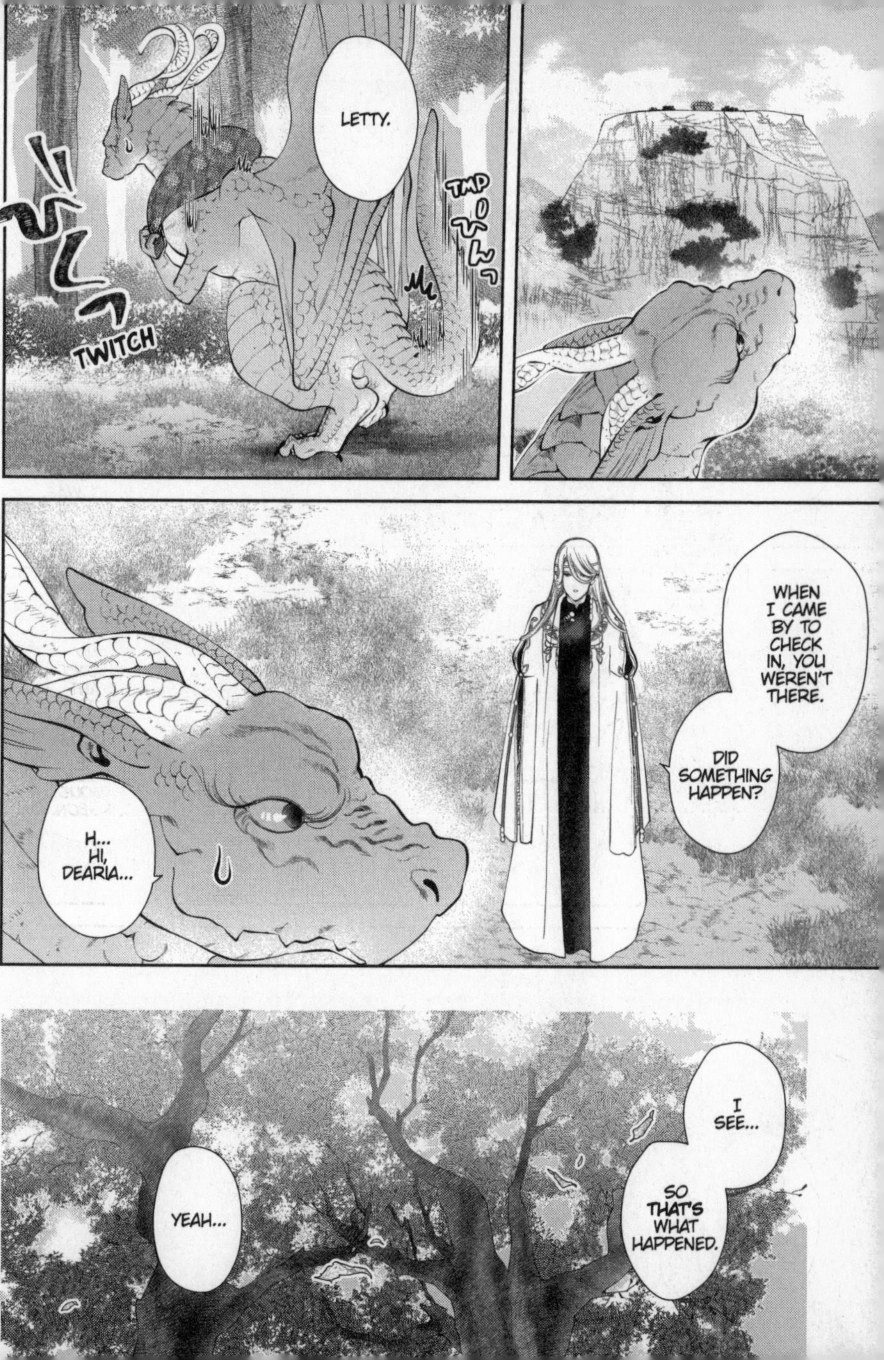
LETTY.
TMP
TWITCH
WHEN I CAME BY TO CHECK IN, YOU WEREN'T THERE.
DID SOMETHING HAPPEN?
H... HI, DEARIA...
I SEE...
SO THAT'S WHAT HAPPENED.
YEAH...

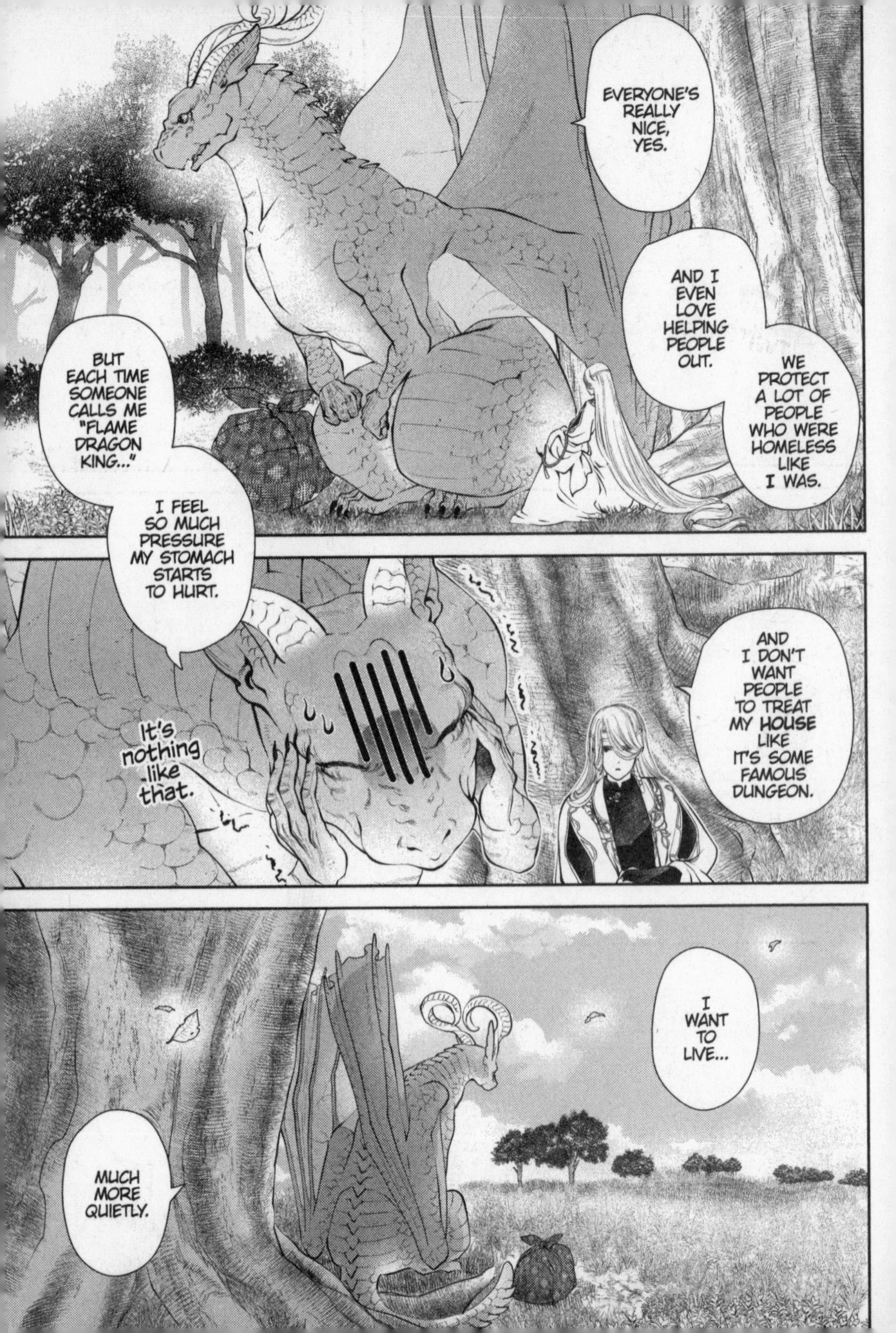
EVERYONE'S REALLY NICE, YES.
AND I EVEN LOVE HELPING PEOPLE OUT.
WE PROTECT A LOT OF PEOPLE WHO WERE HOMELESS LIKE I WAS.
BUT EACH TIME SOMEONE CALLS ME "FLAME DRAGON KING..."
I FEEL SO MUCH PRESSURE MY STOMACH STARTS TO HURT.
AND I DON'T WANT PEOPLE TO TREAT MY HOUSE LIKE IT'S SOME FAMOUS DUNGEON.
It's nothing like that.
I WANT TO LIVE...
MUCH MORE QUIETLY.

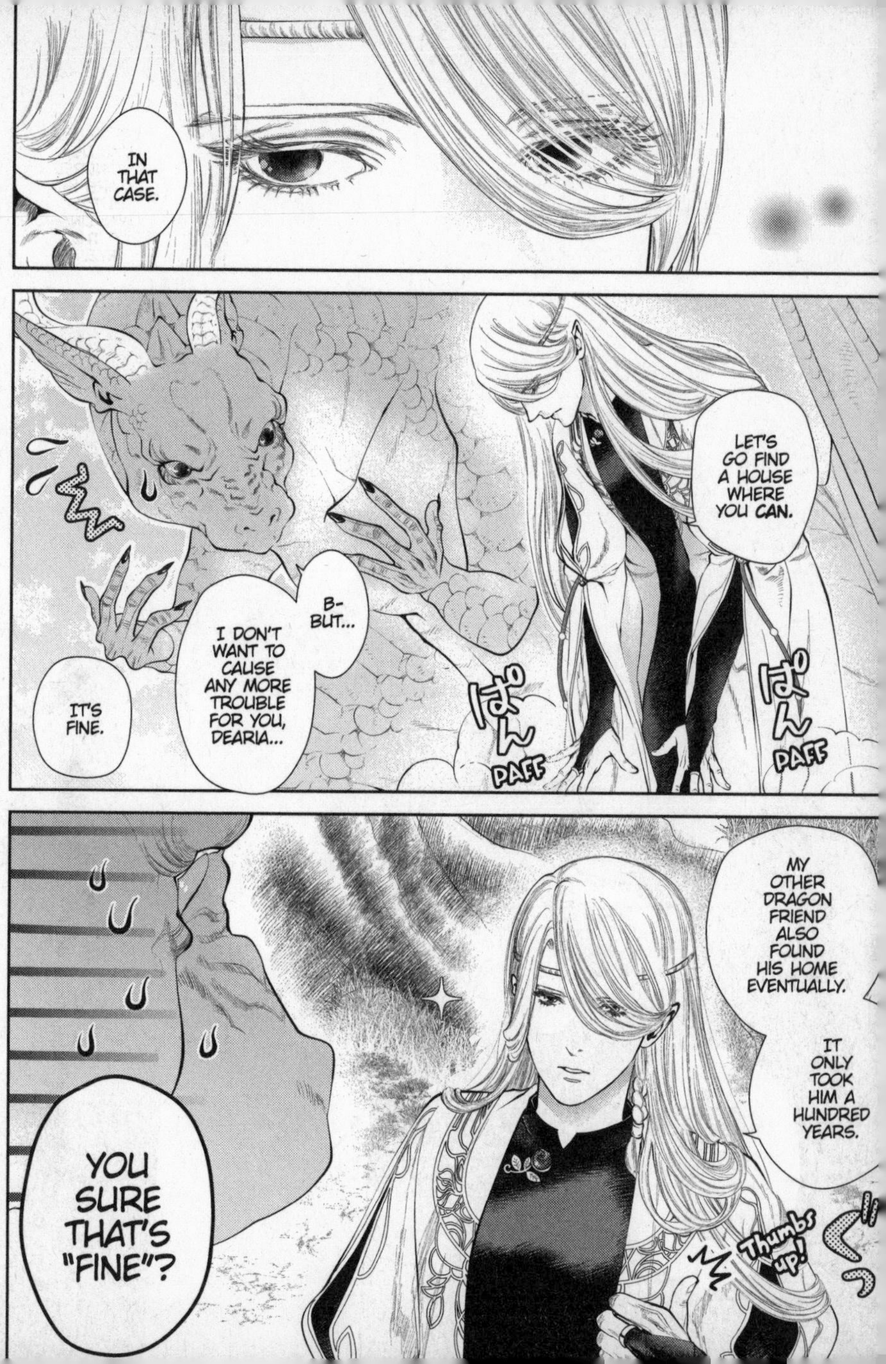
IN THAT CASE.
LET'S GO FIND A HOUSE WHERE YOU CAN.
ぱん PAFF
ぱん PAFF
B-BUT...
I DON'T WANT TO CAUSE ANY MORE TROUBLE FOR YOU, DEARIA...
IT'S FINE.
MY OTHER DRAGON FRIEND ALSO FOUND HIS HOME EVENTUALLY.
IT ONLY TOOK HIM A HUNDRED YEARS.
Thumbs up!
YOU SURE THAT'S "FINE"?

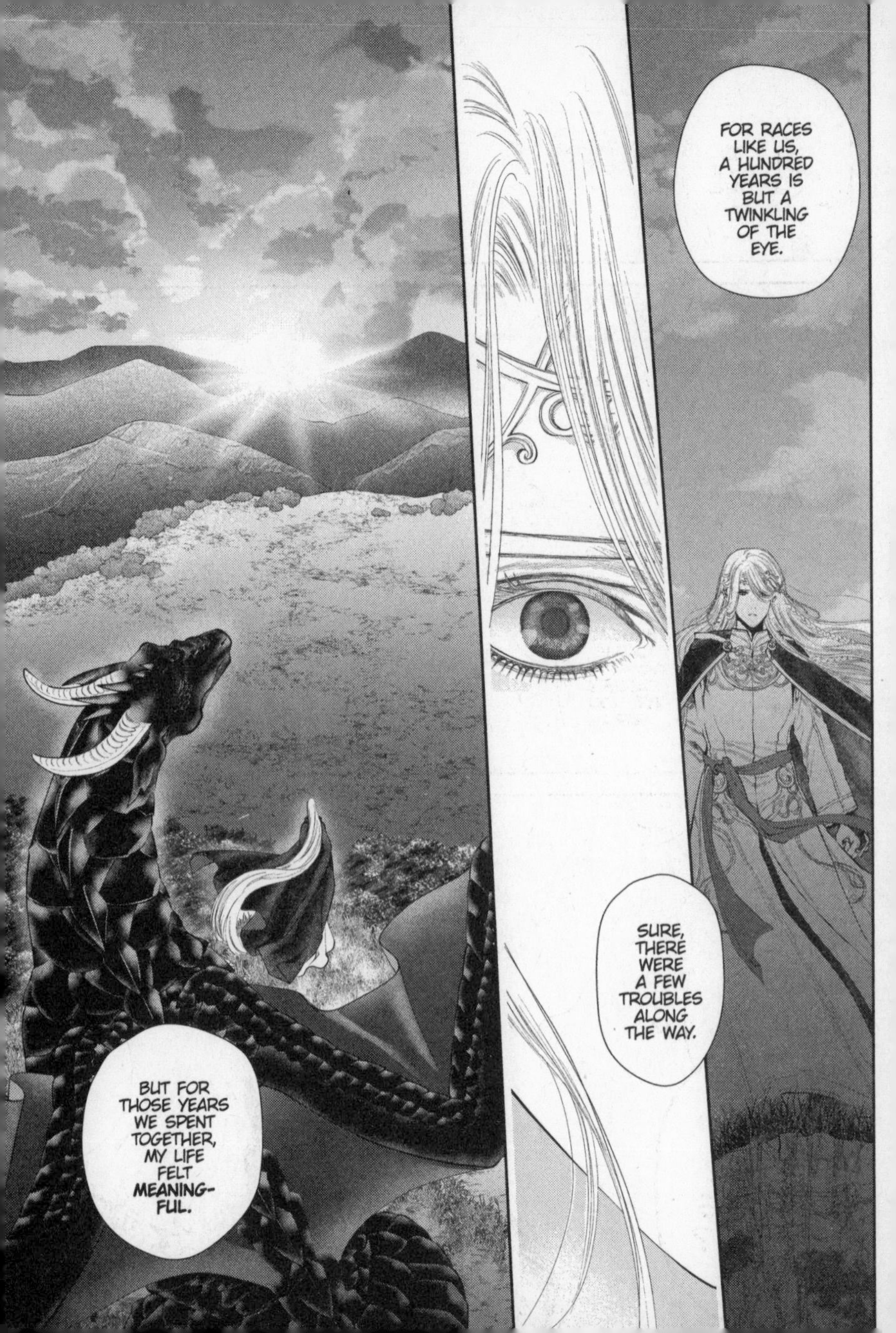
FOR RACES LIKE US, A HUNDRED YEARS IS BUT A TWINKLING OF THE EYE.
SURE, THERE WERE A FEW TROUBLES ALONG THE WAY.
BUT FOR THOSE YEARS WE SPENT TOGETHER, MY LIFE FELT MEANING-FUL.

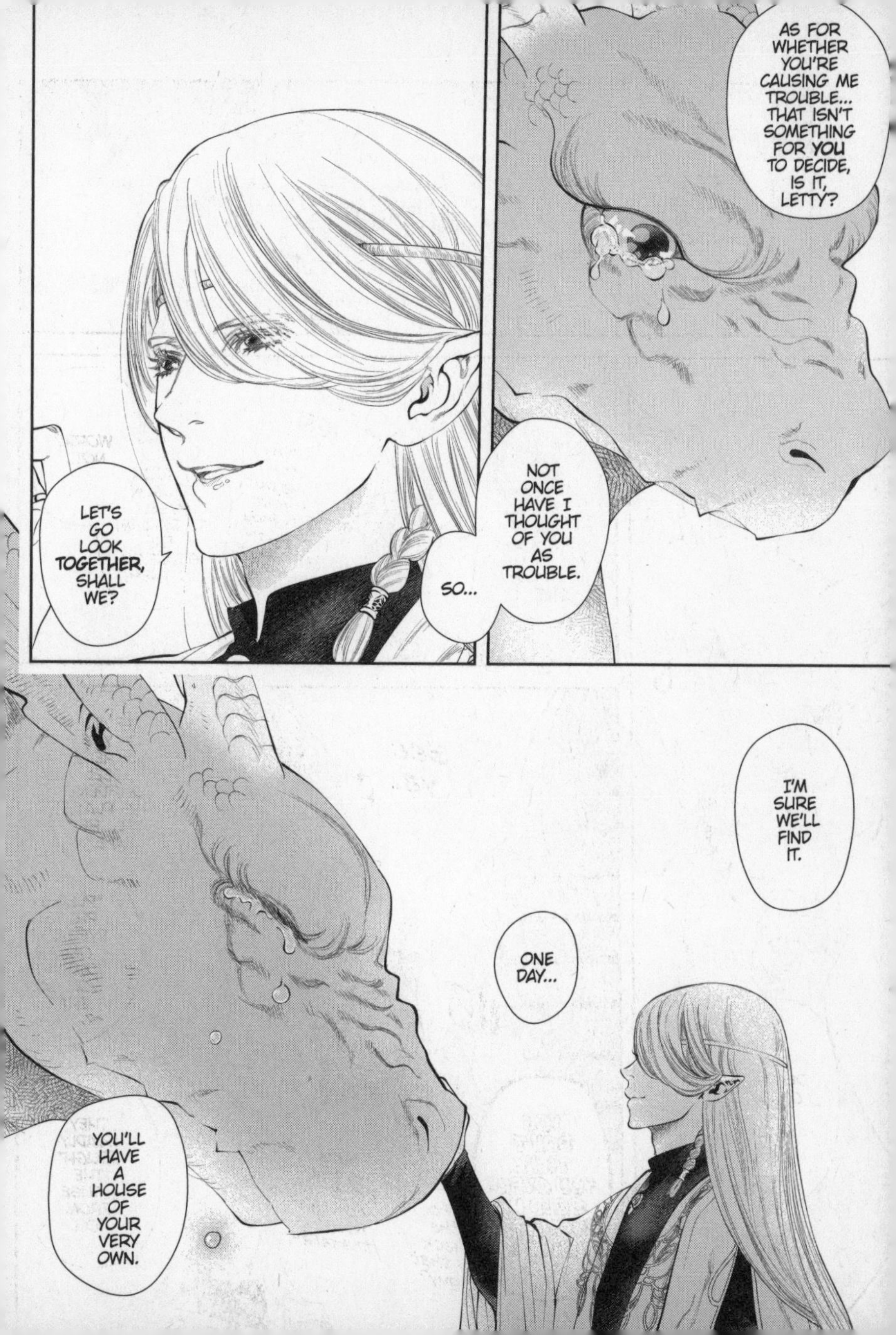
AS FOR WHETHER YOU'RE CAUSING ME TROUBLE... THAT ISN'T SOMETHING FOR YOU TO DECIDE, IS IT, LETTY?
NOT ONCE HAVE I THOUGHT OF YOU AS TROUBLE.
SO...
LET'S GO LOOK TOGETHER, SHALL WE?
I'M SURE WE'LL FIND IT.
ONE DAY...
YOU'LL HAVE A HOUSE OF YOUR VERY OWN.

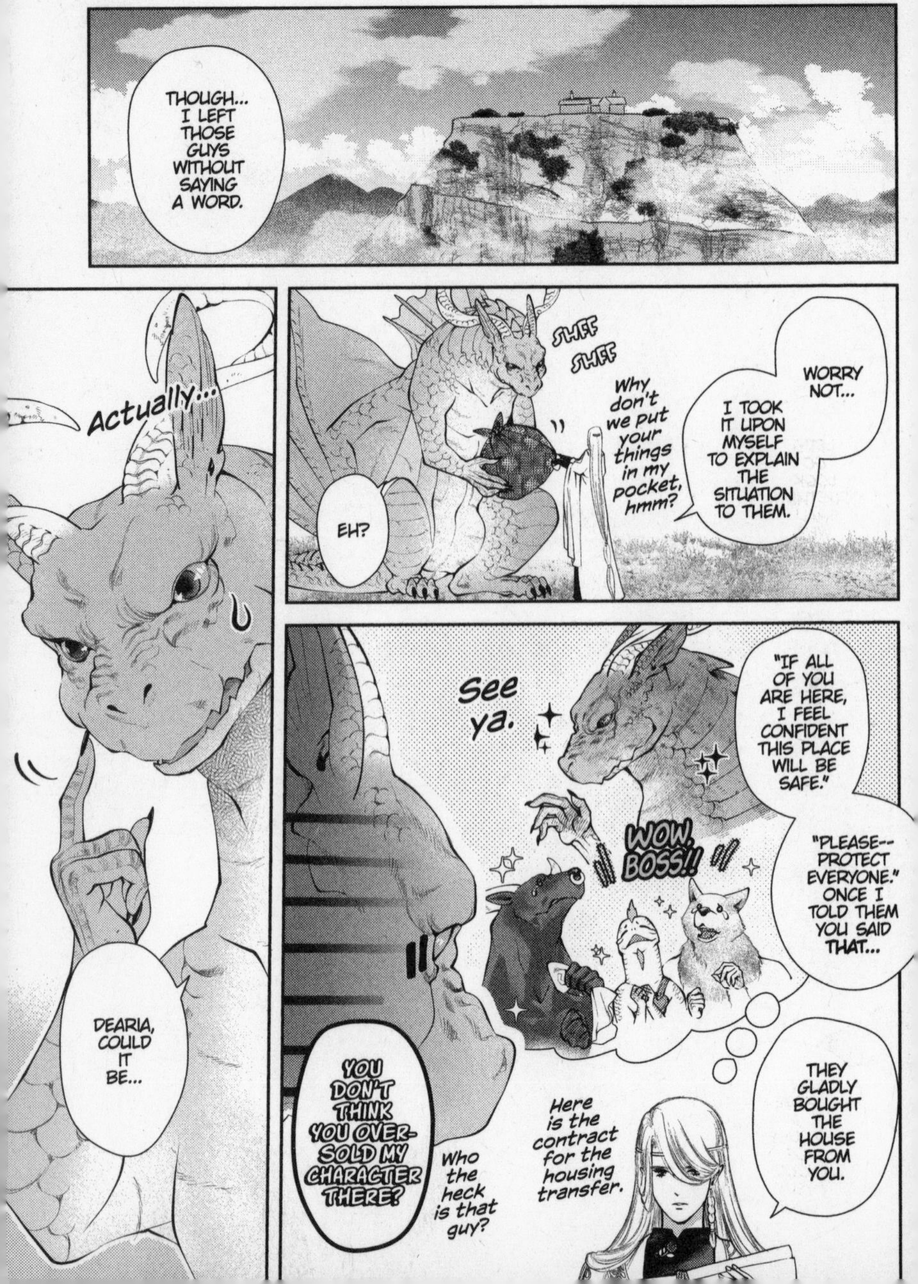
THOUGH... I LEFT THOSE GUYS WITHOUT SAYING A WORD.
WORRY NOT...
I TOOK IT UPON MYSELF TO EXPLAIN THE SITUATION TO THEM.
SHFF
SHFF
Why don't we put your things in my pocket, hmm?
EH?
"IF ALL OF YOU ARE HERE, I FEEL CONFIDENT THIS PLACE WILL BE SAFE."
"PLEASE--PROTECT EVERYONE." ONCE I TOLD THEM YOU SAID THAT...
WOW. BOSS!!
See ya.
THEY GLADLY BOUGHT THE HOUSE FROM YOU.
Here is the contract for the housing transfer.
Who the heck is that guy?
YOU DON'T THINK YOU OVER-SOLD MY CHARACTER THERE?
Actually...
DEARIA, COULD IT BE...

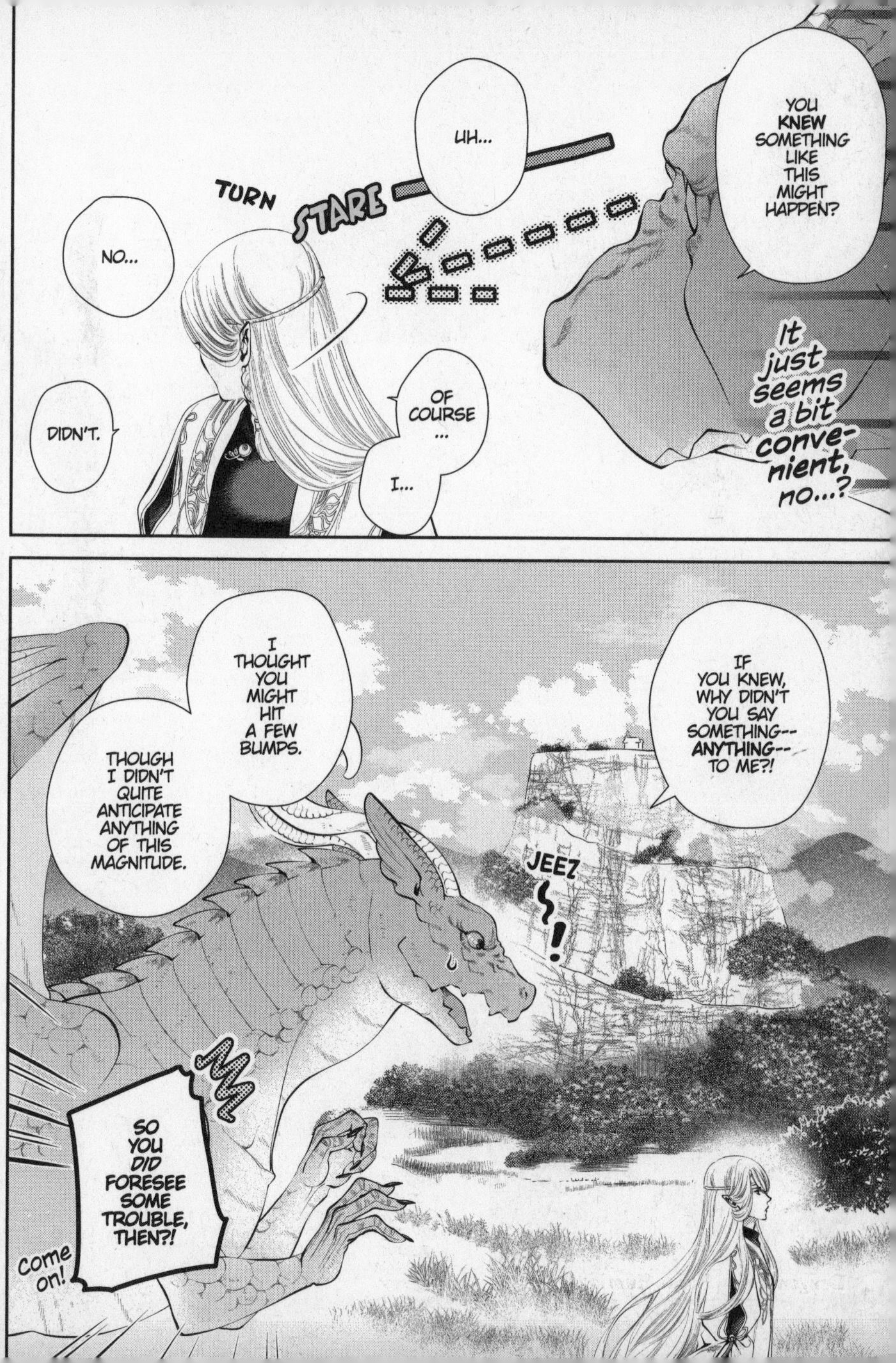
YOU KNEW SOMETHING LIKE THIS MIGHT HAPPEN?
It just seems a bit conve-nient, no...?
STARE
UH...
TURN
OF COURSE... I...
NO...
DIDN'T.
IF YOU KNEW, WHY DIDN'T YOU SAY SOMETHING-- ANYTHING-- TO ME?!
JEEZ~!
I THOUGHT YOU MIGHT HIT A FEW BUMPS.
THOUGH I DIDN'T QUITE ANTICIPATE ANYTHING OF THIS MAGNITUDE.
MM
SO YOU DID FORESEE SOME TROUBLE, THEN?!
Come on!

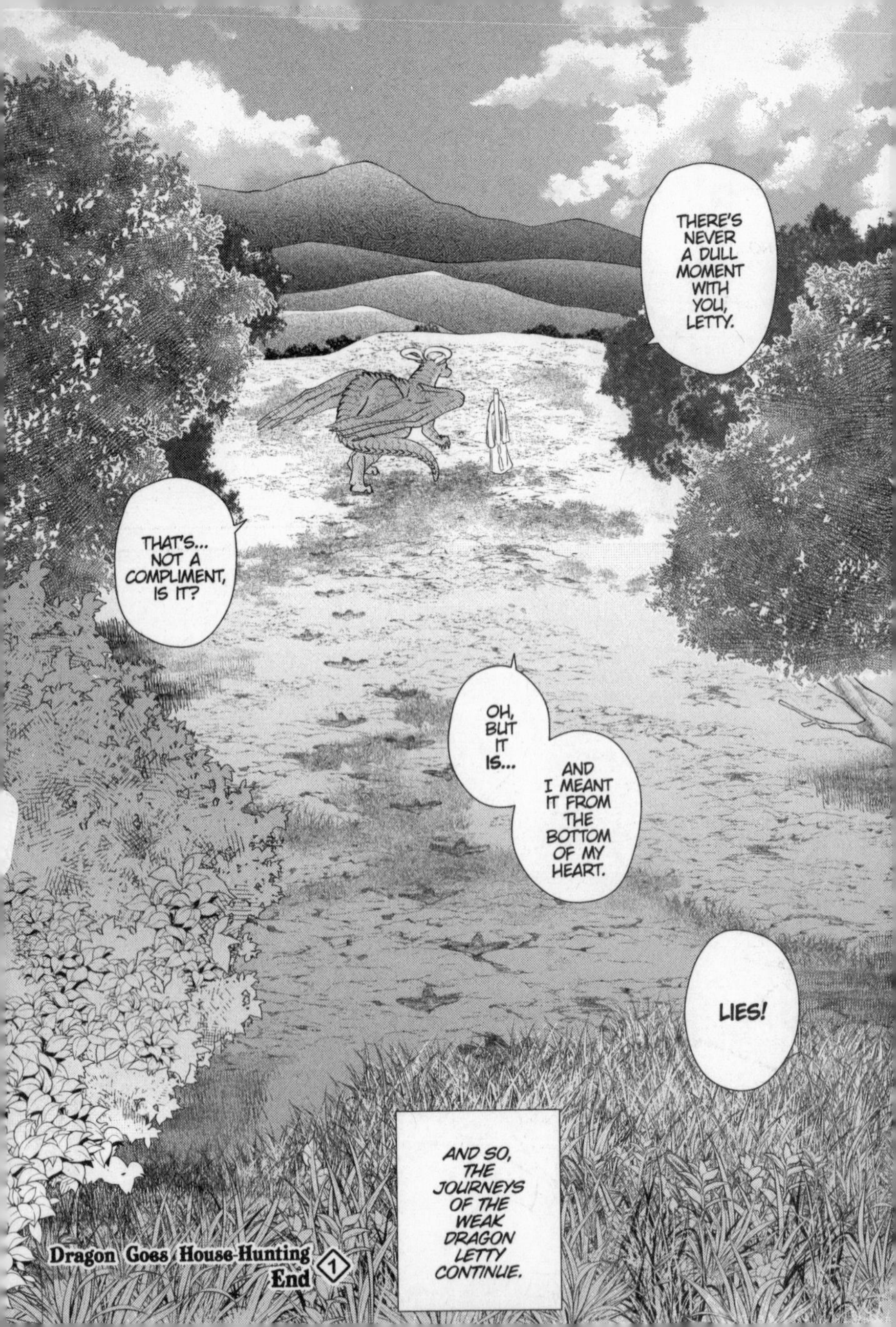
THERE'S NEVER A DULL MOMENT WITH YOU, LETTY.
THAT'S... NOT A COMPLIMENT, IS IT?
OH, BUT IT IS...
AND I MEANT IT FROM THE BOTTOM OF MY HEART.
LIES!
AND SO, THE JOURNEYS OF THE WEAK DRAGON LETTY CONTINUE.
Dragon Goes House-Hunting 1 End

SEVEN SEAS ENTERTAINMENT PRESENTS

VOLUME 1

Dragon Goes House-Hunting

story by KAWO TANUKI art by CHOCO AYA

TRANSLATION
Nan Rymer

ADAPTATION
T Campbell

LETTERING
Alexandra Gunawan

COVER DESIGN
KC Fabellon

PROOFREADER
Shanti Whitesides

EDITOR
J.P. Sullivan

PRODUCTION ASSISTANT
CK Russell

PRODUCTION MANAGER
Lissa Pattillo

EDITOR-IN-CHIEF
Adam Arnold

PUBLISHER
Jason DeAngelis

DRAGON, IE WO KAU. VOLUME 1

Originally published in Japan in 2017 by MAG Garden Corporation, Tokyo.
English translation rights arranged through TOHAN CORPORATION, Tokyo.

Seven Seas books may be purchased in bulk for promotional, educational, or business use. Please contact your local bookseller or the Macmillan Corporate and Premium Sales Department at 1-800-221-7945, extension 5442, or by e-mail at MacmillanSpecialMarkets@macmillan.com.

ISBN: 978-1-626928-85-5

Printed in Canada

First Printing: September 2018

10 9 8 7 6 5 4 3 2 1

FOLLOW US ONLINE: ***www.sevenseasentertainment.com***

READING DIRECTIONS

This book reads from ***right to left***, Japanese style. If this is your first time reading manga, you start reading from the top right panel on each page and take it from there. If you get lost, just follow the numbered diagram here. It may seem backwards at first, but you'll get the hang of it! Have fun!!

1
2
3
4
5
6
7
8
9

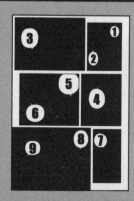